Freedom of the Press

from Hamilton to the Warren Court

THE AMERICAN HERITAGE SERIES

THE

American Heritage

Series

UNDER THE GENERAL EDITORSHIP OF

LEONARD W. LEVY AND ALFRED YOUNG

Freedom of the Press

from Hamilton to the Warren Court

EDITED BY

HAROLD L. NELSON

The University of Wisconsin

THE BOBBS-MERRILL COMPANY, INC.

A Subsidiary of Howard W. Sams & Co., Inc.

INDIANAPOLIS · NEW YORK

Printed in the United States of America
Library of Congress Catalog Card Number 66-22578
Designed by Stefan Salter Associates
Second Printing

For Ann, Susan, and Eric

Foreword

Freedom of the press, like any vital liberty, is one of the grand themes of American history, indeed of human history. The case for freedom of the press and the reason for its special protection in the First Amendment is clear enough: it is simply indispensable to democratic self-government and, broadly conceived, to individual creativity in art and literature. We cherish it, favor it, promote it, and protect it because we cannot do without it and we cannot do well, in government or culture, unless it flourishes. It is one of the ground rules by which the majority governs, bitted and bridled for the protection of the minority and the individual; it is the medium of expression as well as the necessary condition for the search for the truth; but it is also the most dangerous freedom. Democracy can function only with a free, informed, educated electorate; but that electorate cannot exist without freedom of expression even for the thought that may be hateful, licentious, or subversive. Belief in salvation through one church alone, belief in the existence of witches, the flatness of the earth, and the divine right of kings are only a few of the classic fighting faiths that have been discarded in the free exchange of ideas. The thick integuments of ignorance and prejudice are sometimes penetrated by the titanic blows of the moralist, sometimes by the detached empiricism of the scientist. But the indispensable condition for progress achieved at the expense of entrenched beliefs or interests has always been intellectual liberty—and its *sine qua non* is freedom of the press. And despite its abuses, the problems of monopoly, and the growing conformity of opinion, it is still the best hope we have for making political democracy work or for keeping free.

In this book Harold L. Nelson has succinctly described and analyzed the evolution of freedom of the press in America from the watershed of the early nineteenth century to the present. Earlier developments are described in a companion volume in this series by Leonard W. Levy. Nelson's introduction is a remarkable compression of its record, its vicissitudes, and its complexities; his documentary selections are a richly diversified, absorbing collection of materials that will in turn edify, perplex, provoke, dismay, and hearten. Old landmarks are here and an astonishing number of fresh, important documents that reveal, at the very least, how much is yet to be done with this significant subject. The risks of an unfettered freedom and the risks of fettering it pose problems of enduring difficulty that have not yielded to satisfactory solutions. Professor Nelson, in his editing of the materials and his guide to them, has contributed to our understanding of the problems, if not to the solutions.

This book is part of a series whose aim is to provide the essential primary sources of the American experience, especially of American thought, from the colonial period to the present. The series when completed will constitute a documentary library of our history. Many of these volumes will fill a need among scholars, students, libraries, and even general readers, for authoritative collections of original materials that illuminate the thought of significant individuals, such as James Madison or Louis Brandeis; or of groups, such as Puritan political theorists or American Catholic spokesmen on social policy; or of movements such as that of the Antifederalists or the Populists. There are a surprising number of subjects traditionally studied in American history for which there are no documentary anthologies. This series will be by far the most comprehensive and authoritative of its kind. It will also have the distinction of presenting representative pieces of substantial length which have not been butchered into snippets.

Leonard W. Levy
Alfred Young

Contents

PART THREE

CONTEMPT OF COURT

PART FOUR

PATTERN OF RESTRAINT: ATTACK ON THE OPPONENTS OF SLAVERY

The Laws

Mobs and Vigilance Committees

The Mails

PART FIVE

FREEDOM IN LEASH: WARTIME COMPROMISES

Civil War

PART SEVEN

RADICALS, LABOR, AND SEDITION

PART EIGHT

THE ECONOMIC FACTOR

PART NINE

THE PROBLEM OF SECRECY IN GOVERNMENT

PART TEN

FREEDOM AND RESPONSIBILITY

Introduction

Two years of experience under the Alien and Sedition Acts ended in 1801 with a blunt verdict from philosophical libertarians and the public that the law had violated freedom of the press. President Jefferson released from jail those who were still serving sentences for such crimes as printing "peace and retirement to the President [Adams]," and the federal government abandoned the field of legislating against its critics. For one hundred and forty years nothing short of assassination or war would drive it to pass another such law. And since after 1816 the government was blocked by the Supreme Court from the use of the common law of crimes, including that of sedition, its room for maneuver against the words of its critics was almost obliterated, at least in peacetime.[1]

The federal government was sufficiently cowed that for thirty-five years it refrained from almost all restraint of the press, not merely from sedition actions. That by no means meant that the field of press control was vacant, for state legal actions against words ordinarily did not arouse popular protest as did the actions of a remote central government. Operative along with state control, moreover, were the real if often impalpable compulsions of public opinion upon printers, at times as

[1] James Morton Smith, *Freedom's Fetters* (Ithaca, 1956), chaps. 12, 18; Leonard W. Levy, *Legacy of Suppression* (Cambridge, 1960), chap. 6, pp. 238–246. The latter-day sedition law is the Alien Registration Act of 1940, 54 *U.S. Statutes* 670.

despotic as any government's.[2] Nevertheless, in retrospect, freedom of expression seems impressive throughout the first third of the century; and its philosophical undergirding was strong in terms of the natural rights of individuals to develop their capacities, and of self-governing societies' need to communicate ideas and information.[3]

1800-1835

State restraint of the press produced a little punishment for blasphemy, a little for obscenity, and more for garden-variety criminal libel—state prosecution for defamation of any citizen, existing alongside the civil suit by the damaged party.[4] Seditious libel and criminal libel—nearly indistinguishable from each other where the target of verbal attack was a government official—were weakened early in the century. The idea that a self-governing society could accept the crime of sedition on principle had been heavily discounted in the adverse reaction to the Alien and Sedition Acts. In addition, the famous case of *People* v. *Croswell* spread widely a principle that in the long run helped vitiate an underlying assumption in libel prosecutions: that they tended to cause breaches of the peace by persons seeking revenge for harsh words, and that the truer the words, the greater the tendency to breach the peace.

Defense Attorney Alexander Hamilton argued in the Cros-

---

[2] Levy, *Legacy*, pp. 218–219, 235; Joseph T. Buckingham, *Personal Memoirs, and Recollections of Editorial Life* (Boston, 1852), II, 117–121; Gerald W. Johnson, "Freedom of the Newspaper Press," *Annals of the American Academy of Political and Social Science*, CC (Nov. 1938), 70–71.

[3] The two positions for the worth of expression tended to get united in the disquisitions of the early nineteenth century: Thomas Cooper, *A Treatise on the Law of Libel and the Liberty of the Press* (New York, 1830), pp. 48–49; Francis L. Holt, *The Law of Libel . . . in the Law of England*, edited by Anthony Bleecker (1st American ed.; New York, 1818) pp. 59–61.

[4] Reported blasphemy cases number not more than two dozen for the entire nineteenth century. Two famous ones of the early period are *People* v. *Ruggles*, 8 Johnson's Cases 290 (N. Y., 1811), and *Commonwealth* v. *Kneeland*, 20 Pick. 206 (Mass., 1838). Obscenity cases were also few at this time: *Knowles* v. *State*, 3 Day 103 (Conn., 1808).

well case that truth, published with good motives and for justifiable ends, ought to be a good defense against a libel charge. He did not win his case, but the State of New York accepted the principle in a statute passed the following year, and other states followed. The logic of the new rule was that truth was acceptable, not to be frowned upon as irrelevant or as contributory to breaching the peace; and the state statutes, adopted as decades passed, ignored the tendency toward breach of the peace as part of the test of libelous words. Truth might be a help, of course, on the occasions when the offending words could be proved as "facts," though of little help where the words were "opinions."[5]

Also in the early years of the century, Pennsylvania and New York passed laws curbing judges' powers to cite and convict for constructive contempt of court—written criticism of judges, sometimes called "out-of-doors contempt." Congress agreed on this limitation where federal judges were concerned. In 1831 it passed a law limiting federal judges' power to punish for misbehavior "in the presence of the . . . courts, or so near thereto as to obstruct the administration of justice." Behind the law lay an exhaustive airing of the issues involved, brought out by the impeachment of Federal Judge James H. Peck that resulted from his punishing an attorney who wrote a newspaper article attacking one of Peck's decisions. The Senate exonerated Peck and then joined the House in passing the law. The intent was to insure that federal judges' summary power could not reach to the summoning, accusing, prosecuting, and pronouncing guilt on a writer who criticized the very judge involved. It looked like tyranny and like sedition.[6]

[5] *People* v. *Croswell,* 3 Johnson's Cases 337 (N.Y., 1804); Anon., "Constitutionality of the Law of Criminal Libel," *Columbia Law Review,* LII, No. 4 (April 1952), 521–534; [Kimball, Edmund], *Reflections upon the Law of Libel* (Boston, 1832), pp. 37–42.

[6] Walter Nelles and Carol Weiss King, "Contempt by Publication in the United States," *Columbia Law Review* XXVIII, No. 4 (April 1928), 415, 421; Arthur S. Stansbury, *Report of the Trial of James H. Peck* (Boston, 1833), *passim; 4 U.S. Statutes* 487 (1831).

For a third of a century, then, government powers to punish reached newspapers and pamphleteers largely through the prosecution for criminal libel at the state level. It was a period when some of the worst gutter language to which the American newspaper and pamphlet have resorted was taken as a matter of course. There was vast freedom to accuse, charge, question motives, and comment as one wished, subject largely to civil libel suits and an occasional criminal libel action.[7]

But restraint from a force outside government was real as applied to one topic and one section of the nation. The force of public opinion and taboo was keeping an effective lid on the public questioning and discussion of slavery throughout most of the South during this period. There were local or temporary exceptions; but "the most delicate and difficult subject of state concernment," as editor Thomas Ritchie of the Richmond (Virginia) *Enquirer* wrote, was beyond the pale of permissible print in the eyes of most Southerners.[8]

1830-1865

The Southern consensus after 1830 was protected and reinforced by threats and violence directed against speakers and writers and by specific laws of the Southern states; it was buttressed further by federal administrative acquiescence in the suppressing of "incendiary" material in the mails. Meanwhile, for several years following 1830, the Abolitionist-haters of the North formed their own vigilance committees and mobs to harry the speakers and printers whose words and spirit the vigilantes punished with tar brush, club, firebrand, whip, and gun. William Lloyd Garrison was marched half-naked in Boston; the printing shop for James G. Birney's *Philanthropist* was burned in Cincinnati; Elijah Lovejoy was killed by the mob in

---

[7] Frank Luther Mott, *American Journalism* (revised edition; New York, 1950), pp. 168–173.

[8] Richmond (Virginia) *Enquirer*, Jan. 19, 1832; Clement Eaton, *Freedom of Thought in the Old South* (Durham, 1940), chaps. 4, 5.

Alton, Illinois, as he resisted a fourth destruction of his press. It was the last of these outrages that most jolted the North into revulsion and recognition of the consequences of mob rule. It helped to spread appreciation for the inestimable contributions of the Abolitionists to the cause of free expression.[9]

Committed to slavery as generally as the South was, its spokesmen perhaps felt little need to develop and refine the thought that would support denial of freedom of speech and the press to Southern dissenters and to Northern Abolitionists. Thomas Ritchie, who in 1832 wanted the slavery question aired, was answered by an opponent bitterly hostile to discussion of the subject:

> Let us pay no regard to the claim which may be asserted for the independence of the press: if, in the exercise of *their* independence, they choose to print, we, in the exercise of *our* independence, may choose to suppress, to the uttermost of our power, what we deem inflammatory, dangerous, mischievous. . . . The claim to such independence of the press, as not only gives it freedom to publish, but a right to free unrestrained circulation among those whom the circulation may injure, is, in truth, a claim to absolute dominion; which I shall never acknowledge. . . . [10]

The spokesman for the vigilance committee that dismantled and shipped away the press of Cassius M. Clay from Lexington, Kentucky, in 1845 justified the act to the mob in these terms: Clay, a native Kentuckian turned now into an "agent of an incendiary sect," had used his *True American* to make ruthless attacks on individuals, and to "terrify resistance of his course"; he had helped foment hate and discord in Kentucky's pattern of "mild slavery"; he had printed statements that called on "laborers of all classes" to support him in the battle between

---

[9] *Ibid.*; Russel B. Nye, *Fettered Freedom* (East Lansing, 1949), pp. 115–121; William Lloyd Garrison, *Selections from the Writings and Speeches of William Lloyd Garrison* (Boston, 1852), pp. 375–387; James G. Birney, *Narrative of the Late Riotous Proceedings Against the Liberty of the Press, in Cincinnati* (Cincinnati, 1836).

[10] Richmond (Virginia) *Enquirer,* Feb. 4, 1832, "Appomatox."

liberty and slavery—and he was no longer tolerable to the community. Legal measures could not reach him, and the only course for a self-respecting community was the orderly, non-destructive procedure of bundling up his press and shipping it away. It was truly a gentlemanly mob.[11]

That which was labeled "incendiary" or "inflammatory" came to be synonymous with "provoking servile insurrection," and the South was willing that its vigilance committees judge what was incendiary. Powerful allies in the federal government were anxious to lend a hand in suppressing the spread of the literature of abolition and called it "incendiary," although the Abolitionists tried unceasingly and unsuccessfully to demonstrate that they abhorred the thought of "servile revolt."[12]

More than a century of administrative decision-making in control of the press began in 1835 with the support of President Andrew Jackson and Postmaster General Amos Kendall. A Charleston, South Carolina, mob had seized and destroyed a large shipment of abolitionist mail, and Postmaster Huger wrote Kendall that he was withholding delivery of similar materials pending instructions. Kendall knew that no law empowered him to authorize the withholding of mail, but his sympathies were Southern; he wrote Huger that he could neither sanction nor condemn the postmaster's act. With Jackson and John C. Calhoun, Kendall sought a law that would permit blocking delivery to Southern addresses. Congress chose instead to accept Daniel Webster's and Henry Clay's view that this would invade freedom of the press, and passed a law that ran counter to Kendall's wish; but it was the Postmaster General's spirit that prevailed nevertheless. As Southern vigilance

---

[11] W. L. Barre, *Speeches and Writings of Hon. Thomas F. Marshall* (Cincinnati, 1858), pp. 196–210.

[12] "Address of the Anti-Slavery Society to the Public," *Niles' Register*, XLIX (Sept. 12, 1835), 28; William Goodell, *Slavery and Anti-Slavery* (New York, 1853), pp. 416–417; Massachusetts Anti-Slavery Society, *Fourth Annual Report* (Boston, 1836), p. 17.

committees were being formed by the hundreds, Southern laws were passed contradicting the federal statute, Southern postmasters co-operated fully, and effective suppression was the result.[13]

By 1857, Attorney General Caleb Cushing had upheld the principle of nullification of the federal postal act by Southern laws; by 1859 Postmaster General J. Holt had approved Cushing; and in 1863 Postmaster General Montgomery Blair told Congress that he assumed such precedents gave him power to remove from the mails or forbid delivery of anti-Union writings, and of materials he considered obscene.[14] He got away with it, and a long line of his successors asserted and exercised the power of interpreting their mandates liberally.

This was the period of the greatest peacetime restraint of speech and press in American history. Advances on the side of expanding freedom seem small alongside the suppressions, but they are not to be ignored. The federal government eliminated its stable of "captive" newspapers, passing a law under which its printing would be done by the Government Printing Office. Immunity from successful libel suits was first extended to reports of legislative and other official proceedings, in addition to reports of court proceedings. Potentially most important, no doubt, was the fact that the newspaper was being made available to huge new audiences by popularizing its appeal, cutting its cost to one penny instead of six, and introducing into its columns accounts of areas of life hitherto ignored. All this amounted to practical recognition of the "right to read," how-

---

[13] Kendall to Huger, *Niles' Register,* XLVIII (Aug. 22, 1835), 448; Kendall to Jackson, *Correspondence of Andrew Jackson,* edited by J. S. Bassett (Washington, D. C., 1931), V, 359; *Register of Debates in Congress,* 24 Cong., 1 Sess., June 8, 1836, pp. 1,721–1,737.

[14] Yazoo City Post Office Case, 8 Op. Atty. Gen. 489 (1857); Postmaster General J. Holt to Postmaster Charles Orton, Dec. 5, 1859, *Cong. Rec.,* 53 Cong. 2 Sess., 26:9, App. Part 1 (1894), 4; *House Miscellaneous Documents,* No. 16, 37 Cong., 3 Sess., Jan. 20, 1863, "Postmaster General's Authority over Mailable Matter," pp. 4–8.

ever much it was highly profitable business; and the new content was not entirely froth.[15]

Civil War

It is easy to view the period of the Civil War itself as one of dark restraint and a twilight of freedom. Yet there was actually much freedom attending much restraint in the North. The South had the freedom of consensus, and a dearth of Northern antislavery mail and roving Abolitionists to restrain.

The presence of restraint during this period cannot be entirely equated with the absence of freedom. Although ultimately the "Copperhead" editor might be disciplined, his often rabid attacks on President Lincoln, on the conduct of the war, and on the goals of the North might go on for months without check. Major newspapers of general circulation—not the marginal organs of deprived classes as in World War I—called into question the motives of the North and the worth of union, and kept it up.[16]

Tolerance on the part of government and people was great but exhaustible. Lincoln reluctantly ordered newspapers closed and editors jailed. Military commanders of Northern districts did the same with far less reluctance and forbade entry of mailed "Copperheadism" into their districts. The postmaster general barred some newspapers from the mail. One grand jury investigated "Copperhead" newspapers and hoped they would be punished; another indicted anti-Union editors. Through it all ran the gang or mob that threatened, manhandled, or tarred editors, required changes in editorial policy, burned print shops, and had its way. A comprehensive list of instances of restraint by government and people apparently is

---

[15] 12 *U.S. Statutes* 117 (1860); *New York Laws,* 1854, chap. 130; Mott, *American Journalism,* chaps. 12, 13.

[16] Frank L. Klement, *The Copperheads of the Middle West* (Chicago, 1960), chaps. 3–6.

yet to be made, but there were at least sixty cases of threats and violence against Northern newspapers and editors from angered citizens and soldiers during the war.[17]

The thought behind the North's plans for a field censorship that would protect the security of strategy and armies was primitive, and the system worked badly through most of the war. The press, now reaching a far greater percentage of the population than in previous wars, was riding high on a system of aggressive news-gathering developed with pride during the previous twenty-five years. It was enamored of freedom and insensitive to the damage that battle plans and armies might suffer from news reports that got into print within hours or days after dispatch. The government, its armies dependent as in no previous war upon the efforts and support of the whole people, was insensitive to the people's need for maximum information about the war. There were times when it was uncertain where responsibility lay for systematizing field censorship, and the assignment bounced from one cabinet member to another. Tried briefly, voluntary censorship by the press under these circumstances was almost hopeless. By war's end, there was perhaps the dawn of understanding within both institutions: in the press, that total war meant some compromise of democratic forms, including even freedom of the press; in the government, that a people tutored in access to news needed information when war came if its maximum support was to be elicited.[18]

---

[17] A. C. Cole, "Lincoln and the American Tradition of Civil Liberty," *Illinois State Historical Society Journal*, XIX (Oct. 1926–Jan. 1927), 102–114; "Freedom of the Press," *American Annual Cyclopaedia* . . . (New York, 1861–1902), I, 328–330, II, 480–481. I am indebted to Mr. Emil Fisher, graduate student at the University of Wisconsin, for his compilation and analysis of instances of threats and violence, in an unpublished paper of January 1964.

[18] Edwin Emery, *The Press and America* (second edition; Englewood Cliffs, New Jersey, 1962), pp. 284–301; *House Report* No. 64, 37 Cong., 2 Sess., March 20, 1862, "Telegraph Censorship."

1865-1900

America did not carry a stringent restraint of expression into the decades after the Civil War. Real or imagined threats to national existence, of the kind that were to follow world war in the twentieth century, were lacking. Freedom of speech and press entered a period of health—qualified in some respects, as always. No broad source of potential violation of freedom of the press was inactive: government, the public, and the press itself contributed. But as freedom goes, it was going here.

Reconstruction brought the growth of a "kept press" in the South, kept perhaps in grandest style in South Carolina, where many newspapermen sold out to the largesse of the Republican government. It was the judgment of later investigators that of all public frauds during the state's deeply corrupt reconstruction period, the printing fraud was the worst. The North could also furnish examples of editors seeking to sell their pens to whatever party might win power in state government, and thus have lucrative public printing contracts to award its favorites. Until territories and states began to let printing contracts to the lowest bidder, conditions were good for the growth of the government "house organ" newspaper. Much as these "sell-outs" violated the public interest, however, the low cost of establishing competing papers helped minimize the total effect. Throughout most of the century, indeed, it was common practice for newspapers to be established and run as subsidized arms of political parties or candidates; but partisan conviction, rather than the prospect of loot, motivated most editors under the ordinary partisan system.[19]

Prosecutions for criminal libel increased rapidly during the last quarter of the century, and at the same time, the legal

---

[19] *South Carolina Reports and Resolutions, 1877–1878,* Report of the Joint Investigating Committee on Public Frauds, Public Printing, pp. 213–331; W. A. Katz, "Public Printers of Washington Territory, 1863–1889," *Pacific Northwest Quarterly,* LI, No. 4 (Oct. 1960), 171–181; Mott, *American Journalism,* chap. 14.

assault on obscenity was intensified. The first sharp increase in reported criminal libel cases appeared between 1880 and 1890; the number reached its peak in the next decade, held there until World War I, and then fell off steadily until it almost vanished by mid-twentieth century. It is hard to explain why the number jumped from about twenty between 1871 and 1880, to almost seventy-five between 1881 and 1890, and to more than a hundred during the last decade of the century.[20]

"Obscenity" caught Congress's attention briefly in 1865 when the postmaster general asked for a law to help him check the flow in the mails of materials he thought obscene—and which he had been suppressing without sanction of law for some years. He obtained a law that permitted prosecution of offenders. Eight years later, the stimulus of the nation's greatest smut-hunter, Anthony Comstock, shortly to become executive secretary of the New York Society for the Suppression of Vice, effected a broadening of the law's provisions and a national awareness of an untiring crusader's concern that physical, mental, and moral ruin awaited countless youths exposed to printed materials dealing with sex. The statute of 1873 was given his name, the "Comstock law," and its descendants carry the same name today.[21]

To say that "Victorianism" or "Puritanism" was the force that lay behind public and government support of the growth of suppression that followed explains little. There may have been widespread anxiety over the state of the nation's morality: the scandals of the Grant administration, Reconstruction frauds, and the shocking graft of Boss Tweed's Tammany Hall were spectacular evidences of corruption. The conditions that

---

[20] Tabulations from the West Publishing Co. *American Digest, Decennial Digest,* and *General Digest* (St. Paul, 1902–   ).

[21] James C. N. Paul and Murray L. Schwartz, *Federal Censorship: Obscenity in the Mail* (New York, 1961), pp. 17–24, 249–252; 17 *U.S. Statutes* 598 (1873); Heywood Broun and Margaret Leech, *Anthony Comstock, Roundsman of the Lord* (New York, 1927); Anthony Comstock, *Traps for the Young* (third edition; New York, 1884).

fostered the new concern probably included a considerable increase in the output of pornography.[22]

Among the instruments of suppression, particularly significant was the "Hicklin test" of obscenity, laid down by Chief Justice Cockburn of England in 1868. Words in any part of a written work that might have a tendency to "deprave and corrupt" even the most immature or pathological mind were obscene.[23] And equally or even more important was the broad discretion given to or assumed by the Post Office Department to bar from the mails whatever its officials thought obscene, quite apart from any criminal prosecution. Congress may have meant to bestow such power, but it has never been clear that this was the case, or that Congress planned to have the Post Office become the nation's strong arm of censorship by suppression in advance of distribution.[24]

Meanwhile, Congress's power to say what content could be excluded from the mail was confirmed; the states' power to punish those involved in the sale of "obscenity" was employed; and the Customs' power to bar the literature of sex at the nation's borders—first bestowed by Congress in 1842, or twenty-three years before the first postal obscenity act—was actively wielded. By 1900, all branches of federal and state government were represented in the suppression of obscenity and printed material dealing with sex. Accompanying the official restraint was the work of voluntary citizens' groups, early Watch-and-Warders. The groundwork had been laid solidly for official and unofficial expansion of restraint in the first thirty-odd years of the twentieth century.[25]

[22] Paul and Schwartz, *Federal Censorship*, pp. 17–18.

[23] *Queen* v. *Hicklin*, L. R. 3Q.B. 360 (1868). Acceptance by federal courts came in *U.S.* v. *Bennett*, 24 Fed. Cas. 1,093 (1879).

[24] Paul and Schwartz, *Federal Censorship*, pp. 253–262; Eberhard P. Deutsch, "Freedom of the Press and of the Mails," *Michigan Law Review*, XXXVI, No. 5 (March 1938), 730–739; Exclusion from the Mails, 19 Op. Atty. Gen. 667 (1890).

[25] *Ex parte Jackson*, 96 U.S. 728 (1878); Lindsay Rogers, *The Postal Power of Congress* (Baltimore, 1916), pp. 115–120; Morris L. Ernst and William Seagle, *To the Pure* (New York, 1928), pp. 9–13.

1900–1930

Measuring the extent of restraint on the press in any period is heavily guesswork. If the number of avenues being used and the amount of traffic on them are the gauge, America never experienced greater government restrictions on the press than during the first quarter of the twentieth century. Actions for obscenity plagued the world of books and magazines especially; actions for sedition harried the pamphlets and periodicals of radicalism; actions for contempt of court increasingly reached the standard newspapers; criminal libel prosecutions diminished hardly at all from their peak rate during the decade 1890–1900.

To take contempt first, the spirit of the federal statute of 1831 that circumscribed federal judges' contempt power had been giving way in the states, decade by decade, since approximately 1860. In *State* v. *Morrill,* the Arkansas Supreme Court had furnished a rationale that appealed widely to other courts, for punishing out-of-court writing that might have a tendency to interfere with the orderly administration of justice. It asserted that the contempt power was "inherent" in the courts, that legislative enactments were powerless to limit it, and that by immemorial usage the power extended to words outside the courtroom.[26] It became a leading case in other state courts' adoption of its principles. And in 1918, its spirit was embraced as the rule for federal courts: in *Toledo Newspaper Co.* v. *U.S.*, the United States Supreme Court upheld a federal judge's power to punish printed criticism, despite the words of the 1831 statute that seemed to limit the power to punishment of misbehavior in the near environs of the court.[27] While a case was pending, comment on it could be dangerous and was often punished.

With obscenity and sex, the strictures grew and so did the administrative grip. Unless there was a manifest "abuse of dis-

[26] *State* v. *Morrill,* 16 Ark. 384 (1855); Nelles and King, "Contempt by Publication," pp. 535–540.

[27] *Toledo Newspaper Co.* v. *U.S.*, 247 U.S. 402 (1918).

cretion" by the legal functionaries of the Post Office Department, courts would not interfere with their decision about what was nonmailable. Refinements of the postal power were added by Congress. And ultimately the postmaster general decided that it was in his power to withdraw the low, second-class mail rate from magazines that had a history of including nonmailable matter. In the Customs, informal procedures and, after 1926, accretions in the powers of a special Customs Court added to the port-of-entry barriers. Balzac, Boccaccio, Pierre Louys, Flaubert, George Moore, James Joyce, D. H. Lawrence, and others were not fit writers for Americans to read, and their works were stopped at the border along with printed pornography and pictured perversion. The mails rejected Margaret Sanger's works, Mary Ware Dennett's essay on sex education for youth, "The Sex Side of Life," and the Chicago Vice Report prepared by an official agency for distribution among editors, social workers, and clergymen. In Boston, the Watch and Ward Society grew.[28]

The morals of the people and the good name and work of the courts were perhaps sufficiently armed, by 1900, against the written word or picture. But arising from the deprived condition of large numbers of people who were left behind in the rushing advance of industrial society or in the agrarian backwashes was a challenge to free enterprise and in part to democracy. Variants of socialism, anarchism, and syndicalism, growing in the late decades of the nineteenth century, had raised the specter of revolution in the minds of millions of Americans. Whatever the real threat, apprehension over the Emma Goldmans, the Big Bill Haywoods, and the Daniel de Leons was widespread. The assassination of President William McKinley by Leon Czolgosz, widely believed to

---

[28] Paul and Schwartz, *Federal Censorship*, pp. 34–49; Deutsch, "Freedom of the Press and the Mails," pp. 738–744; Sidney Grant and S.E. Angoff, "Massachusetts and Censorship," *Boston University Law Review*, X (Jan. 1930), 36.

be an anarchist, was the signal for national and state legislation to curb speech against the government. At President Theodore Roosevelt's call, Congress passed the Immigration Act of 1903 to bar from the country or to deport those who believed in or advocated the overthrow by force and violence of the United States government. The state of New York had already passed its own anti-anarchist act, and New Jersey and Wisconsin followed. It was a resumption of sedition legislation after the lapse of a century.[29]

With 1914 and the start of world war, radicals and right-wing Socialists denounced the conflict as a gigantic and grotesque extension of "the capitalists'" instruments for profit-making. When the war reached America and the nation closed ranks, their antiwar theme, coupled with their long attack on free enterprise, placed these people outside the ring of consensus. With them were the farmers' Non-partisan League, the pacifists, and the pro-Germans. By 1918, alarm at the success of revolutionary communism in Russia was added to fear of German victory.[30]

The familiar story of World War I suppression starts with a rush of sedition laws: the Espionage Act of 1917 and its 1918 amendment, state statutes passed with the dispatch of fear, the Trading-with-the-Enemy Act, and others. The main categories of proscribed words, as the story worked out, were in the Espionage Act: attempts by talk or print to cause insubordination or disloyalty in the armed forces or to obstruct enlistment or recruiting. Offenders might be prosecuted directly or their materials banned from the mails. There were some 1,900 prosecutions, primarily of speakers; and perhaps a hundred news-

[29] William Preston, *Aliens and Dissenters* (Cambridge, 1963), pp. 30–32; Zechariah Chafee, Jr., *Free Speech in the United States* (Cambridge, 1941), pp. 163–164, 573, 597; Exclusion of Seditious Publications from the Mails, 26 Op. Atty. Gen. 555 (1908).

[30] H. C. Peterson and Gilbert C. Fite, *Opponents of War* (Madison, Wis., 1957), chaps. 1, 2; Harry N. Scheiber, *The Wilson Administration and Civil Liberties, 1917–1921* (Ithaca, 1960), pp. 3–5.

papers, an unknown number of pamphlets, and some books were disciplined by courts or Post Office.[31]

The spirit of the times is reflected in the work of the Post Office Department and in the attitude of its chief, Postmaster General Albert S. Burleson. For material in print, the most impressive power to control was the postal power. Decades of practice in largely unhindered suppression of obscenity, fraud, and lottery served Post Office administrators well as they hunted the newly proscribed content. And Burleson was disposed to use all the generously broad discretion that earlier Congresses and court decisions had bestowed upon him. Civil War restraint of "Copperheadism" had sometimes been severe but was often preceded by long official sufferance; now Burleson announced a policy of no sufferance for words he thought might affect army discipline or enlistments. He announced that print could not say[32]

> that this government got in the war wrong, that it is in it for wrong purposes, or anything that will impugn the motives of the Government for going into the war. They can not say that this Government is the tool of Wall Street or the munitions-makers. That kind of thing makes for insubordination in the Army and Navy and breeds a spirit of disloyalty through the country. . . . There can be no campaign against conscription and the Draft Law, nothing that will interfere with enlistments or raising of an Army.

In this censorial spirit, Burleson confirmed, by means of the approval of the Supreme Court, his power to use an important economic weapon against periodical print: withdrawal of the

---

[31] *Ibid.*, chap. 2; Chafee, *Free Speech in the United States*, pp. 3, 100–102, 298–305; Lucille B. Milner and Groff Conklin, "Wartime Censorship in the United States," *Harper's*, CLXXX (Jan. 1940), 193. The Espionage Act is 40 *U.S. Statutes* 217; the Sedition Act is 40 *U.S. Statutes* 553.

[32] "Mr. Burleson to Rule the Press," *Literary Digest*, LV, No. 2 (Oct. 6, 1917), 12; Donald O. Johnson, *The Challenge to American Freedom* (University of Kentucky Press, 1963), chap. 3; William Hard, "Mr. Burleson, Espionagent," *New Republic*, XIX (May 10, 1919), 42–45.

low-cost, second-class mail rate from publications that he declared nonmailable under the Espionage Act. It was a striking extension of the postal power over print.[33]

In the same spirit, citizens, newspapers, and congressmen denounced all criticism of the nation's purpose and pursuit of the war; mobs threatened, tarred, painted, and even lynched speakers, and attacked an occasional newspaper; and courts swept a broad range of words into the sphere of proscribed expression.[34] War's end eased the pursuit, but a flood of state sedition acts was passed, directed against domestic espousal of the Russian revolutionary theme. Wartime convictions working their way through the judicial appeals process, and subsequent convictions under the new laws, were generally upheld in the Supreme Court through the 1920's.[35]

But two major assaults on past attitudes and rulings of the Supreme Court made their appearance in the postwar decade, and while they had little effect on convictions for that decade, their impact in later years was to be large. One was the clear and present danger test that tempered an ancient mode in which lawmakers, judges, and others explicated the kinds of words that could be punished—those that had a "tendency" or "reasonable tendency" to bring about some undesired or illegal result. The old rule had been assailed by American libertarians for many decades as capable of ensnaring the most innocent speech, but it held fast. Now, in his landmark opinion in *Schenck* v. *United States,* Justice Oliver Wendell Holmes, Jr., expressed another test: "The question in every case is whether

---

[33] *U.S. ex. rel. Milwaukee Social Democratic Publishing Co.* v. *Burleson,* 255 U.S. 407 (1921); Deutsch, "Freedom of the Press and the Mails," pp. 741–746.

[34] Robert M. LaFollette, "Free Speech in Wartime," in *We Hold These Truths,* edited by Stuart G. Brown (New York, 1948), pp. 291–295; National Civil Liberties Bureau, *War-Time Prosecutions and Mob Violence* (New York, 1919), pp. 1–13; Chafee, *Free Speech in the United States,* chaps. 2, 3, 7.

[35] Chafee, *ibid.,* chaps. 6–10.

the words used are used in such circumstances and are of such a nature as to create a clear and present danger that they will bring about the substantive evils that Congress has a right to prevent." In its expansive thrust it gave libertarians a new vision, and in its later judicial elaboration it evoked some of the greatest American statements on the democratic ideal.[36]

The second change was the Supreme Court's acceptance in 1925 of a position long urged upon it: that the "liberty" protected from invasion by the states in the Fourteenth Amendment to the U.S. Constitution included liberty of speech and press. Heretofore, the Supreme Court had reasoned that states' control of expression had been their own province; but after *Gitlow* v. *New York*, state governments would be under the federal Constitution in regulating words. Zechariah Chafee, Jr., was to say thirty years later that it was the greatest victory for free speech in his lifetime.[37]

Besides these two disruptions of old ways in the law during this period, a growing protest against restraint issued from powerful thinkers and writers. Theodore Schroeder, probably America's most prolific advocate of a radically free speech and press, had begun by 1906 his tireless attacks on the censorship of writings on sex and the suppression of radical agitation. Roger Baldwin, Walter Nelles, Albert de Silver, and others started the great unflagging effort of the American Civil Liberties Union and its precursor, the National Civil Liberties Bureau. Zechariah Chafee, Jr., wrote his basic *Freedom of Speech.*

---

[36] 249 U.S. 47 (1919). Attacks on the "tendency" principle were made by Thomas Jefferson, *The Papers of Thomas Jefferson,* edited by Julian P. Boyd, *et al.,* (Princeton, 1950–) II, 545–553; by William Ellery Channing in 1836, *Works* (Boston, 1887), pp. 745-746; by Theodore Schroeder, who called it the idea "productive of the most injury to mankind" in all history.

[37] *Gitlow* v. *New York,* 268 U.S. 652 (1925); Charles Warren, "The New 'Liberty' under the Fourteenth Amendment," *Harvard Law Review,* XXXIX, No. 4 (Feb. 1926), 431; Chafee, *Freedom of Speech and Press* (New York, 1955), p. 54.

The strong voices of Charles Evans Hughes and Alfred E. Smith cut through foggy rationalizations for punishing radicals, and Senator Bronson Cutting of New Mexico stated basic rebuttals to the justifications for Customs censorship. Meanwhile, the great opinions of Justices Holmes and Louis D. Brandeis spoke a spirit and language of freedom that later majorities were to accept.[38]

1930–1950

In all this there was focus on discovering—anew, some said; at last, according to others—what the term "freedom of speech and press" meant in the eyes of the law. The Supreme Court stood at the apex of the effort, and beginning in 1931 and extending to the post-World War II period, its decisions gave content to the First and Fourteenth Amendments. In its major outlines that content was clearly libertarian in spirit and effect.

The scrutinies of the Supreme Court exposed flaws in ancient dogma about the states as bulwarks and central depositories of our liberties. The Gitlow decision of 1925 having cleared the way for review of free press cases from the states, the Supreme Court examined and struck down provision after provision for restraint by the states. Under Chief Justice Charles Evans Hughes from 1930 to 1941, it relied very little on the Holmes and Brandeis test of "clear and present danger," but the court's liberating thrust was theirs, and their test was to start its career of use by majorities in 1940.

Beginning with Hughes's milestone decision in *Near* v. *Min-*

---

[38] Nancy Sanky-Jones, *Theodore Schroeder on Free Speech, a Bibliography* (New York, 1919); D. O. Johnson, *The Challenge to American Freedom;* Chafee, *Freedom of Speech* (New York, 1920); *New York Times,* Jan. 21, 1920, p. 2; Norman Hapgood and Henry Moskowitz, *Up from the City Streets: Alfred E. Smith* (New York, 1927), pp. 192–198; *Cong. Rec.,* 71 Cong., 1 Sess., Oct. 11, 1929, pp. 4,445–4,456. Notable opinions of Holmes and Brandeis include those in *Abrams* v. *U.S.,* 250 U.S. 616; *Gilbert* v. *Minn.,* 254 U.S. 325; *Gitlow* v. *New York,* 268 U.S. 652; *Whitney* v. *Calif.,* 274 U.S. 357.

nesota in 1931, the Supreme Court worked at the adhesive, obscuring crust around the outlines of "freedom of the press":

Restraint in advance of publication, it ruled, is almost always unconstitutional (*Near* v. *Minnesota,* 283 U.S. 697, 1931).

Freedom of the press means more than freedom from restraint in advance of publication (*Near* v. *Minnesota,* 283 U.S. 697, 1931).

"Taxes on knowledge"—here in the form of a discriminatory tax on large newspapers, levied as punishment for political opposition—were tyranny to the American colonists and were surely intended by the framers of the Constitution to be outlawed (*Grosjean* v. *American Press Co.,* 297 U.S. 233, 1936).

Freedom of the press includes freedom of distribution as much as freedom from prior restraint (*Lovell* v. *Griffin,* 303 U.S. 444, 1938).

Freedom of the press is as applicable to pamphlets and leaflets as it is to newspapers, books, and magazines (*Lovell* v. *Griffin,* 303 U.S. 444, 1938); and picketing by labor unions also deserves the protection of the Constitution as a form of expression (*Thornhill* v. *Alabama,* 310 U.S. 88, 1940).

A court's power to convict out-of-court publication as contemptuous cannot rest on a "reasonable tendency" in the words to interfere with justice; there must be in the words a "clear and present danger" to the orderly processes of justice (*Bridges* v. *California,* 314 U.S. 252, 1941).

On the eve of America's entry into World War II, there were grave warnings that fear of fascism and communism was driving government and people to take measures that threatened civil liberties. One evidence was the sweeping and indiscriminate attack on persons accused of disloyalty and subversion that issued from the Special House Committee on Un-American Activities. And in 1940 the first federal peacetime sedition law since the Alien and Sedition Acts of 1798–1800 was passed by Congress—the Alien Registration Act. This made it a crime to advocate violent overthrow of government.

Libertarians raised the specter of World War I suppressions.[39]

But when war came, it was soon evident that speakers and writers were to escape the fury of prosecution and persecution that had so characterized World War I. Some actions were brought against speakers and writers, indeed, but far fewer than during the earlier war. Mob violence was almost totally lacking. Each year the American Civil Liberties Union examined the record and found it vastly different from that of 1917–1920. There was good evidence that "our democracy can fight even the greatest of all wars and still maintain the essentials of liberty," the ACLU reported in 1943. It felt that important factors in the change were a national outlook that far more nearly approached consensus about war aims than did that of twenty-five years earlier, and the enlightened attitude of the United States Department of Justice and the Supreme Court.[40]

The Supreme Court did, indeed, carry into the war years and after its expansion of the area of permitted expression. Not since the Schenck case of 1919 had a majority of the court relied upon Justice Holmes's "clear and present danger" test, but from 1940 to 1950, it was used in decisions protecting the use of speech and press and in dissents and concurring opinions. Justice Felix Frankfurter found it a doctrinaire formula in the hands of the court and repeatedly attacked its use.[41]

Early and again late in this period, striking intrusions were

---

[39] Roscoe Pound, "Government in Time of War," *Vital Speeches*, VII, No. 2, 375–376; Milner and Conklin, "Wartime Censorship in the United States," pp. 194–195; 54 *U.S. Statutes* 670.

[40] See the annual reports of the ACLU, especially the report of 1943, *Freedom in Wartime* (New York, 1943), pp. 3–10. The major exception to a careful regard for civil liberties was the removal of Japanese-Americans from their homes on the Pacific Coast and their confinement in camps.

[41] Cases in which majorities relied on it include *Thornhill* v. *Ala.*, 310 U.S. 88 (1940); *Cantwell* v. *Conn.*, 310 U.S. 296 (1940); *Bridges* v. *Calif.*, 314 U.S. 252 (1941); *W. Va. State Board of Education* v. *Barnette*, 319 U.S. 624 (1943); *Pennekamp* v. *Fla.*, 328 U.S. 331 (1946). Frankfurter attacked the use of the test in the last three.

made upon old configurations in obscenity law and enforcement. Federal District Judge John Woolsey sat in 1933 when yet another attempt was made to breach the Customs barrier against James Joyce's *Ulysses,* this time with the tireless champion of civil liberties, Morris Ernst, as the defending attorney. The literate Woolsey was convinced: the imported "Hicklin test" of obscenity of 1868 should not rule. The "work as a whole," not isolated passages, should be judged; and the person of average sex instincts, not the most susceptible minds, should be the standard.[42]

In 1946 Postmaster General Robert E. Hannegan, understandably confident of his censorial powers in view of the wide discretion accorded his office for many decades, assayed to define the quality of a periodical's content that warranted the low, second-class mail rate. The "smoking-room" humor of *Esquire,* he said, did not deserve it. The Supreme Court routed him.[43]

In these decades of deep depression and major adjustments in government's relation to business, labor, and society, economic issues inevitably confronted the court in decisions on free expression. In one case, the court told the Associated Press that there was no warrant in the First Amendment to fire a newsman for union activity.[44] In another, it told the same organization that "The First Amendment affords not the slightest support for the contention that a combination to restrain trade in news and views has any constitutional immunity."[45]

The economic issues reached far beyond the courts' purview; as never before, the great newspaper and magazine publishing industries became the target of critics who saw in shrinking numbers of owners a threat to the public's stake in freedom of the press. They charged that "monopoly" newspapers, unstimu-

---

[42] *U.S.* v. *One Book Called "Ulysses,"* 5 F. Supp. 182 (1933).
[43] *Hannegan* v. *Esquire,* 327 U.S. 146 (1946).
[44] *Associated Press* v. *NLRB,* 301 U.S. 103 (1937).
[45] *Associated Press* v. *U.S.,* 326 U.S. 1, 20 (1945).

lated and unscrutinized in the absence of competition, had reduced the diversity of available mental fare, had biased that fare heavily on the side of the economic and political *status quo,* and had failed to upgrade their content to meet the needs of a mid-twentieth-century people standing in a position of world leadership.[46]

Local competition did not necessarily provide diversity, balance, and depth of content for the public's right to know. Owners of great communications industries tended to be like-minded whatever the competition; and, further, some of the worst abuses of press freedom had attended competitive press battles for more than a half-century. Moreover, if competition among local communications media was valuable to the public, by the mid-1950's competition was vigorous between newspapers and television, to say nothing of radio.[47]

Major voices among the guardians of the public's right to information placed only modest faith in a rebirth of competition. In 1947 the Commission on Freedom of the Press—thirteen men, of whom most were scholars and none was connected with the mass media—reported the results of several years' deliberations on freedom and responsibility in mass communication. Their central theme was not the need for a rebirth of competition, but for a greater sense of responsibility on the part of the owners and personnel of the mass media. They said that the people would surely demand regulation of a press that did not meet more fully the needs of society for mass communications services. The fullest, most orderly, and perhaps most basic statement of the problem and of suggestions for change among American analyses, the report was attacked

---

[46] Harold Ickes (ed.), *America's House of Lords* (New York, 1939); Morris Ernst, *The First Freedom* (New York, 1946).

[47] William Allen White, Presidential Address, "Problems of Journalism," *Proceedings of 17th Annual Convention of the American Society of Newspaper Editors,* 1939, pp. 15–20; Raymond B. Nixon, "The Problem of Newspaper Monopoly," in Wilbur Schramm (ed.), *Mass Communications* (second edition; Urbana, Ill., 1960), pp. 241–250.

heavily by the press as unfair, badly informed, and unfriendly to freedom of the press. Much of the world of the press was to mellow somewhat in its attitude toward the Commission; some publishers even came to agree with most of its report.[48] And while the Commission was of course talking about long-range tendencies, in 1965 it was as hard to find evidence of increased public clamor for regulation of the press as it was to measure whether the press had become more responsible.

1950–1965

As postwar years turned to cold war and then to the Korean War, the nation was convulsed by waves of alarm over the supposed advance of domestic communism. With most other civil liberties, freedom of expression was subjected to the restraints of public opinion intolerant of unorthodoxy, and to the restraints of a government search for signs of subversion. Whether considered as the individual's right to print or as the people's right to read and know, freedom of the press was hedged.

The Internal Security Act of 1950 (McCarran Act) requiring the Communist Party to register names and addresses with the U.S. Attorney General was passed over a veto by President Truman. He called it "the greatest danger to freedom of speech, press, and assembly since the Alien and Sedition Laws of 1798." Before the McCarran Act was tested in the courts, however, the Smith Act of 1940 had been upheld in *Dennis* v. *U.S.*, under which eleven Communist leaders were convicted of conspiracy to teach and advocate the violent overthrow of government. In the Supreme Court's opinion, if the interest (here, protection from violent overthrow) is of high enough importance, the government may punish expression even

---

[48] Commission on Freedom of the Press, *A Free and Responsible Press* (Chicago, 1947); *Editor & Publisher,* LXXX, No. 21 (May 17, 1947), 46; John W. Cowles, "The Responsibility of a Free Press in a World Crisis," *University of Missouri Bulletin,* LII, No. 33 (Nov. 20, 1951), 11.

though the words carry no clear and present danger to that vital interest. Concurring and dissenting justices added their interpretations of the clear and present danger test, with a diversity that helped erode its usefulness. In few decisions since have majorities relied upon it.[49]

By the mid-1950's, approximately one hundred Communists had gone to prison under the Smith Act, and by 1961, the McCarran Act had been declared constitutional by the Supreme Court.[50]

Meanwhile the "loyalty" committees of Congress were investigating certain newspapers and newsmen, notably James Wechsler, editor of the *New York Post,* and several reporters on the *New York Times.* Wechsler was called by the Senate Subcommittee on Investigations under Senator Joseph McCarthy, whose propensities were unmatched for "exposing" those who, like Wechsler, opposed him. There was heavy evidence that this was the central motive at work in the questioning of Wechsler, who for fifteen years had been a militant anticommunist but was vulnerable to McCarthy's methods because of a previous youthful membership in the Communist Party. "The hearing was manifestly intended as a harassment to me and as a warning to other editors who have displayed inadequate respect for the committee chairman," Wechsler wrote.[51]

If government was restraining advocates and writers by prosecution and investigation, it was also, according to many newsmen, restricting freedom of the press considered as the "people's right to know." By 1950 the news press had launched a continuing offensive that charged that great areas of informa-

---

[49] The McCarran Act is 64 *U.S. Statutes* 987. The Dennis case is 341 U.S. 494 (1951). "Clear and present danger" was used in a contempt case, *Wood* v. *Ga.,* 370 U.S. 375 (1962).

[50] Zechariah Chafee, Jr., *The Blessings of Liberty* (Philadelphia and New York, 1956), p. 22; *Communist Party* v. *Subversive Activities Control Board,* 367 U.S. 1 (1961).

[51] James Wechsler, *The Age of Suspicion* (New York, 1953), chap. 7, pp. 249–316; *New York Times,* Jan. 6, 1956, p. 2; Jan. 7, 1956, pp. 1, 6.

tion were being hidden by the people's servants at every level of government. Although secrecy was generally acknowledged by the press to be appropriate to matters of vital military security, the practice of secrecy had spread beyond security measures necessary during World War II and the cold war. It now served not only security, newsmen found, but also the arrogance of bureaucrats, the functionary's fear of "underclassifying," the hope of hiding inefficiency or graft, and the convenience of not working in a goldfish bowl. It was easy to find all these motives at work—especially in the executive and administrative arenas, but by no means exclusively there. Some voices called for First-Amendment protection for a public right to access to government information.[52]

Quite apart from government, a censorious and vocal minority of the public was giving vent to fears of a "communist takeover" of America and began an assault on books and libraries. Citizens' groups and zealous individuals demanded suppression of the literature of socialism and communism. In many towns and cities, public and school libraries and newsstands and bookstores were canvassed for the polemics and scholarship of "alien ideologies" and were pressured to remove them. The sweep of the hunt spread; publications of the United Nations, UNESCO, and the American Civil Liberties Union, and distinguished American historians were examples of works and men reviled as less than American.[53]

While the ancient, elusive crime of sedition thus occupied government and people, another almost indefinable area of proscribed utterance was causing dismay to millions of Ameri-

---

[52] James Russell Wiggins, *Freedom or Secrecy* (New York, 1956); Jacob Scher, "Access to Information: Recent Legal Problems," *Journalism Quarterly*, XXXVII, No. 1 (Winter, 1960), pp. 41–52; Harold L. Cross, *The People's Right to Know* (New York, 1953).

[53] See *Censorship Bulletin* (as of March, 1962, *Freedom to Read Bulletin*) I (May 1956), 3; I (July 1956), 4; II (July 1957), 2; V (March 1962), 1. W. J. Hempel and P. M. Wall, "Extralegal Censorship of Literature," *New York University Law Review*, XXXIII (Nov. 1958), 989.

cans who thought they knew it when they saw it: "the obscene." The latitude given to the discussion of sex, to erotica, and to prurience during the 1950's flew in the face of custom. Floods of paperback and comic book violence, and scabrous periodicals and girlie magazines were in evidence as never before; under-the-counter, hard-core pornography (perhaps as indefinable as "the obscene") flourished. Citizens' groups rose to combat this kind of material, and church organizations and police joined in formal prosecution and informal suppression. True to familiar pattern, accompanying the attack on the crude and the pornographic was the squelching of works by serious artists: Mailer, Salinger, Hemingway, Faulkner, Wilson, Maugham, O'Hara, Dos Passos, Farrell, Kantor, Steinbeck, were some of them.[54]

In Congress, investigations were undertaken; in the courts, obscenity prosecutions mounted in number. One hundred and fifteen years after the first federal obscenity legislation, the Supreme Court in 1957 delivered its first definition and test of obscenity, and for the first time ruled that the obscene deserves no constitutional protection. In *Roth* v. *U.S.* it said "the test of obscenity is whether to the average person, applying contemporary community standards, the dominant theme of the material taken as a whole appeals to prurient interest." Although applying the test brought predictably uneven results, under it there was a steady liberation of works that had been barred to Americans for decades: Lawrence's *Lady Chatterly's Lover,* Miller's *Tropic of Cancer,* Cleland's *Fanny Hill.* The turbulent conflict over what was legitimate treatment of sex, however, emerged from the pages of subsequent Supreme Court decisions as it did from pulpits and advice columns. *Roth* v. *U.S.* had said much, but decisions of the next decade showed that it had settled little: Was permissiveness to extend to all

[54] William B. Lockhart and Robert C. McClure, "Literature, the Law of Obscenity, and the Constitution," *Minnesota Law Review,* XXXVIII, No. 4 (March 1954), 302–320.

words, to all except "hardcore pornography," to anything except "pandering" or "commercial exploitation" of sex? Although the Supreme Court's attitude toward sex had become expansive, the legal specifics of obscenity remained unfinished business.[55]

Tradition stemming from American Revolutionary thought and experience had customarily placed government prosecutions at the heart of threats to freedom of the press; history had found government's record of suppression more accessible, more available for study and telling, than that of the citizenry or of the press itself. But the fact was that by the 1960's, the ancient law of criminal words offered scarcely more than a blush of restriction to print. Obscenity charges continued to harass and convictions could sometimes be gotten; but the appeal process following the Roth decision in 1957 generally brought reversal. The assault on the obscene—the most persistent legal pursuit of criminal words since 1800—now moved with an uncertainty it had not revealed since Anthony Comstock gave it life.

Sedition was at the heart of the mid-twentieth-century laws intended to curb domestic communism, under the rubric of advocating violent overthrow of government. Clearly, central interests on which the laws impinged were First-Amendment freedoms of expression and assembly. It was difficult, and perhaps of small importance, to sort out the free-press implications of one hundred-odd convictions obtained during the first twenty-five years of the Smith Act's life: it was a crime under the Act to belong to an organization that advocated violent overthrow of government, as it was to advocate such overthrow. Speech, print, and assembly all were, of course, curbed by such provisions, but by 1955 the "Warren Court"—called this for Chief Justice Earl Warren, who had been appointed in 1953—was plainly reluctant to uphold Smith Act convictions.

---

[55] *Roth* v. *U.S.*, 354 U.S. 476 (1957); M. L. Ernst and A. U. Schwartz, *Censorship: the Search for the Obscene*, pp. 220–229; *Ginzburg* v. *U.S.*, 86 S. Ct. 942 (1966).

And in 1965 the court rendered unenforcible the provisions of the McCarran Act of 1950 that reinforced the Smith Act: It said that the provisions of the former, which required members of the Communist Party to register and thus admit membership, were out of joint with the protection of the self-incrimination clause of the Fifth Amendment. The Warren Court made its striking record in the protection of civil liberties through its free-expression decisions, as well as through those that recognized the Negro race as equal under the laws to the white.

Of the three other major word-crimes of English tradition, blasphemy had been the rarest of rare charges in the twentieth century and was a dead letter by the 1920's. Contempt of court by publication flourished from the third quarter of the nineteenth century until 1941, when the Supreme Court sent it into retreat under the clear and present danger test. Criminal libel gained and held momentum from 1880 until World War I, and then declined swiftly until, by mid-century, hardly a dozen cases in a decade reached the states' high courts.

So far as these ancient legal restraints of English origin and American adoption were concerned, never since 1800 had the American printing press been freer than it was by 1960. Moreover, antiquity's law of civil libel was shaken in its bastion of complexity and confusion, and its power to intimidate reduced, when in 1964 the Supreme Court sharply limited the range of words that could be held to be defamatory of public officials. It said that words must be proved malicious to permit recovery of damages by officials, and in its authoritative definition of malice—knowing falsehood or reckless disregard of the truth or falsity of words—chose a standard of some clarity and rigor where there had previously been more than a dozen opaque and elastic definitions.[56]

Of course, twentieth-century government could power the restraint of expression with levers other than the encrusted law of criminal words and civil libel. Publishers of the New Deal

[56] *New York Times* v. *Sullivan*, 376 U.S. 254, 279–280; 53 *Corpus Juris Secundum* 35–37.

era who issued grave warnings of the death of freedom as the result of employment of antitrust, tax, and labor laws against the print media, however, proved inaccurate prophets. There was more cause for concern in a quite different government propensity—the impulse to secrecy which became an issue after World War II. The mid-twentieth-century newsman, likely to discern and decry a large increase in government refusal of access to information of public affairs, saw such hedging of the "right to know" as the modern threat to freedom. But in the absence of historical study of the right to know, it was impossible to see it in perspective and to weigh its general condition as of 1960 against that of fifty or a hundred years earlier.

Also of uncertain implication in the 1960's was a growing national concern over the effects of news media publicity on trials and especially on the prejudicing of trial juries. The Supreme Court largely limited its focus on the press to lecturing it for circus treatment of sensational criminal cases. A few press groups established voluntary codes of proper practice. High courts and attorneys general tried to cure some of the illness at the prime source by telling trial judges and prosecutors to stanch the flow of publicity from witnesses, district attorneys, police, and lawyers involved in the cases. The libertarian cry that throttling sources of news was in effect damaging the free press was loud in the land, but by no means universally found among media spokesmen.[57]

Of all the restraints, public sentiment had most strikingly supported the attack on obscenity and sedition. Acting as moral and economic pressure-groups against obscenity, citizens had been far more likely to resort to physical threat or violence when they suspected sedition, as during the Civil War and

---

[57] *Report of the President's Commission on the Assassination of President John F. Kennedy* (Washington, D.C.: Government Printing Office, 1964), pp. 240–242; *Irvin* v. *Dowd,* 366 U.S. 717 (1961); *Sheppard* v. *Maxwell, New York Times,* June 7, 1966, p. 1; *Editor & Publisher,* Aug. 15, 1964, p. 11.

World War I. The public always, of course, had its own categories of words that it would not tolerate; nowhere was this plainer than in its direct action against the proponents of racial equality in the South, whether in 1835 or in 1960. Citizens' approval for freedom of the press in the abstract fell off sharply in the practical application of the principle to their taboos and prejudices.[58]

It was possible that public tolerance for unorthodoxy in times of tension and anxiety was greater in 1965 than it had been in 1800.[59] But the whip and club and gun emerged in explosions of violence against the spokesmen for racial equality as the nation undertook the hard labor of desegregation in the 1950's and 1960's. It was education that Jefferson had relied on for the growth of tolerance, and the mid-twentieth century generally said the same. A notable force unknown to Jefferson but at work after 1920 was the institutionalized drive for civil liberty. "Eternal vigilance" was organized, in the form of the American Civil Liberties Union and other associations. As public educators, pressure groups, and constant watchmen, these groups were invaluable.

Years of stress in the life of the nation ordinarily had brought increased restrictions and diminished freedom. Fluctuation in liberty with stress and release, however, told only part of the story. Regionalism and localism could throttle discussion of a social problem or issue almost permanently, as much of the South did with the plight of the Negroes. Furthermore, even so cataclysmic an event as World War II had not tortured restraint of the press into outright oppression. The Civil War system of suppression was widespread, but it left great gaps through which uninhibited if often irresponsible writers spoke

---

[58] Charles E. Swanson, "Midcity Daily: What the People Think a Newspaper Should Be," *Journalism Quarterly*, XXVI, No. 3 (June 1949), 173; Hadley Cantril (ed.), *Public Opinion 1935–1946* (Princeton, 1951), pp. 244–245.

[59] John P. Roche, *The Quest for the Dream* (New York, 1963), chaps. 1, 11.

their minds. There is little to indicate that increased social stress was related to contempt or criminal libel convictions.

The times of most marked restraint may be roughly designated as the middle third of the nineteenth century and the first third of the twentieth. Freedom of the press ran strongest during the first and last thirds of the nineteenth century, and the period between 1930 and 1965, with an interrupting spasm in the early and middle 1950's. No period had seen an "absolute" freedom, and at no time had a segment of the society sought it. Always there were thinkers who wanted no punishment for words unless the words could be plainly attached to overt criminal acts. In the 1950's and 1960's, Supreme Court Justice Hugo Black espoused the most drastic libertarian position of any major American spokesman for freedom of the press since 1800: No words should be punished, he said, and even civil libel actions should be abandoned.[60] Supreme Court majorities, however, even when they approved a "preferred position" for First-Amendment freedoms, insisted on balancing these freedoms against other social interests. The court's libertarian thrust, growing since shortly after World War I, eschewed Black's absolute.

The Supreme Court could not extinguish the creativity of postal administrators in devising tools for censorship; nor take cognizance of the public's countless extralegal ways with libraries and with those who sought aggressively to change the social and economic *status quo;* nor force the communications industries to increase the diversity of their content. It had not found reason to declare unconstitutional the sedition laws that Congress passed. But for thirty-five years it had proved to be the nation's foremost agency for the furtherance of freedom of the press, and in 1965 there were no portents that it was retreating.

---

[60] "Justice Black and First Amendment 'Absolutes': a Public Interview," *New York University Law Review*, XXXVII, No. 4 (June 1962), 549—563.

Chronology of Freedom and Restraint

1801	Alien and Sedition Acts expire.
1804	Alexander Hamilton pleads truth with good motives and justifiable ends as defense in criminal libel in *People* v. *Croswell.*
1805	New York legislature enacts law adopting Hamilton's phrase.
1812	Supreme Court rejects principle of a federal common law of crimes in *U.S.* v. *Hudson and Goodwin.*
1829–1830	Southern states begin enactment of laws punishing expression intended to incite slaves to insurrection.
1831	Congress passes statute restricting punishment for contempt of court to misbehavior in the presence of the court or so near thereto as to obstruct administration of justice.
1835	Rapid growth of vigilance committees to control antislavery expression begins.
1835–1836	Congress rejects President Jackson's request for a law barring "incendiary publications" from mails.
1837	The Reverend Elijah Lovejoy, editor of Alton, Illinois, *Telegraph,* is killed by a mob for his antislavery publications.
1842	First federal obscenity law is passed, barring obscene pictures from entry to the United States.

1861 Congress enacts statute making conspiracy to overthrow the government by force a crime.

1861–1865 Civil War suppressions: military, presidential, judicial, postal, and mob control of speech and press.

1865 First postal obscenity law is passed, barring obscene materials from mails.

1873 "Comstock Act" passed, strengthening act of 1865.

1890 Attorney General declares the power of the Post Office to use the Comstock Act as a censorship statute.

1890–1900 Criminal libel actions in state supreme courts reach their peak, with more than one hundred cases.

1902–1905 Four states pass laws to punish anarchists' advocacy of violent overthrow of government.

1908–1909 Federal government prosecution of the New York *World* and the Indianapolis *News* for criminal libel is instituted by President Theodore Roosevelt, and fails.

1917–1918 Espionage Act of 1917 and Amendment of 1918 ("Sedition Act") are passed as the first federal sedition legislation since 1800, followed by similar and farther-reaching state enactments. Prosecutions of almost 2,000 persons follow, with almost 900 convictions; postal control is exerted upon approximately 100 newspapers.

1917 National Civil Liberties Bureau, forerunner of the American Civil Liberties Union, is established under the direction of Roger Baldwin.

1919 Supreme Court accepts "clear and present danger" test stated by Justice Oliver Wendell Holmes in *Schenck* v. *U.S.*

1921 Power of Postmaster General to withdraw second-class mail rate from newspapers on the basis of their content is confirmed by Supreme Court in *U.S. ex rel. Milwaukee Social Democratic Publishing Co.* v. *Burleson.*

1925 Supreme Court rules that freedom of speech and press as guaranteed by the First Amendment, is protected against state invasion by the due process clause of the Fourteenth Amendment, in *Gitlow* v. *State of New York.*

1931 Supreme Court rules in *Near* v. *Minnesota* that censorship before publication is almost always unconstitutional.

1933 Restrictive "Hicklin test" of obscenity is rejected in *U.S.* v. *One Book Called "Ulysses."*

1940 Alien Registration Act of 1940 is passed by Congress as the first federal peacetime sedition law since 1800.

1940 *Thornhill* v. *Alabama* marks the beginning of a decade of reliance on "clear and present danger" by the Supreme Court.

1941–1945 Crisis of World War II passed without severe restraints on expression.

1951 Supreme Court upholds constitutionality of Alien Registration Act of 1940 in *Dennis* v. *U.S.;* "clear and present danger," diversely interpreted in concurring and dissenting opinions, loses its force and begins to decline.

1957 "Roth test" for obscenity is stated by the Supreme Court in *Roth* v. *U.S.*

1964 Supreme Court rules that public officials cannot recover damages in civil libel cases unless the publication is made with malice—with knowledge of the falsity of the words, or reckless disregard for truth or falsity: *New York Times Company* v. *Sullivan.*

Selected Bibliography

ORIGINAL SOURCES

General

ANONYMOUS. "Freedom of the Press," *American Annual Cyclopaedia and Register of Important Events, 1861–1864*. New York: D. Appleton & Company, 1865, 1867. I, 328–330; II, 480–481; III, 423–425; IV, 389–394.

———. "Requests for Censorship by Press of Certain War News," *The Official Bulletin*, Dec. 31, 1917.

BARRE, W. L., ed. *Speeches and Writings of Hon. Thomas F. Marshall.* Cincinnati: Applegate & Company, 1858.

BEECHER, EDWARD. *Narrative of Riots at Alton.* Alton, Ill.: George Holton, 1838.

BIRNEY, JAMES G. *Narrative of the Late Riotous Proceedings Against the Liberty of the Press, in Cincinnati.* Cincinnati, 1836. Pamphlet.

BUCKINGHAM, JOSEPH T. *Personal Memoirs and Recollections of Editorial Life.* 2 vols. Boston: Ticknor, Reed, and Fields, 1852.

CHAFFE, ZECHARIAH, JR. *Freedom of Speech.* New York: Harcourt, Brace and Howe, 1920.

CHANNING, WILLIAM E. *Works.* Boston: American Unitarian Association, 1887.

COMMISSION ON FREEDOM OF THE PRESS. *A Free and Responsible Press.* Chicago: University of Chicago Press, 1947.

COMSTOCK, ANTHONY. *Traps for the Young.* 3rd edition. New York: Funk & Wagnalls, 1884.

COOLEY, THOMAS M. *A Treatise on the Constitutional Limitations.* 1st edition. Boston: Little, Brown, and Company, 1868.

COOPER, THOMAS. *Political Essays.* 2nd edition. Philadelphia: Printed for Robert Campbell, 1800.

———. *A Treatise on the Law of Libel and the Liberty of the Press.* New York: G. F. Hopkins & Son, 1830.

EDITORS OF THE RICHMOND (VA.) *Compiler.* "Canons for the Management of the Press," *Niles' Register,* XIII (Nov. 29, 1817), 210–211.

FISK, THEOPHILUS. *The Nation's Bulwark, an Oration, on the Freedom of the Press.* New Haven: Examiner and Watch Tower of Freedom, 1832. Pamphlet.

GOODELL, WILLIAM. *Slavery and Anti-Slavery.* New York: William Goodell, 1853. Chap. 34.

GREELEY, HORACE, ed. *The Writings of Cassius Marcellus Clay.* New York: Harper, 1848.

HOCKING, WILLIAM E. *Freedom of the Press.* Chicago: University of Chicago Press, 1947.

HOLT, FRANCIS LUDLOW. *The Law of Libel . . . in the Law of England.* ANTHONY BLEECKER, ed. 1st American edition. New York: Stephen Gould, 1818.

HUME, JOHN F. *The Abolitionists.* New York and London: G. P. Putnam's Sons, 1905.

INVESTIGATORS TO THE COMMISSION OF INQUIRY, THE INTERCHURCH WORLD MOVEMENT. *Public Opinion and the Steel Strike.* New York: Harcourt, Brace and Company, 1921.

JACKSON, ANDREW. Message to Congress of Dec. 1835. In J. D. RICHARDSON, *A Compilation of the Messages and Papers of the President.* N. P.: Bureau of National Literature, 1913. II, 1,394–1,395.

———. Letter to Postmaster General Amos Kendall, Aug. 9, 1835. In J. S. BASSETT, ed., *Correspondence of Andrew Jackson.* Washington, D.C.: Carnegie Institution, 1931. V, 360–361.

JEFFERSON, THOMAS. *The Papers of Thomas Jefferson,* ed. JULIAN P. BOYD, *et. al.* Princeton: Princeton University Press, 1950–

"Justice Black and First Amendment 'Absolutes': a Public Interview," *New York University Law Review,* XXXVII No. 4 (June 1962), 549–563.

KENDALL, POSTMASTER GENERAL AMOS. Letter to Andrew Jackson. In J. S. BASSETT, ed., *Correspondence of Andrew Jackson.* Washington, D.C.: Carnegie Institution, 1931. V, 359.

———. Letter to Postmaster Samuel L. Gouverneur of New York City, Aug. 22, 1835. In *Niles' Register,* XLIX (Sept. 5, 1835), 8–9.

KENT, JAMES. *Commentaries on American Law.* 11th edition. Boston: Little, Brown, and Company, 1867.

[KIMBALL, EDMUND]. *Reflections upon the Law of Libel, in a Letter Addressed to 'A Member of the Suffolk Bar.' By a Citizen.* Boston: Wells and Lilly, 1823. Pamphlet.

LIEBER, FRANCIS. *On Civil Liberty and Self-Government.* 2 vols. Philadelphia: Lippincott, Grambo and Co., 1853.

———. *Manual of Political Ethics.* Boston: C. C. Little and J. Brown, 1838–1839.

LOVEJOY, ELIJAH. "To My Fellow Citizens," *St. Louis Observer,* Nov. 5, 1835.

MCCORMICK, ROBERT R. *The Freedom of the Press.* New York: D. Appleton-Century Company, 1936.

MEIKLEJOHN, ALEXANDER. *Free Speech and Its Relation to Self-Government.* New York: Harper, 1948.

NATIONAL CIVIL LIBERTIES BUREAU. *War-Time Prosecutions and Mob Violence Involving the Rights of Free Speech, Free Press, and Peaceful Assemblage.* New York: Civil Liberties Bureau, March 11, 1919. Pamphlet.

NELLES, WALTER. *Espionage Act Cases.* New York: National Civil Liberties Bureau, July 1918. Pamphlet.

PHILLIPS, WENDELL. Maiden speech, on the death of Elijah Lovejoy. In HENRY TANNER, *The Martyrdom of Lovejoy.* Chicago: Fergus Printing Company, 1881.

[PLUMER, WILLIAM]. *Freedom's Defence: or a Candid Examination of Mr. Calhoun's Report on the Freedom of the Press. By Cincinnatus.* Worcester: Dorr, Howland & Co., 1836. Pamphlet.

ROOSEVELT, THEODORE. Letter to Henry L. Stimson, Dec. 9, 1908. In ELTING E. MORISON, ed., *The Letters of Theodore Roosevelt.* Cambridge: Harvard University Press, 1951–1954. VI, 1,415–1,417.

SCHOFIELD, HENRY. "Freedom of the Press in the United States," *Publications of the American Sociological Society,* IX (1915), 67–116.

SCHROEDER, THEODORE. *Free Speech for Radicals.* New York: The Free Speech League, 1916.

———. *"Obscene" Literature and Constitutional Law: A Forensic Defense of Freedom of the Press.* New York: privately published, 1911.

STANSBURY, ARTHUR J. *Report of the Trial of James H. Peck.* Boston: Hilliard, Gray and Company, 1833.

STORY, JOSEPH. *Commentaries on the Constitution* (Boston: Hilliard, Gray, and Company, 1833. Vol. III.

THOMSON, JOHN. *An Enquiry, Concerning the Liberty, and Licentiousness of the Press, and the Uncontroulable Nature of the Human Mind.* New York: Printed by Johnson and Stryker, for the author, 1801.

TOCQUEVILLE, ALEXIS DE. *Democracy in America.* New York: J. & H. G. Langley, 1841. Vol. I.

TUCKER, ST. GEORGE. "Of the Right of Conscience; And of the Freedom of Speech and of the Press." In Tucker's *Blackstone's Commentaries: with Notes of Reference, to the Constitution and Laws, of the Federal Government of the United States: and of the Commonwealth of Virginia.* 5 vols. Philadelphia: William Young Birch and Abraham Small, 1803. Appendix to Vol. I, part 2, Note G.

The War of the Rebellion: Official Records of the Union and Confederate Armies. 4 series, 128 vols. Washington, D.C.: Government Printing Office, 1880–1901.

WORTMAN, TUNIS. *Treatise Concerning Political Enquiry, and the Liberty of the Press.* New York: Printed by George Forman, for the Author, 1800.

Court Decisions

Abrams v. *U.S.*, 250 U.S. 616 (1919).

Associated Press v. *National Labor Relations Board,* 301 U.S. 103 (1937).

Beauharnais v. *Illinois,* 343 U.S. 250 (1952).

Bridges v. *California,* 314 U.S. 252 (1941).

Butler v. *Michigan,* 352 U.S. 380 (1957).

Case of Lysander Barrett, 36 Va. 665 (1839).

Chaplinsky v. *New Hampshire,* 315 U.S. 568 (1942).

Commonwealth v. Blanding, 3 Pick. 304 (Mass., 1825).

Commonwealth v. *Clap,* 4 Tyng 163 (Mass., 1808).
Dennis v. *U.S.,* 341 U.S. 494 (1951).
Ex parte Jackson, 96 U.S. 727 (1877).
Gilbert v. *Minn.,* 254 U.S. 325 (1920).
Gitlow v. *New York,* 268 U.S. 652 (1925).
Grosjean v. *American Press Co.,* 297 U.S. 233 (1936).
Grove Press v. *Christenberry,* 276 F.2d 433 (1960).
Hannegan v. *Esquire,* 327 U.S. 146 (1946).
Irvin v. *Dowd,* 366 U.S. 717 (1961).
Kneeland's Case, 20 Pick. 206 (Mass., 1838).
Lovell v. *Griffin,* 303 U.S. 444 (1938).
Near v. *Minnesota,* 283 U.S. 697 (1931).
New York Times Company v. *Sullivan,* 376 U.S. 254 (1964).
Patterson v. *Colorado,* 205 U.S. 454 (1907).
People v. *Croswell,* 3 Johnson's Cases 337 (N.Y., 1804).
Queen v. *Hicklin,* L.R. 3 Q.B. 360 (1868).
Respublica v. *Dennie,* 4 Yeates 267 (Pa., 1805).
Roth v. *U.S.,* 354 U.S. 476 (1957).
Schenck v. *U.S.,* 249 U.S. 47 (1919).
State v. *Morrill,* 16 Ark. 384 (1855).
Thornhill v. *Alabama,* 310 U.S. 88 (1940).
Toledo Newspaper Co. v. *U.S.,* 247 U.S. 402 (1918).
U.S. ex rel. Milwaukee Social Democratic Publishing Co. v. *Burleson,* 255 U.S. 407 (1921).
U.S. v. *Associated Press,* 52 F.Supp. 362 (1943).
U.S. v. *Associated Press,* 326 U.S. 1 (1945).
U.S. v. *Bennett,* 24 Fed. Cas. 1093 (2d. cir., 1879).
U.S. v. *Hudson and Goodwin,* 7 Cranch 32 (1812).
U.S. v. *One Book Called "Ulysses,"* 5 F.Supp. 182 (1933).
U.S. v. *Press Publishing Co.,* 219 U.S. 1 (1911).
U.S. v. *Smith,* 173 Fed. Rep. 227 (1909).
Whitney v. *California,* 274 U.S. 357 (1927).

Opinions of Attorney General

Exclusion from the Mails, 19 Op. Atty. Gen. 667 (1890)
Case of Murray, Eddy & Co., 12 Op. Atty. Gen. 399 (1868)
Exclusion of Seditious Publications from the Mails, 26 Op. Atty. Gen. 555 (1908)
Yazoo City Post Office Case, 8 Op. Atty. Gen. 489 (1857)

COLLATERAL READING

ANONYMOUS. "Constitutionality of the Law of Criminal Libel," *Columbia Law Review*, LII, No. 4 (April 1952), 521–534.

———. "Mr. Burleson to Rule the Press," *Literary Digest*, LV, No. 2 (Oct. 6, 1917), 12.

BERNS, WALTER. *Freedom, Virtue and the First Amendment*. Baton Rouge: Louisiana State University Press, 1957.

BROOKS, ALEXANDER D. *Civil Rights and Liberties in the United States, An Annotated Bibliography*. New York: Civil Liberties Educational Foundation, 1962.

BROUN, HEYWOOD, and MARGARET LEECH. *Anthony Comstock, Roundsman of the Lord*. New York: The Literary Guild of America, 1927.

CHAFEE, ZECHARIAH, JR. *Free Speech in the United States*. Cambridge: Harvard University Press, 1941.

———. *Government and Mass Communications*. 2 vols. Chicago: University of Chicago Press, 1947.

———. *Thirty-Five Years with Freedom of Speech*. New York: Roger N. Baldwin Civil Liberties Foundation, 1952. Pamphlet.

CHANDLER, PELEG W., ed. *American Criminal Trials*. 2 vols. Boston: Timothy H. Carter & Co., 1844.

CHEYNEY, EDWARD P. "Freedom and Restraint: A Short History," *Annals of the American Academy of Political and Social Science*, CC (Nov. 1938), 1–12.

———, ed. "Freedom of Inquiry and Expression," *Annals of the American Academy of Political and Social Science*, CC (Nov. 1938).

COLE, A. C. "Lincoln and the American Tradition of Civil Liberty," *Illinois State Historical Society Journal*, XIX, Numbers 3–4 (Oct. 1926–Jan. 1927), 102–114.

CORWIN, E. S. "Freedom of Speech and Press under the First Amendment: a Résumé," *Yale Law Journal*, XXX, No. 1 (Nov. 1920), 48–55.

CROSS, HAROLD L. *The People's Right to Know*. New York: Columbia University Press, 1953.

DANIELS, WALTER M., ed. *The Censorship of Books*. New York: H. W. Wilson Company, 1954.

DEUTSCH, E. P. "Freedom of the Press and of the Mails," *Michigan Law Review*, XXXVI, No. 5 (March 1938), 703.

DUNIWAY, CLYDE AUGUSTUS. *The Development of Freedom of the Press in Massachusetts*. New York: Longmans, Green, and Co., 1906.

EATON, CLEMENT. "Censorship of the Southern Mails," *American Historical Review*, XLVIII, No. 2 (Jan. 1943), 266–280.

———. *Freedom of Thought in the Old South*. Durham: Duke University Press, 1940.

———. "Mob Violence in the Old South," *Mississippi Valley Historical Review*, XXIX, No. 3 (Dec. 1942), 351–370.

EMERSON, THOMAS I. "The Doctrine of Prior Restraint," *Law and Contemporary Problems*, XX, No. 4 (Autumn, 1955), 648–671.

——— and DAVID HABER. *Political and Civil Rights in the United States*. 2 vols. 2nd edition. Buffalo: Dennis & Co., 1958.

ERNST, MORRIS L., and ALAN U. SCHWARTZ. *Censorship: the Search for the Obscene*. New York: Macmillan, 1964.

FELLMAN, DAVID. *The Censorship of Books*. Madison: University of Wisconsin Press, 1957. Pamphlet.

FOX, SIR JOHN C. *The History of Contempt of Court*. Oxford: Clarendon Press, 1927.

GARDINER, HAROLD CHARLES, S. J. *Catholic Viewpoint on Censorship*. Garden City and New York: Hanover House, 1958.

GERALD, J. EDWARD. *The Press and the Constitution*. Minneapolis: University of Minnesota Press, 1948.

GRANT, SIDNEY S., and S. E. ANGOFF. "Massachusetts and Censorship," *Boston University Law Review*, X, No. 1 (Jan. 1930), 36–60.

HOCKING, WILLIAM E. *Freedom of the Press*. Chicago: University of Chicago Press, 1947.

HOLMES, JOHN HAYNES, compiler. *Freedom of Speech and of the Press; Striking Passages from Distinguished Champions of Freedom of Expression*. New York, Washington: National Civil Liberties Bureau, 1918. Pamphlet.

HUDON, EDWARD G. *Freedom of Speech and Press in America*. Washington: Public Affairs Press, 1963.

ICKES, HAROLD L., compiler. *Freedom of the Press Today; A Clinical Examination by 28 Specialists*. New York: Vanguard Press, 1941.

JENSEN, JAY. "Toward a Solution of the Problem of Freedom of the Press," *Journalism Quarterly,* XXVII, No. 4 (Fall 1950), 399–408.

JOHNSON, DONALD O. *The Challenge to American Freedoms.* University of Kentucky Press, 1963.

JOHNSON, GERALD W. "Freedom of the Newspaper Press," *Annals of the American Academy of Political and Social Science,* CC (Nov. 1938), 60–75.

KLEMENT, FRANK. *The Copperheads in the Middle West.* Chicago: University of Chicago Press, 1960.

KONVITZ, MILTON R. *First Amendment Freedoms.* Ithaca: Cornell University Press, 1963.

———. *Fundamental Liberties of a Free People: Religion, Speech, Press, Assembly.* Ithaca: Cornell University Press, 1957.

LEFLAR, ROBERT A. "The Social Utility of the Criminal Law of Defamation," *Texas Law Review,* XXXIV, No. 7 (Oct. 1956), 984–1,035.

LEVY, LEONARD. *Jefferson and Civil Liberties.* Cambridge, Mass.: Belknap Press of Harvard University Press, 1963.

———. *Legacy of Suppression.* Cambridge, Mass.: Belknap Press of Harvard University Press, 1960.

LIPPMANN, WALTER. "The Indispensable Opposition," *Atlantic,* CLXIV, No. 2 (Aug. 1939), 186–190.

———. *Liberty and the News.* New York: Harcourt, Brace and Howe, 1920.

LOCKHART, WILLIAM B., and ROBERT C. MCCLURE. "Censorship of Obscenity: The Developing Constitutional Standards," *Minnesota Law Review,* XLV, No. 1 (Nov. 1960), 5–121.

MARBUT, FREDERICK B. "Decline of the Official Press in Washington," *Journalism Quarterly,* XXXIII, No. 3 (Summer 1956), 335–341.

MCCORMICK, JOHN, and MAIRI MACINNES. *Versions of Censorship.* Garden City, N. Y.: Doubleday & Company, Inc., 1962.

MCKEON, RICHARD, ROBERT K. MERTON, and WALTER GELLHORN. *Freedom to Read: Perspective and Program.* New York: R. R. Bowker, 1957.

MENDELSON, WALLACE. "Clear and Present Danger—From Schenck to Dennis," *Columbia Law Review,* LII, No. 3 (March 1952), 313–333.

MILNER, LUCILLE B., and GROFF CONKLIN. "Wartime Censorship in the United States," *Harper's*, CLXXX (Jan. 1940), 187–195.

MOCK, JAMES R. *Censorship 1917*. Princeton: Princeton University Press, 1941.

MOTT, FRANK LUTHER. *Jefferson and the Press*. Baton Rouge: Louisiana State University Press, 1943.

MURRAY, ROBERT K. *Red Scare: A Study in National Hysteria, 1919–1920*. Minneapolis: University of Minnesota Press, 1955.

NELLES, WALTER, and CAROL WEISS KING. "Contempt by Publication in the United States," *Columbia Law Review*, XXVIII, No. 4 (April 1928), 401–431; and XXVIII, No. 5 (May 1928), 525–562.

NYE, RUSSEL B. *Fettered Freedom*. East Lansing, Mich.: State College Press, 1949.

OUTLAND, ETHEL R. *The "Effingham" Libels on Cooper: A Documentary History of the Libel Suits of James Fenimore Cooper Centering Around the Three-Mile Point Controversy and the Novel* Home as Found, *1837–1845*. Madison: University of Wisconsin Press, 1929.

PATERSON, JAMES. *The Liberty of the Press, Speech, and Public Worship*. London: Macmillan and Co., 1880.

PATTERSON, GILES J. *Free Speech and a Free Press*. Boston: Little, Brown and Company, 1939.

PAUL, JAMES C. N., and MURRAY L. SCHWARTZ. "Foreign Communist Propaganda in the Mails: A Report on Some Problems of Federal Censorship," *University of Pennsylvania Law Review*, CVII, No. 5 (March 1959), 621–666.

———. *Federal Censorship; Obscenity in the Mail*. New York: Free Press of Glencoe, 1961.

PETERSON, H. C., and GILBERT C. FITE. *Opponents of War, 1917–1918*. Madison: University of Wisconsin Press, 1957.

PRESTON, WILLIAM, JR. *Aliens and Dissenters, Federal Suppression of Radicals, 1903–1933*. Cambridge: Harvard University Press, 1963.

RANDALL, JAMES G. *Constitutional Problems under Lincoln*. Revised edition. Urbana: University of Illinois Press, 1951.

ROCHE, JOHN P. *The Quest for the Dream*. New York: Macmillan, 1963.

WAITE, EDWARD F. "The Debt of Constitutional Law to Jehovah's Witnesses," *Minnesota Law Review*, XXVIII, No. 4 (March 1944), 209–246.

WARREN, CHARLES. "The New 'Liberty' under the Fourteenth Amendment," *Harvard Law Review*, XXXIX, No. 4 (Feb. 1926), 431–465.

WECHSLER, JAMES. *The Age of Suspicion*. New York: Random House, 1953.

WHIPPLE, LEON. *The Story of Civil Liberty in the United States*. New York: Vanguard Press, 1927.

WIGGINS, JAMES RUSSELL. *Freedom or Secrecy*. New York: Oxford University Press, 1956.

WILSON, QUINTUS C. "Voluntary Press Censorship During the Civil War," *Journalism Quarterly*, XIX, No. 3 (Sept. 1942), 251–261.

Periodicals

The Alton, Illinois, *Telegraph*, 1836, 1837.

Annual Report. American Civil Liberties Union, 1940–1964.

Cincinnati, Ohio, *Republican*, 1836.

Cincinnati, Ohio, *Weekly Herald and Philanthropist*, 1836–1846.

Freedom-to-Read Bulletin (Occasional; New York, American Book Publishers Council) 1962–1964.

The Nation, 1917–1921.

The National Anti Slavery Standard, 1856.

The New Republic, 1917–1921.

New York Evening Post, 1835–1837, 1917–1921.

The *New York World*, 1917–1921.

Niles' Register, 1835–1840.

The Official Bulletin, 1917–1918.

Richmond, Virginia, *Enquirer*, 1832, 1836.

Richmond, Virginia, *Whig*, 1836.

St. Louis, Missouri, *Observer*, 1835.

MILNER, LUCILLE B., and GROFF CONKLIN. "Wartime Censorship in the United States," *Harper's*, CLXXX (Jan. 1940), 187–195.

MOCK, JAMES R. *Censorship 1917*. Princeton: Princeton University Press, 1941.

MOTT, FRANK LUTHER. *Jefferson and the Press*. Baton Rouge: Louisiana State University Press, 1943.

MURRAY, ROBERT K. *Red Scare: A Study in National Hysteria, 1919–1920*. Minneapolis: University of Minnesota Press, 1955.

NELLES, WALTER, and CAROL WEISS KING. "Contempt by Publication in the United States," *Columbia Law Review*, XXVIII, No. 4 (April 1928), 401–431; and XXVIII, No. 5 (May 1928), 525–562.

NYE, RUSSEL B. *Fettered Freedom*. East Lansing, Mich.: State College Press, 1949.

OUTLAND, ETHEL R. *The "Effingham" Libels on Cooper: A Documentary History of the Libel Suits of James Fenimore Cooper Centering Around the Three-Mile Point Controversy and the Novel* Home as Found, *1837–1845*. Madison: University of Wisconsin Press, 1929.

PATERSON, JAMES. *The Liberty of the Press, Speech, and Public Worship*. London: Macmillan and Co., 1880.

PATTERSON, GILES J. *Free Speech and a Free Press*. Boston: Little, Brown and Company, 1939.

PAUL, JAMES C. N., and MURRAY L. SCHWARTZ. "Foreign Communist Propaganda in the Mails: A Report on Some Problems of Federal Censorship," *University of Pennsylvania Law Review*, CVII, No. 5 (March 1959), 621–666.

———. *Federal Censorship; Obscenity in the Mail*. New York: Free Press of Glencoe, 1961.

PETERSON, H. C., and GILBERT C. FITE. *Opponents of War, 1917–1918*. Madison: University of Wisconsin Press, 1957.

PRESTON, WILLIAM, JR. *Aliens and Dissenters, Federal Suppression of Radicals, 1903–1933*. Cambridge: Harvard University Press, 1963.

RANDALL, JAMES G. *Constitutional Problems under Lincoln*. Revised edition. Urbana: University of Illinois Press, 1951.

ROCHE, JOHN P. *The Quest for the Dream*. New York: Macmillan, 1963.

ROGERS, LINDSAY. *The Postal Power of Congress: A Study in Constitutional Expansion.* Baltimore: Johns Hopkins Press, 1916.

ROURKE, FRANCIS E. *Secrecy and Publicity.* Baltimore: Johns Hopkins Press, 1961.

SALMON, LUCY MAYNARD. *The Newspaper and Authority.* New York: Oxford University Press, 1923.

SAVAGE, W. S. *The Controversy over the Distribution of Abolition Literature.* Washington: Association for the Study of Negro Life and History, Inc., 1938.

SCHEIBER, HARRY N. *The Wilson Administration and Civil Liberties, 1917–1921.* Ithaca: Cornell University Press, 1960. Pamphlet.

SCHER, JACOB. "Access to Information: Recent Legal Problems," *Journalism Quarterly,* XXXVII, No. 1 (Winter 1960), 41–52.

SCHROEDER, THEODORE, compiler. *Free Press Anthology.* New York: Free Speech League and Truth Seeker Publishing Co., 1909.

———. *Free Speech Bibliography: Including Every Discovered Attitude toward the Problem, Covering Every Method of Transmitting Ideas and of Abridging Their Promulgation upon Every Subject Matter.* New York: H. W. Wilson Company, 1922.

SIEBERT, FREDERICK S. *Freedom of the Press in England, 1476–1776.* Urbana: University of Illinois Press, 1952.

SIEBERT, FREDERICK S., THEODORE PETERSON, and WILBUR SCHRAMM. *Four Theories of the Press.* Urbana: University of Illinois Press, 1956.

SMITH, JAMES MORTON. *Freedom's Fetters; the Alien and Sedition Laws and American Civil Liberties.* Ithaca: Cornell University Press, 1956.

SUMMERS, ROBERT E., compiler. *Federal Information Controls in Peacetime.* New York: H. W. Wilson Co., 1949.

———. *Wartime Censorship of Press and Radio.* New York: H. W. Wilson Co., 1942.

SWINDLER, WILLIAM F. *Problems of Law in Journalism.* New York: Macmillan, 1955.

THAYER, FRANK. *Legal Control of the Press.* 4th edition. Brooklyn: The Foundation Press, 1962.

VANCE, W. R. "Freedom of Speech and of the Press," *Minnesota Law Review,* II, No. 4 (March 1918), 239–260.

Editor's Note

The documents used here appear without change in spelling, punctuation, and capitalization. Ellipses may indicate the deletion of a segment or all of a sentence, or more than a sentence. In the decisions of courts I have sometimes eliminated almost all references to cited cases, but have retained citations where they lead the reader to cases that seem to me particularly important in understanding the development of legal doctrine.

For the great gaps inevitable in a book of documents covering more than a century and a half in the history of a subject as vital as freedom of the press, I make no apologies. I have chosen what I consider seminal works and important statements in major phases of the subject, illustrating change where possible. In several cases I have rejected the famous but accessible and often-printed document in favor of another that seems to me as important but is generally unknown or hard to get: thus, for example, neither President James Madison nor Elijah Lovejoy is represented here, while Thomas Cooper and William Ellery Channing are.

My thanks go particularly to Dean Leonard W. Levy of Brandeis University and Professor J. Edward Gerald of the University of Minnesota, who have been generous with advice and suggestions for which I have asked. They are in no way responsible for shortcomings of the work; the decisions have been my own.

I am deeply grateful to Donald Shaw for his help in checking references and making many a document copy, and also to Robert Kahan and Peter Knights, all of whom have been students in my seminar. Miss Ruth H. Davis and Miss Ellen Burke of the Library of the State Historical Society of Wisconsin have never failed in their willing and untiring help in locating documents. Most of all, I thank my wife—organizer, typist, and keen and patient critic.

H.L.N.

Freedom of the Press

from Hamilton to the Warren Court

Part One

GENERAL PRINCIPLES

The Case for Freedom: The Social and the Individual Good

1. ON THE PROPRIETY AND EXPEDIENCY OF UNLIMITED ENQUIRY

Thomas Cooper, 1800

Dr. Thomas Cooper left his native England in 1793 for America, a country where his contentious, aggressive spirit and his agitations for reform might have more room for expression. With other Jeffersonians, he found that room sharply circumscribed by the Alien and Sedition Acts of 1798–1800 under which criticism of government was made a federal crime. His natural reaction

---

From Thomas Cooper, *Political Essays* (2nd ed.; Philadelphia: Printed for R. Campbell, 1800), pp. 71–88.

was to object, and writing in the Northumberland, Pennsylvania, *Gazette* in 1799, he became one of the earliest libertarians in America to state publicly a rationale for a radical freedom of expression. Shortly thereafter, he himself was convicted under the Sedition Act for criticism of President John Adams. For the next thirty-odd years, his uncompromising stand that no criminal action for libel ought to be permitted was expressed in letters, newspapers, pamphlets, and books. He was to modify his radical position only in 1835 when, as a good Southerner (and the belligerent but respected former president of South Carolina College), he favored the exclusion of abolitionist literature from the mails. In the selection below, he argues the values of free speech and press in terms of the society's political good.

. . . But some topics have been urged, and some laws have been adopted, even in this free country, that strangely counteract the freedom of discussion we thought ourselves entitled to, and mysteriously shield the characters and conduct of our rulers from the unhallowed attacks of public investigation. I shall state, as fairly as I can, the common topics which are urged to protect the conduct of government (that is, of the citizens whom the people have elected to manage their public concerns) from general enquiry, and suggest the replies to which, in my opinion, they obviously lie open.

It may be said, that the freedom of the press, and the licentiousness of the press, are two very different things: that the liberty of propagating falshood [*sic*] may do as much harm, as the propagation of truth may do good; and that whatever encouragement the latter may deserve, it is surely right, even by penalties and prohibitions, to discourage the former.

It may be said, that rulers in every country are compelled to act from motives, and under circumstances, which it is impossible always to make public; that hence arises the necessity of reposing confidence in them, till time shall develope the motives of their actions: it is therefore injustice toward them, to license injurious accusations that may be founded in so many instances, on imperfect knowledge, even when the motive may be good.

That without respect for governors, and confidence in their conduct, it is impossible for the business of the people to be carried on: that calumnies against governors tend materially to lessen this necessary respect and confidence, and to obstruct the operations of government.

That if calumnious accusations could always be answered, they might perhaps do little harm: but that governors have their time so much occupied by affairs of state, that they cannot attend or reply to the numerous aspersions to which their conduct might be subject, from ignorance, from ambition, from disappointment, or malevolence: that it is unfair, therefore, to put them in a situation to be attacked with impunity, where they have not leisure for defence.

That a good public character is of more consequence to a public man, and of more consequence to the public also, than the private character of any private man: that the characters of our rulers deserve protection, therefore, from their superior importance both to themselves and to the public.

That no person of feeling would submit to fill an office of government, if he were perpetually liable to promiscuous unresented calumny, while he was exerting his best abilities, to benefit the community. Such an irritating situation would tend to exclude some of the best and most capable men, from accepting it.

It may be farther urged, that the privilege of unrestrained discussion of the measures of government, and the conduct of governors, is at least unnecessary in such countries as Great Britain, America, or France; where the constitution recognizes the representatives of the people, as the proper tribunal for the investigation of the conduct of government-officers: a tribunal, which has a right to demand every necessary evidence on both sides of the question—which need not proceed upon half information—which will hear deliberately the defence as well as the charge—and which decides upon a fullness of evidence that the public at large could no otherwise obtain.

That at all events, however allowable, or even desirable, would be such an uncontrouled licence of discussion in an Utopian state of society, where the mass of the people might have sufficient leisure to examine, and sufficient knowledge to understand, what might be offered to the consideration of the public, yet, in the actual state of society, which in all probability will never be much altered, the mass of the people, in every country, are necessarily ignorant and bigotted; guided by their passions and prejudices, and not by cool reasoning or the result of patient investigation. That this cannot be expected from them, and therefore all attempts to excite their passions and their prejudices against their governors, and against measures they cannot understand, is an unfair advantage taken of the multitude, which it is the duty of government to guard them from. That, in fact, all governments (even the American and French republics) have found it necessary to put such limits to political discussion, as should prevent popular tumult from being excited, by an appeal to popular prejudice. That in this most republican country, the western insurrection, and the riots in Northampton county, have proved the absolute necessity of the restriction contended for.

That although violent declamation, or fallacious argument, may break no bones, they are the parents of tumult; they excite to disturbance; they endanger internal tranquillity and sometimes external safety. Nor can government pay due attention to these most important objects, without keeping a check on the means by which they may be shaken.

That permitting the truth of the facts, of which a public officer is accused, to be given in evidence on the trial of the author or publisher, is a sufficient guard to freedom of enquiry, and a sufficient check on the officers of government. Nor ought any man to claim the privilege of accusing another, before the tribunal of the public, without being able to substantiate his charge.

Such are the arguments of those who are unfriendly to unlimited enquiry on political subjects. I have stated them as fairly as I am able, and shall proceed to reply to the substance of them. . . .

I. The propagation of falsehood is as injurious, as the propagation of truth is beneficial.

No. The evils that arise from the propagation of falsehood are transient; when the falsehood is detected they cease: the way to get rid of these evils is to permit discussion, that falsehood may be the sooner detected. The good derived from truth is permanent as truth itself.

Again. Who is to be the judge of truth or falsehood? The lawgivers who sedulously screen their own conduct from the public eye? If those who arrogate the right to decide on the truth or falsehood of opinion (for of facts we will speak presently) are liable to be mistaken, do they not deal out their punishments in the dark? And who can pretend to political infallibility?

Again. No error can be forcibly suppressed but at the hazard of suppressing truth also. Galileo was imprisoned. Locke was interdicted in an English university. Common Sense was sedition in America, and the Rights of Man are sedition in Great Britain. In how many countries was the perusal of the Bible prohibited?

II. Governors may act from motives not publicly known and not proper to be publicly communicated.

I would observe, that the more we understand of the science of government, the less necessity we find for governmental secrets. State-craft and priest-craft are fond of hidden mysteries: they delight in their esoteric and exoteric doctrines and measures; but hidden motives are always suspicious in a republican government. In such a government, so far as we have experienced, secrecy is the child of misconduct and the parent of mischief. Let any man consider the treaties of Pilnitz and Pavia, or read Monroe's View of the conduct of the Executive, and, comparing it with our present situation, form his own opinion on this subject. Where a statesman chuses to conceal his motives, it is at least an equal chance that he is *afraid* to disclose them, as that he *ought not* to disclose them.

The cases where secrecy is expedient are very few: they occur but rarely; and unless there be something apparently wrong, or some good reason for previous distrust, the people generally (far too generally) acquiesce without suspicion. The objection, therefore, amounts at the most to an exception only of small extent, to a general rule. Nor can a right of so much consequence as the right contended for, be overthrown by a few cases of possible inconvenience, and even these of so dubious a complexion.

III. Respect and confidence in our governors are necessary for the business of government to be carried on with effect.

Where respect and confidence are really due from having been earned, the public is never backward at paying them; on the contrary, the people are notoriously apt to err on the opposite side, and to pay an exuberance of homage approaching to adulation, where there exist the evidences of public merit. Had Washington, has Buonaparte, any reason to complain on this score? Do not the silly idolaters that compose a British mob, harness themselves like brutes to the carriage of a popular character? Have not Mr. Pitt and Mr. Fox their respective adorers equally devoted and blind? It is evident, then, that respect and confidence will be cheerfully paid where they are due; but ought they to be paid where they are not due? And how can it be ascertained whether they are really due or not, unless by means of perfect freedom of discussion of those characters to which they are said to be due?

IV. Governors have not leisure to answer calumnious accusations, however false and ill-founded they may really be.

In every government where the people, from having a due share in it, feel interested, as they really are, in every measure of their rulers, there will always be two parties among the public. There always has been, and therefore we have a right to say it is probable there always will be, some who defend against those who attack the conduct and characters of men in power. There is no fear, therefore, of the prevalence of unmerited or unrefuted calumny. Besides, unless the proofs of delinquency are glaring, the public are never influenced by general charges, by declamatory accusation, or by mere party appeals. In proportion to the freedom with which these are permitted, they do the less injury to those who are exposed to them. Moreover, is it not always in the power of governors, to procure able persons to state the truth to the public, and prevent any long continued mistake or deception?

V. The public characters of men in high situations, are of more importance to the public, than private character is to private individuals.

Granted. But a good public character should be founded upon integrity and ability: it should not be given if it be not deserved. Nor can that character deserve well of the public which will not bear public investigation. Whether it be merited or not, can only be known by such an investigation, if there be any circumstance of doubt.

VI. The right of unlimited discussion, or rather accusation, would tend to exclude valuable men from public offices: for they would be cautious of exposing themselves to situations of unmerited calumny.

Every situation has its peculiar advantages and disadvantages, which arise from the same source, and are generally proportionate to each other. Elevated stations attach distinction and celebrity, but in cases of real or supposed dereliction of duty, they incur a proportionate degree of reproach and obloquy. The man who enjoys the one, must run the risk of the other. Indeed, persons in these cases seem prone enough to think the former, a sufficient compensation for the latter; nor do we find that offices of profit or of honour are frequently rejected from this refined delicacy.

Ingratitude is not a vice common to the public mind; but excessive, unreasonable gratitude and veneration of high civil rank, is a weakness to which in all ages it has been peculiarly prone. Aristides, it is true, was banished, and Socrates put to death; but the annals of every nation testify, that while a single meritorious act in a prince or magistrate, will often excite veneration approaching to idolatry, a thousand instances of the wanton abuse of power—or arbitrary and oppressive conduct, have passed unnoticed.

VII. An appropriate tribunal for the investigation of public misconduct, is provided by the constitution of Great Britain, and of this country, and therefore the right contended for is unnecessary. It is sufficiently vested in the houses of legislature.

In the first place, the right of investigation is not exclusively vested in the legislature of either country, but conjointly belongs to the people at large, according to the acknowledged constitutions of both. The right of *impeachment,* so as to induce actual punishment, does indeed belong to the legislative tribunals, but the freedom of the press includes at least the freedom of enquiry into public delinquency.

In the next place, every citizen of a free government is as much interested as a legislator, in the public conduct of public men; and therefore ought not to be precluded from expressing his opinion where his interest is equally concerned.

Thirdly, many topics and remarks may occur to intelligent writers on public measures, who are not legislators, that may not occur to those who are. This is so notoriously the case, that the expediency of permitting the public at large to discuss political topics, has never been openly denied in any free government, but it has always been indirectly attacked by its opposers with plausible and insidious restrictions.

Fourthly, How are the people in a representative government, to judge of the respective merits of those whom they are to reject or appoint to public situations, if the liberty in question be not granted? The political merits or demerits of public characters, cannot be known without this liberty. And in proportion to the general exercise of it, such will be the general diffusion of knowledge; and of course in such proportion will the electors be qualified to choose, and the persons chosen, to act, with superior discernment and ability. A nation thus generally enlightened on public topics, must derive advantages in her public career, that never could be obtained where the jealousy of despotism, or public ignorance, or national prejudice, has obstructed this grand source of all human improvement.

We may urge, fifthly, that experience has shewn there is room for the question, Quis custodiet ipsos custodes? Do the elected guardians of public liberty never require watching? We have heard of venal commons, and corrupted representatives; nay more, we know them to be possible evils. It may sometimes be made the interest of these representative tribunals to screen, instead of to punish delinquency; and they may sometimes think it right to place artificial ramparts even round their own characters, against the attacks of public enquiry. It may be their interest, or the interest of some of their leaders, to deceive the people; but it never can be the interest of the people to deceive themselves. Upon the servants of the public, in whatever situation, there is no effectual check but public opinion: this can never be well grounded, but on public investigation, on perfect unrestricted discussion. Hence all the eulogia of patriots of every enlightened country, on the freedom of the press; and hence the pertinacious never-ending attacks, open and concealed, plausible and daring, of governors in every age and in every nation, against this grand safeguard of public liberty, this scourge and terror of public delinquency. Experience has presented us with no truth more confirmed or important, than that from the moment a man in public trust begins to talk about the licentiousness of the press, and sacredness of public character, he is to be suspected. Hic niger est, hunc tu Romane caveto.

VIII. The mass of the people are, and always will be ignorant, and therefore we ought not to permit their prejudices to be worked upon by designing men. Witness the Western insurrection and the Northampton riots.

The most effectual way to keep the people ignorant, if they are so, is to perpetuate those restrictions on freedom of enquiry, which this objection is intended to support. Diffuse knowledge—enable the people to read, and incite them to think, and the objection is done away: they are no longer Mr. Sedgwick's ignorant herd, or Mr. Burke's swinish multitude. I know, and allow, that the modern doctrines of the perfectibility of man, can never take away the necessity of human labour, or make every blacksmith a Newton; but every man may and OUGHT to be taught to read, to write, and to be familiar with the common operations of arithmetic: he ought to have the *means* of knowledge put in his power; nor does any station imply, of necessity, such unremitting labour as not to afford some leisure to make use of these means. The country where this unremitting labour is necessary to the comfortable subsistence of any class of the community, is a bad one; in some shape or other there is despotism in it. The country where every man and woman cannot read and write, has reason to complain of its rulers. These truths require no defence in the present day, however they may be neglected, and in this country shamefully neglected, in practice. The objection then destroys itself; if the people are ignorant it is for want of the general diffusion and practice of the truths which discussion would bring incessantly into view. And when it is considered that the cautious opinions of philosophers of half a century ago, are now common axioms, especially on political subjects, the argument from ignorance can be of little weight.

As to the Western insurrection, and the riots in Northampton county, much as was made of them at the time, and most grossly as they have been exaggerated, they would never have happened at all, if reasoning and argument, if fair representation and mild and conciliatory remonstrance, had been sufficiently the precursors of military force. But that military force has taught the people to think as well as to obey, and in those counties where its effects have been experienced, there are few indeed so ignorant, as not to feel the extreme importance of public investigation, unlimited by the powerful jealousy of those whose conduct is obnoxious to it.

It is the general diffusion of knowledge—it is free discussion, that eradicates the prejudices of the people: a prejudice, or pre-judgment, is a view of one side of a question, and an opinion formed and acted on from this partial view, before all the facts and arguments that may be conveniently obtained, are fairly considered. It is self-evident that the right we contend for is the cure of prejudice. In like manner, people will be governed by their passions, if they are not governed by their reason. What is the cure for *this* evil? Surely to call their reason into play—to incite them to reflect—to teach them that every question has two sides—that as their neighbour is not infallible, so neither are they. In short, to accustom them to free enquiry on all subjects.

In a government in which the people have a voice—in all governments not completely despotic, it will surely be allowed that some knowledge is requisite in the people at large. The better they are informed, the more readily may they be expected to approve and acquiesce in wise measures. Ignorance, we grant, is the certain parent of error and obstinacy, nor can there be a more effectual means of removing it, than the free exercise of the right in question. If the complaints of the multitude, be they well or ill founded, are forcibly suppressed, there is danger: for people will think, though they may be prohibited from speaking; and sometimes they will act: but in nine cases out of ten, let the ebullitions of political opinion evaporate as they arise, and they will not acquire force enough to justify apprehension.

IX. An author is sufficiently protected where he is permitted to defend himself, as in this country, by giving in evidence the truth of the facts stated.

This is not a sufficient protection; for, a public fact may be notorious, and yet strict legal proof almost impossible to be procured by an individual. Suppose it commonly known and believed in England, that Lord Hawkesbury has declared there is a British party in this country; or that such a sentiment were expressed in a report of the council, how could an author here bring forward legal evidence of the fact?

Secondly, The expence of producing such evidence, even where it could be obtained, is sufficient to discourage any author from stating a known fact, where the purse of the government is to be employed against him. Suppose I were to assert, that Mr. Pickering wrote a letter to Judge Bee, stating that it was the advice and request of the President that Jonathan Robbins should be given up to the British, must I not (legally speaking) resort to Carolina or to Braintree for evidence, should the President be gone home?

Thirdly, This liberty still leaves *opinion* open to punishment. We cannot draw conclusions with impunity, if they tend directly or indirectly, in the cautious language of our sedition law, to criminate the persons whose characters are sheltered by that law.

For the investigation of public characters and measures, I think no action for libel ought to be permitted: but if it must, the accused should have the right of producing, unchecked by the court, any evidence whatever, that he may think will prove his case; and the jury should have the right of determining what weight is due to it.

After all, the most cautious must acknowledge that public officers ought to be amenable to those they serve; and that public opinion is a salutary check on those who guide the helm of state. What should we think of an agent who forbad his employers to examine his accounts, or scrutinize his conduct, in cases where their interest was materially concerned, and respecting the business they had entrusted to his care?

Every page of history attests the proneness of mankind to abuse power; and if the conduct of governors be not to be open to investigation and reprehension, room is left for the introduction of every abuse. What avails a good constitution, if the spirit of it may be counteracted, and its essential principles infringed with impunity, by those who administer it? Nor are the people in any country addicted to suspicion or unreasonable complaint; on the contrary, it is well known they will bear much, before they have recourse to opposition. In all the struggles of the English against the extension of prerogative, from the earliest period of their history to the present time, do we not in every instance wonder that oppression could proceed so far unresisted? Will any person contend that there was not abundant reason for complaint whenever they did complain? and yet the English have been more remarkable for their tenacious jealousy of liberty than any other modern nation, and would consequently have been particularly prone to this kind of excess.

But men will in time be persuaded that the cautious jealousy of persons in power, here as well as elsewhere, lest the freedom of the press should degenerate into licentiousness, is founded much more upon considerations of their own interest and safety, than the interest and safety of the public: it is not usually the people who encroach on the rights of their governors, it is the encroachment of the latter that history points out as the object of dread. Every day's experience brings some new proof of this; and the citizens of a free state should be at least as jealous and tenacious of their rights as their servants are of their own characters.

2. OF THE LIBERTY OF THE PRESS

Francis Ludlow Holt, 1818

English law for the regulation of speech and press reached early America in considerable part as a result of the writings of barristers Francis Ludlow Holt of the Middle Temple and Thomas Starkie of Lincoln's Inn. In 1818 a New York publisher obtained Holt's *The Law of Libel . . . in the Law of England,* copied the entire work and procured Anthony Bleecker, counselor at law, to add such notes on American cases "as are analogous or nonconformable to the English doctrine." Bleecker found nothing with which to take exception in Holt's primary emphasis on freedom of the press as one of the "rights of nature . . . that is to say, of the free exercise of our faculties." But while he thus expressed the freedom of the press as the individual's sacred natural right—a point of view much more congenial, of course, to the nineteenth century than to the twentieth—he was also at pains to depict the benefits of a free press to the society.

Having already shown that the common law recognised the offence of libel from the earliest times, it remains to be con-

---

From Francis Ludlow Holt, *The Law of Libel . . . in the Law of England,* edited by Anthony Bleecker (first American edition, taken from the second London edition; New York: Stephen Gould, 1818), pp. 57–61.

sidered, whether the invention of printing, a new and enlarged means of libel, in any way altered the legal acceptance of the offence; whether it abridged the rights of reputation, and, from respect to the general utility of the newly discovered instrument, absolved those who might employ it, from the responsibility attached to them in every other way. And this leads us to what is loosely called the doctrine of the Liberty of the Press, a term which has become elemental in all free Governments.

As this liberty is opposed to the power of the licenser, the term is correct. It is loose only, when distinctively used as a new peculiar right of the press. The liberty of the press is only the liberty of those who use it. It is only one of the personal rights of the printer.

When we have termed the press a new and enlarged instrument of publication, whether of good or evil, we have, in fact, pointed out that part of its nature which defines and circumscribes the law which attaches to it. The law of libel was not altered by the discovery of printing; nor is there any reason that it should be altered. The rights of personal reputation, and the rights of free discussion, remained the same. Printing is but the mechanical art of extending such discussion into a wider sphere. It was a new power, but no new right. It left, therefore, every thing as it found it, with the exception, that the acquisition of such power, and the greater facility of mischief, demanded an increase of vigilance on the part of the law.

In fact, the discovery of printing produced only the same changes in the law of libel, which commerce, agriculture, and the other improved circumstances of society, introduced into other penal laws.

An increased facility of commission, and the difficulty in the detection of crimes, are the two main circumstances from which it is usual with lawyers to justify the severity of our penal code. In the case of libels, however, this increased rigour must rather be looked for in the administration and construction of the law, than in any change in the letter. Hence, what has often been adverted to with another purpose, the greater frequency of prosecution for libels in modern times.

With respect to the correct acceptance of the popular notion of the liberty of the press, it is what is necessarily included in its equivalent and progressive terms, thinking, speaking, and writing.

In regard to human tribunals, every one is at liberty to think as he pleases. Human cognizance cannot reach what is beyond human evidence. It is contrary to the first law of nature to put a man upon his own confession. If you accuse, and he deny, there is at once an end of all trial. Upon these grounds it has been the maxim of every code that thinking is beyond its capacity.[g]

When these thoughts are embodied in words, they become in that shape moral substances; they produce palpable and material effects upon the personal rights of others. Hence the peculiar felicity of the expression of the Roman law, which, in its technical description of an injury similar to our assaults, employs the words, *pulsas et verberas me lingua.* In this shape, therefore, as being naturally capable of injury, they become cognizable by law. Writing is the further publication of words, as printing is the further publication of writing. They are all different forms of the same thing, namely, publicly speaking. They are all therefore, comprehended within the same term; have all the same extent of right, the same limits from the rights of others, and are all contained under the same compass of law.

The liberty of the press, therefore, properly understood, is the personal liberty of the writer to express his thoughts in the

---

[g] "Despotism however knows no such maxim. Dyonisius the tyrant of Syracuse, put to death *Marsyas,* whom he had advanced to a considerable military command, merely because Marsyas dreamed that he killed him; for he concluded that this dream by night was occasioned by some similar suggestion of the day" (Plutarch, *Lives,* "Dion" IX. 4–5).

more improved way invented by human ingenuity in the form of the press. This definition, or rather description, will lead us not only to an accurate conception of the thing, but to the origin of those notions, and which some writers have deemed prejudices, entertained in favour of it in a popular constitution.

The press, it has been said, is the creature of human ingenuity exerted in an improved, and therefore in a late progress of society; it is not, nor can be supposed, contemporary with the state of nature; how, therefore, it is demanded, can the liberty of the press be a natural right? What do you intend therefore when you speak of the sacredness of this right, and employ terms which are only appropriate to our absolute and inalienable rights? To this it may be answered, that the rights of nature, that is to say, of the free exercise of our faculties, must not be invidiously narrowed to any single form or shape. They extend to every shape, and to every instrument, in which, and by whose assistance, those faculties can be exercised. I have a right to walk, I have the same right to run, and, if by the exertion of ingenuity I could invent any way to fly, I have the same natural right to fly. The same character, therefore, of natural rights is conveyed to every right which is natural in its origin and principle through all the possible modes and instruments of exercising and launching it into action and employment. In this manner the liberty of the press may be regarded as a natural right, and in the language of our best lawyers, and the daily acceptance of the constitution, it is, under this notion, invested with a corresponding sacredness. Such is one of the reasons of the partiality of the English law and constitution towards this right.

Another reason for this partiality is in the evident benefit, which our constitution, in particular, has derived from the exercise of this natural principle of liberty in the acquired organ of the press. The constitution herein pays back what it has received. Our constitution, in fact, as it at present exists, in a church reformed from the errors of superstition, and in a system of liberty, equally remote from feudal anarchy, and monarchical despotism, is almost entirely, under Providence, the fruit of a free press. It was this which awakened the minds of men from that apathy, in which ignorance of their rights, and of the duties of their rulers, had left them. It was by these means, that moral and religious knowledge, the foundations of all liberty, was refracted, multiplied, and circulated; and instead of existing in masses, and in the single points of schools and universities, was rendered the common atmosphere in which we all live and breathe. It was from the press that originated what is, in fact, the main distinction of the ancient and modern world, public opinion. A single question will be sufficient to put the importance of this subject in the strongest point of view. In the present state of knowledge and manners, is it possible that a Nero or Tiberius would be suffered to reign or live?

It is a maxim of policy in favour of natural liberty, that in every case of the deprivation or restraint of personal rights, the burthen is upon the Governors to show the necessity of such diminution and restriction.

It is therefore a maxim of the English constitution, that no liberty of the subject, either in itself, or in any instrument by which it may be exercised, shall be repealed, restricted, or abridged, unless the magistrate shall show, upon his part, a full and sufficient civil reason for such diminution.

This is, in fact, the main distinction between tyranny and liberty. A free Government is in the daily habit of repealing and restricting our natural rights; and this too, in a greater degree, and in more frequency, than any scheme of despotism whatever. No man complains that such acts of our governors are an invasion of our liberties. The reason of this is, that society, like the individual, is under the obligation of reason, and whatever is required by such reason, in other words, by general or individual prudence, constitutes our duty, and not our servitude.

Obedience to reason is the great moral law of our nature. The reasonableness of any civil rule is a sufficient foundation of the right of the magistrate, who has authority to impose it. Rights, in truth, are nothing more than such qualities of acts as render them obligatory upon the reason of the agent. A right is only a legal term for a reason.

Conditions of Freedom

3. INDEPENDENCE OF THE PRESS

Joseph T. Buckingham, 1852

Joseph T. Buckingham owned and edited newspapers and magazines in Massachusetts for more than forty years. He was one of the most outspoken editors of his day; his extraordinary independence was almost legendary, and his caustic character evaluations led to several libel actions. A biographer of his predecessors and contemporaries in New England printing, Buckingham also wrote his memoirs and recollections, a valuable record of the practice of journalism in his time, including the perils and difficulties confronting an editor. In this excerpt from *Personal Memoirs* is angry recognition of the subservience to political parties and partisan subscribers of many mid-nineteenth century newspapers.

From Joseph T. Buckingham, *Personal Memoirs, and Recollections of Editorial Life* (Boston: Ticknor, Reed, and Fields, 1852), II, 117–121.

Nothing has ever excited my indignation more than attacks made upon the Press by writers and speakers, who wanted a subject on which to pour out the filthy dregs of ill-nature,—nothing has more quickly provoked me to the utterance of the strongest language I could command. Scribblers, whose communications have been rejected, may be expected to take their revenge in scolding, or by insulting the offending editor with anonymous letters. Some men of *high standing* have been known to descend from their elevated positions in the pulpit or at the bar to abuse a poor printer, who had the audacity to refuse a compliance with their wishes, and may possibly have thrown an effusion of their spleen or stupidity into the fire. I remember that, at the trial of a supposed murderer, in the state of Rhode-Island, some fifteen, or perhaps twenty, years ago, one of the most celebrated lawyers in New-England pronounced an unmanly and undignified sentence of condemnation upon the press, accusing the newspaper printers, indiscriminately, with wilful falsehood and misrepresentation in regard to his client, and cautioning the jury against believing any thing they might see in the newspapers,—for "a newspaper was the last place in which an honest man should look for truth,"—or words to that effect. On one occasion, having refused to insert a certain communication, a professedly religious editor in Boston was pleased to take up the cause of the aggrieved writer, and, after accusing me of servility and want of independence, (as if the independence of an editor consisted altogether in submission to the wishes of correspondents,) very charitably undertook to represent all those who supported the paper as reprobates and sinners, and outcasts from all moral and civil associations. While fretting under this charge of want of independence, my choler gained vent and was emitted in this wise:—

"It is said that the Press of our country is free,—nay, we boast of its freedom. Why?—because any one may establish a press of his own?—or because printers and publishers are responsible only to the undefinable law of libel? Is it because the proprietor may use his press as his passions or his fancies invite him? Is it because he possesses the sovereign power of making it the channel of truth and virtuous communication, or the foul and pestilent sewer of falsehood and moral contamination? Is it because he may wield it as an instrument of good or an engine of evil? Is it because its rapidly multiplying power affords a ready means of gratifying the benevolence of the heart, or satiating the malevolence of the passions?—How fallacious are such opinions! The Press free, and the Editor and Publisher dependent for their subsistence upon the shifting and weathercock opinions of some one or two thousand subscribers, who pay the paltry pittance of their subscription, as an ungrateful convalescent pays the fees of his physician, with most graceless reluctance;—who deem the paper, which they honor with their *patronage*, as a part of their personal property, over which they possess the same power of control as of their wardrobe;—in which they have a right to demand the insertion of *their* opinions, upon all subjects, whether political, poetical, mechanical, or *rigmarolical*,—whilst the poor half paid and sometimes wholly starved Editor or Printer must pay for his refusal to insert by the forfeiture of his correspondent's subscription.

"An occurrence of some interest calls forth editorial commentary. The article contains opinions too indigestible for pampered appetites, and the wounded *sensibilities* of some fifty or a hundred subscribers are quieted by a fractious order to 'stop the paper.' And yet the Press is free?—so it is;—very free; as free as mechanical industry and uncontrolled power of printing and publishing can make it; but, alas for the proprietor! *his* freedom may well be questioned; he truly may be pardoned, if he should sometimes lose his identity in the vexatious struggles between his duty and his interest. Still the Press is free!—Blessed freedom! blessed independence!—where the dungeons of the Inquisition live only in story, and the frowns of Censors are as little cared for as the age of a sparrow. O how free is the American Press! how boldly it pours forth its volumes of wrath against rulers and aspirants! how fearlessly it canvases [*sic*] the demerits of the living and the merits of the dead! How smooth and uninterrupted is its course, whilst whole columns of lying paragraphs float quietly along, impelled by the propitious gales of partizan applause! How sure and how secure seem the secular interests of the proprietor, whilst his diurnal folio circulates in the broad field of party patronage! What boots it whether honest Paul pays for the paper, or damns the impertinence of the collector? It is sufficient that there is an end to be obtained, and the paper must be pushed into circulation at any hazard, or by any sacrifice, until the printer is compelled to "look to his bond," and be grateful for a barren indemnity, where he had been taught by the *managers* of the farce to expect a profitable harvest. The fact is, too many of our presses are the exclusive property of sects and parties, and their editors but the twilight shadows of bodies without souls. They assume the responsibility of opinions which belong to them only by adoption; and feel,—whilst writhing under a conviction that all is not so honest as it should be,—that there is no alternative but to hoodwink their consciences or to starve. Hence the multiplicity of presses; hence the clamorous appeals to the public for support and patronage; hence the crouching and cringing to the aristocratical sensibility of one class, and the unceasing and active irritation applied to the jacobinical prejudices of another; hence all the wild effusions of illiberality and dogmatism,—all the madness and licentiousness of atheism. There seems to be no room for neutrality, no time for pause in the warfare of the passions; no rest for the high-strung cords of embittered feelings;—war, war to the utterance. Such is the blessed freedom of the Press. And why is this? Is it necessary that an editor should exhaust his intellect in a constant endeavor to furnish the poison of pestilent excitement,—or, by unceasing study, how best to minister to the craving appetite of slander and defamation? Is the taste of the public so entirely vitiated, that nothing but caustic applications, bitter satire, unchristian reproach,—garbled and mutilated extracts, patched and pieced until the nakedness of truth is hid beneath the many-colored mantle of falsehood,—will satisfy its cormorant appetite? Is it possible?—but we desist, satisfied that there is yet a redeeming principle in our people,—a counteracting power,— abundantly sufficient to set at nought the rabid venom of the party Press, and restore its columns to the cause of truth, and save its conductors from the curse of purchased dependence."

4. ESSENTIAL CONDITIONS FOR THE MAINTENANCE OF A HEALTHY PUBLIC OPINION

Zechariah Chafee, Jr., 1947

The contributions of the late Zechariah Chafee, Jr., to the understanding of free speech and press in America are unsurpassed. His first article on the subject appeared during World War I, when his duties as a Harvard law professor turned him, as he said more than thirty years later, to "something I could not ever

From Zechariah Chafee, Jr., *Government and Mass Communications* (Chicago: University of Chicago Press, 1947), I, 21–29. Reprinted from *Government and Mass Communications* by Zechariah Chafee, Jr., by permission of The University of Chicago Press.

stop." A classic work in the field of free expression in America is his *Free Speech in the United States* (1941), a heavily revised version of his book of 1920, *Freedom of Speech*. Other books appeared before his death in 1957, each illuminating the law and the court decisions and the social climate in which they were made, and analyzing their effects; each setting forth the product of his penetrating reflection and study in lucid, strong prose. The selection printed below is from the book published in 1947 as part of his contribution to the work of the Commission on Freedom of the Press.

Do the Essential Conditions for the Maintenance of a Healthy Public Opinion Now Exist in the United States?

Although the foregoing survey shows a predominance of trends toward governmental interference with mass communications, these trends will not inevitably prevail. The chances for successful resistance depend greatly on the existence of a healthy public opinion. It is when society and the press are in a bad way that despotism finds its golden opportunity. Consequently, we need to concern ourselves about the preservation of the essential conditions of healthy public opinion. Two main conditions, somewhat interrelated, may be called the two-way process and the self-righting process.

1. *The two-way process.*—Communication is a two-way process of mutual response between the members of the community. The right to speak implies a readiness to listen and give consideration to what the other man says. A community is a universe of discourse in which the members participate by speaking and listening, writing and reading. In a free community the members establish and re-establish, examine and re-examine, in response to one another, their formulations of man's ultimate ends, the standards of their behavior, and their application to concrete issues. Thus the society in a con-

tinuous enterprise of inquiry and discussion gropes its way through changing tasks and conditions; the individual, even if not free from the pressures of his own circumstances, can feel "free" by participating in that enterprise. The First Amendment takes the universe of discourse for granted. It is doubtful whether and to what extent it can be taken for granted under the conditions of life in a modern industrial society. Hence it must be defended.

In Germany during the Hitler regime there was a significant change in the process of communication from two-way discussion to one-way propaganda. As Goebbels formulated it: "We no longer want the formation of public opinion, but rather the public formation of opinion." The universe of discourse had broken apart—no discussion or argument was permitted to the Nazis by their leaders. A public opinion which thus is *made* is to be distinguished from one which *grows*.

Therefore, it is not enough to have the right of a free press on parchment in the Constitution. As we look toward the future of this freedom, it is important to know the extent to which this two-way process is working actively. The country is not without dangers in this respect. One danger, already mentioned, is the way we are divided into racial, religious, and economic groups. In every industrial society of large size, forces arise that tend to separate sections of the community from the universe of discourse and thus split the community into parts between which discussion dies out. Workers, farmers, racial minorities, the *gens bien nés* or *bien pensant*, the members of the Union League Club, may finally move in separate worlds.

Fortunately, the process of growth of opinion is still rather strong in the United States (though too little studied in comparison with the manipulation of opinion). Discussion in this country is still vigorous and alive, and the universe of discourse has not yet been shattered. Consequently the dangers just indicated can still be met by a deliberate and consistent effort of the national community. The possibilities of action must be constantly explored.

2. *The self-righting process.*— This is the process by which in the long run truth is to emerge from the clash of opinions, good and bad. Milton described it in a famous passage: "And though all the winds of doctrine were let loose to play upon the earth, so Truth be in the field, we do injuriously by licensing and prohibiting to misdoubt her strength. Let her and Falsehood grapple; who ever knew Truth put to the worse, in a free and open encounter?"

The importance of the satisfactory operation of this process for the freedom of the press was constantly stressed at meetings of the Commission. One membeı said: "A free society presupposes a self-righting process, some sort of ballast. The assumption is that free action in rational minds will result in self-correction, social as well as individual. Now the problem is not whether freedom is good, but whether, given freedom, the self-righting process is in good order, whether the above assumption is being realized. Discussion is not self-correcting in a society which does not use the criteria of a serious search for truth. It is like a cattle ship with the cattle broken loose from their halters. Perhaps we are getting like that. What we want therefore [in our inquiry] is a formulation of the dangers arising from failure to understand and to realize in practice the assumptions which are essential to the workings of a democratic society."

Expressions of similar ideas by others were: "It is material to consider how much immunity to harmful lies the public possesses. This immunity may vary with education and other qualities of readers." And, again: "It is important to determine the level at which public discussion is carried on. How far can we count on society to take care of itself?"

That this self-righting process is not working well at the present time was plain to the Commission. It was unquestionably demonstrated to us that the output of the press includes an appallingly large quantity of irresponsible utterances and even deliberate lying. Consequently, some members feared that it is a matter of manipulation or luck what conclusions will emerge from such a tangle. They came to regard Milton's vision of victorious Truth as an illusion. The natural inference was that the government must step in as an umpire in the contest of conflicting opinions and allegations.

Although others were less pessimistic, we were all gravely concerned. To be more specific, the Commission was disturbed by three obstacles to the satisfactory operation of the self-righting process today:

First and foremost is the drift toward concentration of power which has already been mentioned and is fully set forth in *A Free and Responsible Press.* This is exemplified by the large number of cities with only one newspaper, the common ownership of newspapers and radio stations, and the growth of newspaper chains. Now, diversity in the effective communication of facts and opinions is a fundamental presupposition of the self-righting process. That point is stressed by Judge Learned Hand in the recent case which prevented the Associated Press from denying its services to competing newspapers:

> . . . The newspaper industry . . . serves one of the most vital of all general interests: the dissemination of news from as many different sources, and with as many different facets and colors as is possible. That interest is closely akin to, if indeed it is not the same as, the interest protected by the First Amendment; it presupposes that right conclusions are more likely to be gathered out of a multitude of tongues, than through any kind of authoritative selection. To many this is, and always will be, folly; but we have staked upon it our all.

And Justice Black in the Supreme Court said of the First Amendment:

> That Amendment rests on the assumption that the widest possible dissemination of information from diverse and antagonistic sources is essential to the welfare of the public. . . .

This fundamental presupposition is seriously weakened by concentration of power. Instead of several views of the facts and several conflicting opinions, newspaper readers in many cities, or, still worse, in wide regions, may get only a single set of facts and a single body of opinion, all emanating from one owner.

A second obstacle lies in the present prevalence of sales talk in American life, so that it naturally flows into the press. There is a significant distinction between discussion, which tries to uncover the facts, and sales talk, which is interested in the facts only so far as they further the sale. If the spirit of sales talk prevails over the spirit of discussion, talk can no longer be met with talk. Freedom of speech loses its self-regulating power.

Thirdly, the public reads unfavorable news and opinions about people and policies with more appetite than the favorable. Hence an unfavorable item may be insufficiently counteracted because the opposing item (*a*) will not be printed or (*b*) will not be read. As one informant said about news from government departments and business: "Peace, harmony, and brotherly love are not news; a fight is." And we were told that, even when an editor requests an abundant flow of information about Latin America from the Associated Press, he does not print what he gets unless it is unfavorable to the particular country; then he gobbles it up. This inclination of the public to hear about quarrels and excitement and the unusual makes it hard for them to get a well-rounded understanding of important situations at home and abroad. Often it is the long-run facts which really matter. In the pithy words of one of our number: "The fact that no more dogs are biting men should be bigger news than 'Man bites dog.'"

One existing remedy for this partial presentation of life is that longer articles do get favorable and constructive information to interested readers. The monthly magazines and books are a better vehicle for this than the daily press. Even so, is there adequate counteraction to untrue or lopsided derogatory news?

For such reasons the Commission became critical of the principle of laissez faire, according to which the solution for problems of freedom is more freedom. The following attitude of one of our members fairly expressed our apprehensions: The press fails to bring about that kind of communication of fact and idea which leads to a rational discussion of ends and means. Our society rests upon the assumption that, through the freedom of one to speak and the readiness of others to listen and consider, any divagation of our people from a just course will be corrected by themselves. Today there is reason to suppose that this self-correcting process, although commonly considered to function fully, does not in fact function, to our danger. The eighteenth-century champions of liberty assumed *human* nature to be like the rest of nature, with an inner tendency toward harmony, but today men cannot be so complacent. Human society knows no limits to its desires, hence any value can become a peril—even liberty. An analysis of the problem of democracy in general and of the free press in particular proves that there are no such natural harmonies and balances in a community as democratic theory used to assume. Whatever harmony exists at a particular moment may be disturbed by the emergence of new factors and vitalities. Our people have put too much trust in the automatic tendencies of our society to right itself. We have found that we cannot depend on unmanaged processes, whether in economics or in communications. We need more effective methods of self-correction. We cannot rely merely on automatic action. The unity of a society is partly the fruit of moral and political contrivance and is not the inevitable consequence of freedom per se. Since purely political contrivance is bound to destroy freedom for the sake of unity, it follows that the preservation of both unity and freedom depends partly upon the achievement of self-control and a sense of high responsibility on the part of the forces which direct the instruments of a society. But the preservation of such unity also depends partly upon the careful and discriminating establishment of such public and political controls as are least inimical to the value of freedom.

The repeated insistence in the foregoing passages on some sort of management of discussion does not necessarily require the government to predominate in the managing, but it implies that, if others do not manage, the government will. Toward the end of Part II, in chapter 24, I shall consider the desirability of governmental intervention for the purpose of improving the quality and accuracy of mass communications. For the time being, I shall merely say that there are alternative private influences such as the will of individuals, and schools and colleges, and the press itself, which are capable of raising the level of discussion if they are sufficiently intelligent and vigorous. Even though the self-righting process clanks along pretty jerkily, I am far from ready to abandon the case against abridging the freedom of speech and of the press. How self-righting was England when Milton wrote the *Areopagitica* in 1644?

Some reflections I wrote five years ago still represent my own beliefs:

"Speech should be fruitful as well as free. . . . Lack of interference alone will not make discussion fruitful. We must take affirmative steps to improve the methods by which discussion is carried on. Of late years the argument of Milton and Mill has been questioned, because truth does not seem to emerge from a controversy in the automatic way their logic would lead us to expect. For one thing, reason is less praised nowadays than a century ago; instead, emotions conscious and unconscious are said to dominate the conduct of men. . . .

"Nevertheless, the main argument of Milton and Mill still holds good. All that this disappointment means is that friction is a much bigger drag on the progress of Truth than they supposed. Efforts to lessen that friction are essential to the success of freedom of speech. It is a problem, not for law, but for education in the wide sense that includes more than schools and youngsters. . . .

"Reason is more imperfect than we used to believe. Yet it still remains the best guide we have."

The foregoing discussion has brought out many reasons why the impulse toward governmental activity in the field of communications will grow stronger in the near future. If that impulse is allowed free play, very great dangers will arise, not only to the press, but also to the continuance of democracy.

So much stress has been laid of late on various economic pressures and forces which warp mass communications that there is some risk that the American people will lose sight of the evils of a government-controlled press. It is right to emphasize these economic influences, as the general report of the Commission does. Immunity from state action is not enough; the press should also be independent of private forces which prevent it from giving society the kind of mass communications which society needs. Yet nobody should fall into the opposite error of assuming that economic obstacles are the only impairments of freedom or that a press which is dominated by the state is free merely because it is dissevered from all capitalistic controls. The meaning which our ancestors gave to liberty of the press, namely, freedom from the will of legislators and officials, is just as vital today as it was in 1791. It is constantly important for the public to realize the indispensability of freedom of the press from governmental control so that they can fight for it with a clear idea of what they must defend.

This does not mean that all state activity in the field of communications is necessarily bad. The rest of this book will be largely devoted to determining what governmental participation is wise, and what is unwise so that the evils ought to be remedied in other ways.

The point is that unwise state activity must be steadily

resisted, because otherwise it is likely to come to pass in response to numerous conditions of the United States today. The First Amendment is a gun behind the door which must never be allowed to rust.

5. TOWARD A THEORY OF FREEDOM OF THE PRESS

Frederick S. Siebert, 1952

Professor of journalism, attorney, and student of the law of mass communications in the United States and Europe, Frederick Siebert has examined especially political conditions under which freedom and restraint of expression thrive. In the following excerpt from the Introduction to his most significant contribution to the study of the press, Siebert states propositions on the relation between freedom of the press and the theory and stability of governments.

The present study of the rise and decline of government control of the press during three hundred years of English history points up a number of postulates which should be useful in the formulation of a comprehensive statement of the principles of freedom of the press.

One basic assumption appears to be common to all theories

From Frederick S. Siebert, *Freedom of the Press in England, 1476–1776* (Urbana: University of Illinois Press, 1952), pp. 9–13. By permission of the copyright holder.

of liberty of the press, whether it is the theory of the Tudors, or of the eighteenth century as stated by Blackstone and Mansfield, or the theory of the late eighteenth- and early nineteenth-century libertarians. This assumption is that freedom of the press is not and never can be absolute. All agree that some forms of restraint are necessary and that the government has a legitimate function to define the limitations. They differ only as to the nature and number of these limitations.

Government must necessarily exert some control over the press as it must over all other types of institutions operating in society. All agree that it is the function of government to protect private reputations, to control to some unspecified degree the distribution of obscene matter, and to regulate to a still more vague degree publications which undermine the basic structure of organized society. Henry VIII, John Milton, John Locke, Walpole, George III, and even Lord Erskine agree that some government control of the press is necessary. The principal disagreements arise over the standards to be applied in devising and administering controls designed to protect the third objective mentioned above, the preservation of the basic structure of organized society. With this assumption in mind, the following propositions are advanced:

Proposition I. *The extent of government control of the press depends on the nature of the relationship of the government to those subject to the government.* This relationship, which in its nature provides for a greater or a lesser degree of accountability, has been identified under such general terms as Monarchy (absolute or enlightened), Democracy (more or less direct), and Totalitarianism (Communist or Fascist).

All types of government consider themselves responsible for the welfare of their peoples. The more direct the accountability of the governors to the masses, the greater the freedom of the press. As England progressed from a relatively absolute monarchy under Henry VIII to the more limited administration of Charles II, to the still more democratic government under

George I, the area of freedom enjoyed by the press expanded. The contest to accomplish this expansion was long and arduous and not without retreats. As democratic forms superseded the ancient relationship between the government and its constituents, the press as a necessary corollary took on an extra-legal function, that of an informant and a watchdog of public affairs. The nature of this relationship between the central government and its subjects determines the degree of freedom from control under all types of government, monarchical, democratic, or totalitarian.

Proposition II. *The area of freedom contracts and the enforcement of restraints increases as the stresses on the stability of the government and of the structure of society increase.* This appears to be true for all types of governments. The more secure the existing government, the less restraint is imposed on the press. Henry VIII's insecurity due to the shift in religious allegiance prompted the enforcement of many of the controls during his reign. Elizabeth's insecurity during her early years caused by the flaw in her title to the crown was the primary cause of her interest in the products of the printing press. The stability of the government under Walpole in the eighteenth century was accompanied by few restrictions and lax enforcement. It is axiomatic that government does not exert itself in its own protection unless it is attacked or believes itself seriously threatened.

The three well-defined theories of the relation of the government to the press as described above are all based on these two propositions.

The first, the Tudor-Stuart theory of control, was derived directly from the first proposition, and its implementation and administration were based on the second.

The traditional, conservative, and Tory attitude toward democratic participation in government provides the foundation for the Blackstone-Mansfield theory of liberty of the press. Arbitrary monarchy was no longer tenable, but freedom was extended only to the abolition of licensing, leaving such restraints as the common law and the legislature provided.

The late eighteenth-century position, that of Lord Erskine and Lord Camden, also recognizes the two basic propositions. This theory, the dominant one in the nineteenth century in both England and America, insists on the right to discuss the government in a rational manner provided such discussion derives from a sincere belief in the necessity for a change. Jefferson went even further than Erskine and appears to approve of an absolute freedom to discuss political questions even if such discussion is intemperate and might result in the complete dissolution of the existing form of government. Such a position, however, has been modified in operation to coincide with the second proposition and with Erskine's stand, that the discussion must be addressed to reason and must urge change as an orderly rather than as a revolutionary process. The safety of the state is still a criterion for measuring the amount of freedom allotted to the press.

In addition to the three theories which grew out of the experiences of three hundred years, three additional positions on the relation of the government to the press have made their appearance in modern times. The first of these is the position on the question of the allowable area of freedom taken by the Supreme Court of the United States in a series of decisions since 1919. Justices Oliver W. Holmes and Louis D. Brandeis were largely responsible for the rule which interprets freedom of the press as prohibiting all types of restrictions on political discussion unless there is a clear and present danger that the government will be subverted or that other recognized evils which the government has a right to prohibit will ensue. This vague standard is the one in operation in the United States today. Like the others it is based on the principle that the people in a democracy have a right to speak and print on government affairs but that this right is limited by the immediate conditions under which such speaking and writing take place.

Congress and state legislatures can prohibit certain types of speaking and writing under certain conditions. The "certain" as used here is far from certain as that word is defined in standard dictionaries.

Two additional positions on the question of press freedom are implicit in the operation of the two basic principles in the modern world. The first of these grows out of the assumption that in his relation to his government, the citizen or subject has special duties and responsibilities. The principal duty is to participate in periodic decisions and selections in government affairs. As a participant, the citizen has an obligation to inform himself on the merits of current issues and on the qualifications of candidates for public office. Out of this grows the proposition that it is the duty of the press and of other media of mass communications to inform the citizen and to make available to him such materials as will enable him to arrive at sound and rational conclusions on public affairs. This is the theory of the Hutchins Commission on Freedom of the Press (1947) which would go so far as to intimate the use of government controls in the event that the press itself does not undertake to fulfill this obligation. This theory of social responsibility of the press is echoed in the Report of the Royal Commission on the Press (1949), but the British inquiry group unlike the American commission makes a firm statement that the social objectives stated above can be accomplished only through a private enterprise system of press ownership. The question of how the obligation to furnish the citizen with full, complete, and accurate information and interpretation can be met without government participation or enforcement is a problem for the twentieth century.

The third theory of press freedom in the modern world is that of the Communist government of Soviet Russia. Here again the two basic principles are at work. Because of the nature of the relation of the government to the people (much like that of Tudor times), the central administration takes the responsibility of providing for the welfare of the people as identified by the proletariat. As such it assumes more or less complete control of communications media. Nothing that tends to undermine the soviet system is allowed to appear. Bitter and widespread criticism of the operation of policies and of the administration of operating officials is permitted, but even mild questionings of the economic basis of the soviet system are severely punished.

A modern contribution of the soviet system of press control is the contention that emotional appeals as presented in nonverbal artistic productions have definite and powerful political and economic implications. As such, the more abstract arts such as painting, music, and the dance are included under the theory of press control. In England and America these same nonverbal forms have been excluded from the freedom of the press on the ground that such arts have no political implications and should be regulated by an entirely different set of standards.

What applications or modifications of the principles of freedom of the press from government control will develop during the remainder of the twentieth century? Will the principles of Thomas Jefferson and John Stuart Mill be able to survive the ideological contest between democratic capitalism and totalitarian communism? Already we have seen instances of conflict. The second basic proposition mentioned above seems to have come into operation again in our own day. Whether with reason or not, the fear of communism is a powerful force both in England and in America. This fear places severe strains on the control system. As the stress from this fear and from other more tangible sources increases, the area of freedom of the press will contract. How much freedom we shall enjoy will depend on how widespread are the threats and the feeling of insecurity and instability.

Limits of Freedom

6. NEW YORK'S ACT CONCERNING LIBELS

1805

To discourage criticism of government and its officers and laws, English and early American law called such criticism a crime—"seditious libel"—and punished it. No government could stand, it was argued, if it could be brought freely into disrepute; and further, an attack on an official tended to cause him or others to breach the peace in seeking revenge for the attack.

The latter rationale was also the basis of the crime of libeling individuals who were not in government. And whether the libeled were government or John Doe, the truth of the offending words was an aggravation of the offense, for true defamation would make revenge even more sought after than would a lie, which could be disproved.

In trials for both crimes, the jury was there only to decide the fact of who did the printing. The judge would find the law—whether the words were, indeed, criminal.

In 1805, heavily influenced by the arguments of Alexander Hamilton and the reasoning of Judge James Kent in the 1804 seditious libel case of *People* v. *Croswell*, the New York legislature agreed that truth—at least when published with good motives and for justifiable ends—ought to be a defense for the

---

An Act Concerning Libels, Laws of the State of New York (Albany, 1805).

accused, not an exacerbation of a supposed crime. It passed a law saying so and also gave the jury the right to find the law in criminal prosecutions for libel.

For seditious libel, the law was to matter little: the idea that criticism of government could be a crime had been widely discredited in the bludgeoning prosecutions of the Alien and Sedition Acts of 1798–1800, and seditious libel was about to enter a long eclipse as a legal offense. But the principles of the New York law, widely copied in other states, had a dampening effect on prosecutions for criminal libel of the plain citizen. Even though truth might be of little help in justifying defamatory opinions (who can prove an *opinion* true?) it could be a bulwark where the offending words were *facts*. And perhaps even more useful was its role in undermining breach of the peace as an excuse for punishing words: now the law approved of truth, rather than viewing it as an inducement to violence.

An Act concerning Libels.

Passed April 6, 1805.

Whereas doubts exist whether on the trial of an indictment or information for a libel, the jury have a right to give their verdict on the whole matter in issue.

I. *Be it therefore declared and enacted by the People of the State of New-York, represented in Senate and Assembly,* That on every such indictment or information, the jury, who shall try the same, shall have a right to determine the law and the fact, under the direction of the court, in like manner as in other criminal cases, and shall not be directed or required by the court or judge, before whom such indictment or information shall be tried, to find the defendant guilty, merely on the proof of the publication by the defendant of the matter charged to be libellous, and of the sense ascribed thereto, in such indictment or information: *Provided nevertheless,* That nothing herein contained shall be held or taken to impair or destroy the right and privilege of the defendant to apply to the court to have the judgment arrested as hath heretofore been practised.

II. *And be it further declared and enacted,* That in every prosecution for writing or publishing any libel, it shall be lawful for the defendant, upon the trial of the cause, to give in evidence in his defence, the truth of the matter contained in the publication charged as libellous: *Provided always,* That such evidence shall not be a justification, unless on the trial it shall be further made satisfactorily to appear, that the matter charged as libellous, was published with good motives and for justifiable ends.

III. *And be it further enacted,* That any person or persons who shall, after the passing of this act, be convicted of writing or publishing a libel, such person or persons shall not be sentenced to an imprisonment exceeding the term of eighteen months, or to pay a fine exceeding the sum of five thousand dollars.

IV. *And be it further enacted,* That from and after the passing of this act, it shall not be lawful to prosecute any person or persons by information for writing or publishing any libel.

7. FREEDOM OF THE PRESS IN THE UNITED STATES

Henry Schofield, 1914

The American Sociological Society held a symposium on freedom of assembly and freedom for speakers, teachers, and the press in 1914. Among the distinguished participants was Professor Henry Schofield of the Northwestern University Law School. A specialist on the American Constitution, Schofield presented a paper that has become one of the classics in American writing on freedom of the press. The paper is remarkable for its clear structuring of the classes of criminal words and their treatment by courts in England and the United States in the eighteenth and nineteenth centuries.

At least as striking is the influence that the work has had on Americans who deplore the tendencies of courts to view narrowly the scope of freedom of the press. Schofield's thesis—that declarations by American revolutionary patriots and governments obliterated the restrictive English common law of sedition and blasphemy and common-law rules in prosecutions for defamation—has had weight with jurists and legal writers into the mid-twentieth century. That his evidence supporting this thesis is light is apparent on close scrutiny, and that the founding fathers meant to wipe out the common law by the First Amendment has been subjected to convincing attack. But his reasoning is heavy ammunition for support of today's libertarians, and is given here in its first and most essential part.

Immediately after the Declaration of Independence, the several states reorganized under written constitutions, most of them containing declarations or bills of rights, and liberty of the press among the rights declared. Today all state constitutions declare in some phrase the right of liberty of the press, and the bill of rights of the federal Constitution, as the first ten amendments are commonly called, has a declaration of the right of liberty of the press. Side by side with the declaration, preceding or following it closely, we find in the earliest and

---

From Henry Schofield, "Freedom of the Press in the United States," *Freedom of Communication, Publications of the American Sociological Society,* IX (1915), 67-81. Reprinted by permission of The American Sociological Society.

present state constitutions and in the federal Constitution a declaration of the twin-sister right of religious liberty. The First Amendment to the federal Constitution declares:

> Congress shall make no law respecting an establishment of religion or prohibiting the free exercise thereof; or abridging the freedom of speech, or of the press.

This federal declaration is typical of the declaration in the original state constitutions, as, for example, that of Massachusetts in 1780, still in force, which says:

> The liberty of the press is essential to freedom in a state. It ought not, therefore, to be restricted in this commonwealth.

Very many state constitutions today adopt the definition of liberty of the press given by Hamilton in his argument in *Croswell's case* in New York in 1804.[1] As fairly typical of these present Hamiltonian state constitutions, we may take the declaration of liberty of the press in the present Illinois constitution of 1870, which reads as follows:

> Every person may freely speak, write, and publish on all subjects, being responsible for the abuse of that liberty; and in all trials for libel, both civil and criminal, the truth, when published with good motives and for justifiable ends, shall be a sufficient defense.[2]

The nearly if not quite unanimous expressed view of our judges always has been, and is, that the constitutional declarations of liberty of the press are only declaratory of the English common-law right protected by the English courts at the time of the Revolution, like, for example, the declaration of the right of trial by jury, and are not expansive of that right or creative

[1] *People* v. *Croswell,* 3 Johns. Cas. 337.

[2] See Thorpe, *American Charters, Constitutions and Organic Laws;* Poore, *Federal and State Constitutions.* New York and New Jersey had no constitutional declarations of liberty of the press until 1821 and 1844. Connecticut and Rhode Island lived under Charles II's charters of 1662 and 1663 until 1818 and 1842.

of a new right unknown to the English common law. They accept the definition of the right given by Blackstone, Lord Mansfield, and Lord Kenyon as the right line of constitutional law separating liberty from license. Blackstone said in the fourth book of his *Commentaries*, first published in 1769:

> The liberty of the press is indeed essential to the nature of a free state; but this consists in laying no *previous* restraints upon publications; and not in freedom from censure for criminal matter when published.[3]

In 1784 Lord Mansfield said:

> The liberty of the press consists in printing without any previous license, subject to the consequences of law.
>
> The licentiousness of the press is Pandora's Box, the source of every evil. Miserable is the condition of individuals, dangerous is the condition of the state if there is no certain law (or what is the same thing), no certain administration of law to protect individuals or to guard the state.[4]

In 1799, seven years after Fox's Libel act of 1792, Lord Kenyon said:

> The liberty of the press is dear to England. The licentiousness of the press is odious to England. The liberty of it can never be so well protected as by beating down the licentiousness. I said that the liberty of the press was dear to Englishmen, and I will say that nothing can put that in danger but the licentiousness of the press.

> The liberty of the press is neither more nor less than this, that a man may publish anything which twelve of his countrymen think is not blameable, but that he ought to be punished if he publishes that which is blameable.[5]

---

[3] 4 Bl. Com. 151–153. Lord Mansfield, like Blackstone, thought a man's mind could be free though the law forbade him to publish his thoughts. See citations in footnote 14, below.

[4] *Dean of St. Asaph's case,* or *Rex* v. *Shipley,* 4 Douglas 73, 170.

[5] *Rex* v. *Cuthill,* 27 St. Tr. 674. See the comment in 2 Stephen, *History of the Criminal Law of England,* 348, note 1, concluding: "Hobbes is nearly the only writer who seems to me capable of using the word 'liberty' without talking nonsense."

American judges early took the view that this English common-law definition that "liberty of the press consists in printing without any previous license, subject to the consequences of law," is a correct definition of the right of liberty of the press declared in our first constitutions, and that, therefore, those constitutional declarations left standing the English common law of libel as declared by the English courts after 1694, when the last English licensing act expired and Parliament refused to renew it, and before the American Revolution. This view was first expressed by Chief Justice McKean of Pennsylvania in 1788 in *Oswald's case,* wherein the editor of a newspaper was punished by the summary criminal process of contempt of court for a publication censuring his adversary and one of the judges in a pending case to which the editor was the defendant.[6] The same judge expressed the same view in 1797 in his charge to the grand jury in Philadelphia that indicted *Cobbett* for an alleged seditious publication in *Porcupine's Gazette* censuring the administration at Washington.[7] The view lies at the base of the federal Sedition act of 1798 and its judicial administration by Justices Chase and Patterson of the United States Supreme Court and Judges Griffin, Hitchcock, and Peters of the United States District Court, as appears from their summing up to the juries in the prosecutions of Callender, Cooper, Haswell, and Lyon under that act for alleged seditious publications censuring the administration of John Adams.[8] The view was expressed by Chief Justice Parker of Massachusetts in 1825 in *Blanding's case,* which was a criminal prosecution for a publication in a newspaper defamatory of an innkeeper in his calling.[9] And the view was expressed more or less directly by the judge in prosecutions for blas-

---

[6] *Respublica* v. *Oswald,* 1 Dallas 319.

[7] *Cobbett's case* in Wharton's St. Tr.

[8] The cases of *Callender, Cooper, Haskins* [*sic*], and *Lyon* are in Wharton's St. Tr. and in Federal Cases, Nos. 8,646; 14,704; 14,865; 15,834.

[9] *Commonwealth* v. *Blanding,* 3 Pick. 304.

phemous publications in the courts of different states, by Chief Justice Kent in *Ruggles' case* in New York in 1811, Judge Duncan in *Updegraph's case* in Pennsylvania in 1824, by Chief Justice Clayton in *Chandler's case* in Delaware in 1837, and by Chief Justice Shaw in *Kneeland's case* in Massachusetts in 1838.[10] The view forms the whole of the foundation of the modern and rather numerous cases in state courts wherein strangers to pending and not pending lawsuits were fined or imprisoned under the summary criminal process of contempt of court for publications censuring judges for their administration of the law. And the view perhaps accounts in part for the common judicial classification of the right of liberty of the press under the head of "qualified privilege" in the ordinary law of libel along with the privilege of an employer giving the character of a servant to publish defamatory falsehood about the servant in the honest belief it is truth. One of the latest judicial expressions of the view is by Mr. Justice Holmes speaking for the majority of the United States Supreme Court in 1906 in *Senator Patterson's case,* on error to the Colorado Supreme Court under the Fourteenth Amendment, wherein the learned Justice said:

> The main purpose of such constitutional provisions [declaring liberty of the press] is "to prevent all such *previous restraints* upon publications as had been practiced by other governments," and they do not prevent the subsequent punishment of such as may be deemed contrary to the public welfare."[11]

The work which the constitutional declarations threw upon the judges was to draw the line of law that separates liberty from license, and the question here is whether the judges are

[10] 8 Johns. Rep. 290; 11 Serg. and R. 394; 2 Harr. 553; 20 Pick. 206.

[11] 205 U.S. 454. Text-writers state the law in the same way. See, e.g., Willoughby, *Constitution,* student's ed., pp. 327–328; Townshend, *Slander and Libel,* 2d ed., sec. 252. That constitutional liberty of the press means more than freedom from previous censorship, see *State* v. *McKee,* 73 Conn. 19, 28, and carrying it much further and perhaps too far, see *Louthan* v. *State,* 79 Va. 196; *Ex parte Harrison,* 212 Mo. 88.

right in saying Blackstone, Lord Mansfield, and Lord Kenyon did the work for them by anticipation.

At the time of the Revolution the English common law divided unlawful publications into four species of libel, viz.: defamatory libels, or publications defamatory of personal or professional reputation; seditious libels, or publications defamatory of existing public officers, government, institutions, and laws; blasphemous libels, or publications defamatory of the Christian religion; obscene and immoral libels, or publications defamatory of England's existing standard of public morality. If a given publication did not encounter any one of these four species of libel, then it was a lawful publication in exercise of the right of liberty of the press. By that negative process of exclusion, the sphere of liberty of the press was outlined.

The great subjects of public discussion in England at the time were religion and politics, and especially politics. The King's Bench was the criminal court of practically exclusive jurisdiction of all criminal prosecutions for libel. Lord Mansfield became its lord chief justice in 1756, holding the office until 1788, when he was succeeded by Lord Kenyon, who held the office until 1802. Lord Mansfield laid it down clearly that the English common-law test to be applied to determine the seditious character of publications on politics was their tendency as opinion-makers to create and diffuse among the people an ill opinion of existing public officers, government, institutions, and laws. The same rule governed publications on religion; their tendency to create and diffuse among the people an ill opinion of the Christian religion was the test to be applied to determine whether they were unlawful as blasphemous libels. Likewise publications were unlawful as obscene and immoral libels if their tendency was to create and diffuse among the people an ill opinion of existing standards of morality; and publications were unlawful as defamatory libels if their tendency was to create and diffuse among the people an ill opinion of the personal or professional reputations of the persons referred to, though here it seems actual objective tendency as a matter of fact was more emphasized and important than in the other cases of seditious, blasphemous, and obscene and immoral libels, where supposed tendency as a matter of abstract, subjective speculation seems to have been controlling and decisive. The remedy for a publication alleged to be a defamatory libel was either a civil action for damages by the person whose personal or professional reputation was involved, or a criminal prosecution by the Attorney-General. The remedy for a publication alleged to be a seditious libel, a blasphemous libel, or an obscene and immoral libel, was a criminal prosecution. In a civil action for a defamatory libel the truth of the publication was a decisive answer, the burden of proving the truth being on the defendant author and publisher. In all criminal prosecutions, whether for defamatory libel, seditious libel, blasphemous libel, or obscene and immoral libel, the truth or falsity of the publication was of no importance. "The greater the truth the greater the libel" was the maxim in all criminal prosecutions.

When the legal test of the lawfulness of a publication is its tendency as an opinion-maker to create and diffuse among the people an ill opinion of existing things, the tribunal to apply the test is a matter of great importance. Lord Mansfield laid it down with his usual simplicity and lucidity of expression that the exclusive tribunal to apply the test of tendency was the judges of the King's Bench sitting *in banc* to hear and decide a motion by the defendant in arrest of judgment after the verdict of a jury finding the defendant guilty; that the jury had nothing whatever to do with the tendency of the publication as an opinion-maker, and consequently that the trial judge had no right to leave the question of tendency to the jury in any shape or form, but must withdraw that question from the jury by directing the members of the jury that they had nothing to do with it and must not assume to pass on it.

Erskine's fight for liberty of the press at the bar of the King's Bench was from a legal point of view a procedural fight to substitute the twelve men in the jury-box in the place of the judges on the bench on the issue of libel or no libel. Taking his stand on the maxim dividing the province of the jury from the province of the judge, assigning questions of fact within the issue to the jury and questions of law to the judge, Erskine first contended for the substantive-law point that the "intent" or "criminal intent" of the author and publisher was the true test of libel or no libel, and the question of "intent" or "criminal intent" was a question of fact for the jury exclusively. Erskine was defeated by the opinion of Lord Mansfield in the *Dean of St. Asaph's case* in 1784, Mr. Justice Willes alone dissenting but disagreeing with Erskine. The fight for the tribunal was transferred to Parliament. In Fox's Libel act of 1792 Parliament declared in favor of Mr. Justice Willes' view of the English common law on the procedural point of the tribunal authorized to apply the test of tendency. The act required the trial judge to submit the question of tendency to the jury, and declared the jury was the exclusive tribunal on the question of tendency only when it decided the question *in favor of* the defendant, but left the judges as the exclusive tribunal when the jury found the question *against* the defendant. In short, after Fox's act the prosecution had to convince both the jury and the judges of the bad tendency of the publication as an opinion-maker, while the defendant had to convince only the jury of its good or indifferent or harmless tendency as an opinion-maker. The result of the fight for the tribunal was, as Lord Kenyon expressed it, that before Fox's act liberty of the press in England meant nothing more nor less than that a man could publish anything the judges sitting *in banc* as subsequent or *ex post facto* censors of the press thought was not blamable, while after Fox's act a man could publish anything a jury sitting as subsequent *ex post facto* censors of the press thought was not blamable; but if the jury thought the publication was blamable, there was a second thought coming from the judges, who could set aside the verdict of the jury against the defendant and substitute in its place their own verdict in his favor if they thought the publication was not blamable, meaning by "not blamable" having no bad tendency as an opinion-maker to excite and move the people to change existing things, and by "the people" the multitude or "the masses."

Lord Mansfield and his associates did fine men and send them to jail for their published political opinions because they thought the published political opinions in question had a bad tendency to excite the people to put men out of office and put others in their places, to subvert the existing government, institutions, and laws of the country as it was called by creating and diffusing through the community an ill opinion of them. And they did in fact fine men and send them to jail for their published opinions on the Christian religion, because they thought the published opinions in question had a bad tendency to subvert Christianity by creating and diffusing an ill opinion of it among the people.[12]

As to publications on religion at the time of the Revolution, the English judges were pronouncing them blasphemous under the law laid down by Lord Hale in 1676, viz.:

> Christianity being parcel of the laws of England, therefore to reproach the Christian religion is to speak in subversion of the law.[13]

---

[12] For the English common law of libel at the time of the Revolution, see 2 Stephen, *History of the Criminal Law of England*, chaps. 24 and 25, on "Sedition" and "Blasphemy"; the first editions of Starkie on *Libel* and Holt's *Libel Laws*. And see 1 May, *Constitutional History of England*, chaps. 9 and 10, on "The Press, and Liberty of Opinion"; Bury, *A History of Freedom of Thought*, in "Home University Library" published by Henry Holt & Co. Fox's Libel act is 32 Geo. III, c. 60, and is in Stephen's *History, supra*. p. 344. See Lord Blackburn's explanation of the legal effect of Fox's act, in *Capital and Counties Bank* v. *Henty* (1882), 7 App. Cas. 741, 770–776.

[13] *Rex* v. *Taylor*, 3 Keble 607.

In 1767 Lord Mansfield said:

The eternal principles of natural religion are part of the common law; the essential principles of revealed religion are part of the common law; so that any person reviling, subverting, or ridiculing them may be prosecuted at common law.[14]

In 1797 Lord Kenyon told the jury in the prosecution of a publisher of Paine's *Age of Reason* that "the Christian religion is part of the law of the land."[15] As it was popularly put, the English judges were proceeding on the view that God had a reputation to maintain and needed the help of the English common law to support it.

At the time of the Revolution, then, the line of English common law separating liberty of the press from licentiousness was the opinion of the judges of the King's Bench on the tendency of publications, true or false, to excite and move the people to change the existing order; and that meant the opinion of Lord Mansfield, whose influence in the King's Bench was commanding and controlling. Is it true, as our judges keep telling us, that the original declarations of liberty of the press did nothing but forbid previous censorship, putting American judges into the shoes of Lord Mansfield as subsequent or *ex post facto* censors of publications, true or false?

With reference to the English common law of seditious publications, Sir James Fitzjames Stephen begins his story of it in his *History of the Criminal Law of England* with these observations.[16]

Two different views may be taken of the relation between rulers and their subjects. If the ruler is regarded as the superior of the subject, as being by the nature of his position presumably wise and

---

[14] *Chamberlain of London* v. *Evans*, cited by C. J. Clayton in *State* v. *Chandler*, 2 Harr. (Del.) 556, and in Odgers, *Libel and Slander*, 2d ed., 443.

[15] *Rex* v. *Williams*, 26 St. Tn., 653, 704.

[16] II, 299.

good, the rightful ruler and guide of the whole population, it must necessarily follow that it is wrong to censure him openly; that even if he is mistaken his mistakes should be pointed out with the utmost respect, and that whether mistaken or not no censure should be cast upon him likely or designed to diminish his authority.

If on the other hand the ruler is regarded as the agent and servant, and the subject as the wise and good master who is obliged to delegate his power to the so-called ruler because being a multitude he cannot use it himself, it is obvious that this sentiment must be reversed. Every member of the public who censures the ruler for the time being exercises in his own person the right which belongs to the whole of which he forms a part. He is finding fault with his servant. If others think differently they can take the other side of the dispute, and the utmost that can happen is that the servant will be dismissed and another put in his place, or perhaps that the arrangements of the household will be modified. To those who hold this view fully and carry it out to all its consequences, there can be no such offence as sedition. There may indeed be breaches of the peace which may destroy or endanger life, limb, or property, and there may be incitements to such offences, but no imaginable censure of the government, short of a censure which has an immediate tendency to produce such a breach of the peace, ought to be regarded as criminal.

Sir James goes on to say that the present English law of seditious publications as stated by him in his *Digest of the Criminal Law of England* is the result of a "compromise" between these two "extreme views" of the relation between governors and the governed.[17] The second view, however, that the governed are the master and the governors are the servants, cannot be regarded as "extreme" by an American judge. That view was promulgated in the Declaration of Independence, was vindicated by the Revolutionary War, and was made the foundation stone of the law of the land by our written constitutions. The supreme power of the people always has been a

---

[17] II, 298, note 1, and 300.

fixed legal fact in the United States, admitting of no discussion inside the courts. As related to this fixed legal fact, the constitutional declarations of liberty of the press do not involve any theory that the people are "wise and good" as Sir James Stephen suggests. They simply involve the idea that power denotes duty, expressed over and over again in English lawbooks, commencing with the second one by Bracton, saying that the holder of the supreme power in the community ought to use it to display his reason and judgment rather than the vigor of his power.[18] When the supreme power is definitely lodged by law in the people, to enable them to exercise their power and perform their duty with reason and judgment and not with the vigor of mere power, they must have education and the means of education. The framers of our written constitutions did not leave this legal idea to rest for security on a necessary legal inference from the legal fact of the supremacy of the people, but expressly declared it in the constitutional declarations of the right of liberty of speech and of the press.

Many of the publications on politics in the Colonies before the Revolution were seditious and even treasonable under the English common law and its administration. One of the objects of the Revolution was to get rid of the English common law on liberty of speech and of the press. The first Continental Congress in 1774 enumerated the right of liberty of the press as one of five invaluable rights without which a people cannot be free, and declared its importance consisted—

in the advancement of truth, science, morality, and arts in general, and in the diffusion of liberal sentiments on the administration of government, the ready communication of thought between subjects, and the consequential promotion of union among them whereby

[18] 1 Bracton, *Laws and Customs of England,* trans. by T. Twiss, 39, 41; Coke's report of his interview with James I telling him that the king cannot sit on the bench to decide cases in his own proper person, *Prohibitions Del Roy,* 12 Coke's Rep. 63.

oppressive officers are shamed or intimidated into more honorable and just modes of conducting affairs.[19]

This declaration evidences the view that the right of liberty of the press is confined to matters of public concern such as those enumerated, viz.: the arts and sciences, morality, public officers and their conduct of public affairs, and does not extend to matters of private concern.

The declaration also evidences the view that truth and the right of liberty of the press are one and inseparable, the duty to publish the truth being the right expressed in terms of duty. As obedience to law is liberty, so obedience to truth is liberty of the press.

The Virginia Religious Liberty statute of 1777 declared not only the right of liberty to profess religion and to worship God, but also the right of liberty of opinion, of speech, and of the press on the subject of religion, and eliminated the English common-law subjective test of supposed bad tendency in the following words:

> It is time enough for the rightful purposes of civil government for its officers to interfere when principles break out into overt acts against peace and good order.

The distinction is brought out more fully in one of Dr. Furneaux's letters to Blackstone published in England and in Philadelphia before the Virginia Religious Liberty statute, wherein Dr. Furneaux said:

> If it be objected, that when the tendency of principles is unfavorable to the peace and good order of society, as it may be, it is the magistrate's duty then, and for that reason, to restrain them by penal laws; I reply, that the tendency of principles, though it be *unfavorable,* is not *prejudicial* to society, till it issues in some overt acts against the public peace and order; and when it does, *then* the

---

[19] Cited by Kent, J., in *People* v. *Croswell,* 3 Johns. cases, 337, 391.

magistrate's authority to punish commences; that is, he may punish the *overt acts,* but not the tendency, which is not actually hurtful; and therefore his penal laws should be directed against *overt acts only,* which are detrimental to the peace and good order of society, let them spring from what principles they will; and not against *principles,* or the *tendency* of principles.

The distinction between the tendency of principles, and the overt acts arising from them is, and cannot but be, observed in many cases of a civil nature, in order to determine the bounds of the magistrate's power, or at least to limit the exercise of it, in such cases. It would not be difficult to mention customs and manners, as well as principles, which have a tendency unfavorable to society; and which, nevertheless, cannot be restrained by penal laws, except with the total destruction of civil liberty. And here the magistrate must be contented with pointing his penal laws against the evil overt acts resulting from them. . . . Punishing a man for the tendency of his *principles* is punishing him *before* he is guilty, for fear he *should be guilty.*[20]

While this distinction between the tendency of principles and overt acts arising from principles had special reference to the subject of religion and to nonconformists in the Christian religion, yet it applies equally to any matter of public concern within the sphere of the right of liberty of the press. There is no difference between principles and opinions. And as respects the phrase "overt acts," since speaking is acting, and writing, printing, and publishing are acting, all publications are overt acts. But publications are not overt acts against peace and good order simply because of their supposed bad tendency

---

[20] Cited and quoted by Clayton, C. J., in *State* v. *Chandler,* 2 Harr. (Del.) 553, 576. For an account of Dr. Furneaux, see the *Dictionary of National Biography,* edited by Leslie Stephen. See Locke's first "Letter concerning Toleration" in 1689. As Jefferson himself said, there is not an original thought or word in the Virginia Religious Liberty statute. Jefferson drew it from the laws of Rhode Island, Maryland, and Pennsylvania, and from the best English literature on religious liberty and liberty of the press. I do not know that Jefferson used Dr. Furneaux's letter to Blackstone, but he was looking for literature like that.

as opinion-makers. As illustrating the practical application of the distinction, reference may be made to the *Mormon cases* in the United States Supreme Court holding the practice of polygamy, and publications teaching and advising the practice of polygamy, to be overt acts against peace and good order though arising out of opinions called religious,[21] and to *Most's case* in the New York Court of Appeals holding anarchists' publications teaching and advising the use of force to be overt acts against peace and good order.[22]

Reading the original declarations of the right of liberty of the press in the light of their history and without reference to judicial opinions, evidently they obliterated the English common-law test of supposed bad tendency to determine the seditious or blasphemous character of a publication, and hence obliterated the English common-law crimes of sedition and blasphemy; shifted the law of obscene and immoral publications from the region of libel to the region of public nuisance;[23] and left standing only the law of defamatory publications, materially modifying that. Separating publications as they do into those on matters of public concern and those on matters of private concern, and applying only to the former, and truth being the dividing line between lawful and unlawful publications, the declarations wiped out the English common-law rule in criminal prosecutions for defamatory libel, "The greater the truth the greater the libel." The declarations threw

---

[21] *Davis* v. *Beason*, 133 U.S. 333; *Mormon Church* v. *United States*, 136 U.S. 1.

[22] *People* v. *Most*, 171 N.Y. 423. It has been decided that constitutional religious liberty protects "eternity celestial polygamy" in the next world (*Hilton* v. *Roylance*, 25 Utah 129); that it does not protect a Salvation Army drummer beating his drum out of season (*State* v. *White*, 64 N.H. 48), nor a Christian Scientist healing the sick without a doctor's license (*State* v. *Marble*, 72 Oh. St. 21; *People* v. *Pierson*, 176 N.Y. 201), nor a fortune teller (*State* v. *Neitzel*, 69 Wash. 567).

[23] A standard English lawbook, 2 Russell, *Law of Crimes*, 7th English and 1st Canadian eds., 1875, classifies indecent, obscene and immoral publications as public nuisances, not as libels as in former editions.

on American judges in civil and criminal actions for defamatory libel the new work of drawing the line between matters of public concern and matters of private concern, and of determining what is truth in a publication on a matter of public concern.[24]

When, as ordinarily happens, a publication on a matter of public concern reflecting on personal or professional reputation, as by imputing disgraceful motives and conduct, contains both statements of fact and expressions of opinions, the two have to be separated. It is not true that liberty of the press makes lawful every published expression of opinion on matters of public concern. Published opinions may be true, or false and defamatory, just as published statements of facts may be true, or false and defamatory. If published opinions on matters of public concern are false and defamatory because of their tendency to infuse into the minds of men suspicion, distrust, and dislike for other men, and so influence their conduct, such published false opinions are just as unlawful as false

[24] It must be remembered that the accepted judicial view is that the constitutional declarations did not touch the English common-law rules making truth a defense to a civil action for defamatory libel, and of no importance in a criminal action. See *Com.* v. *Blanding*, 3 Pick. 304, in 1825; *Patterson* v. *Colorado*, 205 U.S. 454, in 1906. In most if not all the states constitutional or statutory provisions, following the New York statute of 1805, hereinafter referred to, expressly make truth a defense in criminal as well as civil actions for defamatory libel, many putting on the defense of truth Hamilton's rider, hereinafter considered, viz., "truth, with good motives, for justifiable ends." There is a wide difference between a rule of substantive law shutting out the truth altogether, and a procedural rule placing the burden of proving truth on the defendant, instead of making the plaintiff prove falsity, the latter being the more natural and logical procedural rule. The true reasons for the English common-law rules about truth in libel cases are unknown, so far as I can see. Reasons as plenty as blackberries are given in the lawbooks, but they are obvious inventions. Lord Campbell's act in 1843, 6 and 7 Vict. c. 96, s. 6, provides that in a *criminal* prosecution for a *defamatory* libel, "the truth of the matters charged may be inquired into, but shall not amount to a defense, unless it was for the public benefit that the said matters charged should be published."

statements of fact having the same tendency. An opinion ordinarily is but an inference from facts. The correct test of the truth or falsity of an opinion on a matter of public concern seems to be the one laid down by the better modern English judges in the law of fair comment on matters of public concern, viz.: Assuming the facts to be true, is the inference or opinion an allowable one? Is it an inference or opinion capable of being drawn from those facts? In other words, could or might a fair-minded average man draw the inference or opinion in question from the facts proved or admitted to be true? This leaves a wide margin for the play and action of conflicting opinions on matters of public concern, leaving the restraint of truth as to matters of fact until removed by the legislature.[25]

The true view of the original declarations of liberty of the press would appear to be, then, that they wiped out the English common-law test of supposed bad tendency as opinion-makers, and substituted the test of truth, as the dividing line between lawful and unlawful publications on matters of public concern, the restraint of truth being inflexible as applied to matters of fact until altered by the legislature,[26] but flexible enough as applied to matters of opinion to legalize any allow-

---

[25] *Campbell* v. *Spottiswoode,* 3 B. and S. 769 (1863), especially the opinion of Blackburn, J. *Hunt* v. *Star Newspaper Co.*[1908], 2 K. B. 309. The right of liberty of the press originated outside the English courts, for all practical purposes in Milton's "Speech for the Liberty of Unlicensed Printing," in 1644, but it did not really begin to become a legal right protected by the English courts until the opinions of Lord Ellenborough in *Tabbert* v. *Tipper,* 1 Campbell 350, in 1808, and in *Carr* v. *Wood,* 1 Campbell 354, note, in 1813, commencing what is called the law of "fair comment on matters of public concern," on which see generally the article on "Fair Comment" by W. Blake Odgers, Q.C., in 6 *Encyc. of the Laws of England,* 2d ed., 5, and Pollock, *The Law of Torts,* 9th ed., 262. Note that it has been written in *civil* actions for *defamatory libel* exclusively, where the rule that truth, *simpliciter,* is a defense has obtained for a long time.

[26] The constitutional declarations only forbid the *abridgment* of liberty of the press, and a legislative removal of the restraint of truth enlarges the liberty, and hence is constitutional.

able opinion on any matter of public concern which any fair-minded average man could or might form from the facts, thus securing to every man the right to publish truth on any matter of public concern, the right of the editor and owner of a newspaper being no greater than the right of any other individual; and making the right to own and operate a printing press a common private-property right, because the public-education right can be exercised practically and conveniently only through the printing press.

The practical securities provided by existing law to compel observance of the restraint of truth in publications on matters of public concern, are the English common-law civil action for damages and criminal prosecution for defamatory publications. Unless published falsehood on matters of public concern has a tendency to defame personal or professional reputation or to cast suspicion on the title or quality of property, it cannot be the foundation of either a civil action for damages or a criminal prosecution. Published truth on matters of public concern cannot be defamatory, under the original declarations at least, as distinguished from the Hamiltonian declarations. . . .

8. SCHENCK v. UNITED STATES

1919

The first federal law punishing a citizen's criticism of government since the death in 1800 of the Alien and Sedition Acts was passed by Congress in 1917, in the form of the Espionage Act.

From *Schenck* v. *U.S.*, 249 United States Reports 47.

It forbade attempts to cause insubordination in the armed forces or to obstruct recruiting, and conspiracy to use the mails for the same purposes. Charles T. Schenck and Elizabeth Baer were convicted under its provisions for their part in the printing and mailing of circulars to draftees, calling conscription despotism arranged in the interest of Wall Street, and urging the right to assert opposition to the draft. Their appeal reached the Supreme Court of the United States.

Justice Oliver Wendell Holmes, Jr., wrote the decision for a unanimous court. And while the conviction was upheld, Holmes stated in his decision for the first time the "clear and present danger" test for allegedly criminal words—the test that was to make the decision one of the most famous in American law and liberty. "The question in every case," Holmes wrote, "is whether the words used are used in such circumstances and are of such a nature as to create a clear and present danger that they will bring about the substantive evils that Congress has a right to prevent."

During the thirty-five years that followed, the test was to be assailed as too lenient, too harsh, too vague for use; to be interpreted in a bewildering variety of ways; to be used more often, perhaps, in cases that convicted for expression than in cases that protected expression; and to undergo a decline in usage by the courts after the 1951 case of *Dennis* v. *U.S.* But that it served the cause of free speech and press in notable ways was hard to dispute: in loosening the grip of the "bad tendency" test of ancient odium; in serving as an opening wedge that helped force courts to think out the content of the First Amendment; in evoking, with its elaboration and refinement, some of the noblest thought and language about the democratic ideal that the American judiciary has produced. Expressed in subsequent opinions such as Holmes's dissents in *Abrams* v. *U.S.* and *Gitlow* v. *New York,* and Justice Brandeis' concurrence in *Whitney* v. *California,* it had an impact far beyond the judicial arena, serving as a rallying point for the foes of restraint and giving them a phrase (no doubt at times a catch phrase used as a substitute for thought) for their banner. In one area especially relevant to the news media—contempt of court—it was used by the Supreme Court to restrain repressive tendencies of the judicial branch itself. And in the opinion of the great student of the First Amendment, Zechariah Chafee, Jr., its presence unquestionably staved off many prosecutions which would otherwise have been pressed.

Mr. Justice Holmes delivered the opinion of the court:

This is an indictment in three counts. The first charges a conspiracy to violate the Espionage Act of June 15, 1917, c. 30, § 3, 40 Stat. 217, 219, by causing and attempting to cause insubordination, &c., in the military and naval forces of the United States, and to obstruct the recruiting and enlistment service of the United States, when the United States was at war with the German Empire, to-wit, that the defendants wilfully conspired to have printed and circulated to men who had been called and accepted for military service under the Act of May 18, 1917, a document set forth and alleged to be calculated to cause such insubordination and obstruction. The count alleges overt acts in pursuance of the conspiracy, ending in the distribution of the document set forth. The second count alleges a conspiracy to commit an offence against the United States, to-wit, to use the mails for the transmission of matter declared to be non-mailable by Title XII, § 2 of the Act of June 15, 1917, to-wit, the above mentioned document, with an averment of the same overt acts. The third count charges an unlawful use of the mails for the transmission of the same matter and otherwise as above. The defendants were found guilty on all the counts. They set up the First Amendment to the Constitution forbidding Congress to make any law abridging the freedom of speech, or of the press, and bringing the case here on that ground have argued some other points also of which we must dispose.

It is argued that the evidence, if admissible, was not sufficient to prove that the defendant Schenck was concerned in sending the documents. According to the testimony Schenck said he was general secretary of the Socialist party and had charge of the Socialist headquarters from which the documents were sent. He identified a book found there as the minutes of the Executive Committee of the party. The book showed a resolution of August 13, 1917, that 15,000 leaflets should be printed on the other side of one of them in use, to be mailed to men who had passed exemption boards, and for distribution. Schenck personally attended to the printing. On August 20 the general secretary's report said "Obtained new leaflets from printer and started work addressing envelopes" &c.; and there was a resolve that Comrade Schenck be allowed $125 for sending leaflets through the mail. He said that he had about fifteen or sixteen thousand printed. There were files of the circular in question in the inner office which he said were printed on the other side of the one sided circular and were there for distribution. Other copies were proved to have been sent through the mails to drafted men. Without going into confirmatory details that were proved, no reasonable man could doubt that the defendant Schenck was largely instrumental in sending the circulars about. As to the defendant Baer there was evidence that she was a member of the Executive Board and that the minutes of its transactions were hers. The argument as to the sufficiency of the evidence that the defendants conspired to send the documents only impairs the seriousness of the real defence. . . .

The document in question upon its first printed side recited the first section of the Thirteenth Amendment, said that the idea embodied in it was violated by the Conscription Act and that a conscript is little better than a convict. In impassioned language it intimated that conscription was despotism in its worst form and a monstrous wrong against humanity in the interest of Wall Street's chosen few. It said "Do not submit to intimidation," but in form at least confined itself to peaceful measures such as a petition for the repeal of the act. The other and later printed side of the sheet was headed "Assert Your Rights." It stated reasons for alleging that any one violated the Constitution when he refused to recognize "your right to assert your opposition to the draft," and went on "If you do not assert and support your rights, you are helping to deny or disparage rights which it is the solemn duty of all citizens and residents of the United States to retain." It described the arguments on the other side as coming from cunning politicians and a mercenary capitalist press, and even silent consent to the conscription law as helping to support an infamous conspiracy. It denied the power to send our citizens away to foreign shores to shoot up the people of other lands, and added that words could not express the condemnation such cold-blooded ruthlessness deserves, &c., &c., winding up "You must do your share to maintain, support and uphold the rights of the people of this country." Of course the document would not have been sent unless it had been intended to have some effect, and we do not see what effect it could be expected to have upon persons subject to the draft except to influence them to obstruct the carrying of it out. The defendants do not deny that the jury might find against them on this point.

But it is said, suppose that that was the tendency of this circular, it is protected by the First Amendment to the Constitution. Two of the strongest expressions are said to be quoted respectively from well-known public men. It well may be that the prohibition of laws abridging the freedom of speech is not confined to previous restraints, although to prevent them may have been the main purpose, as intimated in *Patterson* v. *Colorado,* 205 U. S. 454, 462. We admit that in many places and in ordinary times the defendants in saying all that was said in the circular would have been within their constitutional rights. But the character of every act depends upon the circumstances in which it is done. *Aikens* v. *Wisconsin,* 195 U. S. 194, 205, 206. The most stringent protection of free speech would not protect a man in falsely shouting fire in a theatre and causing a panic. It does not even protect a man from an injunction against uttering words that may have all the effect of force. *Gompers* v. *Bucks Stove & Range Co.*, 221 U. S. 418, 439. The question in every case is whether the words used are used in such circumstances and are of such a nature as to create a clear and present danger that they will bring about the substantive evils that Congress has a right to prevent. It is a question of proximity and degree. When a nation is at war many things that might be said in time of peace are such a hindrance to its effort that their utterance will not be endured so long as men fight and that no Court could regard them as protected by any constitutional right. It seems to be admitted that if an actual obstruction of the recruiting service were proved, liability for words that produced that effect might be enforced. The statute of 1917 in § 4 punishes conspiracies to obstruct as well as actual obstruction. If the act, (speaking, or circulating a paper,) its tendency and the intent with which it is done are the same, we perceive no ground for saying that success alone warrants making the act a crime. *Goldman* v. *United States*, 245 U. S. 474, 477. Indeed that case might be said to dispose of the present contention if the precedent covers all *media concludendi*. But as the right to free speech was not referred to specially, we have thought fit to add a few words.

It was not argued that a conspiracy to obstruct the draft was not within the words of the Act of 1917. The words are "obstruct the recruiting or enlistment service," and it might be suggested that they refer only to making it hard to get volunteers. Recruiting heretofore usually having been accomplished by getting volunteers the word is apt to call up that method only in our minds. But recruiting is gaining fresh supplies for the forces, as well by draft as otherwise. It is put as an alternative to enlistment or voluntary enrollment in this act. The fact that the Act of 1917 was enlarged by the amending Act of May 16, 1918, c. 75, 40 Stat. 553, of course, does not affect the present indictment and would not, even if the former act had been repealed. Rev. Stats., § 13.

Judgments affirmed.

9. TO ADVOCACY, THE FIRST AMENDMENT GUARANTEES FREEDOM; TO INCITEMENT, IT GUARANTEES NOTHING

Alexander Meiklejohn, 1955

The philosopher and teacher Alexander Meiklejohn here speaks his absolutist views of the meaning of free speech and press: where the sovereign citizen is engaging in political discussion, there can be no exceptions to unlimited freedom under the First Amendment. Meiklejohn's writings have had wide influence on thoughtful Americans, including politicians, scholars, and Supreme Court justices. Among the last—and one of those who have asserted their debt to Meiklejohn—is Justice Hugo Black, who carried freedom beyond the position of absolute freedom in *political* discussion and expounded a perfect freedom in almost any sphere where expression is not irrelevant to the occasion.

In the statement below, Meiklejohn was testifying before a

From U.S. Senate, Committee on Judiciary, Sub-Committee on Constitutional Rights, "Security and Constitutional Rights," Testimony of Alexander Meiklejohn, Nov. 14, 1955, pp. 14–21.

Senate subcommittee at a time when compulsions to orthodoxy during a period of acute, nationwide fear of domestic communism put free expression in jeopardy with other civil rights. His attack on the clear and present danger doctrine is here. With it, he states his position that only *incitement* to illegal acts is punishable under the First Amendment, and seems to say that "incitement" has not occurred unless the illegal act has been performed and the prior words can be directly connected with it. When that happens, act and words may be punished.

. . . It may clarify my own part in our conference if I tell you at once my opinion concerning this much-debated subject. The first amendment seems to me to be a very uncompromising statement. It admits of no exceptions. It tells us that the Congress and by implication, all other agencies of the Government are denied any authority whatever to limit the political freedom of the citizens of the United States. It declares that with respect to political discussion, political advocacy, political planning, our citizens are sovereign, and the Congress is their subordinate agent. That agent is authorized, under strong safeguards against the abuse of its power, to limit the freedom of men as they go about the management of their private, their nonpolitical affairs. But the same men, as they endeavor to meet the public responsibilities of citizenship in a free society, are in a vital sense, which is not easy to define, beyond the reach of legislative control. Our common task, as we talk together today, is to determine what that sense is. . . .

Mr. Chairman, I have now stated for your consideration the thesis that the first amendment is not "open to exceptions," that our American "freedom of speech" is not, on any grounds whatever, subject to abridgement by the representatives of the people. May I next, try to answer two arguments which are commonly brought against that thesis in the courts and in the wider circle of popular discussion?

The first objection rests upon the supposition that freedom

of speech may on occasion, threaten the security of the Nation. And when these two legitimate national interests are in conflict, the Government, it is said, must strike a balance between them. And that means that the first amendment must, at times, yield ground. The freedom of speech must be abridged in order that the national order and safety may be secured.

In the courts of the United States, many diverse opinions have asserted that balancing doctrine. One of these often quoted, reads as follows:

"To preserve its independence, and give security against foreign aggression and encroachment, is the highest duty of every nation, and to attain these ends nearly all other considerations are to be subordinated. It matters not in what form such aggression comes * * * the government, possessing the powers which are to be exercised for protection and security is clothed with authority to determine the occasion on which the powers shall be brought forth."

That opinion tells us that the Government of the United States has unlimited authority to provide for the security of the Nation, as it may seem necessary and wise. It tells us, therefore that, constitutionally, the Government which has created the defenses of political freedom may break down those defenses. We, the people, who have enacted the first amendment, may by agreed-upon procedure modify or annul that amendment. And, since we are, as a government, a sovereign nation, I do not see how any of these assertions can be doubted or denied. We Americans, as a body politic, may destroy or limit our freedom whenever we choose. But what bearing has that statement upon the authority of Congress to interfere with the provisions of the first amendment? Congress is not the Government. It is only 1 of 4 branches to each of which the people have denied specific and limited powers as well as delegated such powers. And in the case before us, the words, "Congress shall make no law * * * abridging the freedom of speech," gives plain evidence that, so far as Congress is concerned, the power to limit our political freedom has been explicitly denied.

There is, I am sure, a radical error in the theory that the task of balancing the conflicting claims of security and freedom has been delegated to Congress. It is the failure to recognize that the balancing in question was carefully done when, 170 years ago, the Constitution was adopted and quickly amended. The men who wrote the text of that Constitution knew, quite as well as we do, that the program of political freedom is a dangerous one. They could foresee that, as the Nation traveled the ways of self-Government, the freedom of speech would often be used irresponsibly and unwisely, especially in times of war or near war, and that such talking might have serious consequences for the national safety.

They knew, too, that a large section of the voting population was hostile to the forms of government which were then being adopted. And, further, they had every reason to expect that, in a changing world, new dissatisfactions would arise and might in times of stress, break out into open and passionate disaffection. All these considerations, I am saying, were as clearly and as disturbingly present to their minds as they are to our minds today. And, because of them, the first amendment might have been written, not as it is, but as the courts of the United States have rewritten it in the war-maddened years since 1919. The amendment might have said, "Except in times and situations involving clear and present danger to the national security, Congress shall make no law abridging the freedom of speech." Or it might have read, "Only when, in the judgment of the Legislature, the interests of order and security render such action advisable shall Congress abridge the freedom of speech." But the writers of the amendment did not adopt either of these phrasings or anything like them. . . .

The second objection which must be met by one who asserts the unconditional freedom of speech rests upon the well-known fact that there are countless human situations in which, under the Constitution, this or that kind of speaking may be limited or forbidden by legislative action. Some of these cases have been listed by the courts in vague and varying ways. Thus libels, blasphemies, attacks upon public morals or private reputation have been held punishable. So, too, we are told that "counseling a murder" may be a criminal act, or "falsely shouting 'fire' in a theater, and causing a panic." Offensive or provocative speech has been denied legislative immunity. Contempt of court, shown by the use of speech or by refusal to speak, may give basis for prosecution. Utterances which cause a riot or which incite to it may be subject to the same legal condemnation. And this listing of legitimate legislative abridgements of speech could be continued indefinitely. Their number is legion.

In view of these undoubted facts, the objection which we must now try to meet can be simply stated. In all these cases, it says, inasmuch as speaking is abridged, exceptions are made to the first amendment. The amendment is thus shown to be, in general, open to exceptions. And from this it follows that there is no reason why a Legislature which has authority to guard the public safety should be debarred from making an exception when faced by the threat of national danger.

Now, the validity of that argument rests upon the assumed major premise that whenever, in any way, limits are set to the speaking of an individual, an exception is made to the first amendment. But that premise is clearly false. It could be justified only if it were shown that the amendment intends to forbid every form of governmental control over the act of speaking. Is that its intention? Nothing could be further from the truth. May I draw an example from our own present activities in this room? You and I are here talking about freedom within limits defined by the Senate. I am allowed to speak only because you have invited me to do so. And just now everyone else is denied that privilege. But further, you have assigned me a topic to which my remarks must be relevant. Your schedule, too, acting with generosity, fixes a time within which my remarks must be made. In a word, my speaking, though free in the first amendment sense, is abridged in many ways. But your speaking, too, is controlled by rules of procedure. You may, of course, differ in opinion, from what I am saying. To that freedom there are no limits. But, unless the chairman intervenes, you are not allowed to express that difference by open speech until I have finished my reading. In a word, both you and I are under control as to what we may say and when and how we may say it. Shall we say, then, that this conference, which studies the principle of free speech, is itself making exceptions to that principle? I do not think so. Speech as a form of human action, is subject to regulation in exactly the same sense as is walking, or lighting a fire, or shooting a gun. To interpret the first amendment as forbidding such regulation is to so misconceive its meaning as to reduce it to nonsense. . . .

Mr. Chairman, in the first section of this paper I spoke of the negative fact that the first amendment forbids the Legislature to limit the political freedom of the people. May I now, surveying the same ground from its positive side, discuss with you the active powers and responsibilities of free citizens, as these are described or taken for granted in the general structure of the Constitution as a whole? If I am not mistaken, we shall find here the reason why the words of the great proclamation are so absolute, so uncompromising, so resistant of modification or exception.

The purpose of the Constitution is, as we all know, to define and allocate powers for the governing of the Nation. To that end, three special governing agencies are set up, and to each of them are delegated such specific powers as are needed for doing its part of the work.

Now that program rests upon a clear distinction between the political body which delegates powers and the political bodies, legislative, executive, and judicial, to which powers are delegated. It presupposes, on the one hand, a supreme governing agency to which, originally, all authority belongs. It specifies, on the other hand, subordinate agencies to which partial delegations of authority are made. What, then, is the working relation between the supreme agency and its subordinates? Only as we answer that question shall we find the positive meaning of the first amendment.

First of all, then, what is the supreme governing agency of this Nation? In its opening statement the Constitution answers that question. "We the People of the United States," it declares, "do ordain and establish this Constitution. . . ." Those are the revolutionary words which define the freedom which is guaranteed by the first amendment. They mark off our Government from every form of despotic polity. The legal powers of the people of the United States are not granted to them by someone else—by kings or barons or priests, by legislators or executives or judges. All political authority, whether delegated or not, belongs constitutionally, to us. If anyone else has political authority, we are lending it to him. We, the people, are supreme in our own right. We are governed directly or indirectly, only by ourselves.

But now what have we, the people, in our establishing of the Constitution done with the powers which thus inhere in us? Some of them we have delegated. But there is one power, at least, which we have not delegated, which we have kept in our own hands, for our own direct exercise. Article I, section 2, authorizes the people, in their capacity as electors, to choose their Representatives. And that means that we, the people, in a vital sense, do actively govern those who, by other delegated powers, govern us. In the midst of all our assigning of powers to legislative, executive, and judicial bodies, we have jealously kept for ourselves the most fundamental of all powers. It is the power of voting, of choosing—by joint action—those representatives to whom certain of our powers are entrusted. In the view of the Constitution, then, we the people, are not only the supreme agency. We are, also, politically, an active electorate—a fourth, or perhaps better, a first branch which, through its reserved power governs at the polls. That is the essential meaning of the statement that we Americans are, in actual practice, politically, a free people. Our first amendment freedom is not merely an aspiration. It is an arrangement made by women and men who vote freely and, by voting, govern the Nation. That is the responsibility, the opportunity, which the Constitution assigns to us, however slackly and negligently we may at times, have exercised our power.

It follows from what has just been said that, under the Constitution, we Americans are politically free only insofar as our voting is free. But to get the full meaning of that statement we must examine more closely what men are doing when they vote, and how they do it.

The most obvious feature of activity at the polls is the choosing among candidates for office. But, under our election procedures, with their party platforms and public meetings, with the turmoil and passion of partisan debate, the voters are also considering and deciding about issues of public policy. They are thinking. As we vote we do more than elect men to represent us. We also judge the wisdom or folly of suggested measures. We plan for the welfare of the Nation. Now it is these judging activities of the governing people which the first amendment protects by its guaranties of freedom from legislative interference. Because, as self-governing women and men, we the people, have work to do for the general welfare, we make two demands. First, our judging of public issues, whether done separately or in groups, must be free and independent—must be our own. It must be done by us and by no one else. And, second, we must be equally free and independent in expressing, at the polls, the conclusions, the beliefs, to which our judging has brought us. Censorship over our thinking, duress over our voting, are alike forbidden by the first amendment. A legislative body, or any other body, which, in any way, practices such censorship or duress, stands in contempt of the sovereign people of the United States. . . .

What, then, as seen against this constitutional background, is the purpose of the first amendment, as it stands guard over our freedom? That purpose is to see to it that, in none of these . . . activities of judging shall the voter be robbed, by action of other, subordinate branches of the Government, of the responsibility, the power, the authority, which are his under the Constitution. What shall he read? What he himself decides to read. With whom shall he associate in political advocacy? With those with whom he chooses to associate. Whom shall he oppose? Those with whom he disagrees. Shall any branch of the Government attempt to control his opinions or his vote, to drive him by duress or intimidation into believing or voting this way or that? To do this is to violate the Constitution at its very source. We, the people of the United States, are self-governing. That is what our freedom means. . . .

Mr. Chairman, I have tried to state and defend the assertion that constitutional guaranty of political freedom is not open to exceptions. Judgment upon the theoretical validity of that position I now leave in your hands.

But, as between conflicting views of the first amendment, there is also a practical question of efficiency. May I, in closing, speaking with the tentativeness becoming to a nonlawyer, offer three suggestions as to the working basis on which decisions about political freedom should rest?

First, the experience of the courts since 1919 seems to me to show that, as a procedural device for distinguishing forms of speech and writing and assembly which the amendment does protect from those which it does not protect, the clear and present danger test has failed to work. Its basic practical defect is that no one has been able to give it dependable, or even assignable meaning. Case by case, opinion by opinion, it has shifted back and forth with a variability of meaning which reveals its complete lack of constitutional basis. In his opinion confirming the conviction of Eugene Dennis and others for violation of the Smith Act, Judge Learned Hand reviewed the long series of judicial attempts to give to the words "clear and present" a usable meaning. His conclusion reads, in part, as follows:

"The phrase 'clear and present danger' * * * is a way to describe a penumbra of occasions, even the outskirts of which are indefinable, but within which, as is so often the case, the courts must find their way as they can. In each case they must ask whether the gravity of the evil, discounted by its improbability, justifies such an invasion of free speech as is necessary to avoid the danger."

And to this bewildering interpretation of the words, "clear and present," he adds: "That is a test in whose application the utmost differences of opinion have constantly arisen, even in the Supreme Court. Obviously it would be impossible to draft a statute which should attempt to prescribe a rule for each occasion; and it follows, as we have said, either that the act is definite enough as it stands, or that it is practically impossible to deal with such conduct in general terms."

Those words, coming from the penetrating and powerful mind of Learned Hand show how intolerable it is that the most precious, most fundamental, value in the American plan of Government should depend, for its defense, upon a phrase which, not only has no warrant in the Constitution, but has no dependable meaning, either for a man accused of crime or for the attorneys who prosecute or defend him or for the courts which judge him. That phrase does not do its work. We need to make a fresh start in our interpreting of the words which protect our political freedom.

Second, as we seek for a better test, it is, of course, true that no legal device can transform the making of decisions about freedom into a merely routine application of an abstract principle. Self-government is a complicated business. And yet, the "no exception" view which I have offered seems to me to promise a more stable and understandable basis for judicial decision than does the 1919 doctrine which the courts have been trying to follow. For example, the most troublesome issue which now confronts our courts, and our people, is that of the speech and writing and assembling of persons who find, or think they find, radical defects in our form of government, and who devise and advocate plans by means of which another form might be substituted for it. And the practical question is, "How far, and in what respects, is such revolutionary planning and advocacy protected by the first amendment?"

It is, of course, understood that if such persons or groups proceed to forceful or violent action, or even to overt preparation for such action, against the Government, the first amendment offers them, in that respect, no protection. Its interest is limited to the freedom of judgment making, of inquiry and belief and conference and persuasion and planning and advocacy. It does not protect either overt action or incitement to such action. It is concerned only with those political activities by which, under the Constitution, freemen govern themselves.

From what has just been said it follows that, so far as speech and writing are concerned, the distinction upon which the application of the first amendment rests is that between "advocacy of action" and "incitement to action." To advocacy the amendment guarantees freedom, no matter what may be advocated. To incitement, on the other hand, the amendment guarantees nothing whatever.

This distinction was sharply drawn by Justice Brandeis when, in the Whitney case, he said:

"Every denunciation of existing law tends in some measure to increase the probability that there will be violations of it. Condonation of a breach enhances the probability. Expressions of approval add to the probability. Propagation of the criminal state of mind by teaching syndicalism increases it. Advocacy of lawbreaking heightens it still further. But even advocacy of violation, however reprehensible morally, is not a justification for denying free speech where the advocacy falls short of incitement and there is nothing to indicate that the advocacy would be immediately acted on."

Those words, I think, point the way which decisions about our political freedom can, and should, follow. An incitement, I take it, is an utterance so related to a specific overt act that it may be regarded and treated as a part of the doing of the act itself, if the act is done. Its control, therefore, falls within the jurisdiction of the legislature. An advocacy, on the other hand, even up to the limit of arguing and planning for the violent overthrow of the existing form of government, is one of those opinion forming, judgment-making expressions which freemen need to utter and to hear as citizens responsible for the governing of the nation. If men are not free to ask and to answer the question, "Shall the present form of our Government be maintained or changed?" If, when that question is asked, the two sides of the issue are not equally open for consideration, for advocacy, and for adoption, then it is impossible to speak of our Government as established by the free choice of a self-governing people. It is not enough to say that the people of the United States were free 170 years ago. The first amendment requires, simply and without equivocation, that they be free now.

Third, and finally, if we say, as this paper has urged, that, in many situations, speech and writing and assembly may be controlled by legislative action, we must also say that such control may never be based on the ground of disagreement with opinions held or expressed. No belief or advocacy may be denied freedom if, in the same situation, opposing beliefs or advocacies are granted that freedom.

If, then, on any occasion in the United States, it is allowable to say that the Constitution is a good document, it is equally allowable, in that situation, to say that the Constitution is a bad document. If a public building may be used in which to say, in time of war, that the war is justified, then the same building may be used in which to say that it is not justified. If it be publicly argued that conscription for armed service is moral and necessary, it may be likewise publicly argued that it is immoral and unnecessary. If it may be said that American political institutions are superior to those of England or Russia or Germany, it may, with equal freedom, be said that those of England or Russia or Germany are superior to ours. These conflicting views may be expressed, must be expressed, not because they are valid, but because they are relevant. If they are responsibly entertained by any one, we, the voters, need to hear them. When a question of policy is "before the house," freemen chose [*sic*] to meet it, not with their eyes shut, but with their eyes open. To be afraid of ideas, of any idea, is to be unfit for self-government. Any such suppression of ideas about the common good, the first amendment condemns with its absolute disapproval. The freedom of ideas shall not be abridged.

10. GITLOW v. PEOPLE OF NEW YORK

1925

The state legislature of New York had joined the frantic rush in almost all states to legislate against the speech of revolutionary communism during World War I and its aftermath. But the state dusted off its unused criminal anarchy statute of 1902 to prosecute and convict the radical Benjamin Gitlow in 1920. His "Left-

From *Gitlow* v. *People of New York*, 268 United States Reports 652.

Wing Manifesto," published in the organ of the far-left Socialists, *The Revolutionary Age,* had advocated violent overthrow of the government.

To the United States Supreme Court majority, the ancient "bad tendency" rule and the right of self-preservation gave New York the power to penalize such advocacy; the high court would not interfere. Its approval of restraint of expression in this case, however, was not what made *Gitlow* live in later years. For one thing, a short but splendid dissent by Justice Oliver Wendell Holmes, Jr., added lasting words to the literature of free expression. But more important, in a single brief paragraph the court majority itself now accepted the principle long and unsuccessfully urged by a few and here pressed upon it by attorney Walter H. Pollack: that the "liberty" which the Fourteenth Amendment protects against state invasion includes the liberties of the First Amendment. Zechariah Chafee, Jr., was to say thirty years later that it was the greatest victory for free speech in his lifetime.

Mr. Justice Sanford delivered the opinion of the court:

The correctness of the verdict is not questioned, as the case was submitted to the jury. The sole contention here is, essentially, that as there was no evidence of any concrete result flowing from the publication of the Manifesto or of circumstances showing the likelihood of such result, the statute as construed and applied by the trial court penalizes the mere utterance, as such, of "doctrine" having no quality of incitement, without regard either to the circumstances of its utterance or to the likelihood of unlawful sequences; and that, as the exercise of the right of free expression with relation to government is only punishable "in circumstances involving likelihood of substantive evil," the statute contravenes the due process clause of the Fourteenth Amendment. The argument in support of this contention rests primarily upon the following propositions: 1st, That the "liberty" protected by the Fourteenth Amendment includes the liberty of speech and of the press; and 2nd, That while liberty of expression "is not absolute," it may be restrained "only in circumstances where its exercise bears a causal relation with some substantive evil, consummated, attempted or likely," and as the statute "takes no account of circumstances," it unduly restrains this liberty and is therefore unconstitutional.

The precise question presented, and the only question which we can consider under this writ of error, then is, whether the statute, as construed and applied in this case by the state courts, deprived the defendant of his liberty of expression in violation of the due process clause of the Fourteenth Amendment.

The statute does not penalize the utterance or publication of abstract "doctrine" or academic discussion having no quality of incitement to any concrete action. It is not aimed against mere historical or philosophical essays. It does not restrain the advocacy of changes in the form of government by constitutional and lawful means. What it prohibits is language advocating, advising or teaching the overthrow of organized government by unlawful means. These words imply urging to action. Advocacy is defined in the Century Dictionary as: "1. The act of pleading for, supporting, or recommending; active espousal." It is not the abstract "doctrine" of overthrowing organized government by unlawful means which is denounced by the statute, but the advocacy of action for the accomplishment of that purpose. It was so construed and applied by the trial judge, who specifically charged the jury that: "A mere grouping of historical events and a prophetic deduction from them would neither constitute advocacy, advice or teaching of a doctrine for the overthrow of government by force, violence or unlawful means. [And] if it were a mere essay on the subject, as suggested by counsel, based upon deduction from alleged historical events, with no teaching, advice or advocacy of action, it would not constitute a violation of the statute. . . ."

The Manifesto, plainly, is neither the statement of abstract doctrine nor, as suggested by counsel, mere prediction that industrial disturbances and revolutionary mass strikes will result spontaneously in an inevitable process of evolution in the economic system. It advocates and urges in fervent language mass action which shall progressively foment industrial disturbances and through political mass strikes and revolutionary mass action overthrow and destroy organized parliamentary government. It concludes with a call to action in these words: "The proletariat revolution and the Communist reconstruction of society—*the struggle for these*—is now indispensable. . . . The Communist International calls the proletariat of the world to the final struggle!" This is not the expression of philosophical abstraction, the mere prediction of future events; it is the language of direct incitement.

The means advocated for bringing about the destruction of organized parliamentary government, namely, mass industrial revolts usurping the functions of municipal government, political mass strikes directed against the parliamentary state, and revolutionary mass action for its final destruction, necessarily imply the use of force and violence, and in their essential nature are inherently unlawful in a constitutional government of law and order. That the jury were warranted in finding that the Manifesto advocated not merely the abstract doctrine of overthrowing organized government by force, violence and unlawful means, but action to that end, is clear.

For present purposes we may and do assume that freedom of speech and of the press—which are protected by the First Amendment from abridgment by Congress—are among the fundamental personal rights and "liberties" protected by the due process clause of the Fourteenth Amendment from impairment by the States. We do not regard the incidental statement in *Prudential Ins. Co.* v. *Cheek*, 259 U. S. 530, 543, that the Fourteenth Amendment imposes no restrictions on the States concerning freedom of speech, as determinative of this question.

It is a fundamental principle, long established, that the freedom of speech and of the press which is secured by the Constitution, does not confer an absolute right to speak or publish, without responsibility, whatever one may choose, or an unrestricted and unbridled license that gives immunity for every possible use of language and prevents the punishment of those who abuse this freedom. 2 Story on the Constitution, 5th ed., § 1580, p. 634. . . . Reasonably limited, it was said by Story in the passage cited, this freedom is an inestimable privilege in a free government; without such limitation, it might become the scourge of the republic.

That a State in the exercise of its police power may punish those who abuse this freedom by utterances inimical to the public welfare, tending to corrupt public morals, incite to crime, or disturb the public peace, is not open to question. . . . Thus it was held by this Court in the *Fox Case,* that a State may punish publications advocating and encouraging a breach of its criminal laws; and, in the *Gilbert Case,* that a State may punish utterances teaching or advocating that its citizens should not assist the United States in prosecuting or carrying on war with its public enemies.

And, for yet more imperative reasons, a State may punish utterances endangering the foundations of organized government and threatening its overthrow by unlawful means. These imperil its own existence as a constitutional State. Freedom of speech and press, said Story (*supra*) does not protect disturbances to the public peace or the attempt to subvert the government. It does not protect publications or teachings which tend to subvert or imperil the government or to impede or hinder it in the performance of its governmental duties. . . . It does not protect publications prompting the overthrow of government by force; the punishment of those who publish articles which tend to destroy organized society being essential to the security of freedom and the stability of the State. . . . And a State may penalize utterances which openly advocate the overthrow of the representative and constitutional form of government of the United States and the several States, by violence or other unlawful means. . . . In short this freedom does not deprive a State of the primary and essential right of self preservation; which, so long as human governments endure, they cannot be denied. . . .

By enacting the present statute the State has determined, through its legislative body, that utterances advocating the overthrow of organized government by force, violence and unlawful means, are so inimical to the general welfare and involve such danger of substantive evil that they may be penalized in the exercise of its police power. That determination must be given great weight. Every presumption is to be indulged in favor of the validity of the statute. *Mugler* v. *Kansas,* 123 U. S. 623, 661. And the case is to be considered "in the light of the principle that the State is primarily the judge of regulations required in the interest of public safety and welfare;" and that its police "statutes may only be declared unconstitutional where they are arbitrary or unreasonable attempts to exercise authority vested in the State in the public interest." *Great Northern Ry.* v. *Clara City,* 246 U. S. 434, 439. That utterances inciting to the overthrow of organized government by unlawful means, present a sufficient danger of substantive evil to bring their punishment within the range of legislative discretion, is clear. Such utterances, by their very nature, involve danger to the public peace and to the security of the State. They threaten breaches of the peace and ultimate revolution. And the immediate danger is none the less real and substantial, because the effect of a given utterance cannot be accurately foreseen. The State cannot reasonably be required to measure the danger from every such utterance in the nice balance of a jeweler's scale. A single revolutionary spark may kindle a fire that, smouldering for a time, may burst into a sweeping and destructive conflagration. It cannot be said that the State is acting arbitrarily or unreasonably when in the exercise of its judgment as to the measures necessary to protect the public peace and safety, it seeks to extinguish the spark without waiting until it has enkindled the flame or blazed into the conflagration. It cannot reasonably be required to defer the adoption of measures for its own peace and safety until the revolutionary utterances lead to actual disturbances of the public peace or imminent and immediate danger of its own destruction; but it may, in the exercise of its judgment, suppress the threatened danger in its incipiency. In *People* v. *Lloyd*, . . . [304 Ill. 23, 35], it was aptly said: "Manifestly, the legislature has authority to forbid the advocacy of a doctrine designed and intended to overthrow the government without waiting until there is a present and imminent danger of the success of the plan advocated. If the State were compelled to wait until the apprehended danger became certain, then its right to protect itself would come into being simultaneously with the overthrow of the government, when there would be neither prosecuting officers nor courts for the enforcement of the law."

We cannot hold that the present statute is an arbitrary or unreasonable exercise of the police power of the State unwarrantably infringing the freedom of speech or press; and we must and do sustain its constitutionality.

This being so it may be applied to every utterance—not too trivial to be beneath the notice of the law—which is of such a character and used with such intent and purpose as to bring it within the prohibition of the statute. . . . In other words, when the legislative body has determined generally, in the constitutional exercise of its discretion, that utterances of a certain kind involve such danger of substantive evil that they may be punished, the question whether any specific utterance coming within the prohibited class is likely, in and of itself, to bring about the substantive evil, is not open to consideration. It is sufficient that the statute itself be constitutional and that the use of the language comes within its prohibition.

It is clear that the question in such cases is entirely different from that involved in those cases where the statute merely prohibits certain acts involving the danger of substantive evil, without any reference to language itself, and it is sought to apply its provisions to language used by the defendant for the purpose of bringing about the prohibited results. There, if it be contended that the statute cannot be applied to the language used by the defendant because of its protection by the freedom of speech or press, it must necessarily be found, as an original question, without any previous determination by the legislative body, whether the specific language used involved such likelihood of bringing about the substantive evil as to deprive it of the constitutional protection. In such cases it has been held that the general provisions of the statute may be constitutionally applied to the specific utterance of the defendant if its natural tendency and probable effect was to bring about the substantive evil which the legislative body might prevent. *Schenck* v. *United States,* [249 U.S. 47, 51]. . . . And the general statement in the *Schenck Case* (p. 52) that the "question in every case is whether the words are used in such circumstances and are of such a nature as to create a clear and present danger that they will bring about the substantive evils,"—upon which great reliance is placed in the defendant's argument—was manifestly intended, as shown by the context, to apply only in cases of this class, and has no application to those like the present, where the legislative body itself has previously determined the danger of substantive evil arising from utterances of a specified character.

The defendant's brief does not separately discuss any of the rulings of the trial court. It is only necessary to say that, applying the general rules already stated, we find that none of them involved any invasion of the constitutional rights of the defendant. It was not necessary, within the meaning of the statute, that the defendant should have advocated "some definite or immediate act or acts" of force, violence or unlawfulness.

It was sufficient if such acts were advocated in general terms; and it was not essential that their immediate execution should have been advocated. Nor was it necessary that the language should have been "reasonably and ordinarily calculated to incite certain persons" to acts of force, violence or unlawfulness. The advocacy need not be addressed to specific persons. Thus, the publication and circulation of a newspaper article may be an encouragement or endeavor to persuade to murder, although not addressed to any person in particular. *Queen* v. *Most,* L. R., 7 Q. B. D. 244.

We need not enter upon a consideration of the English common law rule of seditious libel or the Federal Sedition Act of 1798, to which reference is made in the defendant's brief. These are so unlike the present statute, that we think the decisions under them cast no helpful light upon the questions here.

And finding, for the reasons stated, that the statute is not in itself unconstitutional, and that it has not been applied in the present case in derogation of any constitutional right, the judgment of the Court of Appeals is

Affirmed.

Mr. Justice Holmes, dissenting.

Mr. Justice Brandeis and I are of opinion that this judgment should be reversed. The general principle of free speech, it seems to me, must be taken to be included in the Fourteenth Amendment, in view of the scope that has been given to the word 'liberty' as there used, although perhaps it may be accepted with a somewhat larger latitude of interpretation than is allowed to Congress by the sweeping language that governs or ought to govern the laws of the United States. If I am right, then I think that the criterion sanctioned by the full Court in *Schenck* v. *United States,* 249 U. S. 47, 52, applies. "The question in every case is whether the words used are used in such circumstances and are of such a nature as to create a clear and present danger that they will bring about the substantive evils that [the State] has a right to prevent." It is true that in my opinion this criterion was departed from in *Abrams* v. *United States,* 250 U. S. 616, but the convictions that I expressed in that case are too deep for it to be possible for me as yet to believe that it and *Schaefer* v. *United States,* 251 U. S. 466, have settled the law. If what I think the correct test is applied, it is manifest that there was no present danger of an attempt to overthrow the government by force on the part of the admittedly small minority who shared the defendant's views. It is said that this manifesto was more than a theory, that it was an incitement. Every idea is an incitement. It offers itself for belief and if believed it is acted on unless some other belief outweighs it or some failure of energy stifles the movement at its birth. The only difference between the expression of an opinion and an incitement in the narrower sense is the speaker's enthusiasm for the result. Eloquence may set fire to reason. But whatever may be thought of the redundant discourse before us it had no chance of starting a present conflagration. If in the long run the beliefs expressed in proletarian dictatorship are destined to be accepted by the dominant forces of the community, the only meaning of free speech is that they should be given their chance and have their way.

If the publication of this document had been laid as an attempt to induce an uprising against government at once and not at some indefinite time in the future it would have presented a different question. The object would have been one with which the law might deal, subject to the doubt whether there was any danger that the publication could produce any result, or in other words, whether it was not futile and too remote from possible consequences. But the indictment alleges the publication and nothing more.

11. NEAR v. MINNESOTA

1931

J. M. Near published a scandal sheet in Minneapolis that exuded hatred for Jews and contempt for law-enforcement officers. An extraordinary Minnesota law stopped him. It provided that the regular, ongoing publication of a "malicious, scandalous and defamatory" periodical was a public nuisance and could be stopped by the state and permanently suppressed. If the publisher, enjoined from further publication of similar material, disobeyed the injunction, his resumed efforts could be punished as contempt of court. All this was in addition to existing libel laws providing for punishment of the libeler or recovery of damages.

Near was enjoined, and arguing that the statute was a restraint on freedom of the press, he appealed to the United States Supreme Court. Chief Justice Charles Evans Hughes wrote the decision that declared the law unconstitutional. What the statute provided for, he said, was "of the essence of censorship"—restraint in advance of publication. Despite the long history of hostility to "prior restraint" in the Anglo-American experience, it was the first time that the Supreme Court had been faced with ruling on this method of control, and Hughes laid it down at length and in strong terms that such control almost always violates the First and Fourteenth Amendments. Public officers may find remedies for false defamation in libel actions, he ruled; even extravagant and reprehensible charges by "miscreant purveyors

---

From *Near* v. *Minnesota,* 283 United States Reports 697.

of scandal" do not warrant suppression and pre-publication restraint.

Mr. Chief Justice Hughes delivered the opinion of the court:

. . . If we cut through mere details of procedure, the operation and effect of the statute in substance is that public authorities may bring the owner or publisher of a newspaper or periodical before a judge upon a charge of conducting a business of publishing scandalous and defamatory matter—in particular that the matter consists of charges against public officers of official dereliction—and unless the owner or publisher is able and disposed to bring competent evidence to satisfy the judge that the charges are true and are published with good motives and for justifiable ends, his newspaper or periodical is suppressed and further publication is made punishable as a contempt. This is of the essence of censorship.

The question is whether a statute authorizing such proceedings in restraint of publication is consistent with the conception of the liberty of the press as historically conceived and guaranteed. In determining the extent of the constitutional protection, it has been generally, if not universally, considered that it is the chief purpose of the guaranty to prevent previous restraints upon publication. The struggle in England, directed against the legislative power of the licenser, resulted in renunciation of the censorship of the press. The liberty deemed to be established was thus described by Blackstone: "The liberty of the press is indeed essential to the nature of a free state; but this consists in laying no *previous* restraints upon publications, and not in freedom from censure for criminal matter when published. Every freeman has an undoubted right to lay what sentiments he pleases before the public; to forbid this, is to destroy the freedom of the press; but if he publishes what is improper, mischievous or illegal, he must take the consequence of his own temerity." 4 Bl. Com. 151, 152; see Story on the

Constitution, §§ 1884, 1889. The distinction was early pointed out between the extent of the freedom with respect to censorship under our constitutional system and that enjoyed in England. Here, as Madison said, "the great and essential rights of the people are secured against legislative as well as against executive ambition. They are secured, not by laws paramount to prerogative, but by constitutions paramount to laws. This security of the freedom of the press requires that it should be exempt not only from previous restraint by the Executive, as in Great Britain, but from legislative restraint also." Report on the Virginia Resolutions, Madison's Works, vol. IV, p. 543. This Court said, in *Patterson* v. *Colorado,* 205 U. S. 454, 462: "In the first place, the main purpose of such constitutional provisions is 'to prevent all such *previous restraints* upon publications as had been practiced by other governments,' and they do not prevent the subsequent punishment of such as may be deemed contrary to the public welfare. . . . The preliminary freedom extends as well to the false as to the true; the subsequent punishment may extend as well to the true as to the false. This was the law of criminal libel apart from statute in most cases, if not in all. . . ."

The criticism upon Blackstone's statement has not been because immunity from previous restraint upon publication has not been regarded as deserving of special emphasis, but chiefly because that immunity cannot be deemed to exhaust the conception of the liberty guaranteed by state and federal constitutions. The point of criticism has been "that the mere exemption from previous restraints cannot be all that is secured by the constitutional provisions"; and that "the liberty of the press might be rendered a mockery and a delusion, and the phrase itself a by-word, if, while every man was at liberty to publish what he pleased, the public authorities might nevertheless punish him for harmless publications." 2 Cooley, Const. Lim., 8th ed., p. 885. But it is recognized that punishment for the abuse of the liberty accorded to the press is essential to the protection of the public, and that the common law rules that subject the libeler to responsibility for the public offense, as well as for the private injury, are not abolished by the protection extended in our constitutions. . . . The law of criminal libel rests upon that secure foundation. There is also the conceded authority of courts to punish for contempt when publications directly tend to prevent the proper discharge of judicial functions. *Patterson* v. *Colorado, supra; Toledo Newspaper Co.* v. *United States,* 247 U. S. 402, 419. In the present case, we have no occasion to inquire as to the permissible scope of subsequent punishment. For whatever wrong the appellant has committed or may commit, by his publications, the State appropriately affords both public and private redress by its libel laws. As has been noted, the statute in question does not deal with punishments; it provides for no punishment, except in case of contempt for violation of the court's order, but for suppression and injunction, that is, for restraint upon publication.

The objection has also been made that the principle as to immunity from previous restraint is stated too broadly, if every such restraint is deemed to be prohibited. That is undoubtedly true; the protection even as to previous restraint is not absolutely unlimited. But the limitation has been recognized only in exceptional cases: "When a nation is at war many things that might be said in time of peace are such a hindrance to its effort that their utterance will not be endured so long as men fight and that no Court could regard them as protected by any constitutional right." *Schenck* v. *United States,* 249 U. S. 47, 52. No one would question but that a government might prevent actual obstruction to its recruiting service or the publication of the sailing dates of transports or the number and location of troops. On similar grounds, the primary requirements of decency may be enforced against obscene publications. The security of the community life may be protected against incitements to acts of violence and the overthrow by force of orderly government. The constitutional guaranty of free speech does not "protect a man from an injunction against uttering words that may have all the effect of force. *Gompers* v. *Buck Stove & Range Co.*, 221 U. S. 418, 439." *Schenck* v. *United States, supra.* These limitations are not applicable here. Nor are we now concerned with questions as to the extent of authority to prevent publications in order to protect private rights according to the principles governing the exercise of the jurisdiction of courts of equity.

The exceptional nature of its limitations places in a strong light the general conception that liberty of the press, historically considered and taken up by the Federal Constitution, has meant, principally although not exclusively, immunity from previous restraints or censorship. The conception of the liberty of the press in this country had broadened with the exigencies of the colonial period and with the efforts to secure freedom from oppressive administration. That liberty was especially cherished for the immunity it afforded from previous restraint of the publication of censure of public officers and charges of official misconduct. As was said by Chief Justice Parker, in *Commonwealth* v. *Blanding*, 3 Pick. 304, 313, with respect to the constitution of Massachusetts: "Besides, it is well understood, and received as a commentary on this provision for the liberty of the press, that it was intended to prevent all such *previous restraints* upon publications as had been practiced by other governments, and in early times here, to stifle the efforts of patriots towards enlightening their fellow subjects upon their rights and the duties of rulers. The liberty of the press was to be unrestrained, but he who used it was to be responsible in case of its abuse." In the letter sent by the Continental Congress (October 26, 1774) to the Inhabitants of Quebec, referring to the "five great rights" it was said: "The last right we shall mention, regards the freedom of the press. The importance of this consists, besides the advancement of truth, science, morality, and arts in general, in its diffusion of liberal sentiments on the administration of Government, its ready communication of thoughts between subjects, and its consequential promotion of union among them, whereby oppressive officers are shamed or intimidated, into more honourable and just modes of conducting affairs." Madison, who was the leading spirit in the preparation of the First Amendment of the Federal Constitution, thus described the practice and sentiment which led to the guaranties of liberty of the press in state constitutions:

"In every State, probably, in the Union, the press has exerted a freedom in canvassing the merits and measures of public men of every description which has not been confined to the strict limits of the common law. On this footing the freedom of the press has stood; on this footing it yet stands. . . . Some degree of abuse is inseparable from the proper use of everything, and in no instance is this more true than in that of the press. It has accordingly been decided by the practice of the States, that it is better to leave a few of its noxious branches to their luxuriant growth, than, by pruning them away, to injure the vigour of those yielding the proper fruits. And can the wisdom of this policy be doubted by any who reflect that to the press alone, chequered as it is with abuses, the world is indebted for all the triumphs which have been gained by reason and humanity over error and oppression; who reflect that to the same beneficent source the United States owe much of the lights which conducted them to the ranks of a free and independent nation, and which have improved their political system into a shape so auspicious to their happiness? Had 'Sedition Acts,' forbidding every publication that might bring the constituted agents into contempt or disrepute, or that might excite the hatred of the people against the authors of unjust or pernicious measures, been uniformly enforced against the press, might not the United States have been languishing at this day under the infirmities of a sickly Confederation? Might they not, possibly, be miserable colonies, groaning under a foreign yoke?"

The fact that for approximately one hundred and fifty years there has been almost an entire absence of attempts to impose previous restraints upon publications relating to the malfeasance of public officers is significant of the deep-seated conviction that such restraints would violate constitutional right. Public officers, whose character and conduct remain open to debate and free discussion in the press, find their remedies for false accusations in actions under libel laws providing for redress and punishment, and not in proceedings to restrain the publication of newspapers and periodicals. The general principle that the constitutional guaranty of the liberty of the press gives immunity from previous restraints has been approved in many decisions under the provisions of state constitutions.

The importance of this immunity has not lessened. While reckless assaults upon public men, and efforts to bring obloquy upon those who are endeavoring faithfully to discharge official duties, exert a baleful influence and deserve the severest condemnation in public opinion, it cannot be said that this abuse is greater, and it is believed to be less, than that which characterized the period in which our institutions took shape. Meanwhile, the administration of government has become more complex, the opportunities for malfeasance and corruption have multiplied, crime has grown to most serious proportions, and the danger of its protection by unfaithful officials and of the impairment of the fundamental security of life and property by criminal alliances and official neglect, emphasizes the primary need of a vigilant and courageous press, especially in great cities. The fact that the liberty of the press may be abused by miscreant purveyors of scandal does not make any the less necessary the immunity of the press from previous restraint in dealing with official misconduct. Subsequent punishment for such abuses as may exist is the appropriate remedy, consistent with constitutional privilege.

In attempted justification of the statute, it is said that it deals not with publication *per se*, but with the "business" of publishing defamation. If, however, the publisher has a constitutional right to publish, without previous restraint, an edition of his newspaper charging official derelictions, it cannot be denied that he may publish subsequent editions for the same purpose. He does not lose his right by exercising it. If his right exists, it may be exercised in publishing nine editions, as in this case, as well as in one edition. If previous restraint is permissible, it may be imposed at once; indeed, the wrong may be as serious in one publication as in several. Characterizing the publication as a business, and the business as a nuisance, does not permit an invasion of the constitutional immunity against restraint. Similarly, it does not matter that the newspaper or periodical is found to be "largely" or "chiefly" devoted to the publication of such derelictions. If the publisher has a right, without previous restraint, to publish them, his right cannot be deemed to be dependent upon his publishing something else, more or less, with the matter to which objection is made.

Nor can it be said that the constitutional freedom from previous restraint is lost because charges are made of derelictions which constitute crimes. With the multiplying provisions of penal codes, and of municipal charters and ordinances carrying penal sanctions, the conduct of public officers is very largely within the purview of criminal statutes. The freedom of the press from previous restraint has never been regarded as limited to such animadversions as lay outside the range of penal enactments. Historically, there is no such limitation; it is inconsistent with the reason which underlies the privilege, as the privilege so limited would be of slight value for the purposes for which it came to be established.

The statute in question cannot be justified by reason of the fact that the publisher is permitted to show, before injunction issues, that the matter published is true and is published with good motives and for justifiable ends. If such a statute, authorizing suppression and injunction on such a basis, is constitutionally valid, it would be equally permissible for the legislature to provide that at any time the publisher of any newspaper could be brought before a court, or even an administrative officer (as the constitutional protection may not be regarded as resting on mere procedural details) and required to produce proof of the truth of his publication, or of what he intended to publish, and of his motives, or stand enjoined. If this can be done, the legislature may provide machinery for determining in the complete exercise of its discretion what are justifiable ends and restrain publication accordingly. And it would be but a step to a complete system of censorship. The recognition of authority to impose previous restraint upon publication in order to protect the community against the circulation of charges of misconduct, and especially of official misconduct, necessarily would carry with it the admission of the authority of the censor against which the constitutional barrier was erected. The preliminary freedom, by virtue of the very reason for its existence, does not depend, as this Court has said, on proof of truth. *Patterson* v. *Colorado, supra.*

Equally unavailing is the insistence that the statute is designed to prevent the circulation of scandal which tends to disturb the public peace and to provoke assaults and the commission of crime. Charges of reprehensible conduct, and in particular of official malfeasance, unquestionably create a public scandal, but the theory of the constitutional guaranty is that even a more serious public evil would be caused by authority to prevent publication. "To prohibit the intent to excite those unfavorable sentiments against those who administer the Government, is equivalent to a prohibition of the actual excitement of them; and to prohibit the actual excitement of them is equivalent to a prohibition of discussions having that tendency and effect; which, again, is equivalent to a protection of those who administer the Government, if they should at any time deserve the contempt or hatred of the people, against being exposed to it by free animadversions on their characters and conduct." [James Madison's Works, IV, 549.] There is nothing new in the fact that charges of reprehensible conduct may create resentment and the disposition to resort to violent means of redress, but this well-understood tendency did not alter the determination to protect the press against censorship and restraint upon publication. As was said in *New Yorker Staats-Zeitung* v. *Nolan,* 89 N. J. Eq. 387, 388; 105 Alt. 72: "If the township may prevent the circulation of a newspaper for no reason other than that some of its inhabitants may violently disagree with it, and resent its circulation by resorting to physical violence, there is no limit to what may be prohibited." The danger of violent reactions becomes greater with effective organization of defiant groups resenting exposure, and if this consideration warranted legislative interference with the initial freedom of publication, the constitutional protection would be reduced to a mere form of words.

For these reasons we hold the statute, so far as it authorized the proceedings in this action under clause (b) of section one, to be an infringement of the liberty of the press guaranteed by the Fourteenth Amendment. We should add that this decision rests upon the operation and effect of the statute, without regard to the question of the truth of the charges contained in the particular periodical. The fact that the public officers named in this case, and those associated with the charges of official dereliction, may be deemed to be impeccable, cannot affect the conclusion that the statute imposes an unconstitutional restraint upon publication.

Judgment reversed.

12. NEW YORK TIMES COMPANY v. SULLIVAN

1964

In April 1964, the *New York Times* reported that at least seventeen civil libel actions brought by public officials of three southern states were pending against newspapers, magazines, and television. The incredible total in damages sought was $288 million, and although one suit in the name of 275 Mississippi highway patrolmen accounted for all but $12 million of the total, the remainder alone was indicative of a trend in the law of civil libel in the 1960's: huge damages were being sought and in some cases were awarded.

The *Times* itself was the target of two suits asking millions of dollars. One of them was brought by L. B. Sullivan, a Commissioner of the city of Montgomery, Alabama, asking $500,000 from the *Times* and four Negro clergymen. The offending words were in an advertisement in the *Times,* describing alleged police violence against demonstrators who opposed discrimination in Montgomery, and carrying the names—without their knowledge, they said—of the four clergymen. The trial jury awarded $500,000 and the Alabama Supreme Court upheld the judgment. The United States Supreme Court granted certiorari, and, in a decision that must be considered a landmark in freedom of expression in the United States, reversed the state courts.

Justice William J. Brennan wrote that the court considered the

---

From *New York Times Company* v. *Sullivan,* 376 U.S. Reports 254.

case "against a profound national commitment to the principle that debate on public issues should be uninhibited, robust, and wide-open. . . . " An official can recover damages, said Brennan, only if he can prove that actual malice attended the statement, and he defined actual malice not in terms of "intent to defame" or "ill-will," but with the relatively rigorous test of "knowledge that it [the statement] was false or with reckless disregard of whether it was false or not." In raising a barrier to the official's recovering for all except malice, and in defining that opaque and protean concept that had fouled the libel law for generations, the Supreme Court provided new protection for print and a measure of clarity and stability. It decreased the relevancy of and the need for reliance upon the confounding defense device called fair comment, and confirmed the insufficiency of the defense of truth. And the full implications of its decision rested in the future.

Mr. Justice Brennan delivered the opinion of the court:

Because of the importance of the constitutional issues involved, we granted the separate petitions for certiorari of the individual petitioners and of the Times. . . . We reverse the judgment. We hold that the rule of law applied by the Alabama courts is constitutionally deficient for failure to provide the safeguards for freedom of speech and of the press that are required by the First and Fourteenth Amendments in a libel action brought by a public official against critics of his official conduct. We further hold that under the proper safeguards the evidence presented in this case is constitutionally insufficient to support the judgment for respondent. . . .

Under Alabama law as applied in this case, a publication is "libelous per se" if the words "tend to injure a person * * * in his reputation" or to "bring [him] into public contempt"; the trial court stated that the standard was met if the words are such as to "injure him in his public office, or impute misconduct to him in his office, or want of official integrity, or want of fidelity to a public trust * * *." The jury must find that the words were published "of and concerning" the plaintiff, but where the plaintiff is a public official his place in the governmental hierarchy is sufficient evidence to support a finding that his reputation has been affected by statements that reflect upon the agency of which he is in charge. Once "libel per se" has been established, the defendant has no defense as to stated facts unless he can persuade the jury that they were true in all their particulars. . . . His privilege of "fair comment" for expressions of opinion depends on the truth of the facts upon which the comment is based. . . . Unless he can discharge the burden of proving truth, general damages are presumed, and may be awarded without proof of pecuniary injury. A showing of actual malice is apparently a prerequisite to recovery of punitive damages, and the defendant may in any event forestall these by a retraction meeting the statutory requirements. Good motives and belief in truth do not negate an inference of malice, but are relevant only in mitigation of punitive damages if the jury chooses to accord them weight. . . .

The question before us is whether this rule of liability, as applied to an action brought by a public official against critics of his official conduct, abridges the freedom of speech and of the press that is guaranteed by the First and Fourteenth Amendments. . . .

In the only previous case that did present the question of constitutional limitations upon the power to award damages for libel of a public official, the Court was equally divided and the question was not decided. Schenectady Union Pub. Co. v. Sweeney, 316 U.S. 642. . . . In deciding the question now, we are compelled by neither precedent nor policy to give any more weight to the epithet "libel" than we have to other "mere labels" of state law. . . . Like "insurrection," contempt, advocacy of unlawful acts, breach of the peace, obscenity, solicitation of legal business, and the various other formulae for the repression of expression that have been challenged in this Court, libel can claim no talismanic immunity from constitutional limitations. It must be measured by standards that satisfy the First Amendment.

The general proposition that freedom of expression upon public questions is secured by the First Amendment has long been settled by our decisions. The constitutional safeguard, we have said, "was fashioned to assure unfettered interchange of ideas for the bringing about of political and social changes desired by the people." Roth v. United States, 354 U.S. 476, 484. . . . "The maintenance of the opportunity for free political discussion to the end that government may be responsive to the will of the people and that changes may be obtained by lawful means, an opportunity essential to the security of the Republic, is a fundamental principle of our constitutional system." Stromberg v. California, 283 U.S. 359, 369. . . . "[I]t is a prized American privilege to speak one's mind, although not always with perfect good taste, on all public institutions," Bridges v. California, 314 U.S. 252, 270 . . . and this opportunity is to be afforded for "vigorous advocacy" no less than "abstract discussion." N. A. A. C. P. v. Button, 371 U.S. 415, 429. . . . The First Amendment, said Judge Learned Hand, "presupposes that right conclusions are more likely to be gathered out of a multitude of tongues, than through any kind of authoritative selection. To many this is, and always will be, folly; but we have staked upon it our all" United States v. Associated Press, 52 F.Supp. 362, 372 (D.C.S.D.N.Y.1943). Mr. Justice Brandeis, in his concurring opinion in Whitney v. California, 274 U.S. 357, 375–376 . . . gave the principle its classic formulation:

> Those who won our independence believed * * * that public discussion is a political duty; and that this should be a fundamental principle of the American government. They recognized the risks to which all human institutions are subject. But they knew that order cannot be secured merely through fear of punishment for its infraction; that it is hazardous to discourage thought, hope and imagina-

tion; that fear breeds repression; that repression breeds hate; that hate menaces stable government; that the path of safety lies in the opportunity to discuss freely supposed grievances and proposed remedies; and that the fitting remedy for evil counsels is good ones. Believing in the power of reason as applied through public discussion, they eschewed silence coerced by law—the argument of force in its worst form. Recognizing the occasional tyrannies of governing majorities, they amended the Constitution so that free speech and assembly should be guaranteed.

Thus we consider this case against the background of a profound national commitment to the principle that debate on public issues should be uninhibited, robust, and wide-open, and that it may well include vehement, caustic, and sometimes unpleasantly sharp attacks on government and public officials. . . . The present advertisement, as an expression of grievance and protest on one of the major public issues of our time, would seem clearly to qualify for the constitutional protection. The question is whether it forfeits that protection by the falsity of some of its factual statements and by its alleged defamation of respondent.

Authoritative interpretations of the First Amendment guarantees have consistently refused to recognize an exception for any test of truth, whether administered by judges, juries, or administrative officials—and especially not one that puts the burden of proving truth on the speaker. . . . The constitutional protection does not turn upon "the truth, popularity, or social utility of the ideas and beliefs which are offered." N. A. A. C. P. v. Button, 371 U.S. 415, 445. . . . As Madison said, "Some degree of abuse is inseparable from the proper use of every thing; and in no instance is this more true than in that of the press." 4 Elliot's Debates on the Federal Constitution (1876), p. 571. In Cantwell v. Connecticut, 310 U.S. 296, 310 . . . , the Court declared:

In the realm of religious faith, and in that of political belief, sharp differences arise. In both fields the tenets of one man may seem the rankest error to his neighbor. To persuade others to his own point of view, the pleader, as we know, at times, resorts to exaggeration, to vilification of men who have been, or are, prominent in church or state, and even to false statement. But the people of this nation have ordained in the light of history, that, in spite of the probability of excesses and abuses, these liberties are, in the long view, essential to enlightened opinion and right conduct on the part of the citizens of a democracy.

That erroneous statement is inevitable in free debate, and that it must be protected if the freedoms of expression are to have the "breathing space" that they "need * * * to survive," N. A. A. C. P. v. Button, 371 U.S. 415, 433, . . . was also recognized by the Court of Appeals for the District of Columbia Circuit in Sweeney v. Patterson, 128 F.2d 457, 458 (1942). Judge Edgerton spoke for a unanimous court which affirmed the dismissal of a Congressman's libel suit based upon a newspaper article charging him with anti-Semitism in opposing a judicial appointment. He said:

> Cases which impose liability for erroneous reports of the political conduct of officials reflect the obsolete doctrine that the governed must not criticize their governors. * * * The interest of the public here outweighs the interest of appellant or any other individual. The protection of the public requires not merely discussion, but information. Political conduct and views which some respectable people approve, and others condemn, are constantly imputed to Congressmen. Errors of fact, particularly in regard to a man's mental states and processes, are inevitable. * * * Whatever is added to the field of libel is taken from the field of free debate.

Just as factual error affords no warrant for repressing speech that would otherwise be free, the same is true of injury to official reputation. Where judicial officers are involved, this Court has held that concern for the dignity and reputation of the courts does not justify the punishment as criminal contempt of criticism of the judge or his decision. Bridges v. California, 314 U.S. 252. . . . This is true even though the utterance contains "half-truths" and "misinformation." Pennekamp v. Florida, 328 U.S. 331, 342, 343, n. 5, 345 . . . ; such repression can be justified, if at all, only by a clear and present danger of the obstruction of justice. . . . If judges are to be treated as "men of fortitude, able to thrive in a hardy climate," Craig v. Harney, supra, 331 U.S., at 376, . . . surely the same must be true of other government officials, such as elected city commissioners. Criticism of their official conduct does not lose its constitutional protection merely because it is effective criticism and hence diminishes their official reputations.

If neither factual error nor defamatory content suffices to remove the constitutional shield from criticism of official conduct, the combination of the two elements is no less inadequate. This is the lesson to be drawn from the great controversy over the Sedition Act of 1798, 1 Stat. 596, which first crystallized a national awareness of the central meaning of the First Amendment. See Levy, Legacy of Suppression (1960), at 258 et seq.; Smith, Freedom's Fetters (1956), at 426, 431 and *passim.* That statute made it a crime, punishable by a $5,000 fine and five years in prison, "if any person shall write, print, utter or publish * * * any false, scandalous and malicious writing or writings against the government of the United States, or either house of the Congress * * *, or the President * * *, with the intent to defame * * * or to bring them or either of them, into contempt or disrepute; or to excite against them, or either or any of them, the hatred of the good people of the United States." The Act allowed the defendant the defense of truth, and provided that the jury were to be judges both of the law and the facts. Despite these qualifications, the Act was vigorously condemned as unconstitutional in an attack joined in by Jefferson and Madison. In the famous Virginia Resolutions of 1798, the General Assembly of Virginia resolved that it

doth particularly protest against the palpable and alarming infractions of the Constitution, in the two late cases of the 'Alien and Sedition Acts,' passed at the last session of Congress * * *. Congress

[The Sedition Act] exercises * * * a power not delegated by the Constitution, but, on the contrary, expressly and positively forbidden by one of the amendments thereto—a power which, more than any other, ought to produce universal alarm, because it is levelled against the right of freely examining public characters and measures, and of free communication among the people thereon, which has ever been justly deemed the only effectual guardian of every other right. 4 Elliot's Debates, supra, pp. 553-554.

Madison prepared the Report in support of the protest. His premise was that the Constitution created a form of government under which "The people, not the government, possess the absolute sovereignty." The structure of the government dispersed power in reflection of the people's distrust of concentrated power, and of power itself at all levels. This form of government was "altogether different" from the British form, under which the Crown was sovereign and the people were subjects. "Is it not natural and necessary, under such different circumstances," he asked, "that a different degree of freedom in the use of the press should be contemplated?" Id., p. 569–570. Earlier, in a debate in the House of Representatives, Madison had said: "If we advert to the nature of Republican Government, we shall find that the censorial power is in the people over the Government, and not in the Government over the people." 4 Annals of Congress, p. 934 (1794). Of the exercise of that power by the press, his Report said: "In every state, probably, in the Union, the press has exerted a freedom of canvassing the merits and measures of public men, of every description, which has not been confined to the strict limits of the common law. On this footing the freedom of the press has stood; on this foundation it yet stands * * *." 4 Elliot's Debates, supra, p. 570. The right of free public discussion of the stewardship of public officials was thus, in Madison's view, a fundamental principle of the American form of government.

Although the Sedition Act was never tested in this Court, the attack upon its validity has carried the day in the court of history. . . .

What a State may not constitutionally bring about by means of a criminal statute is likewise beyond the reach of its civil law of libel. The fear of damage awards under a rule such as that invoked by the Alabama courts here may be markedly more inhibiting than the fear of prosecution under a criminal statute. . . . Alabama, for example, has a criminal libel law which subjects to prosecution "any person who speaks, writes, or prints of and concerning another any accusation falsely and maliciously importing the commission by such person of a felony, or any other indictable offense involving moral turpitude," and which allows as punishment upon conviction a fine not exceeding $500 and a prison sentence of six months. Alabama Code, Tit. 14, § 350. Presumably a person charged with violation of this statute enjoys ordinary criminal-law safeguards such as the requirements of an indictment and of proof beyond a reasonable doubt. These safeguards are not available to the defendant in a civil action. The judgment awarded in this case—without the need for any proof of actual pecuniary loss—was one thousand times greater than the maximum fine provided by the Alabama criminal statute, and one hundred times greater than that provided by the Sedition Act. And since there is no double-jeopardy limitation applicable to civil lawsuits, this is not the only judgment that may be awarded against petitioners for the same publication. Whether or not a newspaper can survive a succession of such judgments, the pall of fear and timidity imposed upon those who would give voice to public criticism is an atmosphere in which the First Amendment freedoms cannot survive. Plainly the Alabama law of civil libel is "a form of regulation that creates hazards to protected freedoms markedly greater than those that attend reliance upon the criminal law." Bantam Books, Inc. v. Sullivan, 372 U.S. 58, 70. . . .

The state rule of law is not saved by its allowance of the defense of truth. A defense for erroneous statements honestly made is no less essential here than was the requirement of proof of guilty knowledge which, in Smith v. California, 361 U.S. 147 . . . we held indispensable to a valid conviction of a bookseller for possessing obscene writings for sale. We said:

> For if the bookseller is criminally liable without knowledge of the contents, * * * he will tend to restrict the books he sells to those he has inspected; and thus the State will have imposed a restriction upon the distribution of constitutionally protected as well as obscene literature. * * * And the bookseller's burden would become the public's burden, for by restricting him the public's access to reading matter would be restricted. * * * [H]is timidity in the face of his absolute criminal liability, thus would tend to restrict the public's access to forms of the printed word which the State could not constitutionally suppress directly. The bookseller's self-censorship, compelled by the State, would be a censorship affecting the whole public, hardly less virulent for being privately administered. Through it, the distribution of all books, both obscene and not obscene, would be impeded. . . .

A rule compelling the critic of official conduct to guarantee the truth of all his factual assertions—and to do so on pain of libel judgments virtually unlimited in amount—leads to a comparable "self-censorship." Allowance of the defense of truth, with the burden of proving it on the defendant, does not mean that only false speech will be deterred. Even courts accepting this defense as an adequate safeguard have recognized the difficulties of adducing legal proofs that the alleged libel was true in all its factual particulars. . . . Under such a rule, would-be critics of official conduct may be deterred from voicing their criticism, even though it is believed to be true and even though it is in fact true, because of doubt whether it can be proved in court or fear of the expense of having to do so. They tend to make only statements which "steer far wider of the unlawful zone." . . . The rule thus dampens the vigor and limits the variety of public debate. It is inconsistent with the First and Fourteenth Amendments.

The constitutional guarantees require, we think, a federal

rule that prohibits a public official from recovering damages for a defamatory falsehood relating to his official conduct unless he proves that the statement was made with "actual malice"—that is, with knowledge that it was false or with reckless disregard of whether it was false or not. An oft-cited statement of a like rule, which has been adopted by a number of state courts, is found in the Kansas case of Coleman v. MacLennan, 78 Kan. 711. . . . The State Attorney General, a candidate for re-election and a member of the commission charged with the management and control of the state school fund, sued a newspaper publisher for alleged libel in an article purporting to state facts relating to his official conduct in connection with a school-fund transaction. The defendant pleaded privilege and the trial judge, over the plaintiff's objection, instructed the jury that

where an article is published and circulated among voters for the sole purpose of giving what the defendant believes to be truthful information concerning a candidate for public office and for the purpose of enabling such voters to cast their ballot more intelligently, and the whole thing is done in good faith and without malice, the article is privileged, although the principal matters contained in the article may be untrue in fact and derogatory to the character of the plaintiff; and in such a case the burden is on the plaintiff to show actual malice in the publication of the article.

In answer to a special question, the jury found that the plaintiff had not proved actual malice, and a general verdict was returned for the defendant. On appeal the Supreme Court of Kansas, in an opinion by Justice Burch, reasoned as follows (78 Kan., at 724 . . .):

[I]t is of the utmost consequence that the people should discuss the character and qualifications of candidates for their suffrages. The importance to the state and to society of such discussions is so vast, and the advantages derived are so great that they more than counter-balance the inconvenience of private persons whose conduct may be involved, and occasional injury to the reputations of individuals must yield to the public welfare, although at times such injury may be great. The public benefit from publicity is so great and the chance of injury to private character so small that such discussion must be privileged.

The court thus sustained the trial court's instruction as a correct statement of the law, saying:

In such a case the occasion gives rise to a privilege qualified to this extent. Any one claiming to be defamed by the communication must show actual malice, or go remediless. This privilege extends to a great variety of subjects and includes matters of public concern, public men, and candidates for office. 78 Kan., at 723. . . .

Such a privilege for criticism of official conduct is appropriately analogous to the protection accorded a public official when *he* is sued for libel by a private citizen. In Barr v. Matteo, 360 U.S. 564. . . . this Court held the utterance of a federal official to be absolutely privileged if made "within the outer perimeter" of his duties. The States accord the same immunity to statements of their highest officers, although some differentiate their lesser officials and qualify the privilege they enjoy. But all hold that all officials are protected unless actual malice can be proved. The reason for the official privilege is said to be that the threat of damage suits would otherwise "inhibit the fearless, vigorous, and effective administration of policies of government" and "dampen the ardor of all but the most resolute, or the most irresponsible, in the unflinching discharge of their duties." Barr v. Matteo, supra, 360 U.S., at 571. . . . Analogous considerations support the privilege for the citizen-critic of government. It is as much his duty to criticize as it is the official's duty to administer. See Whitney v. California, 274 U.S. 357, 375 . . . (concurring opinion of Mr. Justice Brandeis . . .). As Madison said . . . "the censorial power is in the people over the Government, and not in the Government over the people." It would give public servants an unjustified preference over the public they serve, if critics of official conduct did not have a fair equivalent of the immunity granted to the officials themselves.

We conclude that such a privilege is required by the First and Fourteenth Amendments.

We hold today that the Constitution delimits a State's power to award damages for libel in actions brought by public officials against critics of their official conduct. Since this is such an action, the rule requiring proof of actual malice is applicable. While Alabama law apparently requires proof of actual malice for an award of punitive damages, where general damages are concerned malice is "presumed." Such a presumption is inconsistent with the federal rule. "The power to create presumptions is not a means of escape from constitutional restrictions," Bailey v. Alabama, 219 U.S. 219. . . . Since the trial judge did not instruct the jury to differentiate between general and punitive damages, it may be that the verdict was wholly an award of one or the other. But it is impossible to know, in view of the general verdict returned. Because of this uncertainty, the judgment must be reversed and the case remanded. . . .

Since respondent may seek a new trial, we deem that considerations of effective judicial administration require us to review the evidence in the present record to determine whether it could constitutionally support a judgment for respondent. This Court's duty is not limited to the elaboration of constitutional principles; we must also in proper cases review the evidence to make certain that those principles have been constitutionally applied. This is such a case, particularly since the question is one of alleged trespass across "the line between speech unconditionally guaranteed and speech which may legitimately be regulated." Speiser v. Randall, 357 U.S. 513, 525. . . . In cases where that line must be drawn, the rule is that we "examine for ourselves the statements in issue and the circumstances under which they were made to see * * * whether they are of a character which the principles of the First Amendment, as adopted by the Due Process Clause of the

Fourteenth Amendment, protect." Pennekamp v. Florida, 328 U.S. 331, 335. . . .

Applying these standards, we consider that the proof presented to show actual malice lacks the convincing clarity which the constitutional standard demands, and hence that it would not constitutionally sustain the judgment for respondent under the proper rule of law. The case of the individual petitioners requires little discussion. Even assuming that they could constitutionally be found to have authorized the use of their names on the advertisement, there was no evidence whatever that they were aware of any erroneous statements or were in any way reckless in that regard. The judgment against them is thus without constitutional support.

As to the Times, we similarly conclude that the facts do not support a finding of actual malice. The statement by the Times' Secretary that . . . he thought the advertisement was "substantially correct," affords no constitutional warrant for the Alabama Supreme Court's conclusion that it was a "cavalier ignoring of the falsity of the advertisement [from which], the jury could not have but been impressed with the bad faith of The Times, and its maliciousness inferable therefrom." The statement does not indicate malice at the time of the publication; even if the advertisement was not "substantially correct"—although respondent's own proofs tend to show that it was—that opinion was at least a reasonable one, and there was no evidence to impeach the witness' good faith in holding it. The Times' failure to retract upon respondent's demand . . . is likewise not adequate evidence of malice for constitutional purposes. Whether or not a failure to retract may ever constitute such evidence, there are two reasons why it does not here. *First,* the letter written by the Times reflected a reasonable doubt on its part as to whether the advertisement could reasonably be taken to refer to respondent at all. *Second,* it was not a final refusal, since it asked for an explanation on this point—a request that respondent chose to ignore. . . .

Finally, there is evidence that the Times published the advertisement without checking its accuracy against the news stories in the Times' own files. The mere presence of the stories in the files does not, of course, establish that the Times "knew" the advertisement was false, since the state of mind required for actual malice would have to be brought home to the persons in the Times' organization having responsibility for the publication of the advertisement. With respect to the failure of those persons to make the check, the record shows that they relied upon their knowledge of the good reputation of many of those whose names were listed as sponsors of the advertisement, and upon the letter from A. Philip Randolph, known to them as a responsible individual, certifying that the use of the names was authorized. There was testimony that the persons handling the advertisement saw nothing in it that would render it unacceptable under the Times' policy of rejecting advertisements containing "attacks of a personal character"; their failure to reject it on this ground was not unreasonable. We think the evidence against the Times supports at most a finding of negligence in failing to discover the misstatements, and is constitutionally insufficient to show the recklessness that is required for a finding of actual malice. . . .

We also think the evidence was constitutionally defective in another respect: it was incapable of supporting the jury's finding that the allegedly libelous statements were made "of and concerning" respondent. Respondent relies on the words of the advertisement and the testimony of six witnesses to establish a connection between it and himself. Thus, in his brief to this Court, he states:

> The reference to respondent as police commissioner is clear from the ad. In addition, the jury heard the testimony of a newspaper editor * * *; a real estate and insurance man * * *; the sales manager of a men's clothing store * * *; a food equipment man * * *; a service station operator * * *; and the operator of a truck line for whom respondent had formerly worked * **. Each of these witnesses stated that he associated the statements with respondent * * *. (Citations to record omitted.)

There was no reference to respondent in the advertisement, either by name or official position. A number of the allegedly libelous statements—the charges that the dining hall was padlocked and that Dr. King's home was bombed, his person assaulted, and a perjury prosecution instituted against him—did not even concern the police; despite the ingenuity of the arguments which would attach this significance to the word "They," it is plain that these statements could not reasonably be read as accusing respondent of personal involvement in the acts in question. The statements upon which respondent principally relies as referring to him are the two allegations that did concern the police or police functions: that "truckloads of police * * * ringed the Alabama State College Campus" after the demonstration on the State Capitol steps, and that Dr. King had been "arrested * * * seven times." These statements were false only in that the police had been "deployed near" the campus but had not actually "ringed" it and had not gone there in connection with the State Capitol demonstration, and in that Dr. King had been arrested only four times. The ruling that these discrepancies between what was true and what was asserted were sufficient to injure respondent's reputation may itself raise constitutional problems, but we need not consider them here. Although the statements may be taken as referring to the police, they did not on their face make even an oblique reference to respondent as an individual. Support for the asserted reference must, therefore, be sought in the testimony of respondent's witnesses. But none of them suggested any basis for the belief that respondent himself was attacked in the advertisement beyond the bare fact that he was in overall charge of the Police Department and thus bore official responsibility for police conduct; to the extent that some of the witnesses thought respondent to have been charged with ordering or approving the conduct or otherwise being personally involved in it, they based this notion not on any statements in the advertisement, and not on any evidence that he had in fact been so involved, but solely on the unsupported assumption that, because of his official position, he must have been. This reliance on the bare fact of respondent's official position was made explicit by the Supreme Court of Alabama. That court, in holding that the trial court "did not err in overruling the demurrer [of the Times] in the aspect that the libelous matter was not of and concerning the plaintiffs," based its ruling on the proposition that:

> We think it common knowledge that the average person knows that municipal agents, such as police and firemen, and others, are under the control and direction of the city governing body, and more particularly under the direction and control of a single commissioner. In measuring the performance or deficiencies of such groups, praise or criticism is usually attached to the official in complete control of the body. 273 Ala., at 674-675. . . .

This proposition has disquieting implications for criticism of governmental conduct. For good reason, "no court of last resort in this country has ever held, or even suggested, that prosecutions for libel on government have any place in the American system of jurisprudence." City of Chicago v. Tribune Co., 307 Ill. 595, 601. . . . The present proposition would sidestep this obstacle by transmuting criticism of government, however impersonal it may seem on its face, into personal criticism, and hence potential libel, of the officials of whom the government is composed. There is no legal alchemy by which a State may thus create the cause of action that would otherwise be denied for a publication which, as respondent himself said of the advertisement, "reflects not only on me but on the other Commissioners and the community." Raising as it does the possibility that a good-faith critic of government will be penalized for his criticism, the proposition relied on by the Alabama courts strikes at the very center of the constitutionally protected area of free expression. We hold that such a proposition may not constitutionally be utilized to establish that an otherwise impersonal attack on governmental operations was a libel of an official responsible for those operations. Since it was relied on exclusively here, and there was no other evidence to connect the statements with respondent, the evidence was constitutionally insufficient to support a finding that the statements referred to respondent.

The judgment of the Supreme Court of Alabama is reversed and the case is remanded to that court for further proceedings not inconsistent with this opinion.

Reversed and remanded.

Part Two

CRIMINAL LIBEL

---

13. COMMONWEALTH v. CLAP

1808

Truth as a defense quickly worked its way into the criminal libel proceedings of various states in the early nineteenth century, especially in the terms of Alexander Hamilton's famous qualification: "truth, with good motives, for justifiable ends. . . ." Massachusetts courts, however, were among the reluctant ones, and Chief Justice Parsons would go only part of the distance in a case of 1808 when the defense urged the acceptance of Hamilton's formulation. Parsons was willing to accept truth as a defense where the words were spoken of a public, elective official; but in other cases the "breach-of-the-peace" reasoning held good for him. William Clap was guilty in publishing of auctioneer Caleb Howard that he was "a liar, a scoundrel, a cheat, and a swindler." Not until 1827 was Massachusetts to adopt a statute providing for truth as a defense in all libel actions.

From *Commonwealth* v. *Clap,* 4 Tyng 163 (Massachusetts).

The opinion of the court was afterwards delivered by Parsons, C. J.

The defendant has been convicted, by the verdict of a jury, of publishing a libel. On the trial, he moved to give in evidence, in his defence, that the contents of the publication were true. This evidence the judge rejected, and for that reason, the defendant moves for a new trial.

It is necessary to consider what publication is libellous, and the reason why a libellous publication is an offence against the commonwealth.

A libel is a malicious publication, expressed either in printing or writing, or by signs and pictures, tending either to blacken the memory of one dead, or the reputation of one who is alive, and expose him to public hatred, contempt, or ridicule.

The cause why libellous publications are offences against the state, is their direct tendency to a breach of the public peace, by provoking the parties injured, and their friends and families, to acts of revenge, which it would not be easy to restrain, were offences of this kind not severely punished. And every day's experience will justify the law in attributing to libels that tendency which renders the publication of them an offence against the state. The essence of the offence consists in the malice of the publication, or the intent to defame the reputation of another. In the definition of a libel, as an offence against law, it is not considered whether the publication be true or false; because a man may maliciously publish the truth against another, with the intent to defame his character, and if the publication be true, the tendency of it to inflame the passions, and to excite revenge, is not diminished, but may sometimes be strengthened.

The inference is, therefore, very clear, that the defendant cannot justify himself for publishing a libel, merely by proving the truth of the publication, and that the direction of the judge was right.

If the law admitted the truth of the words in this case to be a justification, the effect would be a greater injury to the party libelled. He is not a party to the prosecution, nor is he put on his defence; and the evidence at the trial might more cruelly defame his character than the original libel.

Although the truth of the words is no justification in a criminal prosecution for a libel, yet the defendant may repel the charge, by proving that the publication was for a justifiable purpose, and not malicious, nor with the intent to defame any man. And there may be cases, where the defendant, having proved the purpose justifiable, may give in evidence the truth of the words, when such evidence will tend to negative the malice and intent to defame.

Upon this principle, a man may apply by complaint to the legislature to remove an unworthy officer; and if the complaint be true, and made with the honest intention of giving useful information, and not maliciously, or with intent to defame, the complaint will not be a libel.

And when any man shall consent to be a candidate for a public office conferred by the election of the people, he must be considered as putting his character in issue, so far as it may respect his fitness and qualifications for the office. And publications of the truth on this subject, with the honest intention of informing the people, are not a libel. For it would be unreasonable to conclude that the publication of truths, which it is the interest of the people to know, should be an offence against their laws.

And every man holding a public elective office may be considered as within this principle; for as a reëlection is the only way his constituents can manifest their approbation of his conduct, it is to be presumed that he is consenting to a reëlection, if he does not disclaim it. For every good man would wish the approbation of his constituents for meritorious conduct.

For the same reason, the publication of falsehood and calumny against public officers, or candidates for public offices, is an offence most dangerous to the people, and deserves punishment, because the people may be deceived, and reject the best citizens, to their great injury, and it may be to the loss of their liberties.

But the publication of a libel maliciously and with intent to defame, whether it be true or not, is clearly an offence against law, on sound principles, which must be adhered to, so long as the restraint of all tendencies to the breach of the public peace, and to private animosity and revenge, is salutary to the commonwealth.

The defendant took nothing by his motion, and was afterwards sentenced to two months' imprisonment, with costs.

14. THEODORE ROOSEVELT'S PROSECUTION OF THE *NEW YORK WORLD* AND THE *INDIANAPOLIS NEWS*

1908

No other president of the United States has so publicly and vigorously sought criminal punishment of the press for criticism of government as Theodore Roosevelt did in the famous Panama Canal Case of 1908–1909. He was enraged by repeated charges in Joseph Pulitzer's *New York World* and by editorial comment in the *Indianapolis News* that deep corruption appeared to be involved in the purchase of the title to the Panama Canal from France. He directed Attorney General Charles J. Bonaparte to bring a libel charge against each, and while the actions were generally labeled with the legal rubric "criminal libel," their identity with *seditious* libel is plain: government and its officers had been scandalized, and the press was to pay.

Two separate legal attempts to punish the publishers were made. The first, to bring both to Washington, D. C., for trial there, failed so thoroughly before District Judge A. B. Anderson in Indianapolis, that Bonaparte dropped the case against Pulitzer. The second began in federal court in New York and was based on the fact that the *World* had circulated twenty-nine copies on the federal reservation at West Point. A motion to quash the indictment against the *World* was approved on grounds that the federal government did not have jurisdiction, and this motion was upheld by the Supreme Court of the United States. The decisions were widely hailed as victories for freedom of the press.

A. The Charges Are a Libel upon the United States Government

Theodore Roosevelt, 1908

President Roosevelt chose to open his case in a special message to Congress. The "string of infamous libels" not only defamed

---

From Special Message of the President of the United States to Congress, House Documents, 60th Congress, 2 Sess., #1213, Dec. 15, 1908, pp. 3–5.

the government, he declared, but also vilified the American people. The feelings that aroused him to the ill-advised prosecutions appear in the opening section of his message.

In view of the constant reiteration of the assertion that there was some corrupt action by or on behalf of the United States Government in connection with the acquisition of the title of the French Company to the Panama Canal, and of the repetition of the story that a syndicate of American citizens owned either one or both of the Panama companies, I deem it wise to submit to the Congress all the information I have on the subject. These stories were first brought to my attention as published in a paper in Indianapolis, called "The News," edited by Mr. Delavan Smith. The stories were scurrilous and libelous in character and false in every essential particular. Mr. Smith shelters himself behind the excuse that he merely accepted the statements which had appeared in a paper published in New York, "The World," owned by Mr. Joseph Pulitzer. It is idle to say that the known character of Mr. Pulitzer and his newspaper are such that the statements in that paper will be believed by nobody; unfortunately, thousands of persons are ill informed in this respect and believe the statements they see in print, even though they appear in a newspaper published by Mr. Pulitzer. A Member of the Congress has actually introduced a resolution in reference to these charges. I therefore lay all the facts before you.

The story repeated at various times by the World and by its followers in the newspaper press is substantially as follows: That there was corruption by or on behalf of the Government of the United States in the transaction by which the Panama Canal property was acquired from its French owners; that there were improper dealings of some kind between agents of the Government and outside persons, representing or acting for an American syndicate, who had gotten possession of the French Company; that among these persons, who it was alleged made "huge profits," were Mr. Charles P. Taft, a brother of Mr. William H. Taft, then candidate for the Presidency, and Mr. Douglas Robinson, my brother-in-law; that Mr. Cromwell, the counsel for the Panama Canal Company in the negotiations, was in some way implicated with the United States governmental authorities in these improper transactions; that the Government has concealed the true facts, and has destroyed, or procured or agreed to the destruction of, certain documents; that Mr. W. H. Taft was Secretary of War at the time that by an agreement between the United States Government and the beneficiaries of the deal all traces thereof were "wiped out" by transferring all the archives and "secrets" to the American Government, just before the holding of the convention last June at which Mr. Taft was nominated.

These statements sometimes appeared in the editorials, sometimes in the news columns, sometimes in the shape of contributions from individuals either unknown or known to be of bad character. They are false in every particular from beginning to end. The wickedness of the slanders is only surpassed by their fatuity. So utterly baseless are the stories that apparently they represent in part merely material collected for campaign purposes and in part stories originally concocted with a view of possible blackmail. The inventor of the story about Mr. Charles P. Taft, for instance, evidently supposed that at some period of the Panama purchase Mr. W. H. Taft was Secretary of War, whereas in reality Mr. W. H. Taft never became Secretary of War until long after the whole transaction in question had been closed. The inventor of the story about Mr. Douglas Robinson had not taken the trouble to find out the fact that Mr. Robinson had not had the slightest connection, directly or indirectly, of any kind or sort with any phase of the Panama transaction from beginning to end. The men who attacked Mr. Root in the matter had not taken the trouble to read the public documents which would have informed them that Mr. Root had nothing to do with the purchase, which was entirely arranged through the Department of Justice under the then Attorney-General, Mr. Knox.

Now, these stories as a matter of fact need no investigation whatever. No shadow of proof has been, or can be, produced in behalf of any of them. They consist simply of a string of infamous libels. In form, they are in part libels upon individuals, upon Mr. Taft and Mr. Robinson for instance. But they are in fact wholly, and in form partly, a libel upon the United States Government. I do not believe we should concern ourselves with the particular individuals who wrote the lying and libelous editorials, articles from correspondents, or articles in the news columns. The real offender is Mr. Joseph Pulitzer, editor and proprietor of the World. While the criminal offense of which Mr. Pulitzer has been guilty is in form a libel upon individuals, the great injury done is in blackening the good name of the American people. It should not be left to a private citizen to sue Mr. Pulitzer for libel. He should be prosecuted for libel by the governmental authorities. In point of encouragement of iniquity, in point of infamy, of wrongdoing, there is nothing to choose between a public servant who betrays his trust, a public servant who is guilty of blackmail, or theft, or financial dishonesty of any kind, and a man guilty as Mr. Joseph Pulitzer has been guilty in this instance. It is therefore a high national duty to bring to justice this vilifier of the American people, this man who wantonly and wickedly and without one shadow of justification seeks to blacken the character of reputable private citizens and to convict the Government of his own country in the eyes of the civilized world of wrongdoing of the basest and foulest kind, when he has not one shadow of justification of any sort or description for the charge he has made. The Attorney-General has under consideration the form in which the proceedings against Mr. Pulitzer shall be brought. . . .

B. If the History of Liberty Means Anything, This Proceeding Must Fail

Judge A. B. Anderson, 1909

Federal District Judge Anderson delivered his opinion orally. He had serious doubts, he said, that the *Indianapolis News* editorial was libelous. Further, Congress' investigation of the Panama Canal purchase left many legitimate doubts unclarified as to the propriety of the purchase of the Panama Canal rights, and it is a newspaper's duty to print the news. He decided the question, however, on Sixth Amendment grounds: Accused persons have a right to be tried in the state where the crime has been committed; any other disposition would be "a strange result of a revolution where one of the grievances complained of was the assertion of the right to send parties abroad for trial."

. . . I was very strongly impressed this morning with Mr. [defense attorney] Winter's argument on the proposition that these articles are not libelous. Up to that time it had not occurred to me that there was any question about their being libelous. But I am not so sure about it. I think, myself, that there is a good deal in the proposition that when articles charge people with swindling, or with thievery, and in the articles there is contained a statement of the facts upon which the charges are based, it does not necessarily follow that, because the words "thieving" and "swindling" are used, the articles are

---

From *United States* v. *Smith,* 173 Federal Reporter 227.

libelous per se. On two other questions that have been discussed I have more definite notions. I will take these up in their order, in the order in which they have been discussed and presented during this hearing.

In the first place, it is seriously contended, earnestly contended here, by the defendants' counsel, that these articles are conditionally privileged. When one undertakes to find a definition of privilege, or conditional privilege, it is very difficult to find one that is satisfactory. Under the head of "Malice," subhead "Privilege and Justification," American and English Encyclopædia of Law, I find this statement:

> The reconciliation of the two classes of cases mentioned above—those in which motive is material and those in which motive is not material—is to be sought in an extension of the concept of privilege, as understood in the law of libel, or in a coherent application of the idea of justification or excuse. The conception of privilege in the law of defamation is that an individual may with immunity commit an act which is a legal wrong, and, but for his privilege, would afford a good cause of action against him; all that is required, in order to raise the privilege and entitle him to protection, being that he shall act honestly in the discharge of some duty which the law recognizes, and shall not be prompted by a desire to injure the person who is affected by his act.

Let us go back a little. I have had occasion to say before that a newspaper has a certain duty to perform. It was well stated by a former President of the United States that it is the duty of a newspaper to print the news and tell the truth about it. It is the duty of a public newspaper, such as is owned and conducted by these defendants, to tell the people, its subscribers, its readers, the facts it may find out about public questions, or matters of public interest; and it is its duty and its right to draw inferences from the facts known—draw them for the people. I might just digress long enough to suggest that it is not everybody that can draw an inference.

Here was a great public question. There are many very peculiar circumstances about the history of this Panama Canal, or Panama Canal business. I do not wish to be understood as reflecting upon anybody, in office or out, in connection with that matter, except such persons as I may name in that way. The circumstances surrounding the revolution in Panama were unusual and peculiar. The people were interested in the construction of a canal. It was a matter of great public concern. It was much discussed. A large portion of the people favored the Nicaragua route. Another portion of those who were interested in it, officially or personally, preferred the Panama route. A committee was appointed to investigate the relative merits of the two routes. They investigated, and reported in favor of the Nicaragua route. Shortly afterwards—I do not now recall just how soon afterward—they changed to the Panama route. Up to the time of that change, as I gathered from the evidence, the lowest sum that had been suggested, at which the property of the Panama Canal Company could be procured, was something over $100,000,000. Then rather suddenly it became known that it could be procured for $40,000,000. There were a number of people who thought there was something not just exactly right about that transaction. And I will say for myself that I have a curiosity to know what the real truth was. Thereupon a committee of the United States Senate was appointed to investigate these matters—about the only way the matter could be investigated. The committee met. As stated in those articles, the man who knew all about it—I think that is the proper way to speak of Mr. Cromwell, who knew all about it—was called before the committee. Mr. Cromwell, upon certain questions being put to him, more or less pertinent, stood upon his privilege as an attorney and refused to answer. That was the state of the case, as shown by the evidence, when we adjourned last June.

At this session certain parts of the record showing the proceedings before the Senate Committee have been introduced by the government, and the impression made upon my mind from such parts as the government has seen fit to introduce is not more favorable to Mr. Cromwell's position than it was upon the former hearing. So far as the record has been read—and that is all the part that I have any acquaintance with—Mr. Cromwell stood upon his privilege whenever questions were asked, the answers to which would or might reflect upon him and his associates. But whenever a question was asked which gave him an opportunity to say something in their behalf, he ostentatiously thanked the examiner for the question and proceeded to answer. To my mind that gave just ground for suspicion. I am suspicious about it now. Subsequently, upon further examination in this matter, I suppose knowing that he would be examined about certain transactions in connection with it, he took the pains to get the privilege released by his then client; and the reasons given for varying his conduct in that instance from his conduct in the former instance, were about as unsubstantial as the reasons given upon the first instance for not answering then. So we have this situation: Here was a matter of great public interest, public concern. I was interested in it. You were interested in it. We were all interested in it. Here was a newspaper printing the news, or trying to. Here was this matter up for discussion, and I cannot say now—I am not willing to say—that the inferences are too strongly drawn. I am not approving of the inferences. I am simply saying that I am not able to say that they were too strongly drawn. Now, if that is the situation—and, as I understand the facts, that is the way it stands—the question is: Did these defendants, under the circumstances, act honestly in the discharge of this duty of which I have spoken, and which the law recognizes? Or were they prompted by a desire to injure the persons who were affected by their acts? If it were necessary to decide this case upon the question of privilege, the lack of malice, I would hesitate quite a while before I would conclude that it was my duty to send these people to Washington for trial.

But that is not all. This indictment charges these defendants with the commission of a crime in the District of Columbia.

The sixth amendment to the Constitution of the United States provides:

> In all criminal prosecutions the accused shall enjoy the right to a speedy and public trial by an impartial jury of the state or district wherein the crime shall have been committed, which district shall have been previously ascertained by law.

I will state what I find the evidence to be, and if I am mistaken about it in any way I will be glad to be corrected, because upon that I shall proceed to a conclusion. The Indianapolis News is owned, the evidence shows, by these defendants, is printed and published by them in the city of Indianapolis, in the state of Indiana, and at the time covered by this indictment it had a daily circulation of about 90,000 copies. All but about 2,000 of these copies were circulated and distributed in the state of Indiana. Some 400 or 500 were distributed in one or two adjoining states, and to the District of Columbia there were sent by mail, daily, about 50 copies, to subscribers and persons who ordered them sent there. The defendants have no agent, or bureau, or office, and maintain no agency, bureau, or office, in the city of Washington, or the District of Columbia, for the circulation of papers within that District. I think that is what the evidence in this case shows as to the way in which these papers are published and circulated. It is perfectly manifest that so far as this case is concerned the publication and the circulation of these papers anywhere except in the District of Columbia may be disregarded for the moment. So the question is: Do the defendants, when they print and publish 50 copies in the city of Indianapolis and deposit them in the United States post office in this building, to be transmitted by mail to 50 subscribers in Washington—do they publish those 50 papers in Washington? If they do, that court has jurisdiction of the offense. I will not go so far as to say that it has jurisdiction of the defendants. But, if they do not, then that court has neither jurisdiction of the offense nor of the defendants. . . .

. . . These defendants, as shown by the evidence, have not committed an act, a part of the doing of which was here and part of it in Washington. It is not that kind of a case. A United States statute, I might stop to say, which would make a case triable in a district different from the district where the act was committed, would be unconstitutional. Their acts are not shown by the evidence to have been acts part of which were committed in this district and part of them in Washington. It is not that kind of a case. Nor are they charged with doing an act here, the effect of which results in Washington. It is not that kind of a case. Everything that the evidence shows that the defendants did, they did in the district of Indiana, in the city of Indianapolis, in the county of Marion. I am not saying that if these defendants had an agent in Washington, to whom they sent for circulation copies of this paper, they might not be amenable to prosecution in Washington, if they could be arrested in Washington. We must distinguish that sort of a case from this.

It seems to me that I am compelled to take one of two views upon this question, and there is no middle ground between them. I cannot compromise it. When a newspaper owner or proprietor does what the evidence in this case shows these defendants did—composed, printed, and deposited in the mails for circulation these papers containing, for the purpose of this statement, libelous articles—either they are guilty here, and in every county and district and jurisdiction into which those papers go, or they are only guilty here. When these defendants put newspapers containing the alleged libelous articles into the post office here in Indianapolis, which went through the mails throughout the country, to various states, counties, and districts of the United States, either they committed a separate crime every time one of those papers went into another county, another state, or another district, or there was but one crime, and that crime was committed here.

In the case put during the argument, where a paper is deposited here in Indianapolis and circulates throughout the 92 counties of Indiana, when I asked counsel for the government whether it would be an offense in each county, he thought it would. And in the absence of the Indiana statute cited by the government's counsel, according to their theory, it would be. Then the question is: Suppose there was a conviction, say in Posey county; would that be a bar to a prosecution in Marion county? Counsel for the government think it would. I do not think it would, at all. Let us see if it would. The theory is that it becomes a crime in each jurisdiction where it is circulated. If so, it must be a separate crime. If there is something in the circulation of it in the other county, or district, or jurisdiction, which makes it a crime there, it must be a separate crime. There is no escape from that. If it is a separate crime, a conviction or acquittal of it, of course, could not be pleaded in bar of a prosecution for another crime. I think that, as between these two views, the view that the offense, if any, was committed here is the more reasonable one, and the correct one. I am not saying, now, that there may not be circumstances where the publisher of a newspaper circulated throughout the country might be guilty of and prosecuted for more than one offense. I am speaking of the facts as shown by the evidence here—where people print a newspaper here, and deposit it in the post office here, for circulation throughout other states, territories, counties, and districts, there is one publication, and that is here. If that is true, then there was no publication, under the evidence, in Washington.

The discussion as to the hardship of taking a man away from his home to a distant place, to be tried, and the discussion pro and con as to the desirability of the District of Columbia and the city of Washington as a place for trial, was interesting. But those considerations, as suggested in one of the decisions of the Supreme Court, are not controlling, and I am not compelled to resort to anything of that kind to satisfy myself about what ought to be done here. To my mind that man has read the history of our institutions to little purpose who does not look with grave apprehension upon the possibility of the success of a proceeding such as this. If the history of liberty means anything, if constitutional guaranties are worth anything, this proceeding must fail.

If the prosecuting officers have the authority to select the tribunal, if there be more than one tribunal to select from, if the government has that power, and can drag citizens from distant states to the capital of the nation, there to be tried, then, as Judge Cooley says, this is a strange result of a revolution where one of the grievances complained of was the assertion of the right to send parties abroad for trial.

The defendants will be discharged.

15. BEAUHARNAIS v. ILLINOIS

1952

While "words that tend to breach the peace" has long since been eliminated from most state statutory definitions of criminal libel, one rare variant of the crime does call these words criminal. This is the offense of "group libel" under which the old assumption that libel is committed only against individuals breaks down. A very few cases had held by mid-twentieth century that groups could be libeled, although strong protests rose from students of free expression. The latter saw, for example, real danger that not only racial and religious groups but also economic, political,

---

From *Beauharnais* v. *Illinois,* 343 United States Reports 250.

occupational, and social groups might be placed beyond the pale of legitimate verbal assessment.

But in 1952 the United States Supreme Court upheld Illinois' statute punishing, among other things, public distribution of printed materials that portrayed depravity or lack of virtue in a class of citizens of any race, color, creed, or religion, if the materials exposed the citizens to contempt or obloquy or produced breach of the peace or riots. The case arose after Beauharnais directed the distribution in Chicago of literature that petitioned authorities to halt the "encroachment, harrasment, and invasion of white people . . . by the Negro." It denounced the "rapes, robberies, knives, guns, and marijuana of the Negro."

Justice Felix Frankfurter's opinion displays his familiar position on the side of judicial restraint and respect for the legislative will. His opinion accepted the statute as a "libel" law although it did not use the word, discounted the likelihood that prohibiting libel of a religious or racial group is only a step from prohibiting libel of a political party, and upheld Beauharnais' conviction.

Illinois itself was to have second thoughts: In 1961 its legislature repealed the statute under which Beauharnais was convicted and did not replace it.

Mr. Justice Frankfurter delivered the opinion of the Court:

. . . The Illinois Supreme Court tells us that § 224a [the statute in question] "is a form of criminal libel law." . . . The defendant, the trial court and the Supreme Court consistently treated it as such. The defendant offered evidence tending to prove the truth of parts of the utterance, and the courts below considered and disposed of this offer in terms of ordinary criminal libel precedents. Section 224a does not deal with the defense of truth, but by the Illinois Constitution, Art. II, § 4, "in all trials for libel, both civil and criminal, the truth, when published with good motives and justifiable ends, shall be a sufficient defense." See also Ill. Rev. Stat., 1949, c. 38, § 404.

Similarly, the action of the trial court in deciding as a matter of law the libelous character of the utterance, leaving to the jury only the question of publication, follows the settled rule in prosecutions for libel in Illinois and other States. Moreover, the Supreme Court's characterization of the words prohibited by the statute as those "liable to cause violence and disorder" paraphrases the traditional justification for punishing libels criminally, namely their "tendency to cause breach of the peace."

Libel of an individual was a common-law crime, and thus criminal in the colonies. Indeed, at common law, truth or good motives was no defense. In the first decades after the adoption of the Constitution, this was changed by judicial decision, statute or constitution in most States, but nowhere was there any suggestion that the crime of libel be abolished. Today, every American jurisdiction—the forty-eight States, the District of Columbia, Alaska, Hawaii and Puerto Rico—punish libels directed at individuals. "There are certain well-defined and narrowly limited classes of speech, the prevention and punishment of which have never been thought to raise any Constitutional problem. These include the lewd and obscene, the profane, the libelous, and the insulting or 'fighting' words—those which by their very utterance inflict injury or tend to incite an immediate breach of the peace. It has been well observed that such utterances are no essential part of any exposition of ideas, and are of such slight social value as a step to truth that any benefit that may be derived from them is clearly outweighed by the social interest in order and morality. 'Resort to epithets or personal abuse is not in any proper sense communication of information or opinion safeguarded by the Constitution, and its punishment as a criminal act would raise no question under that instrument.' *Cantwell* v. *Connecticut*, 310 U.S. 296, 309–310." . . . No one will gainsay that it is libelous falsely to charge another with being a rapist, robber, carrier of knives and guns, and user of marijuana. The precise question before us, then, is whether the protection of "liberty" in the Due Process Clause of the Fourteenth Amendment prevents a State from punishing such libels—as criminal libel has been defined, limited and constitutionally recognized time out of mind—directed at designated collectivities and flagrantly disseminated. There is even authority, however dubious, that such utterances were also crimes at common law. It is certainly clear that some American jurisdictions have sanctioned their punishment under ordinary criminal libel statutes. We cannot say, however, that the question is concluded by history and practice. But if an utterance directed at an individual may be the object of criminal sanctions, we cannot deny to a State power to punish the same utterance directed at a defined group, unless we can say that this is a wilful and purposeless restriction unrelated to the peace and well-being of the State.

Illinois did not have to look beyond her own borders or await the tragic experience of the last three decades to conclude that wilful purveyors of falsehood concerning racial and religious groups promote strife and tend powerfully to obstruct the manifold adjustments required for free, ordered life in a metropolitan, polyglot community. From the murder of the abolitionist Lovejoy in 1837 to the Cicero riots of 1951, Illinois has been the scene of exacerbated tension between races, often flaring into violence and destruction. . . .

In the face of this history and its frequent obligato of extreme racial and religious propaganda, we would deny experience to say that the Illinois legislature was without reason in seeking ways to curb false or malicious defamation of racial and religious groups, made in public places and by means calculated to have a powerful emotional impact on those to whom it was presented. "There are limits to the exercise of these liberties [of speech and of the press]. The danger in these times from the coercive activities of those who in the delusion of racial or religious conceit would incite violence and breaches of the peace in order to deprive others of their equal right to the exercise of their liberties, is emphasized by events familiar to all. These and other transgressions of those limits the States appropriately may punish." This was the conclusion, again of a unanimous Court, in 1940. *Cantwell* v. *Connecticut, supra,* at 310.

It may be argued, and weightily, that this legislation will not help matters; that tension and on occasion violence between racial and religious groups must be traced to causes more deeply embedded in our society than the rantings of modern Know-Nothings. Only those lacking responsible humility will have a confident solution for problems as intractable as the frictions attributable to differences of race, color or religion. This being so, it would be out of bounds for the judiciary to deny the legislature a choice of policy, provided it is not unrelated to the problem and not forbidden by some explicit limitation on the State's power. That the legislative remedy might not in practice mitigate the evil, or might itself raise new problems, would only manifest once more the paradox of reform. It is the price to be paid for the trial-and-error inherent in legislative efforts to deal with obstinate social issues. . . .

We are warned that the choice open to the Illinois legislature here may be abused, that the law may be discriminatorily enforced; prohibiting libel of a creed or of a racial group, we are told, is but a step from prohibiting libel of a political party. Every power may be abused, but the possibility of abuse is a poor reason for denying Illinois the power to adopt measures against criminal libels sanctioned by centuries of Anglo-American law. "While this Court sits" it retains and exercises authority to nullify action which encroaches on freedom of utterance under the guise of punishing libel. Of course discussion cannot be denied and the right, as well as the duty, of criticism must not be stifled. . . .

Libelous utterances not being within the area of constitutionally protected speech, it is unnecessary, either for us or for the State courts, to consider the issues behind the phrase "clear and present danger." Certainly no one would contend that obscene speech, for example, may be punished only upon a showing of such circumstances. Libel, as we have seen, is in the same class.

We find no warrant in the Constitution for denying to Illinois the power to pass the law here under attack. But it bears repeating—although it should not—that our finding that the law is not constitutionally objectionable carries no implication of approval of the wisdom of the legislation or of its efficacy. These questions may raise doubts in our minds as well as in others. It is not for us, however, to make the legislative judgment. We are not at liberty to erect those doubts into fundamental law.

Affirmed.

Part Three

CONTEMPT OF COURT

16. AN ACT DECLARATORY OF THE LAW CONCERNING CONTEMPTS OF COURT

1831

Federal Judge James H. Peck of Missouri in 1826 handed down a decision that jeopardized the shaky claims of speculators to lands once part of Spain's Upper Louisiana. Attorney Luke Lawless, deeply interested in the legitimacy of many claims, wrote a newspaper article on "some of the principal errors" of Peck's decision. The judge cited Lawless for contempt of court, found him guilty, and suspended him from practice for eighteen months. Lawless asked Congress to impeach Peck, and after more than four years his dogged effort succeeded when the House of Rep-

---

4 *U. S. Statutes* 487.

resentatives voted to present articles of impeachment to the Senate.

Through interminable speeches by the five managers of the impeachment, who were led in exhaustiveness of argument and prolixity by Representative James Buchanan of Pennsylvania, the Senate of 1830–1831 heard the case out. Every phase of the subject was canvassed, and the heart of the matter was whether courts could punish only for contempts committed in the presence of the judge and immediately disruptive of proceedings, or as Peck did, for "constructive contempts" outside the courtroom as well. The similarities of the latter to punishment for seditious libel were striking.

The Senate exonerated Peck, but it was at one with the House in wanting no more convictions for constructive contempt. Scarcely a month after the trial Congress passed the statute below, limiting punishment to disturbances that palpably disrupt the administration of justice.

Be it enacted by the Senate and House of Representatives of the United States of America, in Congress assembled, That the power of the several courts of the United States to issue attachments and inflict summary punishments for contempts of court, shall not be construed to extend to any cases except the misbehaviour of any person or persons in the presence of the said courts, or so near thereto as to obstruct the administration of justice, the misbehaviour of any of the officers of the said courts in their official transactions, and the disobedience or resistance by any officer of the said courts, party, juror, witness, or any other person or persons, to any lawful writ, process, order, rule, decree, or command of the said courts.

SEC. 2. *And be it further enacted,* That if any person or persons shall, corruptly, or by threats or force, endeavour to influence, intimidate, or impede any juror, witness, or officer, in any court of the United States, in the discharge of his duty, or shall, corruptly, or by threats or force, obstruct, or impede, or endeavour to obstruct or impede, the due administration of justice therein, every person or persons, so offending, shall be liable to prosecution therefor, by indictment, and shall, on conviction thereof, be punished, by fine not exceeding five hundred dollars, or by imprisonment, not exceeding three months, or both, according to the nature and aggravation of the offence.

Approved, March 2, 1831.

17. STATE OF ARKANSAS v. MORRILL

1855

The spirit of the federal contempt statute of 1831 held good in most of the handful of state cases that arose before the Civil War. But in 1855 the Supreme Court of Arkansas delivered a decision that was to be seized on by the courts in state after state as precedent for nullifying statutes limiting courts' powers in the face of criticism.

Morrill had published an article in the Des Arc *Citizen* questioning the Supreme Court's decision in setting bail for an alleged murderer. The court thought Morrill was suggesting it had been bribed and cited him for contempt. In a long decision, Chief Justice Elbert H. English developed the thesis that courts' "immemorial powers" to try for contempts—including criticism far removed from the courtroom—could be checked only by *constitutional* provision; that statutes such as Arkansas', passed by a co-ordinate branch of government, had no authority over the "inherent powers" of courts—powers springing into existence

From *State of Arkansas* v. *Morrill*, 16 Arkansas Reports 384.

upon creation of the courts. He relied heavily on the English common law and authorities; extolled the liberty of the press and condemned its "licentiousness"; and distinguished the federal contempt statute's force from that of the Arkansas statute. Courts around the nation took note: The Arkansas court had successfully denied the legislature's power to curb it in shielding its own good name.

The statute, on the subject of contempts, declares that "Every court of record shall have power to punish, as for criminal contempt, persons guilty of the following acts, and no others:

First. Disorderly, contemptuous, or insolent behavior, committed during its sitting, in its immediate view and presence, and directly tending to interrupt its proceedings, or to impair the respect due to its authority. *Second.* Any breach of the peace, noise or disturbance, directly tending to interrupt its proceedings. *Third.* Willful disobedience of any process or order lawfully issued, or made by it. *Fourth.* Resistance willfully offered, by any person, to the lawful order or process of the court. *Fifth.* The contumacious and unlawful refusal of any person to be sworn as a witness, and when so sworn, the like refusal to answer any legal and proper interrogatory." *Digest, chap.* 36, *sec.* 1, approved February 28th, 1838.

It is conceded that the act charged against the defendant in this case, is not embraced within either clause of this statute.

It was argued by the counsel for the defendant, that the court must look to the statute for its power to punish contempts, and not to any supposed inherent power of its own, springing from its constitutional organization. That it is controlled by the statute, and cannot go beyond its provisions. In other words, that the will of a co-ordinate department of the government is to be the measure of its power, in the matter of contempts, and not the organic law, which carves out the landmarks of the essential powers to be exercised by each of the several departments of the government.

In response to this position, we say, in the language of Mr. Justice Scott, in *Neil v. The State,* 9 *Ark.* 263, that: "The right to punish for contempts, in a summary manner, has been long admitted as *inherent in all courts of justice,* and in legislative assemblies, founded upon great principles, which are coeval, and must be co-existent with the administration of justice in every country, the power of self-protection. And it is only where this right has been claimed to a greater extent than this, and the foundation sought to be laid for extensive classes of contempts not legitimately and necessarily sustained by these great principles, that it has been contested. It is a branch of the common law, brought from the mother country and *sanctioned by our constitution.* The discretion involved in the power is necessarily, in a great measure, arbitrary and undefinable, and yet, the experience of ages has demonstrated that it is compatible with civil liberty, and auxiliary to the purest ends of justice, and to the proper exercise of the legislative functions, especially when these functions are exerted by a legislative assembly." . . .

Without resorting to the English authorities, where one of the counsel for the defendant supposes a rigorous doctrine prevails on the subject of the power of the courts to [punish] for contempts, in consequence of the fiction that the majesty of the king is deemed to be present in all the courts, in the persons of the judges, it might be shown, were it supposed to admit of serious question on the part of even the learned counsel for the defense themselves, that every enlightened jurist in the United States, who has treated of the subject, has held that the power to punish for contempts, is inherent in courts of justice, springing into existence upon their creation, as a necessary incident to the exercise of the powers conferred upon them.

Had the Legislature never passed the act above quoted, or any act at all on the subject, could it be doubted that this court would possess the constitutional power to preserve order and decorum, enforce obedience to its process, and maintain respect for its judgments, orders and decrees, and as a necessary consequence, punish for contempts against its authority and dignity, without which it could never accomplish the useful purposes for which it was established by the framers of the constitution? . . .

As far as the act in question goes, in sanctioning the power of the courts to punish, as contempts, the "*acts*" therein enumerated, it is merely declaratory of what the law was before its passage. The *prohibitory* feature of the act can be regarded as nothing more than the expression of a judicial opinion of the Legislature, that the courts may exercise and enforce all their constitutional powers, and answer all the useful purposes of their creation, without the necessity of punishing as a contempt any matter not enumerated in the act. As such, it is entitled to great respect, but to say that it is absolutely binding upon the courts, would be to concede that the courts have no constitutional and inherent power to punish any class of contempts, but that the whole subject is under the control of the legislative department; because, if the General Assembly may deprive the courts of power to punish one class of contempts, it may go the whole length, and divest them of power to punish any contempt. . . .

It was further submitted by the counsel for the defense, that the publication of a libel upon the official action of a court, being an out-door affair, was not, by the common law, the subject of contempt, and if it were, it was only so where the publication was made in reference to a cause pending in court; and that inasmuch as the publication in question was made after the case of *Ellis* had been determined by the court; and was, therefore, not *pending*, it does not fall within the definition of common law contempts.

In Neil v. The State, the common law doctrine of contempts was thoroughly examined and discussed by the court, and the rule thus stated as the result: "By the common law, a court may punish for contemptuous conduct toward the tribunal, its process, the presiding judge, or for indignities to the judge while engaged in the performance of judicial duties in vacation, *or for insults offered him in consequence of judicial acts:* but indignities offered to the person of the judge in vacation, when not engaged in judicial business, *and without reference to his official conduct,* are not punishable as contempts."

In the course of the opinion, Mr. Justice Scott said: "It is of no importance whether the contumely be used in open court, at the moment when the occasion occurs, or the moment afterwards, when the sheriff has proclaimed the adjournment. The only real question in either case, is *whether it is the official conduct for which the judge is challenged and insulted.*"

Mr. Blackstone (*Book* 4, *p.* 284), says: "The contempts that are thus punished, are either *direct,* which openly insult or resist the powers of the courts, or the persons of the judges who preside there; or else *consequential,* which (without such gross insolence, or direct opposition) plainly tend to create an universal disregard of their authority."

And then after enumerating the classes of contempts punishable by the courts of England (some of which would not be punished here in consequence of the modifications of the common law, produced by our constitution, and the character of our institutions as above indicated), he remarks further:

"Some of these contempts may arise in the face of the court, as by rude and contemptuous behavior; by obstinacy, perverseness, or prevarication; by breach of the peace; or any wilful disturbance whatever: others, in the absence of the party, as by disobeying or treating with disrespect the king's writ, or the rules or process of the court; by perverting such writ or process to the purposes of private malice, extortion, or injustice; by speaking *or writing contemptuously of the court or judges, acting in their judicial capacity;* by printing false accounts (or even true ones, without proper permission) of causes then depending in judgment; and by anything, in short, *that demonstrates a gross want of that regard and respect, which when once courts of justice are deprived of, their authority* (so necessary for the good order of the kingdom) is entirely lost among the people." . . .

In 1765, a motion was made in the King's Bench, for an attachment against Mr. Almon, for a contempt in publishing a libel upon the court, and upon the Chief Justice. In consequence of the resignation of the Attorney-General, the prosecution was dropped, but *Chief Justice Wilmot* prepared an able opinion in the case, which was left among his papers, and published by his son after his death. It is reported in the *8th vol. of State Trials, p.* 54. After showing that the authority of the courts to punish contempts by attachment was not derived from statute, as seems to have been argued for the defense, he says: "The power which the courts in Westminister [*sic*] Hall have of vindicating their own authority, is coeval with their first foundation and institution; it is a necessary incident to every court of justice, whether of record or not, to fine and imprison for a contempt to the court, acted in the face of it (1 *Vent.* 1), and the issuance of attachments by the supreme courts of justice in Westminister Hall, for contempts out of court, stands upon the same immemorial usage, as supports the whole fabric of the common law; it is as much the "*lex terrœ* [*sic*], and within the exception of *magna charta,* as the issuing any other legal process whatever.

"I have examined very carefully to see if I could find out any vestiges or traces of its introduction, but can find none: it is as ancient as any other part of the common law. And though I do not mean to compare and contrast attachments with trials by jury, yet truth compels me to say, that the mode of proceeding by attachment stands upon the same foundation and basis as trials by jury do, immemorial usage and practice; it is a constitutional remedy in particular cases, and the judges in those cases are as much bound to give an activity to this part of the law as to any other part of it. Indeed it is admitted, that attachments are very properly granted for resistance of process, or a contumelious treatment of it, or any violence or abuse of the ministers, or others employed to execute it.

"But it is said, that the course of justice in those cases is obstructed, and the obstruction must be instantly removed; that there is no such necessity in the case of libels upon courts or judges, which may wait for the ordinary method of prosecution, without any inconvenience whatever. But where the nature of the offense of libeling judges, for *what they do in their judicial capacities,* either in court, or out of court, comes to be considered, it does, in my opinion, become more proper for an attachment than any other case whatever.

"The arraignment of the justice of the judges, * * excites in the minds of the people a general dissatisfaction with all judicial determinations, and indisposes their minds to obey them; and whenever men's alliance to the laws is so fundamentally shaken, it is the most fatal and the most dangerous obstruction of justice; and, in my opinion, calls out for a more rapid and immediate redress than any other obstruction whatever; *not for the sake of the judges as private individuals,* but because they are the channels by which the King's justice is conveyed to the people." . . .

The cases above cited (and many more might be cited, if deemed at all necessary) abundantly show that, by the common law, courts possessed the power to punish, as for contempt, libelous publications, of the character of the one under consideration, upon their proceedings *pending or past,* upon the ground that they tended to degrade the tribunals; destroy that public confidence and respect for their judgments and decrees, so essentially necessary to the good order and well being of society, and most effectually obstructed the free courts of justice.

We have above stated that when the supreme court was created by the constitution, and certain judicial powers conferred upon it, the power to punish contempts of its authority, was impliedly given to it, as a necessary incident to the exercise of its express powers. Otherwise, it would have been powerless of self-preservation, and unable to fulfill the useful purposes of its creation. The question now recurs, is there any feature in the constitution, or in the character of our free institutions, which denies to this court the power to punish, as for contempt, libelous publications however flagrant, and however much they may tend to degrade its authority and destroy public confidence in the integrity of its judgment and decrees? In other words, can it punish no act as a contempt, which is not enumerated in the letter of the statute, for this is the broad issue tendered by the defendant's plea to the jurisdiction in this case? This question was left open in the case of *Neil v. The State*. See *p*. 269.

Such limitation upon the power of the court, is not to be found in the provision of the Bill of Rights, guaranteeing the right of trial by jury, because we have seen that this right existed at common law, by immemorial usage, in harmony with the power of the courts to punish for contempts by attachment, each applying to its appropriate class of cases; and in *Neil v. The State* it was expressly held, that this provision of the constitution did not take away from our courts the power to punish for contempts in a summary mode.

The only provisions to be found in our constitution, on the subject of contempts, are as follows:

"Each house may determine the rule of its proceedings, punish its own members for disorderly behavior; and, with the concurrence of two-thirds of the members elected, expel a member" &c. *Sec*. 16, *art*. 4.

"Each house may punish, by fine and imprisonment, any person, not a member, who shall be guilty of disrespect to the house, by any disorderly or contemptuous behavior in their presence, during their session; but such imprisonment shall not extend beyond the final adjournment of that session." *Sec*. 17, *ib*.

These provisions are not to be regarded as a grant of power

to the two houses to punish contempts, because they would have impliedly possessed such power without the grant (2 *Story on the Const., sec.* 1503); but, by the rules of interpretation, usually applied to such instruments, these provisions must be regarded as a limitation upon such power; and under the rule that the expression of one thing excludes another, it is perhaps safe to state, that the two houses would not possess the power to punish, as for contempt, the authors of libelous publications upon their proceedings.

Had the framers of the constitution inserted in it, a provision similar to the one last above copied, in relation to the courts, the question now under discussion would be at an end.

But the fact that the convention, which framed the constitution, had the subject of contempts before them, placed a limitation upon the power of the two houses to punish contempts, but did not think proper to place any such limitation upon the power of the courts, warrants the conclusion that the courts were left to exercise such common law powers on the subject, as, in their sound discretion, might be found necessary to preserve their authority, and enforce their legal process, orders, judgments and decrees, without which they could not answer the purposes of their creation.

And there is a good reason why the framers of the constitution might well have made this distinction. The legislature is a political body. If its proceedings, and the conduct and motives of its members are unjustly assailed by libelous publications, they may defend their official conduct, and repel attacks through the press, and upon the "*stump,*" but it is not the usage of the country, nor would it comport with the dignity of judicial stations, for judges to resort to newspapers, or the public forum in defense of the integrity of their decisions, &c., and it would be an unwise policy that would drive them to such a course. . . .

The counsel for the defense supposed that the power of the courts to punish, as for contempt, the publication of libels upon their proceedings, was cut off by the *7th sec. of the Bill of Rights,* which is in these words: "That printing presses shall be free to every person; and no law shall ever be made to restrain the rights thereof. The free communication of thoughts and opinions, is one of the invaluable rights of man; and every citizen may freely speak, write and print on any subject—*being responsible for the abuse of that liberty.*"

The last clause of the section, "*being responsible for the abuse of that liberty,*" is an answer to the argument of the learned counsel.

It is a well known fact, that the *bench* and the *bar* have been, in this, and all other countries where the law has existed as a distinct profession, the ablest and most zealous advocates of liberal institutions, the freedom of conscience, and the *liberty of the press;* and none have guarded more watchfully the encroachments of power on the one hand; or deprecated more earnestly tendencies to lawless anarchy and licentiousness on the other. The freedom of the press, therefore, has nothing to fear from the bench in this State. No attempt has ever been made, and we may venture to say, never will be, to interfere with its legitimate province, on the part of the judiciary, by the exercise of the power to punish contempts.

The object of the clause in the *Bill of Rights* above quoted, is known to every well informed man. Although the press is *now* almost as free in England as it is in this country, yet the time was, in by-gone ages, when the ministers of the crown possessed the power to lay their hand upon it, and hush its voice, when deemed necessary to subserve political purposes. A similar clause has been inserted in all the American constitutions, to guard the press against the trammels of political power, and secure to the whole people a full and free discussion of public affairs.

Any citizen has the right to publish the proceedings and decisions of this court, and if he deem it necessary for the public good, to comment upon them freely, discuss their correctness, the fitness or unfitness of the judges for their stations, and the fidelity with which they perform the important public trusts reposed in them, but he has no right to attempt, by defamatory publications, to degrade the tribunal, destroy public confidence in it, and dispose the community to disregard and set at naught its orders, judgments, and decrees. Such publications are an abuse of the liberty of the press, and tend to sap the very foundation of good order and well-being in society, by obstructing the course of justice. If a judge is really corrupt, and unworthy of the station which he holds, the constitution has provided an ample remedy by *impeachment* or *address,* where he can meet his accuser face to face, and his conduct may undergo a full investigation. The liberty of the press is one thing, and licentious *scandal* is another. The constitution guarantees to every man the right to acquire and hold property, by all lawful means, but this furnishes no justification to a man to *rob* his neighbor of his lands or goods. . . .

After the impeachment of Judge Peck, Congress passed an act restricting the power of the courts of the United States in the punishment of contempts, and intended, doubtless, to treat out-door publications of any character as such. See *4th Statutes at Large,* 487. This act was approved 2d March, 1831. In *United States v. Holmes, Wallace Reports* 1, Mr. Justice Baldwin, presiding in the circuit court of the United States, correctly remarked that the act of Congress referred to, was a limitation upon his power to punish contempts.

The judicial power of the United States is vested in one supreme court, and in such inferior courts as the Congress may, from time to time, ordain and establish. *Constitution of United States, art.* 3, *sec.* 1. The supreme court was created by the constitution, the district and circuit courts by acts of Congress. When the latter were established, and vested with certain judicial powers, the authority to punish contempts attached as an incident. 2 *Story on the Constitution, sec.* 1774. But deriving their existence from Congress, it follows that their power to punish contempts is under its control.

The act above referred to, however, applies, in its terms, to all the courts of the United States, but whether the supreme court, deriving its existence and powers from the constitution, has regarded the act as an imperative limitation upon its authority to punish contempts, we have no means of determining, finding no adjudications upon the point by it. Perhaps the supreme court has acquiesced in the act, through that respect due to the Legislative will, without inquiry into the question of power. It may be said, to the credit of the press in this country, that it has generally upheld and maintained respect for the judiciary, and instances of libelous publications upon the courts have rarely occurred.

The case of Judge Peck is familiar to the profession. Presiding in the district court of the United States, for the district of Missouri, in the year 1826, and having decided one of several important land cases pending before him, he published his opinion in the cause. Mr. *Lawless*, an attorney of the court, and engaged in the cases, published a criticism upon the opinion, not impugning the motives or charging corruption upon the judge, but discussing the correctness of his decision, and pointing out what he deemed to be its errors. The judge treated the publication as libelous, and punished its author as for contempt of court, on the grounds that it tended to prejudice the determination of the remaining causes. Mr. *Lawless* complained to the House of Representatives of the Congress of the United States, of the conduct of the judge, and finally he was impeached for an official misdemeanor; and, on full discussion of the law of contempts, acquitted by the Senate upon a close vote. The impression generally prevailed, however, that Judge Peck exceeded his authority, and this doubtless lead [*sic*] to the passage of the act of Congress above referred to.

But we may venture to remark, that independent of any statutory provisions upon the subject, the distinction between the constitutional freedom, and licentious abuse of the press, is now so well understood in this country, that no American judge would consider himself authorized to punish, as for contempt, authors of publications of the character of that made by Mr. *Lawless*. . . .

18. BRIDGES v. CALIFORNIA

1941

The power of courts to convict by summary procedure for criticism of their work that appeared outside the courtroom ("constructive contempt") was asserted in state after state following the Morrill case of 1855. Newspapers were cited and convicted by the very judges who were criticized and who called their constructive contempt power an "immemorial" one despite the fact that highly questionable precedent from the mid-eighteenth-century English common law was their undergirding. Two contempt convictions in the twentieth century were supported in the United States Supreme Court, majorities holding that words having a reasonable tendency to interfere with the orderly process of justice were punishable. The spirit of the federal statute of 1831 gave way to that of the Morrill doctrine in the leading cases of *Patterson* v. *Colorado* in 1907, and *Toledo Newspaper Co.* v. *U.S.* in 1918.

But in 1941 the Supreme Court abandoned the restrictive reasoning and acted to limit sharply the powers of the judicial branch to keep its own "good press." Deciding two California cases at once—those of an antilabor newspaper and of a militant labor leader—the court ruled on the side of vigorous discussion of court cases while they are pending. Contempt convictions ordi-

---

From *Bridges* v. *California*, 314 U. S. Reports 252.

narily "punish utterances made during the pendency of a case," Justice Black said, and "produce their restrictive results at the precise time when public interest . . . would naturally be at its height." The court ruled that it was not enough that words have a "reasonable tendency" to interfere with the orderly process of justice; they must offer a "clear and present danger" of interfering. And whatever the fate of the famous Holmesian formulation in other spheres of the law, where contempt was concerned "clear and present danger" persisted into the 1960's.

Mr. Justice Black delivered the opinion of the Court:

These two cases, while growing out of different circumstances and concerning different parties, both relate to the scope of our national constitutional policy safeguarding free speech and a free press. All of the petitioners were adjudged guilty and fined for contempt of court by the Superior Court of Los Angeles County. Their conviction rested upon comments pertaining to pending litigation which were published in newspapers. In the Superior Court, and later in the California Supreme Court, petitioners challenged the state's action as an abridgment, prohibited by the Federal Constitution, of freedom of speech and of the press; but the Superior Court overruled this contention, and the Supreme Court affirmed. The importance of the constitutional question prompted us to grant certiorari. 309 U. S. 649; 310 U. S. 623.

In brief, the state courts asserted and exercised a power to punish petitioners for publishing their views concerning cases not in all respects finally determined, upon the following chain of reasoning: California is invested with the power and duty to provide an adequate administration of justice; by virtue of this power and duty, it can take appropriate measures for providing fair judicial trials free from coercion or intimidation; included among such appropriate measures is the common law procedure of punishing certain interferences and obstructions through contempt proceedings; this particular measure, devolving upon the courts of California by reason of their creation as courts, includes the power to punish for publications made outside the court room if they tend to interfere with the fair and orderly administration of justice in a pending case; the trial court having found that the publications had such a tendency, and there being substantial evidence to support the finding, the punishments here imposed were an appropriate exercise of the state's power; in so far as these punishments constitute a restriction on liberty of expression, the public interest in that liberty was properly subordinated to the public interest in judicial impartiality and decorum.

If the inference of conflict raised by the last clause be correct, the issue before us is of the very gravest moment. For free speech and fair trials are two of the most cherished policies of our civilization, and it would be a trying task to choose between them. But even if such a conflict is not actually raised by the question before us, we are still confronted with the delicate problems entailed in passing upon the deliberations of the highest court of a state. This is not, however, solely an issue between state and nation, as it would be if we were called upon to mediate in one of those troublous situations where each claims to be the repository of a particular sovereign power. To be sure, the exercise of power here in question was by a state judge. But in deciding whether or not the sweeping constitutional mandate against any law "abridging the freedom of speech or of the press" forbids it, we are necessarily measuring a power of all American courts, both state and federal, including this one.

I

It is to be noted at once that we have no direction by the legislature of California that publications outside the court room which comment upon a pending case in a specified manner should be punishable. As we said in *Cantwell* v. *Connecti-*

cut, 310 U. S. 296, 307–308, such a "declaration of the State's policy would weigh heavily in any challenge of the law as infringing constitutional limitations." But as we also said there, the problem is different where "the judgment is based on a common law concept of the most general and undefined nature." *Id.* 308. Cf. *Herndon* v. *Lowry,* 301 U. S. 242, 261–264. For here the legislature of California has not appraised a particular kind of situation and found a specific danger sufficiently imminent to justify a restriction on a particular kind of utterance. The judgments below, therefore, do not come to us encased in the armor wrought by prior legislative deliberation. Under such circumstances, this Court has said that "it must necessarily be found, as an original question," that the specified publications involved created "such likelihood of bringing about the substantive evil as to deprive [them] of the constitutional protection." *Gitlow* v. *New York,* 268 U. S. 652, 671.

How much "likelihood" is another question, "a question of proximity and degree" that cannot be completely captured in a formula. In *Schenck* v. *United States,* however, this Court said that there must be a determination of whether or not "the words used are used in such circumstances and are of such a nature as to create a clear and present danger that they will bring about the substantive evils." We recognize that this statement, however helpful, does not comprehend the whole problem. As Mr. Justice Brandeis said in his concurring opinion in *Whitney* v. *California,* 274 U. S. 357, 374: "This Court has not yet fixed the standard by which to determine when a danger shall be deemed clear; how remote the danger may be and yet be deemed present."

Nevertheless, the "clear and present danger" language of the *Schenck* case has afforded practical guidance in a great variety of cases in which the scope of constitutional protections of freedom of expression was in issue. It has been utilized by either a majority or minority of this Court in passing upon the constitutionality of convictions under espionage acts, *Schenck*

v. *United States, supra; Abrams* v. *United States,* 250 U. S. 616; under a criminal syndicalism act, *Whitney* v. *California, supra;* under an "anti-insurrection" act, *Herndon* v. *Lowry, supra;* and for breach of the peace at common law, *Cantwell* v. *Connecticut, supra.* And very recently we have also suggested that "clear and present danger" is an appropriate guide in determining the constitutionality of restrictions upon expression where the substantive evil sought to be prevented by the restriction is "destruction of life or property, or invasion of the right of privacy." *Thornhill* v. *Alabama,* 310 U. S. 88, 105.

Moreover, the likelihood, however great, that a substantive evil will result cannot alone justify a restriction upon freedom of speech or the press. The evil itself must be "substantial," Brandeis, J., concurring in *Whitney* v. *California, supra,* 374; it must be "serious," *id.* 376. And even the expression of "legislative preferences or beliefs" cannot transform minor matters of public inconvenience or annoyance into substantive evils of sufficient weight to warrant the curtailment of liberty of expression. *Schneider* v. *State,* 308 U. S. 147, 161.

What finally emerges from the "clear and present danger" cases is a working principle that the substantive evil must be extremely serious and the degree of imminence extremely high before utterances can be punished. Those cases do not purport to mark the furthermost constitutional boundaries of protected expression, nor do we here. They do no more than recognize a minimum compulsion of the Bill of Rights. For the First Amendment does not speak equivocally. It prohibits any law "abridging the freedom of speech, or of the press." It must be taken as a command of the broadest scope that explicit language, read in the context of a liberty-loving society, will allow.

II

Before analyzing the punished utterances and the circumstances surrounding their publication, we must consider an argument which, if valid, would destroy the relevance of the foregoing discussion to this case. In brief, this argument is that the publications here in question belong to a special category marked off by history—a category to which the criteria of constitutional immunity from punishment used where other types of utterances are concerned are not applicable. For, the argument runs, the power of judges to punish by contempt out-of-court publications tending to obstruct the orderly and fair administration of justice in a pending case was deeply rooted in English common law at the time the Constitution was adopted. That this historical contention is dubious has been persuasively argued elsewhere. Fox, *Contempt of Court, passim, e. g.*, 207. See also Stansbury, *Trial of James H. Peck,* 430. In any event it need not detain us, for to assume that English common law in this field became ours is to deny the generally accepted historical belief that "one of the objects of the Revolution was to get rid of the English common law on liberty of speech and of the press." Schofield, *Freedom of the Press in the United States,* 9 Publications Amer. Sociol. Soc., 67, 76.

More specifically, it is to forget the environment in which the First Amendment was ratified. In presenting the proposals which were later embodied in the Bill of Rights, James Madison, the leader in the preparation of the First Amendment, said: "Although I know whenever the great rights, the trial by jury, freedom of the press, or liberty of conscience, come in question in that body [Parliament], the invasion of them is resisted by able advocates, yet their Magna Charta does not contain any one provision for the security of those rights, respecting which the people of America are most alarmed. The freedom of the press and rights of conscience, those choicest privileges of the people, are unguarded in the British Constitution." 1 Annals of Congress 1789–1790, 434. And Madison elsewhere wrote that "the state of the press . . . under the common law, cannot . . . be the standard of its freedom in the United States." VI Writings of James Madison 1790–1802, 387.

There are no contrary implications in any part of the history of the period in which the First Amendment was framed and adopted. No purpose in ratifying the Bill of Rights was clearer than that of securing for the people of the United States much greater freedom of religion, expression, assembly, and petition than the people of Great Britain had ever enjoyed. It cannot be denied, for example, that the religious test oath or the restrictions upon assembly then prevalent in England would have been regarded as measures which the Constitution prohibited the American Congress from passing. And since the same unequivocal language is used with respect to freedom of the press, it signifies a similar enlargement of that concept as well. Ratified as it was while the memory of many oppressive English restrictions on the enumerated liberties was still fresh, the First Amendment cannot reasonably be taken as approving prevalent English practices. On the contrary, the only conclusion supported by history is that the unqualified prohibitions laid down by the framers were intended to give to liberty of the press, as to the other liberties, the broadest scope that could be countenanced in an orderly society.

The implications of subsequent American history confirm such a construction of the First Amendment. To be sure, it occurred no more to the people who lived in the decades following Ratification than it would to us now that the power of courts to protect themselves from disturbances and disorder in the court room by use of contempt proceedings could seriously be challenged as conflicting with constitutionally secured guarantees of liberty. In both state and federal courts, this power has been universally recognized. See *Anderson* v. *Dunn*, 6 Wheat. 204, 227. But attempts to expand it in the post-Ratification years evoked popular reactions that bespeak a feeling of jealous solicitude for freedom of the press. In Pennsylvania and New York, for example, heated controversies arose over alleged abuses in the exercise of the contempt power, which in both places culminated in legislation practically forbidding summary punishment for publications. See Nelles and King, *Contempt by Publication,* 28 Col. L. Rev. 401, 409–422.

In the federal courts, there was the celebrated case of Judge Peck, recently referred to by this Court in *Nye* v. *United States,* 313 U. S. 33, 45. The impeachment proceedings against him, it should be noted, and the strong feelings they engendered, were set in motion by his summary punishment of a lawyer for publishing comment on a case which was on appeal at the time of publication and which raised the identical issue of several other cases then pending before him. Here again legislation was the outcome, Congress proclaiming in a statute expressly captioned "An Act *declaratory* of the law concerning contempts of court," that the power of federal courts to inflict summary punishment for contempt "shall not be construed to extend to any cases except the misbehaviour of . . . persons in the presence of the said courts, or so near thereto as to obstruct the administration of justice. . . . " When recently called upon to interpret this statute, we overruled the earlier decision of this Court in *Toledo Newspaper Co.* v. *United States,* 247 U. S. 402, in the belief that it improperly enlarged the stated area of summary punishment. *Nye* v. *United States, supra.* . . .

III

We may appropriately begin our discussion of the judgments below by considering how much, as a practical matter, they would affect liberty of expression. It must be recognized that public interest is much more likely to be kindled by a controversial event of the day than by a generalization, however penetrating, of the historian or scientist. Since they punish utterances made during the pendency of a case, the judgments below therefore produce their restrictive results at the precise time when public interest in the matters discussed would naturally be at its height. Moreover, the ban is likely to fall not only at a crucial time but upon the most important topics of discussion. . . .

This unfocussed threat is, to be sure, limited in time, terminating as it does upon final disposition of the case. But this does not change its censorial quality. An endless series of moratoria on public discussion, even if each were very short, could hardly be dismissed as an insignificant abridgment of freedom of expression. And to assume that each would be short is to overlook the fact that the "pendency" of a case is frequently a matter of months or even years rather than days or weeks.

For these reasons we are convinced that the judgments below result in a curtailment of expression that cannot be dismissed as insignificant. If they can be justified at all, it must be in terms of some serious substantive evil which they are designed to avert. The substantive evil here sought to be averted has been variously described below. It appears to be double: disrespect for the judiciary; and disorderly and unfair administration of justice. The assumption that respect for the judiciary can be won by shielding judges from published criticism wrongly appraises the character of American public opinion. For it is a prized American privilege to speak one's mind, although not always with perfect good taste, on all public institutions. And an enforced silence, however limited, solely in the name of preserving the dignity of the bench, would probably engender resentment, suspicion, and contempt much more than it would enhance respect.

The other evil feared, disorderly and unfair administration of justice, is more plausibly associated with restricting publications which touch upon pending litigation. The very word "trial" connotes decisions on the evidence and arguments properly advanced in open court. Legal trials are not like elections, to be won through the use of the meeting-hall, the radio, and the newspaper. But we cannot start with the assumption that publications of the kind here involved actually do threaten to change the nature of legal trials, and that to preserve judicial impartiality, it is necessary for judges to have a contempt power by which they can close all channels of public expression to all matters which touch upon pending cases. We must therefore turn to the particular utterances here in question and the circumstances of their publication to determine to what extent the substantive evil of unfair administration of justice was a likely consequence, and whether the degree of likelihood was sufficient to justify summary punishment.

The Los Angeles Times Editorials. The Times-Mirror Company, publisher of the Los Angeles Times, and L. D. Hotchkiss, its managing editor, were cited for contempt for the publication of three editorials. Both found by the trial court to be responsible for one of the editorials, the company and Hotchkiss were each fined $100. The company alone was held responsible for the other two, and was fined $100 more on account of one, and $300 more on account of the other.

The $300 fine presumably marks the most serious offense. The editorial thus distinguished was entitled "Probation for Gorillas?" After vigorously denouncing two members of a labor union who had previously been found guilty of assaulting nonunion truck drivers, it closes with the observation: "Judge A. A. Scott will make a serious mistake if he grants probation to Matthew Shannon and Kennan Holmes. This community needs the example of their assignment to the jute mill." Judge Scott had previously set a day (about a month after the publication) for passing upon the application of Shannon and Holmes for probation and for pronouncing sentence.

The basis for punishing the publication as contempt was by the trial court said to be its "inherent tendency" and by the Supreme Court its "reasonable tendency" to interfere with the orderly administration of justice in an action then before a court for consideration. In accordance with what we have said on the "clear and present danger" cases, neither "inherent tendency" nor "reasonable tendency" is enough to justify a restriction of free expression. But even if they were appropriate measures, we should find exaggeration in the use of those phrases to describe the facts here.

From the indications in the record of the position taken by the Los Angeles Times on labor controversies in the past, there could have been little doubt of its attitude toward the probation of Shannon and Holmes. In view of the paper's long-continued militancy in this field, it is inconceivable that any judge in Los Angeles would expect anything but adverse criticism from it in the event probation were granted. Yet such criticism after final disposition of the proceedings would clearly have been privileged. Hence, this editorial, given the most intimidating construction it will bear, did no more than threaten future adverse criticism which was reasonably to be expected anyway in the event of a lenient disposition of the pending case. To regard it, therefore, as in itself of substantial influence upon the course of justice would be to impute to judges a lack of firmness, wisdom, or honor—which we cannot accept as a major premise. Cf. Holmes, J., dissenting in *Toledo Newspaper Co.* v. *United States*, 247 U. S. 402, 424.

. . . With respect to these [other] two editorials, there is no divergence of conclusions among the members of this Court. We are all of the opinion that, upon any fair construction, their possible influence on the course of justice can be dismissed as negligible, and that the Constitution compels us to set aside the convictions as unpermissible exercises of the state's power. In view of the foregoing discussion of "Probation for Gorillas?", analysis of these editorials and their setting is deemed unnecessary.

The Bridges Telegram. While a motion for a new trial was pending in a case involving a dispute between an A. F. of L. union and a C. I. O. union of which Bridges was an officer, he either caused to be published or acquiesced in the publication of a telegram which he had sent to the Secretary of Labor. The telegram referred to the judge's decision as "outrageous"; said that attempted enforcement of it would tie up the port of Los Angeles and involve the entire Pacific Coast; and concluded with the announcement that the C. I. O. union, representing some twelve thousand members, did "not intend to allow state courts to override the majority vote of members in choosing its officers and representatives and to override the National Labor Relations Board."

Apparently Bridges' conviction is not rested at all upon his use of the word "outrageous." The remainder of the telegram fairly construed appears to be a statement that if the court's decree should be enforced there would be a strike. It is not claimed that such a strike would have been in violation of the terms of the decree, nor that in any other way it would have run afoul of the law of California. On no construction, therefore, can the telegram be taken as a threat either by Bridges or the union to follow an illegal course of action.

Moreover, this statement of Bridges was made to the Secretary of Labor, who is charged with official duties in connection with the prevention of strikes. Whatever the cause might be if a strike was threatened or possible the Secretary was entitled to receive all available information. Indeed, the Supreme Court of California recognized that, publication in the newspapers aside, in sending the message to the Secretary, Bridges was exercising the right of petition to a duly accredited representative of the United States Government, a right protected by the First Amendment.

It must be recognized that Bridges was a prominent labor leader speaking at a time when public interest in the particular labor controversy was at its height. The observations we have previously made here upon the timeliness and importance of utterances as emphasizing rather than diminishing the value of constitutional protection, and upon the breadth and seriousness of the censorial effects of punishing publications in the manner followed below, are certainly no less applicable to a leading spokesman for labor than to a powerful newspaper taking another point of view.

In looking at the reason advanced in support of the judgment of contempt, we find that here, too, the possibility of causing unfair disposition of a pending case is the major justification asserted. And here again the gist of the offense, according to the court below, is intimidation.

Let us assume that the telegram could be construed as an announcement of Bridges' intention to call a strike, something which, it is admitted, neither the general law of California nor the court's decree prohibited. With an eye on the realities of the situation, we cannot assume that Judge Schmidt was unaware of the possibility of a strike as a consequence of his decision. If he was not intimidated by the facts themselves, we do not believe that the most explicit statement of them could have sidetracked the course of justice. Again, we find exaggeration in the conclusion that the utterance even "tended" to interfere with justice. If there was electricity in the atmosphere, it was generated by the facts; the charge added by the Bridges telegram can be dismissed as negligible. The words of Mr. Justice Holmes, spoken in reference to very different facts, seem entirely applicable here: "I confess that I cannot find in all this or in the evidence in the case anything that would have affected a mind of reasonable fortitude, and still less can I find there anything that obstructed the administration of justice in any sense that I possibly can give to those words." *Toledo Newspaper Co.* v. *United States, supra,* 247 U. S. at 425.

Reversed.

Part Four

PATTERN OF RESTRAINT: ATTACK ON THE OPPONENTS OF SLAVERY

The Laws

The South periodically suffered severe tensions over the possibility of "servile insurrections" during the three decades before the Civil War. One spasm occurred in 1829 with the publication of the famous pamphlet by a former slave, David Walker, "Walker's Appeal in Four Articles Together with a Preamble to the Colored Citizens of the World." It plainly appealed to insurrection and revolt, and it set off legislation to curb expression in several states beginning with Georgia. Next came the Nat Turner rebellion of 1831, followed by similar laws in other Southern states. In 1835 the loosing of floods of abolitionist literature on the South helped bring even more severe laws against expression.

The laws reflected the temper and mood of Southerners, but they served largely as warnings to the bold or careless. In the two best-known Virginia prosecutions that involved offending publications—those of Lysander Barrett in 1839 and Samuel Janney in 1850—the judges interpreted the statutes strictly and the men were exonerated. The laws were eminently visible and handy to reach, but the South found quicker and surer instruments for dealing with those who violated its icons.

In the wake of the Nat Turner rebellion, Virginia's legislature went into long debate over slavery and laws to control expression of opinion about slavery, and took the extraordinary step of opening these debates to the public. The taboos on public discussion of the subject were swept aside for a time in 1832, not to be broken in a considerable way again in Virginia before the Civil War.

19. THE BREACH OF THE TABOO ON THE DISCUSSION OF SLAVERY

1832

Among the Southerners who in 1832 looked to eventual emancipation was Thomas Ritchie, the talented and vigorous editor of the *Richmond Enquirer*. When at the instance of the State legislature the ancient silence on the subject of slavery was broken temporarily in that year, he was among the editors of the state who soberly rejoiced at the prospect of public debate. Items below from the important *Enquirer* testify to the long muzzling of discussion, the relief of some at the breach, and the implacable hostility of others to questioning slavery. "Appomattox" was said to be Benjamin Watkins Leigh, a prominent Whig.

Richmond Enquirer

January 19, 1832

The seals are broken, which have been put for fifty years upon the most delicate and difficult subject of state concernment.—We publish speeches in the H.[ouse] of D.[elegates] today, *which, at no other period, would have been delivered but in closed doors.*—In the same spirit the press fearlessly speaks its own sentiments—unawed by the tocsin of denunciation or the menaces of proscription.—What is right, both for the Legislators, the Editors, and all our Politicians, is to speak with forbearance, coolness and moderate [sic] towards each other, and with the utmost discretion in the presence of persons whose destinies are dependent upon the discussion.

The following are the opinions expressed by two of the newspapers in this State—one on the borders of the Atlantic, and the other at the foot of the Blue Ridge:

(From the *Norfolk Herald*)

The subject of our coloured population is now before the Legislature of Virginia, and we are glad to see a disposition in that body to act upon it without the control of those sickly apprehensions and fancied views of danger, which have heretofore restrained our legislators from discussing the monstrous evil which it portends to the commonwealth. Our state has too long shrunk from the agitation of this important subject, and the evil of slavery has increased upon us with fearful rapidity.—Heavens! shall we fear the consequences of a public investigation of the evil with a view to its gradual removal, and not shudder at the inevitable results of permitting it to grow upon us? . . .

We are not so besotted as to ask that the evil be removed at once: if it can be entirely shaken off in 50 or even 100 years, it is as much as we should expect. All that we have in view is, that the number of slaves sent out of the country shall equal their increase for the next 10 years, that a certain per centum of decrease shall be established for the next 10 years, and so on until their entire removal shall be accomplished. . . .

(From the *Charlotteville Advocate*)

We are truly rejoiced that these Editors, have at last, found a field in which their *united talents* may be exerted. The good which they have it in their power to do on this subject is incalculable—by uniting their energies on this momentous question they will confer far more substantial benefits on their native State, than by wrangling on the comparative, but doubtful merits of rival political aspirants. Their labours will meet with the ready co-operation of every true patriot, and merit alike the applause and gratitude of their fellow-citizens. . . .

The rules that we should pursue are—Touch not *private property*. . . . Take time for . . . the consummation of any plan—a Century, if necessary—An evil, that has been so long growing will take a *long time* to eradicate. . . . Let our plan be gradual, but certain—systematic, *but discreet*—Meanwhile, strengthen our police—prevent all combinations, all nocturnal meetings, and even meetings in the day-time in any large number—all itinerant black preachers . . . all teachings, and schools in the towns—Get clear of the free people of colour, the worst, the first, by the strongest inducements we can properly exert—and prevent them from being taught, lest they should teach and mislead the slave. . . .

Richmond Enquirer

February 4, 1832

From a Letter Signed "Appomattox"

I do most earnestly and deliberately recommend to all the people of the slave-holding parts of Virginia—and moreover to all the people of the Southern and Southwestern slaveholding States, who have a common interest with us and are exposed to the same dangers—to discourage every man by his own example, and by advice to his neighbors, the circulation among them of the papers of the Virginia *abolition presses,* upon the like reasons of common prudence, that would not tolerate the dissemination of writings wilfully incendiary. I do not think, and therefore I do not say, that *our* abolition presses are *willfully incendiary;* and, therefore, I entertain no resentment towards the editors. But to *us* it can make no odds, whether their publications are editorial or contributed—in the form of speeches or of essays—dictated by indiscretion, or carelessness of consequences, or blindness to them: to *us* the danger and the mischief are the same, as if they were dictated by the most malignant design. The effusions of inflammatory matter they have already poured forth, and the temper in which they have taken up the subject, should warn us all of the burning lava yet to be discharged upon us; which, like the travail of a volcano in the immediate neighborhood of our dwellings, threatens the more danger and mischief, for coming from *them.* The public sentiment, we see, is to be 'developed'—the subject is to be discussed—and he that does not foresee in what tone it will be discussed in the public prints, cannot be made to take warning. Let us pay no regard to the claim which may be asserted for the independence of the press: if, in the exercise of *their* independence, they choose to print, we, in the exercise of *our* independence, may choose to suppress, to the uttermost of our power, what we deem inflammatory, dangerous, mischievous. Every man has a perfect right to withdraw his subscription from any newspaper, and to discourage the circulation of it; and if he thinks the opinions it maintains, likely to produce evil, he is bound, in duty to his country, to exercise that right. I have been credibly informed, that the publications contained in a certain independent press during the late war, giving an account of the defenceless condition of Washington, were the real incentive to Gen. Ross's visit to that city. The claim to such independence of the press, as not only gives it freedom to publish, but a right to free unrestrained circulation among those whom the circulation may injure, is, in truth, a claim to absolute dominion; which I shall never acknowledge in any man or set of men whatever. I want no sedition laws—I would have none—there is a check, a sufficient check, in the influence of public opinion, if timely, promptly and vigorously exerted; and, in my deliberate judgment, prudence, justice, necessity, require *the people of the whole slave holding country to unite in the exercise of that check, upon the present occasion.* . . .

Richmond Enquirer

February 4, 1832

Editorial Statement Accompanying Letter of "Appomattox"

The author of Appomattox wishes us to exercise a sort of practical bull. He uses the liberty of the Press for the purpose of extinguishing that liberty. He calls upon us to lend him a stick wherewith to break our own heads. Well—he is welcome to use it.—No one is more sensible than we are of the abilities of that gentleman, and of the weight which his pen always carries with it—But we can trust our cause to a cool jury of our countrymen, and fearlessly abide the issue.—Our whole course is before them. What we have published from others, what we have written ourselves, the Debates of the deliberative Assembly of this land in open doors, and even the spicy summary of their arguments from the pen of Appomattox himself, are all before them. They are all, all before them.—What we mean hereafter to do; how far we shall permit or restrict or prohibit the publication of other articles, we shall scarcely venture to say at this time, with such an article staring us in the face, because, like "honest old Jack Falstaff," "were reasons as plenty as blackberries, we would not give one—*upon compulsion*"— The other Virginia Editors are as free as we are—They will take such course as their judgments direct.

20. THE STATUTORY PROGRESSION OF SUPPRESSION

Virginia Law of 1832

The legislature's deliberations of 1832 produced in part the statute below, punishing the counselling in print of insurrection or rebellion among the slaves. It reflected fears generated by Nat Turner.

Chap. 187—An ACT to amend an act, entitled, an act reducing into one the several acts concerning slaves, free negroes and mulattoes. . . .

Section 7. If any person shall hereafter write, print, or cause to be written or printed any book, pamphlet, or other writing,

---

From *Supplement to the Revised Code of the Laws of Virginia* (Richmond: Samuel Shepherd & Co., 1833), pp. 246, 247.

advising persons of colour within this state to make insurrection, or to rebel, or shall knowingly circulate, or cause to be circulated, any book, pamphlet or other writing, written or printed, advising persons of colour in this commonwealth to commit insurrection or rebellion; such person, if a slave, free negro or mulatto, shall, on conviction before any justice of the peace, be punished for the first offence with stripes, in the discretion of the said justice, not exceeding thirty-nine lashes; and for the second offence, shall be deemed guilty of felony, and on due conviction, shall be punished with death without benefit of clergy; and if the person so offending be a white person, he or she shall be punished on conviction, in a sum not less than one hundred nor more than one thousand dollars.

Virginia Law of 1836

The event that spurred Southern states to pass new laws curbing speech and press in 1835–1836 was the first great propaganda drive of the Northern abolitionist societies. The South was deluged with the literature of emancipation, and reacted with outraged demands on Northern governors and legislatures to make such activity illegal. On their own ground, Southern states passed new laws such as Virginia's given below. This was aimed with blunt warning at abolition societies and "evil disposed persons" who might come to Virginia, and at their printed materials that might reach Virginia post offices. Especially proscribed were statements holding that masters "have no property in their slaves." It has been called the most intolerant law that Virginia ever passed. The marginal notes summarize the extent of the prohibitions.

From *Acts of the General Assembly of Virginia, 1835–1836* (Richmond: Thomas Ritchie, 1836), pp. 44–45.

CHAP. 66.—An ACT to suppress the circulation of incendiary publications, and for other purposes.

(Passed March 23, 1836.)

amble.

Whereas attempts have been recently made by certain abolition or anti-slavery societies and evil disposed persons, being and residing in some of the non-slaveholding states, to interfere with the relations existing between master and slave in this state, and to excite in our coloured population a spirit of insubordination, rebellion and insurrection, by distributing among them, through the agency of the United States mail and other means, certain incendiary books, pamphlets, or other writings of an inflammatory and mischievous character and tendency: For remedy whereof, and to provide against the dangers thence arising,

ıalty on mbers or nts of olition ieties aying right property slaves.

1. *Be it enacted by the general assembly,* That any member of an abolition or anti-slavery society, or agent of an abolition or anti-slavery society, who shall come into this state, and shall here maintain, by speaking or writing, that the owners of slaves have no property in the same, or advocate or advise the abolition of slavery, shall be deemed guilty of a high misdemeanor, and on conviction thereof shall be fined in a sum of not less than fifty dollars nor more than two hundred dollars, and shall suffer a term of imprisonment of not less than six months nor more than three years, at the discretion of a jury.

rm of prisonment.

ıalty for iting, printor circulatincendiary ctrines.

2. *And be it further enacted,* That if any person shall hereafter write, print, or cause to be written or printed, any book, pamphlet, or other writing, with intent of advising, enticing, or persuading persons of colour within this commonwealth to make insurrection, or to rebel, or denying the right of masters to property in their slaves, and inculcating the duty of resistance to such right, or shall, with intent to aid the purposes aforesaid of such book, pamphlet, or other writing, knowingly circulate, or cause to be circulated, any such book, pamphlet, or other writing,

ıishment on ves.

such person shall, if a slave or other coloured person, b
punished by stripes, not exceeding thirty-nine, and tran
ported and sold beyond the limits of the United State
under the orders of the executive of this commonwealt
and if a free white person, shall be deemed guilty
felony, and on conviction thereof be punished by impriso
ment in the penitentiary of this commonwealth for a ter
not less than two years nor more than five years.

On white persons.

Post-masters to give notice of reception of incendiary publications.

3. *Be it further enacted,* That if any post-master or de
uty postmaster within this commonwealth, shall give notic
to any justice of the peace that any book, pamphlet,
other writing, hath been received at his office through th
medium of the mail, of the character and description me
tioned in the section of this act immediately preceding,
shall be the duty of such justice of the peace to enqui
into the circumstances of the case, and to have such boo
pamphlet, or other writing, burned in his presence; and
it shall appear to him by satisfactory evidence that th
person to whom the same is directed, subscribed for th
said book, pamphlet, or other writing, knowing its cha
acter and tendency, or agreed to receive it with an inte
tion of circulating it, thereby to aid the purposes of th
abolitionists or anti-slavery societies, the said justice sha
commit him or her to the jail of his county, to be dealt wit
according to law. Any post-master, or deputy post-maste
knowingly violating the provisions of this act, shall forfe
and pay a sum not less than fifty dollars, nor more tha
two hundred dollars, to be recovered with costs, by actic
of debt or information, in any court of record in this con
monwealth, one moiety to the commonwealth, for the u
of the literary fund, the other to the informer, or any pe
son who will sue for the same.

Justice to cause them to be burned.

Punishment on subscriber thereto.

Penalty on post-masters violating provisions of act.

Arrests of offenders how made.

4. *And be it further enacted,* That offenders against th
first section of this act may be arrested by any free whi
person, and by such person carried before any judge
justice of the peace in this commonwealth; and if suc

judge or justice shall be of opinion, after hearing the testimony, that such offender ought to be prosecuted in the courts of this commonwealth, such judge or justice shall commit such offender to the jail of the county where the offence was committed, and be there detained until his final trial, or such judge or justice may admit such offender to bail.

nmitment.

5. This act shall constantly be given in charge to the grand juries by the judges of the superior courts of law, and the county and other inferior courts.

to be n in ge to d juries.

6. This act shall commence and be in force from and after the first day of June next.

mence- t.

Virginia Law of 1848

Virginia's act of 1848 condensed that of 1836, and in some ways modified the punishments for forbidden expression. Essentially, however, the new law was as harsh as the old. And in eliminating the focus on members and agents of abolition societies, the legislature actually was strengthening the act: At least one abolitionist brought to trial under the 1836 statute had been freed because the State could not show that he belonged to an abolition society.

Chap. 120—An ACT to reduce into one the several acts concerning crimes and punishments. . . .

24. Any free person who, by speaking or writing, shall maintain that owners have not right of property in their slaves, shall be punished by confinement in the jail not more than twelve months, and by fine not exceeding five hundred dollars; and such person may be arrested by any white person and carried before a judge or justice to be dealt with according to law.

ying erty wner ave.

nder how sted.

From *Acts of the General Assembly of Virginia, 1847–1848* (Richmond: Samuel Shepherd, 1848), p. 117.

Incendiary publications.

25. Any free person who shall write, print, or cause to b written or printed, any book, pamphlet, or other writin with intent to advise or incite persons of colour within th commonwealth to rebel or make insurrection, or denyin the rights of masters to property in their slaves, and incu cating the duty of resistance to such right, or shall, wi intent to aid the purposes aforesaid of such book, pamphl or other writing, knowingly circulate the same, shall b punished by confinement in the penitentiary for a term n less than one nor more than five years.

Duty of postmasters relative to incendiary publications.

Magistrate to cause them to be burned.

Subscriber therefor punished.

Penalty on postmasters.

26. If any postmaster or deputy postmaster shall kno that any such book, pamphlet or other writing mention in the preceding section has been received at his offic through the medium of the mail, it shall be his duty to gi notice thereof to some justice of the peace, whose duty shall be to enquire into the circumstances, and to have su book, pamphlet or other writing burned in his presenc and if it shall appear to him by satisfactory evidence th the person to whom the same is directed, subscribed ther for, knowing its character and tendency, or agreed to r ceive with intention to circulate it, thereby to aid t purposes of the abolitionists, the said justice shall comn him to the jail to be dealt with according to law. Any po master or deputy postmaster who shall knowingly viola the provisions of this section shall be punished by fine n exceeding two hundred dollars.

Justice to take recognizance for offender's appearance at court.

In default, to commit him.

27. It shall be the duty of any judge, justice of the peac or mayor, before whom any person may be brought for t offence mentioned in the preceding section, to cause su person to enter into a recognizance, with sufficient securi to appear before the circuit superior court of law a chancery having jurisdiction of the offence, at the next te thereof, to answer for the same; and in default of su recognizance, to commit such offender to jail, there remain until discharged by order of the said court.

Mobs and Vigilance Committees

21. NARRATIVE OF THE RIOTS AGAINST THE LIBERTY OF THE PRESS IN CINCINNATI

James G. Birney, 1836

Professor Francis Lieber of South Carolina College wrote to his friend John C. Calhoun concerning the South's ban on discussion of slavery: " . . . If you fear discussion, if you maintain that the South cannot afford it . . . then you admit at the same time that the whole institution is to be kept up by violence only, and is against the spirit of the times and unameliorable, which means, in other words, that violence supports it, and violence will be its end."

It was principally the pressure of public opinion, whose hammer was the vigilance committee or the mob, that kept speakers, writers, and printers in check in the South and that operated to make heroes and martyrs in the North. The formation of vigilance committees in the South to suppress or punish expression grew apace after 1835 and was a familiar phenomenon down to the war. In the North, intense, widespread opposition to abolitionists led to frequent acts of violence, dropping sharply in num-

---

From James G. Birney, "Narrative of the Late Riotous Proceedings against the Liberty of the Press, in Cincinnati" (Cincinnati: 1836), pp. 24–40. Pamphlet.

ber in the excruciating aftermath of the murder of the Rev. Elijah P. Lovejoy, the abolitionist editor of the Alton, Illinois, *Observer*, in 1837.

The justifications, techniques, kinds of supporters, and temper of committees and mobs, and the abolitionists' complete rejection of restraint on freedom of the press, appear below in excerpts from a pamphlet that made James G. Birney known throughout the North for his work as an utterly resolute foe of slavery. Willing to print his opponents' views and scarcely the kind of abolitionist who "gnawed the slave's chains with the madman's tooth," Birney had been editor of the *Philanthropist* in Ohio for about seven months when its printing office was wrecked by a Cincinnati mob. His account, which must be taken in part as that of a man speaking in his own cause, relies heavily on reports from antiabolition newspapers in Cincinnati, the *Whig* and the *Republican*.

Meetings, threats, violence, and newspaper editorials had harassed the *Philanthropist* since July 12; on July 23, 1836, a public meeting (of "not more than 1000 persons," Birney said) was held at the Cincinnati Market House. The *Whig*'s report of the meeting starts the account here.

Anti-Abolition Meeting.

At a very large and respectable meeting of the citizens of Cincinnati, convened at the Lower Market House, in pursuance of a public call, on the 23d day of July, 1836, the following proceedings took place—

William Burke was elected President, Morgan Neville Vice President, and Timothy Walker Secretary.

The following preamble and resolutions were then unanimously adopted:

Whereas, The citizens of Cincinnati are now laboring under a serious excitement, in consequence of the existence of an Abolition

Press in this city, from the influence of which, the most deplorable results may be justly apprehended. *And, whereas,* although we deprecate the existence of slavery as a great evil, yet we hold it to be one for which the present generation is not responsible; and disclaiming all right to interfere with the regulations of our sister states on this subject, we regard the conduct of the abolitionists as justly calculated to excite unfriendly dispositions on their part, and thus to effect injuriously our own business and prosperity. *And whereas,* While we recognize the constitutional right of liberty of speech and of the press, in its utmost extent; yet, being anxious to preserve the peace and tranquility of our city, and continue those amicable relations which have hitherto existed between the States, we deem it our duty to utter a warning voice. . . . Be it therefore

Resolved, That the spirit exhibited by the immediate supporters of the abolition press in this city, is entirely at variance with the feelings and opinions of the great mass of our population, is as unjust to our sister states, as it is prejudicial to our own quiet and prosperity.

Resolved, That the establishment of the said abolition press in this city is in direct violation of the solemn pledge heretofore given by its conductor at a public meeting on this subject.

Resolved, That in the opinion of this meeting nothing short of the absolute discontinuance of the publication of the said abolition paper in this city, can prevent a resort to violence, which may be as disastrous to its publisher and supporters, as it must be to the good order and fair fame of our city.

Resolved, That we will use all lawful means to discountenance and suppress every publication in this city which advocates the modern doctrines of abolitionism.

Resolved, That a committee consisting of twelve persons be appointed by the Chair to wait upon James G. Birney and his associates in the publication of the said paper, to remonstrate with them upon the dangerous tendency of the course they are pursuing, to communicate to them the actual tone of public feeling in the city, to request them by every motive of patriotism and philanthropy to desist from the publication of their paper; and to warn them that if they persist, we cannot hold ourselves responsible for the consequences.

The Chair then appointed the following persons as the above

committee, viz: Jacob Burnet, Josiah Lawrence, Robert Buchanan, Nicholas Longworth, John C. Wright, Oliver M. Spencer, David Loring, David T. Disney, Thomas W. Bakewell, Stephen Burrows, John P. Foote, and William Greene.

To whom on motion the officers of this meeting were afterwards added.

It was then resolved that the committee publish the result of their interview, and that these proceedings be published in all the papers in the city.

The following resolution was then offered by Wilson N. Brown, and adopted.

Resolved, That we entertain the most profound respect for the memories of the venerated Patriots of more than "sixty years since" who in the harbor of Boston, *without* the sanction of law, but in the plenitude of the justness of their cause took the responsibility of re-*shipping* the Tea Cargo, and for which illegal act they were entitled to and did receive the warmest thanks and gratitude of every lover of good order and well-wisher of his country—and that we in imitation of the noble and fearless example set us by those true-hearted Americans, declare that whenever we shall find an existing evil—wicked and mischievous in its conceptions—warring against the best interests and happiness of our common country by its effects—aiming at the destruction and disunion of our happy government; and only prompted and sustained by those untiring engines of human ambition hope of gain and love of notoriety—but shielded from legal enactment according to the usual practice of our laws so as to leave us but one channel through which we can rid our fair land from its withering influence, that in seizing that one tangible point our exertions shall be firm, united, and decided.

WILLIAM BURKE, President.
Morgan Neville, Vice President.
Timothy Walker, Secretary.

From the foregoing extracts it would appear, that from the period of the first assault, when by no means *all* the mischief that was *intended* was perpetrated—there was a continued effort to excite the profligate, and to bring them into the usual mobocratic combination—and that to this purpose the *slavery* press of this city prodigally lent its aid, *after the publication by the Mayor*. If there was ever an occasion when those who are called "leading and influential" men might, with honor to themselves and signal benefit to the country, have made a stand, *on principle,* for the integrity of the laws, for the inviolableness of constitutional right, that occasion was now presented. . . .

If the persons constituting the list nominated in the *call* to act as a committee to prepare resolutions for the meeting on Saturday, had, publicly and at once, refused to have any connexion with a proceeding undisguisedly and avowedly in opposition to the laws, there would have been no *meeting*, and if there had been no meeting there would have been no *mob;* for, notwithstanding the auxiliaries of "*wealth* and *respectability,*" it was, at last, a hard matter to strain it up to the point of action. For this purpose, not only the usual stimulant of ardent spirits was resorted to, but the sons of some of the committee-men entered the ranks as *operatives* in the work of demolition. But in this long list of names, the weight of whose influence we do not at all question, there was not found *one* who came out publicly as the advocate of good order, and the upholder of the laws—although, we believe many of them are truly such—notwithstanding *two whole days and more* intervened between the *call* and the *meeting*. In order that you may the better appreciate the influence which this list of names *might* have exerted had they chosen to make the effort, we subjoin a sketch of the occupations and standing of the committee-men afterwards appointed, taken from the Cincinnati Gazette of the 2d August. In addition to what the Gazette says, we add, that EIGHT of the THIRTEEN who *acted* on the committee are members of the Episcopal, Methodist Episcopal, Wesleyan Methodist, New Jerusalem, and Unitarian churches. Here is the extract:

Jacob Burnet—He is known as a man of wealth, a lawyer of the first eminence, a Supreme Judge, a Senator in Congress, a citizen of extensive influence.

Josiah Lawrence—A merchant of high character, and President of the Lafayette Bank.

Robert Buchanan—Also a merchant of high reputation—late President of the Commercial Bank of Cincinnati.

Nicholas Longworth—A lawyer, retired from practice—the most extensive property holder in the city.

Oliver M. Spencer—A Minister of the Methodist Episcopal Church, a man of wealth, and highly esteemed in the city.

David Loring—A large property holder, one of the most enterprising and active business men of the city.

David T. Disney—Has been a member of both Houses of the Ohio Legislature, and Speaker of both; an influential politician, conversant with the interests of the city, and extensively engaged in business.

Thomas W. Bakewell—A wealthy and highly respectable merchant.

John P. Foote and William Green—Gentlemen of Intelligence and wealth, and proprietors of a large stock in the Cincinnati Water Works. No men stand better in society.

William Burke—Postmaster of the city, and a Minister of the Gospel.

Morgan Neville—Known throughout the country, and esteemed wherever he is known.

Timothy Walker—A respectable lawyer; one of the law lecturers in the Cincinnati College. . . .

The next day, July 26th, the following . . . appeared . . . in the Republican. . . .

The ANTI ABOLITION MEETING which took place in this city on Saturday last, was one of the largest, most orderly, and unanimous assemblages we have ever seen in Cincinnati, notwithstanding it was held in a public market house, in a public part of the city, and in the open day. The proceedings were characterized by great moderation. There were no outbreakings; no violations of the public peace or tranquility; which, considering the vastness of the multitude, is as remarkable as it is creditable to our city.

The abolitionists and their croaking friends were industrious during the day and for several days previous, in creating the belief, that the meeting would result in disturbance and riot. . . . The "raw head and bloody bone" stories of *disturbance, riot,* and *disgrace* were laughed at by the major portion of our citizens. The meeting was held in spite of their remonstrances. With regard to the spirit which pervaded those who participated in the proceedings of the meeting, we cannot better illustrate it than by referring to the resolutions which were adopted upon the occasion. These resolutions, though temperate, are nevertheless strong and conclusive. They speak a language that cannot be misunderstood or misrepresented. They declare in so many words that the doctrine of abolition as preached in this city by a few fanatics, will not receive the countenance of Cincinnatians, and that the open and unblushing advocacy of principles so repugnant to the feelings of more than nine tenths of the community, will not be tolerated. The abolitionists in Cincinnati, the Birneys, the Donaldsons, &c. have doubtless received their *last warning*. If their infatuation has not rendered them both blind and deaf, or if they are not perfectly reckless of consequences, they will now come to a halt in their mad career, adopt the advice and heed the warning which we gave them long since.

There are points beyond which public sentiment, even in a free government, may not be trifled with, with impunity. That the abolitionists have arrived at that point in this city, is plainly indicated in the proceedings of the Saturday's anti-abolition meeting. The proceedings of that meeting show a determination to prohibit—"peaceably if they can, but forcibly if they must,"—the distribution of abolition papers in this city, and if needs be, the publication of them too. . . .

[The Market House Committee requested a conference with the Ohio Anti-Slavery Society's executive committee on July 28.] At the time appointed all the members of the Executive Committee who lived in the city, with the exception of Dr. Colby who was called off by a professional emergency, met, it is believed, *twelve* out of *thirteen* who composed the Market House Committee. Judge Burnet, the chairman commenced by giving a long explanation of the manner in which he had been brought into the position he, at present occupied. This being disposed of, he spoke of the high degree of excitement which pervaded a large portion—nineteen twentieths we believe—of the inhabitants of the city. In proof of it he related a conversation he had held with a man apparently of low condition in life, who had accosted him in the street—though altogether unknown to the judge—in tone and phrase dark and mysterious. We will not undertake to give it in the graphic manner in which it was related by the chairman who seemed still to feel the impression, that the mysterious stranger had made on him. We will give only the result—which was that the stranger on parting with the judge said in reference to the destruction of the Philanthropist press, as it was understood, *make haste—(we)—or I am ready to help you.* Judge Burnet professed himself alarmed at the excitement which he believed was in the city—and we do not in the least call in question the sincerity of the declaration, for his whole manner and language gave proof of it. He further stated, that by report, the excitement pervaded not only the city, but that it had gone some distance into the neighborhood; that there were, between Cincinnati and Columbia (6 miles above on the river) 160 men who were banded together, to destroy the Philanthropist establishment—who had their officers appointed—were fully drilled, and ready, at the first signal, to make the onset. He also stated that for four or five miles the excitement had passed into Kentucky, and that the three towns (Covington, Newport, and Cincinnati) were ready, at any moment, to rise for the same purpose. He further represented, that the mob were becoming impatient,—were beginning, from what they supposed was the dilatory conduct of the Committee, to lose confidence in that body, and to suspect them, of rather a favorable leaning towards the object of their hate. . . .

The next point mooted was the *business of the city.* It was on this ground—and on this solely—that the *merits* of the question seemed to be placed. It was asked by us, if rents were not high—houses to rent scarce, real property on the advance—commercial business brisk for the season of the year, and every body—artizan or common laborer—who would work, employed at high wages? All this was admitted—and it did appear to our plain judgments to be evidence of at least as much prosperity as ought to satisfy reasonable men. But it was insisted on the other hand, that this state of things *(in which all were employed at good wages,)* was not the true criterion of prosperity. All this might be true—yet if abolitionism in Cincinnati had prevented the south from sending her orders for even more work than could be executed by the mechanics now here, it had injured the city,—because these very orders would be the means of introducing among us more artizans from other places. In the solidity of this reasoning the gentlemen on the other side, no doubt had entire confidence—but it seemed to us not more conclusive, than that of the Kentucky farmer who undertook to prove to a neighbor that he had lost a hundred calves that spring, by not having, *as he might have had,* a hundred cows to produce them.

It was asked by us, what evidence there was, that the south was withdrawing her business from us because of the existence of abolitionism here? To this it was replied, that it was to be found in various communications and letters from the south. One of the Market House Committee, (Mr. Buchanan) an extensive and prosperous merchant, who has large connections, in the way of business with the south, said the subject had been frequently mentioned to him by his southern correspondents, and that they were now beginning to present the alternative to this city, either to suppress the abolition discussion, or to be content to lose their southern business. He was asked if the Philanthropist or its editor had ever been specified, as items in the complaint. Mr. B. said they had not—he did not know that either of them was particularly known at the south—but the complaint was one of general character, *that the anti-slavery discussion was entertained in Cincinnati. . . .*

The conversation was at length turned to the main object of the meeting—the *discontinuance of the Philanthropist.*—The first suggestions were, that it should be "postponed," or "suspended for a time." All such modified propositions, however, were at length, put aside as useless—and the demand made, of an *absolute discontinuance,* with the certain alternative in case of refusal, of a mob unusual in its numbers, determined in its purpose, and desolating in its ravages. The chairman expressed it as his opinion, that it would be one of unprecedented character—that it would consist of *four or five thousand persons,* bent on the wide destruction of property, and that *two-thirds of the property holders* of the city would join it. That it would be utterly vain for any man or set of men to attempt to restrain it—it would destroy any one who would set himself in opposition to it.

In order to ascertain, what was the temper of the Market House Committee gentlemen, themselves, they were asked, whether *if a mob could be averted* THEY *would be content that the publication of the Philanthropist should be continued?*—The question was scarcely uttered, when the chairman and several of the other members replied unhesitatingly, *they would not. . . .*

The next morning our Committee assembled, and agreed on the following reply to the request of the Market House Committee. It was handed in at the time mentioned in their resolution.

Cincinnati, July 29, 1836.

J. Burnet, Ch. Com.

Sir:—Whilst we feel ourselves constrained altogether to decline complying with your request, as submitted last evening, *to discontinue the Philanthropist,* we think it but just to ourselves, and respectful to our fellow citizens generally, to offer a brief exposition of the reasons that persuade us to this course.

1. We decline complying—not so much from the fear that the particular cause in which our press is employed may be injured—but because compliance involves a tame surrender of the FREEDOM OF THE PRESS—THE RIGHT TO DISCUSS.

2. The Philanthropist is the acknowledged organ of some twelve thousand, or more, of our fellow citizens of Ohio, who believe that slavery, as it exists in our country, is altogether incompatible with the permanency of her institutions; who believe that the *Slavery* of the *South* or the *Liberty* of the *North* must cease to exist; and who intend to do, what in them lies, to bring about a happy and a peaceful termination of the former—and this as speedily as facts, and arguments, and appeals to the consciences and understandings of the slave-holders can be made instrumental to effect it.

3. The Philanthropist is the only journal in this city or neighborhood, through which these facts, and arguments, and appeals can be fully addressed to the community. It has been conducted with fairness and moderation, as may be abundantly proved by the acknowledgements of those who are opposed to its objects. It has invited the slaveholders themselves to the use of its columns for the defence of slavery, and has given up to a republication of their arguments a large share of its space.

To discontinue such a paper under existing circumstances, would be a tacit submission to the exhorbitant demand of the South, that *Slavery* shall never more be mentioned among us.

4. We decline complying with your request—because if it has originated among our own citizens, it is an officious and unasked for intrusion on the business of others—If among the citizens of other States, it is an attempt at dictation as insolent and high-handed on their part, as a tame submission to it would be base and unmanly on ours.

5. We decline complying with your request—because we would not preclude ourselves, and others, from discussing in the most advantageous manner a subject, which, by the acknowledgement of all is of momentous consequence, and which is now occupying the minds of the whole nation.

6. We decline complying—because the demand is virtually the demand of slave-holders, who, having broken down all the safeguards of liberty in their own States, in order that slavery may be perpetuated, are now, for the fuller attainment of the same object, making the demand of us to follow their example.

[The two remaining reasons were omitted—unintentionally, we have no doubt—in the published report of the Market House Committee. They were part of the letter sent to the Market House Committee, and are here supplied.]

[7.] We decline complying—because the attempt is now first made in our case, formally and deliberately to put down the freedom of speech and of the press. *We* are, to be sure, the object of the attack—but there is not a freeman in the State whose rights are not invaded, in any assault which may be made on us, for refusing to succumb to an imperious demand to surrender our rights.

8. We believe, that a large portion of the people of Cincinnati are utterly opposed to the prostration of the liberty of the press—and that there is among us—whatever may be said to the contrary—enough of correct and sober feeling to uphold the laws, if our public officers faithfully discharge their duty.

With these reasons—to which many more might be added, did time permit—we leave the case with you:—expressing, however, our firm conviction, should any disturbance of the peace occur, that you, gentlemen, must be deeply, if not almost entirely, responsible for it, before the bar of sober and enlightened public opinion.

James C. Ludlow,
Isaac Colby,
Wm. Donaldson,
James G. Birney,
Thos. Maylin,
John Melendy,
C. Donaldson,
Gamal. Bailey.

Executive Committee of the Ohio Anti-Slavery Society.

J. Burnet, Chairman, &c. Cincinnati.

Thereupon, the following resolution was unanimously adopted by the [Market House] Committee:

Resolved, That the members of this Committee reluctantly accepted the responsible trust committed to them, with no other motive than the hope of being able to allay the excitement which they believed to exist, and to prevent the violence which they feared might be its result. That, in discharging their duties, they have used all the measures of persuasion and conciliation in their power. That their exertions have not been successful, the above correspondence will show. It only remains, then, in pursuance of their instructions, to publish their proceedings and adjourn without delay. But ere they do this, they owe it to themselves and those whom they represent, to express their utmost abhorrence of every thing like violence; and earnestly to implore their fellow citizens to abstain therefrom.

The Market House Committee . . . forthwith despatched their report . . . to the city papers for publication next morning. The Cincinnati Gazette refused to publish it till Monday, knowing that Saturday, of all days of the week, is the most favorable for a popular disturbance. It was heralded forth in the Republican on Saturday morning. The same morning the Whig, as if a knowledge of the preliminaries to an attack had not been sufficiently disseminated, and there was need of a signal to begin, sounded the charge in the following strain:

"Lay on M'Duff, and d——d be he
Who first cries hold, enough!"

The editor and publisher of the *"Philanthropist,"* the abolition paper in this city, seem to have fully adopted the above aphorism, and to be determined to put the great mass of the people of this city at utter and contemptuous defiance.

We observe that the offensive paper appeared yesterday, *as usual,* bearing upon its front the name of James G. Birney as editor, and A. *Pugh,* as printer. Publishing office corner of Main and Seventh streets.

What has become of Pugh's recent pledge to the public to have nothing to do with the Philanthropist?

Are the abolitionists in this city mad? Will they not take counsel of what has occurred? Or will they persist in contemning public sentiment until they bring upon themselves the excited vengeance of the multitude? Once more we say to them, *pause!*

Nor was even this sufficient. For at 6 o'clock in the evening a *preparatory* meeting was held at the Exchange, at which Joseph Graham presided, and J. A. D. Burrows acted as Secretary—where it was resolved, 1. That the Press should be destroyed, and the types thrown into the street; and 2. That Mr.

Birney should be notified to leave the city in 24 hours. This meeting, composed mostly of well-dressed young men, having the appearance of clerks, store-boys, &c. adjourned to the Texas meeting held in the Court House, at 8 o'clock.

The following account of the subsequent disturbances is taken from the Cincinnati Gazette, and is, we believe in the main, more correct than any other we have seen.

Destruction of Property.

On Saturday night, July 30, very soon after dark, a concourse of citizens assembled at the corner of Main and Seventh streets, in this city, and upon a short consultation, broke open the printing office of the Philanthropist, the abolition paper, scattered the type into the streets, tore down the presses, and completely dismantled the office. It was owned by A. Pugh, a peaceable and orderly printer, who published the Philanthropist for the Anti-Slavery Society of Ohio. From the printing office the crowd went to the house of A. Pugh, where they supposed there were other printing materials, but found none, nor offered any violence. Then to the Messrs. Donaldsons', where ladies only were at home. The residence of Mr. Birney, the editor, was then visited, no person was at home but a youth, upon whose explanations, the house was left undisturbed. A shout was raised for Dr. Colby's, and the concourse returned to Main street, proposing to pile up the contents of the office in the street, and make a bonfire of them. Joseph Graham mounted the pile, and advised against burning it, lest the houses near might take fire. A portion of the press was then dragged down Main street, broken up and thrown into the river. The Exchange was then visited and refreshments taken. After which the concourse again went up Main street to about opposite the Gazette Office. Some suggestions were hinted that it should be demolished, but the hint was overruled. An attack was then made on the residence of some blacks, in Church alley; two guns were fired upon the assailants, and they recoiled. It was supposed that one man was wounded, but that was not the case. It was some time before a rally could be again made, several voices declaring they did not wish to endanger themselves. A second attack was made, the houses were found empty, and their interior contents destroyed.—It was now about midnight, when the party parading down Main street, was addressed by the Mayor, who had been a silent spectator of the destruction of the printing office. He told them they might as well now disperse. A dispersion to a considerable extent followed: but various other disturbances took place through the night, of the magnitude and particulars of which we are not advised.

22. THE ABOLITIONISTS HAVE TAUGHT THE FOLLY OF ATTEMPTING TO CRUSH OPINION BY FORCE

William Ellery Channing, 1836

The great Unitarian minister, William Ellery Channing, was against slavery in every respect but, like many Northern leaders, he was long repelled by the intemperance and extremes of expression among the abolitionists. Profoundly moved by their courage in speaking and printing in the antislavery cause despite repeated violence against them, however, he became increasingly identified with them through the 1830's and gave them his support. Channing's deep understanding of the im-

---

From "The Abolitionists: a Letter to James G. Birney," *Works of William E. Channing, D.D.* (Boston, 1887), pp. 743–750.

portance of freedom of the press and his devastating analysis of the censorial mind appear in this magnificent tribute and admonishment to James G. Birney and the abolitionists, sent to Birney after Channing saw the pamphlet account of the Cincinnati suppression.

Boston, Nov. 1, 1836

My Dear Sir,—I have not the pleasure of knowing you personally; but your history and writings have given me an interest in you, which induces and encourages me to address you with something of the freedom of acquaintance. I feel myself attracted to the friends of humanity and freedom, however distant; and when such are exposed by their principles to peril and loss, and stand firm in the evil day, I take pleasure in expressing to them my sympathy and admiration. The first accounts which reached me of the violence which drove you from Cincinnati, inclined me to write to you; but your "Narrative of those Riotous Proceedings," which I have lately received and read, does not permit me to remain longer silent. The subject weighs much on my mind. I feel that I have a duty to perform in relation to it, and I cannot rest until I yield to this conviction,—till I obey what seems to me the voice of God. I think it best, however, not to confine myself to the outrage at Cincinnati, but to extend my remarks to the spirit of violence and persecution which has broken out against the abolitionists through the whole country. This, I know, will be more acceptable to you than any expression of sympathy with you as an individual. You look beyond yourself to the cause which you have adopted, and to the much-injured body of men with whom you are associated.

It is not my purpose to speak of the abolitionists as abolitionists. They now stand before the world in another character, and to this I shall give my present attention. Of their merits and demerits as abolitionists, I have formerly spoken. In my short work on Slavery, I have expressed my fervent attachment to the great end to which they are pledged, and at the same time my disapprobation, to a certain extent, of their spirit and measures. I have no disposition to travel over this ground again. Had the abolitionists been left to pursue their object with the freedom which is guarantied to them by our civil institutions; had they been resisted only by those weapons of reason, rebuke, reprobation, which the laws allow, I should have no inducement to speak of them again either in praise or censure. But the violence of their adversaries has driven them to a new position. Abolitionism forms an era in our history, if we consider the means by which it has been opposed. Deliberate, systematic efforts have been made, not here or there, but far and wide, to wrest from its adherents that liberty of speech and the press, which our fathers asserted unto blood, and which our national and state governments are pledged to protect as our most sacred right. Its most conspicuous advocates have been hunted and stoned, its meetings scattered, its presses broken up, and nothing but the patience, constancy, and intrepidity of its members has saved it from extinction. The abolitionists then not only appear in the character of champions of the colored race. In their persons the most sacred rights of the white man and the free man have been assailed. They are sufferers for the liberty of thought, speech, and the press; and, in maintaining this liberty amidst insult and violence, they deserve a place among its most honored defenders. In this character I shall now speak of them.

In regard to the methods adopted by the abolitionists of promoting emancipation, I might find much to censure; but when I regard their firm, fearless assertion of the rights of free discussion, of speech and the press, I look on them with unmixed respect. I see nothing to blame, and much to admire. To them has been committed the most important bulwark of liberty, and they have acquitted themselves of the trust like men and Christians. No violence has driven them from their post. Whilst, in obedience to conscience, they have refrained from opposing force to force, they have still persevered, amidst menace and insult, in bearing their testimony against wrong, in giving utterance to their deep convictions. Of such men I do not hesitate to say, that they have rendered to freedom a more essential service than any body of men among us. The defenders of freedom are not those who claim and exercise rights which no one assails, or who win shouts of applause by well-turned compliments to liberty in the days of her triumph. They are those who stand up for rights which mobs, conspiracies, or single tyrants put in jeopardy; who contend for liberty in that particular form which is threatened at the moment by the many or the few. To the abolitionists this honor belongs. The first systematic effort to strip the citizen of freedom of speech they have met with invincible resolution. From my heart I thank them. I am myself their debtor. I am not sure that I should this moment write in safety had they shrunk from the conflict, had they shut their lips, imposed silence on their presses, and hid themselves before their ferocious assailants. I know not where these outrages would have stopped, had they not met resistance from their first destined victims. The newspaper press, with a few exceptions, uttered no genuine indignant rebuke of the wrong-doers, but rather countenancd, by its gentle censures, the reign of force. The mass of the people looked supinely on this new tyranny, under which a portion of their fellow-citizens seemed to be sinking. A tone of denunciation was beginning to proscribe *all* discussion of slavery; and had the spirit of violence, which selected associations as its first objects, succeeded in this preparatory enterprise, it might have been easily turned against any and every individual who might presume to agitate the unwelcome subject. It is hard to say to what outrage the fettered press of the country might not have been reconciled. I thank the abolitionists that, in this evil day, they were true to the rights which the multitude were ready to betray. Their purpose to suffer, to die, rather than surrender their dearest liberties, taught the lawless that they had a foe to contend with whom it was not safe to press, whilst, like all manly appeals, it called forth reflection and sympathy in the better portion of the community. In the name of freedom and humanity, I thank them. Through their courage, the violence, which might have furnished a precedent fatal to freedom, is to become, I trust, a warning to the lawless of the folly as well as crime of attempting to crush opinion by force.

Of all the powers, the last to be intrusted to the multitude of men is that of determining what questions shall be discussed. The greatest truths are often the most unpopular and exasperating; and were they to be denied discussion till the many should be ready to accept them, they would never establish themselves in the general mind. The progress of society depends on nothing more than on the exposure of time-sanctioned abuses, which cannot be touched without offending multitudes, than on the promulgation of principles which are in advance of public sentiment and practice, and which are consequently at war with the habits, prejudices, and immediate interests of large classes of the community. Of consequence, the multitude, if once allowed to dictate or proscribe subjects of discussion, would strike society with spiritual blindness and death. The world is to be carried forward by truth, which at first offends, which wins its way by degrees, which the many hate and would rejoice to crush. The right of free discussion is therefore to be guarded by the friends of mankind with peculiar jealousy. It is at once the most sacred and most endangered of all our rights. He who would rob his neighbor of it, should have a mark set on him as the worst enemy of freedom.

I do not know that our history contains a page more disgraceful to us as freemen than that which records the violences against the abolitionists. As a people, we are chargeable with other and worse misdeeds, but none so flagrantly opposed to the spirit of liberty, the very spirit of our institutions, and of which we make our chief boast. Who, let me ask, are the men whose offences are so aggravated, that they must be denied the protection of the laws, and be given up to the worst passions of the multitude? Are they profligate in principle and life, teachers of impious or servile doctrines, the enemies of God and their race? I speak not from vague rumor, but from better means of knowledge, when I say, that a body of men and women more blameless than the abolitionists in their various relations, or more disposed to adopt a rigid construction of the Christian precepts, cannot be found among us. Of their judiciousness and wisdom I do not speak; but I believe they yield to no party in moral worth. Their great crime, and one which in this land of liberty is to be punished above all crimes, is this, that they carry the doctrine of human equality to its full extent, that they plead vehemently for the oppressed, that they assail wrong-doing however sanctioned by opinion or intrenched behind wealth and power, that their zeal for human rights is without measure, that they associate themselves fervently with the Christians and philanthropists of other countries against the worst relic of barbarous times. Such is the offence against which mobs are arrayed, and which is counted so flagrant, that a summary justice, too indignant to wait for the tardy progress of tribunals, must take the punishment into its own hands.

How strange in a free country, that the men from whom the liberty of speech is to be torn are those who use it in pleading for freedom, who devote themselves to the vindication of human rights! What a spectacle is presented to the world by a republic, in which sentence of proscription is passed on citizens who labor, by addressing men's consciences, to enforce the truth that slavery is the greatest of wrongs! Through the civilized world, the best and greatest men are bearing joint witness against slavery. Christians of all denominations and conditions, rich and poor, learned and ignorant, are bound in a holy league against this most degrading form of oppression. But, in free America, the language which despots tolerate must not be heard. One would think that freemen might be pardoned, if the view of fellow-creatures stripped of all human rights should move them to vehemence of speech. But, whilst on all other subjects the deeply stirred feelings may overflow in earnest remonstrance, on slavery the freemen must speak in whispers, or pay the penalty of persecution for the natural utterance of strong emotion.

I am aware that the outrages on the abolitionists are justified or palliated by various considerations; nor is this surprising; for when did violence ever want excuse? It is said that abolitionism tends to stir up insurrection at the South, and to dissolve the Union. Of all pretences for resorting to lawless force, the most dangerous is the *tendency* of measures or opinions. Almost all men see ruinous tendencies in whatever opposes their particular interests or views. All the political parties which have convulsed our country have seen tendencies to national destruction in the principles of their opponents. So infinite are the connections and consequences of human affairs, that nothing can be done in which some dangerous tendency may not be detected. There is a tendency in arguments against any old establishment to unsettle all institutions, because all hang together. There is a tendency in the laying bare of deep-rooted abuses to throw a community into a storm. Liberty tends to licentiousness, government to despotism. Exclude all enterprises which *may* have evil results, and human life will stagnate. Wise men are not easily deterred by difficulties and perils from a course of action which promises great good. Especially when justice and humanity cry aloud for the removal of an enormous social evil, it is unworthy of men and Christians to let the imagination run riot among possible dangers, instead of rousing every energy of mind to study how the evil may be taken away, and the perils which accompany beneficial changes may be escaped.

As to the charge brought against the abolitionists, of stirring up insurrection at the South, I have never met the shadow of a proof that this nefarious project was meditated by a single member of their body. The accusation is repelled by their characters and principles as well as by facts; nor can I easily conceive of a sane man giving it belief. As to the "tendency" of their measures to this result, it is such only as we have seen to belong to all human affairs, and such as may easily be guarded against. The truth is, that any exposition of slavery, no matter from whom it may come, may chance to favor revolt. It may chance to fall into the hands of a fanatic, who may think himself summoned by heaven to remove violently this great wrong; or it may happen to reach the hut of some intelligent, daring slave, who may think himself called to be the avenger of his race. All things are possible. A casual, innocent remark in conversation, may put wild projects into the unbalanced or disordered mind of some hearer. Must we, then, live in perpetual silence? Do such chances make it our duty to shut our lips on the subject of an enormous wrong, and never to send from the press a reprobation of the evil? The truth is, that the great danger to the slave-holder comes from slavery itself, from the silent innovations of time, from political conflicts and convulsions, and not from the writings of strangers. I readily grant that the abolitionists, in consequence of their number and their systematic and public efforts, are more likely to be heard of by the slave than a solitary individual who espouses his cause. But when I consider how steadily they have condemned the resort to force on the part of the oppressed; when I consider what power the master possesses of excluding incendiary influences, if such are threatened from abroad; when I remember that, during the late unparalleled excitement at the South, not a symptom of revolt appeared; and when to all this I add the strongly manifested purpose of the free States to put forth their power, if required, for the suppression of insurrection, it seems to me that none but the most delicate nerves can be disturbed by the movements of the abolitionists. Can any man, who has a sense of character, affect to believe that the tendency of abolitionism to stir up a servile war is so palpable and resistless as to require the immediate application of force for its suppression, as to demand the substitution of mobs for the action of law, as to justify the violation of the most sacred right of the citizen?

As to the other charge, that the measures of the abolitionists endanger our National Union, and must therefore be put down by any and every means, it is weaker than the former. Against whom has not this charge been hurled? What party among us has not been loaded with this reproach? Do not we at the North almost unanimously believe that the spirit and measures of nullification have a direct and immediate tendency to dissolve the Union? But are we therefore authorized to silence the nullifier by violence? Should a leader of that party travel among us, is he to be mobbed? Let me further ask, how is it that the abolitionists endanger the Union? The only reply which I have heard is, that they exasperate the South. And is it a crime to exasperate men? Who then so criminal as the Founder and primitive teachers of our faith? Have we yet to learn that, in cases of exasperation, the blame is as apt to lie with those who take, as with those who occasion, offence? How strange the doctrine, that men are to be proscribed for uttering language which gives offence, are to be outlawed for putting their neighbors into a passion! Let it also be considered that the abolitionists are not the only people who exasperate the South. Can the calmest book be written on slavery without producing the same effect? Can the Chief Justice of Massachusetts expound the constitution and laws of that Commonwealth according to their free spirit, and of course in opposition to slavery, without awakening indignation? Is not the doctrine, that Congress has the right of putting an end to slavery in the District of Columbia, denounced as fiercely as the writings and harangues of abolitionists? Where, then, shall mobs stop, if the crime of exasperating the South is so heinous as to deserve their vengeance? If the philanthropist and Christian must be silenced on the subject of slavery, lest they wound the sensitive ears of the South, ought the judge and legislator to be spared? Who does not see that these apologies for lawless force, if they have any validity, will bring every good man under its iron sway?

In these remarks you learn my abhorrence of the violence offered to the abolitionists, and my admiration of the spirit they have opposed to it. May they vindicate to the end the rights which in their persons have been outraged! Allow me now to express my earnest desire and hope that the abolitionists will maintain the liberty of speech and the press, not only by asserting it firmly, but by using it wisely, deliberately, generously, and under the control of the severest moral principle. It is my earnest desire that they will exercise it in the spirit of Christians and philanthropists, with a supreme love of truth, without passion or bitterness, and without that fanaticism which cannot discern the true proportions of things, which exaggerates or distorts whatever favors or conflicts with its end, which sees no goodness except in its own ranks, which shuts itself up in one object, and is blind to all besides. Liberty suffers from nothing more than from licentiousness, and I fear that abolitionists are not to be absolved from this abuse of it. It seems to me that they are particularly open to one reproach. Their writings have been blemished by a spirit of intolerance, sweeping censure, and rash, injurious judgment. I do not mean to bring this charge against all their publications. Yours, as far as I have seen them, are an honorable exception; and others, I know, deserve the same praise. But abolitionism, in the main, has spoken in an intolerant tone, and in this way has repelled many good minds, given great advantage to its opponents, and diminished the energy and effect of its appeals. I should rejoice to see it purified from this stain. . . .

For . . . selfish opponents of abolitionism, I make no apology. Let them be visited with just rebuke. But they, after all, form but a small part of that great body in the free States who look on the present antislavery movement with distrust and disapprobation. The vast majority in the free States, who refuse communion with you, are not actuated by base considerations. The fear of a servile war, the fear of political convulsions, a perception of the difficulties of great social changes, self-distrust, a dread of rashness, these and the like motives have great influence in deterring multitudes from giving their countenance to what seem to them violent movements for the abolition of slavery. That a culpable insensibility to the evils and wrongs of this nefarious institution is too common in the class of which I now speak, I do not mean to deny. Still, how vast a proportion of the intelligence, virtue, and piety of the country is to be found in their ranks! To speak of them slightly, contemptuously, bitterly, is to do great wrong, and such speaking, I fear, has brought much reproach on abolitionism.

The motives which have induced me to make this long communication to you will not, I trust, be misunderstood. I earnestly desire, my dear Sir, that you and your associates will hold fast the right of free discussion by speech and the press, and, at the same time, that you will exercise it as Christians, and as friends of your race. That you, Sir, will not fail in these duties, I rejoice to believe. Accept my humble tribute of respect and admiration for your disinterestedness, for your faithfulness to your convictions, under the peculiar sacrifices to which you have been called. It is my prayer that, by calm, fearless perseverance in well-doing, you may guide and incite many to a like virtue.

It may be said that it is easy for one living, as I do, at a distance from danger, living in prosperity and ease, to preach exposure and suffering to you and your friends. I can only say in reply, that I lay down no rule for others which I do not feel to be binding on myself. What I should do in the hour of peril may be uncertain; but what I ought to do is plain. What I desire to do is known to the Searcher of all hearts. It is my earnest desire that prosperity may not unnerve me, that no suffering may shake my constancy in a cause which my heart approves. I sometimes indeed fear for myself, when I think of untried persecutions. I know not what weaknesses the presence of great danger may call forth. But, in my most deliberate moments, I see nothing worth living for but the divine virtue which endures and surrenders all things for truth, duty, and mankind. I look on reproach, poverty, persecution, and death, as light evils compared with unfaithfulness to pure and generous principles, to the spirit of Christ, and to the will of God. With these impressions, I ought not to be deterred by self-distrust, or by my distance from danger, from summoning and cheering others to conflict with evil. Christianity, as I regard it, is designed throughout to fortify us for this warfare. Its great lesson is self-sacrifice. Its distinguishing spirit is divine philanthropy suffering on the cross. The cross, the cross, this is the badge and standard of our religion. I honor all who bear it. I look with scorn on the selfish greatness of this world, and with pity on the most gifted and prosperous in the struggle for office and power; but I look with reverence on the obscurest man who suffers for the right, who is true to a good but persecuted cause.

With these sentiments, I subscribe myself your sincere friend,

William E. Channing.

23. SKETCH OF THE LIFE OF WILLIAM S. BAILEY, ANTISLAVERY EDITOR

Himself, 1856

William S. Bailey published newspapers of antislavery sentiments in Newport, Kentucky, for nine years, surviving economic reprisals and one destructive visitation from a mob, and existing

From *National Anti Slavery Standard*, Aug. 16, 1856.

in part on the help of abolitionists from across the Ohio river. The second mobbing of his shop, in 1859, put him finally out of business. Here he tells his story, written for the *New York Evening Post* and reprinted in the *National Anti Slavery Standard.*

I was born in the State of Ohio. I am a cotton machinist, and steam engine builder by trade. Established a machine shop in Newport, Kentucky, on the lot where I now live, and which I purchased for a home residence in 1839. While engaged in the machine business, a Mr. Ryan commenced the publication of a small daily paper in that place, and called it *The Newport Daily News.* He continued the publication of it about six weeks, during which time I, with others, wrote some articles for his paper. He complained, after some of my articles were published, that they were too radically liberal for a slave State, and that they had injured his paper, and finally urged upon me to buy him out.

This was a new idea to me; the thought of an iron worker to lay down the hammer and cold-chisel, and to forsake the anvil and vice, and take up the pen, was a startling reflection to me. But I saw an independent press was needed for our place, and the mechanics and working-men of my acquaintance favoured the new idea; and not feeling satisfied that Mr. Ryan should say I had injured his prospects, I purchased his type and press at $650, and put them in the upper story of my machine shop, a large two-story frame building. I increased the size of the paper, and on the 7th day of March, 1850, we issued the first paper, placing for our motto the words, "LIBERTY AND EQUALITY."

This, with what I had before written, caused a sort of zealous inquiry amongst the officers of the law and Doctors of Divinity as to who this Bailey was and what he was about. We, however, gave the general news of the day and went on to encourage public improvements, industry and education; with now and then a good article, showing slavery to be the greatest curse to our general prosperity. (Newport is older than Cincinnati, but is a mere handful compared with the Queen City of free Ohio.)

We employed from seven to eight compositors, two reporters and a proof reader, the first year, and, during that time, all that would "take a jovial glass" and loiter away their time had money furnished them for that end, by our "sharp-sighted" opponents, who thought they saw a tornado of liberty brewing in territory consecrated to bondage and endless oppression, and took that plan to confuse and spoil the interest of our paper, leaving copy half set up and but little ready for the paper. This caused us to call the attention of our daughters and wife to the composing stick, who, with our own aid, managed to get the paper to press towards daylight in the morning on all such occasions.

Finally, when the craft began to find out that we could patch things together and bring out the paper at its regular time, a majority of them clubbed together and passed a resolution that the girls should not set type in the office, as it would injure the craft, and bring its members into contempt. We expostulated with them, and asked only for steadiness and punctuality on their part; and, at this time, found out they had been told that the paper did not fill the wishes of the leading men of Newport —that it opposed the institutions of the State (the "peculiar institution"), and that such a paper was not wanted there.

We soon found that it was useless to employ printers to be thrown into the hands of a wealthy faction and there tutored to defeat the object for which they were employed. So, after consulting our own family, we concluded it was time for us to pass a resolution also, which was "that no more printers should be employed in our office until the influence of our opponents was destroyed." Then girls and boys (four daughters and two sons), wife and self all "pitched in," to the number of eight, all told; leaving the machine-shop entirely to the care of a few hands until the work engaged was completed; after which, we found it expedient to shut it up altogether, having no time to direct the action of the workmen.

Meantime, our little store, containing $800 worth of groceries, was completely run down, the income from the paper being small, owing to the active opposition of our opponents; for it was their custom to watch the advertisements every morning (obtained by our little daughter, then but ten years old), by going into Cincinnati, and stating to the advertisers that they, the influential Kentuckians, would purchase nothing from any house that advertised in the Newport *News*—that they (the advertisers) were indirectly at war with the most respectable and wealthy citizens of Kentucky by supporting such a sheet, and that they would find it to their interest to have nothing to do with it.

This course of action was mortifying to us, and we resolved to issue a weekly paper also, to let the country people know something of the actions of these heartless men. So, on the 4th of August, 1851, having obtained about fifty subscribers, we issued *The Kentucky Weekly News,* in which, as well as the daily paper, we showed up the actions of lazy drones and despots by name, and contrasted them with the industrious working-men of our State. This drew out the sunburnt masses with hardened hands from the sleek and ruddy faces of ease and leisure, and caused them to stand upon the side of Bailey, their fellow-workman and unflinching advocate of equal rights.

The next thing was to try the law of *might* against *right;* but in this they soon found they would be overpowered in numbers, and they shrank from the encounter. What to do they could not tell. "The d——d fools would continue to read Bailey's paper," and another press must be brought to bear against him; this was the word from the "upper ten." The weekly paper had increased its circulation, from the 4th of August to the 6th of October, to about three hundred, and about 1 o'clock of that morning (6th of October, 1851) the whole concern was in flames, having been set on fire in the night by some base incendiary.

Not only the first type and press purchased of Ryan were lost, but a new font and a new press for the weekly sheet, amounting to $1,600 in addition; which, with the machine-shop, blacksmith shop and screw machinery, were all destroyed, and my lot, with a handsome grape bower and valuable fruit trees, &c., all laid waste to the cattle and hogs in the town. Then were deep anguish and sorry hearts in my family. Our clothing and bedding nearly all destroyed; for, having to work night and day, we were obliged to have our bedding in the office to take rest when we could.

On the same morning, after sunrise, while the blue vapour was rising through the beds of burning coals, came Mr. Samuel Pike, editor of the Maysville (Ky.) *Flag*, a strong pro-slavery man, in company with some of his friends. They viewed the ruins awhile, and then walked off up town, with a subscription paper to raise $1,000 to bring his press, &c., from Maysville to Newport, to build himself up upon my ruins. As soon as this was ascertained, it increased the sorrow and indignation of my friends, and they came and consulted with me, and I agreed to start again with their aid. So they raised me $517 in cash within four days, which I paid on the purchase of two new presses, larger than the others, and a sufficiency of type, job letter, &c., amounting to $2,000. This we put into the house where we lived, and got started again in six weeks after the fire; and in a day or two after that, Mr. Pike started his pro-slavery battery (a Daily and Weekly also) against me.

The conflict was sharp and the excitement great, but in three short months his paper and his friends turned against him indignant, and refusing to pay the money they had subscribed, the lack of which had caused him to yield the ground. By this time two more of our daughters (little ones) became pretty active in setting type, and our paper continued to increase in circulation, but we could not make money fast enough to pay the debts then due on the type, and my notes found their way into the hands of my opponents, and the iron law was set in force against me. Friends were looked for in vain among the officers of the law, and my property (house and lot) was sold to pay the debts—for I was resolved not to give up the types and presses.

Pike finally went to Covington, in the adjoining County, and there continued his persecution by his paper. Another, called the *Star,* joined him against me, but both died out. The *Democratic Union,* another pro-slavery sheet in Covington, also died. Another was started against me in Newport, called the *Messenger,* in which all the pens of the Slave Power and lawyers combined were turned against me, but it only lived about eighteen months; it was a tri-weekly. We still continued our regular course of *reason* and *righteousness,* condemning the Slave Power by the perfidy of its own acts, and showing that it had no friendship in common with the toiling millions, white or black, and that they warred against themselves by encouraging ignorance, chains and slavery.

Another pro-slavery paper was started in Newport, called *The Roll,* a perfect fire-eater, in which heaven and earth were moved to gain a victory over the *News,* but it soon *rolled* overboard, and that ended the pro-slavery presses in Newport. There were two others started in Covington, the city joining Newport, Ky., on the west. One was called *The Garland* and the other *The American Sentinel,* both pro-slavery, but more mild; they, too, have gone to the tombs. In the meantime we were sued for $20,000 for telling the truth on a bad man (J. A. Piner, high sheriff of Campbell County, Ky.). He had taken money fraudulently, and came out of court without receiving *one cent* for his character. But it cost us $300 to defend the suit. These things, together with the new printing-house—one that they cannot burn down, and which cost $1,500—have kept us in the background, and crippled our efforts to set Kentucky free.

We have paid in costs, by the various suits brought

against me, about	$800
First type and press	650
Additional new type and press, before fire	1,600
The last new lot since the fire	2,000
Loss in buildings and tools by the fire	3,000
New Printing-house	1,500
	$9,550
In addition to this has been our yearly labour, say four years at $2,000	$8,000
	$17,550

We have now ten children that can set type. Three of the girls, I think, are without a superior for speed. All have tasted the effects of slavery, and feel resolved to banish it from Kentucky, and never cease to encourage its overthrow everywhere. We now issue twenty-eight hundred weeklies and five hundred dailies. Our own family is giving from fifty to sixty dollars a week, in labour, to the cause of freedom in the United States.

WM. S. BAILEY.

The Mails

In 1835 Southern opinion was convulsed at the mailing of a deluge of abolitionist literature to Southerners by the antislavery societies of the North. Violent reaction broke out in Charleston,

South Carolina, where the arrival on July 29, 1835, of a mail steamer carrying the literature of emancipation, aroused a mob. It broke into the post office, seized and burned the abolitionist material, and gave the signal to the South to establish a vigilance-committee censorship of the mails that persisted until the war. What John Quincy Adams called "the seizure of the mail by a mob of southern gentlemen in co-operation with the postmaster" was followed by hundreds of censorships by other communities.

Charleston's Postmaster Huger wrote to Postmaster General Amos Kendall, saying that he was detaining abolitionist material pending instructions. Kendall, his sympathies in the matter entirely with the South but his understanding of his legal powers realistic, answered that "I cannot sanction, and will not condemn the step you have taken." During the following eleven months, Kendall, President Jackson, and John C. Calhoun were among those who actively sought a federal law that would prevent mailed abolitionist materials from reaching addresses in the South. A great Congressional debate followed: Daniel Webster, Henry Clay, and others offered stirring oratory in defense of freedom of the press, and Congress passed a bill in July 1836 that was precisely the reverse of what Jackson and Kendall sought.

But so far as the South was concerned, the President's and the Postmaster General's spirit prevailed: censorship of the mails by local postmasters and vigilance committees continued as a matter of course. And more than twenty years later, effective nullification of the federal law with the participation of postmasters was resoundingly approved in official statements of Attorney General Caleb Cushing and Postmaster General J. Holt.

24. THE POSTMASTER GENERAL WILL NOT CONDEMN THE DELAY OF THE MAILS

Amos Kendall, 1835

Official concurrence in the administrative control of the kinds of words that will be delivered by the United States mails may be said to start here in Postmaster General Amos Kendall's letter to Postmaster Huger of Charleston, South Carolina.

Post office department, August 4th, 1835.

P.M. Charleston, S.C.

Sir: In your letter of the 29th ult. just received, you inform me that by the steamboat mail from New York your office had been filled with pamphlets and tracts upon slavery; that the public mind was highly excited upon the subject; that you doubted the safety of the mail itself out of your possession; that you had determined, as the wisest course, to detain these papers; and now you ask instructions from the department.

Upon a careful examination of the law, I am satisfied that the postmaster general has no legal authority to exclude newspapers from the mail, nor prohibit their carriage or delivery on account of their character or tendency, real or supposed. Prob-

---

Letter of Amos Kendall to postmaster at Charleston, S. C., August 4, 1835, *Niles' Register,* XLVIII (1835), 448.

ably, it was not thought safe to confer on the head of an executive department a power over the press, which might be perverted and abused.

But I am not prepared to direct you to forward or deliver the papers of which you speak. The post office department was created to serve the people of *each* and *all* of the *United States*, and not be used as the instrument of their *destruction*. None of the papers detained have been forwarded to me, and I cannot judge for myself of their character and tendency; but you inform me, that they are, in character, "the most inflammatory and incendiary—and insurrectionary in the highest degree."

By no act, or direction of mine, official or private, could I be induced to aid, knowingly, in giving circulation to papers of this description, directly or indirectly. We owe an obligation to the laws, but a higher one to the communities in which we live, and if the *former* be perverted to destroy the *latter*, it is patriotism to disregard them. Entertaining these views, I cannot sanction, and will not condemn the step you have taken.

Your justification must be looked for in the character of the papers detained, and circumstances by which you are surrounded.

25. NO TWOPENNY POSTMASTER SHOULD JUDGE WHAT SHOULD BE CIRCULATED

William Leggett, 1835

Only a handful of the newspapers in the nation took exception of any kind to the Postmaster General's approving a form of censorship of the mails. However, William Leggett, the brilliant if often rash editor of the *New York Evening Post,* saw the significance of Kendall's letter and attacked it in the following editorial.

. . . We cannot refrain from . . . an expression of our surprise and regret that Mr. Kendall, in an official communication, should have expressed such sentiments as this extraordinary letter contains. If, according to his ideas of the duties of patriotism, every postmaster may constitute himself a judge of the laws, and suspend their operation whenever, in his supreme discretion, it shall seem proper, we trust Mr. Kendall may be permitted to retire from a post where such opinions have extensive influence, and enjoy his notions of patriotism in a private station. A pretty thing it is, to be sure, when the head officer of the Post Office establishment of the United States, and a member, *ex officio,* of the Administration of the General Government, while he confesses in one breath that he has no legal power to prevent the carriage or delivery of any newspaper,

From *New York Evening Post,* Aug. 12, 1835.

whatever be the nature of its contents, declares in the very next, that by no act of his will he aid, directly or indirectly, in circulating publications of an incendiary and inflammatory character. Who gives him a right to judge what is incendiary and inflammatory? Was there any reservation of that sort in his oath of office?

Mr. Kendall has not met the question presented by recent occurrences at the South, as boldly and manfully as we should have supposed he would. He has quailed in the discharge of his duty. He has truckled to the domineering pretensions of the slave-holders. In the trepidation occasioned by his embarrassing position, he has lost sight of the noble maxim, *fiat justitia ruat cœlum*. The course which, by neither sanctioning nor condemning the unlawful conduct of the postmaster at Charleston, he has virtually authorized him and the other postmasters at the South to pursue, is neither more nor less than practical nullification. It is worse than that: it is establishing a *censorship of the press* in its worst possible form, by allowing every twopenny postmaster through the country to be the judge of what species of intelligence it is proper to circulate, and what to withhold from the people. A less evil than this drew forth, in former days, the Areopagitica from the master mind of Milton; but we little dreamed that new arguments in favour of the freedom of speech and of the press would ever become necessary in our country.

We are sorry to say that this letter of Mr. Kendall has materially diminished the very high respect we have heretofore entertained for him. It shows a deficiency of courage and independence which we did not expect to see him betray.

26. MAILING INFLAMMATORY APPEALS TO THE PASSIONS OF SLAVES SHOULD BE STOPPED BY LAW

Andrew Jackson, 1835

President Jackson's seventh annual message to Congress, made on December 7, 1835, contained the since-famous appeal for a censorship of the mails. With most of the South, Jackson believed that the abolitionist societies were addressing their materials to slaves and were seeking to incite the slaves to insurrection—beliefs that the abolitionists, try as they might, were never able to eradicate.

. . . In connection with these provisions in relation to the Post-Office Department, I must also invite your attention to the painful excitement produced in the South by attempts to circulate through the mails inflammatory appeals addressed to the passions of the slaves, in prints and in various sorts of publications, calculated to stimulate them to insurrection and to produce all the horrors of a servile war. There is doubtless no respectable portion of our countrymen who can be so far misled as to feel any other sentiment than that of indignant regret at conduct so destructive of the harmony and peace of the country, and so repugnant to the principles of our national

From Richardson, James D., *Messages and Papers of the Presidents,* (Bureau of National Literature, 1913), II, 1,394–1,395.

compact and to the dictates of humanity and religion. Our happiness and prosperity essentially depend upon peace within our borders, and peace depends upon the maintenance in good faith of those compromises of the Constitution upon which the Union is founded. It is fortunate for the country that the good sense, the generous feeling, and the deep-rooted attachment of the people of the nonslaveholding States to the Union and to their fellow-citizens of the same blood in the South have given so strong and impressive a tone to the sentiments entertained against the proceedings of the misguided persons who have engaged in these unconstitutional and wicked attempts, and especially against the emissaries from foreign parts who have dared to interfere in this matter, as to authorize the hope that those attempts will no longer be persisted in. But if these expressions of the public will shall not be sufficient to effect so desirable a result, not a doubt can be entertained that the nonslaveholding States, so far from countenancing the slightest interference with the constitutional rights of the South, will be prompt to exercise their authority in suppressing so far as in them lies whatever is calculated to produce this evil.

In leaving the care of other branches of this interesting subject to the State authorities, to whom they properly belong, it is nevertheless proper for Congress to take such measures as will prevent the Post-Office Department, which was designed to foster an amicable intercourse and correspondence between all members of the Confederacy, from being used as an instrument of an opposite character. The General Government, to which the great trust is confided of preserving inviolate the relations created among the States by the Constitution, is especially bound to avoid in its own action anything that may disturb them. I would therefore call the special attention of Congress to the subject, and respectfully suggest the propriety of passing such a law as will prohibit, under severe penalties, the circulation in the Southern States, through the mail, of incendiary publications intended to instigate the slaves to insurrection.

27. NULLIFICATION OF THE FEDERAL POSTAL LAW

Postmaster General J. Holt, 1859

John Brown's raid at Harper's Ferry sent a new wave of apprehension over the South in 1859, and to Charles Orton, postmaster at Falls Church, Virginia, "incendiary papers" arriving at his office for distribution were newly threatening. The federal postal law of 1836 forbade his delaying delivery, but Virginia's statute forbade delivery. He appealed to Postmaster General J. Holt, who without a quiver upheld nullification of the federal law as laid out in a decision of Attorney General Caleb Cushing two years earlier.

Post Office Department, December 5, 1859.

Sir: I am in receipt of your letter of the 2d instant in which, after referring to the opinion of the attorney-general of Virginia sustaining the constitutionality of the statute of that State denouncing under heavy penalties the circulation of books, newspapers, pamphlets, etc., tending to incite the slave population to insurrection, you ask to be instructed as to your duty in reference to such documents should they be received through the mails for distribution at the post-office of which you have charge.

From *Congressional Record,* 53 Cong., 2 Sess., XXVI, Part IX, Appendix Part I, p. 4 (1894).

The statute alluded to is in the following words:

SEC. 23. If a free person write, or print, or cause to be written or printed any book or other thing with intent to advise or incite negroes in this State to rebel or make insurrection, or inculcating resistance to the rights of property of masters in their slaves, or if he shall with intent to aid the purposes of any such book or writing knowingly circulate the same, he shall be confined in the penitentiary not less than one nor more than five years.

SEC. 24. If a postmaster or deputy postmaster know that any such book or other writing has been received at his office in the mail, he shall give notice thereof to some justice who shall inquire into the circumstances and have such book or writing burned in his presence. And if it appears to him that the person to whom it was directed, subscribed therefor, knowing its character, or agreed to receive it for circulation to aid the purposes of abolitionists, the justice shall commit such person to jail.

If any postmaster or deputy postmaster violate this section he shall be fined not exceeding $200.

The point raised by your inquiry is whether this statute is in conflict with the act of Congress regulating the administration of this Department which declared that "if any postmaster shall unlawfully detain in his office any letter, package, pamphlet, or newspaper with the intent to prevent the arrival and delivery of the same to the person or persons to whom such package, letter, pamphlet, or newspaper may be addressed or directed, in the usual course of the transportation of the mail along the route, he shall, on conviction thereof, be fined in a sum not exceeding $500 and imprisoned for a term not exceeding six months, and shall, moreover, be forever thereafter incapable of holding the office of postmaster in the United States."

The question thus presented was fully decided by Attorney-General Cushing in the case of the Yazoo City post-office. (Opinion of Attorney-General, volume 8, page 489.) He there held that a statute of Mississippi in all respects analogous to that of Virginia, as cited, was not inconsistent with the act of

Congress quoted prescribing the duties of postmasters in regard to the delivery of mail matter, and that the latter as good citizens were bound to yield obedience to such State laws. You are referred to the luminous discussion of the case, for the arguments urged by that distinguished civilian in the support of the conclusion at which he arrived. The judgment thus pronounced has been cheerfully acquiesced in by the Department, and is recognized as one of the guides of its administration. The authority of Virginia to enact such a law rests upon that right of self-preservation which belongs to every government and people, and which has never been surrendered, nor indeed can it be. One of the most solemn constitutional obligations imposed upon the Federal Government is that of protecting the States against "insurrection" and "domestic violence."

Of course none of its instrumentalities can be lawfully employed in inciting even in the remotest degree to this very crime which involves in its train all others and with the suppression of which it is specially charged. You must under the responsibilities resting upon you as an officer and as a citizen determine whether the books, pamphlets, newspapers, etc. received by you for distribution are of the incendiary character described in the statute, and if you believe they are, then you are not only not obliged to deliver them to those to whom they are addressed, but you are empowered and required by your duty to the State of which you are a citizen to dispose of them in strict conformity to the provisions of the law referred to.

The people of Virginia may not only forbid the introduction and dissemination of such documents within their borders, but if brought there in the mails, they may by appropriate legal proceedings have them destroyed. They have the same right to extinguish firebrands thus impiously hurled into the midst of their houses and altars that a man has to pluck the burning fuse from a bombshell which is about to explode at his feet.

Part Five

FREEDOM IN LEASH: WARTIME COMPROMISES

Civil War

28. THE WEB OF CONTROLS

1861

The Northern press had vast freedom during the Civil War: freedom to criticize civil leaders and generals, to canvass the direction and success of the war effort, and even to urge abandoning the pursuit of war. Yet time after time, toleration of "Copperhead" newspapers ended in explosions of suppression or punishment carried out by government or people, and probably no other war has brought as many instances of restraint of the

---

From *American Annual Cyclopaedia and Register of Important Events* (D. Appleton and Company, 1867), I, 328–330.

American press. An account of the instruments of control and some indication of their widespread use in the year 1861 appeared in the first volume of the *American Annual Cyclopaedia.*

Freedom of the Press

A weekly newspaper, called the "Democratic Standard," published at Concord, New Hampshire, was attacked by a mob of soldiers on the 8th of August, and the office completely stripped of its contents. The soldiers belonged to the First Regiment of returned volunteers. An article was published in the paper which reflected upon them. A retraction was demanded, and refused defiantly.

On the 12th of August, the office of the "Democrat," a weekly newspaper, published at Bangor, Maine, was completely cleared by a crowd of people. No one was injured. The objections against the print by the people were that its views favored the Confederate States.

On the 14th of August, Gen. Fremont declared martial law in St. Louis, and appointed Major J. McKinstry provost-marshal. On the next day the marshal suppressed the publication of the "War Bulletin," and the "Missourian," two newspapers published in that city, which had been, as it was charged, "shamelessly devoted to the publication of transparently false statements respecting military movements in Missouri."

On the 24th of August, the editor of the St. Louis "Christian Advocate" addressed a letter to Marshal McKinstry, stating that he had been informed suggestions were made to him to suppress the publication of the "Advocate," &c.

To this, on the next day, the marshal replied: "In reference to the course of the St. Louis 'Christian Advocate,' permit me to say that in my judgment, in these times of political excitement, and heated discussion, and civil war, it would be more becoming, as well as more consistent, that a public newspaper, belonging to and advocating the doctrines and principles of the Church of Christ, should abstain from publishing articles of a political character, calculated to inflame the passions of men, and evidently hostile to the Government of the country.

"Let your journal be a religious paper, as it professes to be, and it will never come under the discipline of this department."

On the 20th of August, the office of the "Sentinel," a weekly paper, published at Easton, Pa., was destroyed. The alleged motive was stated to be, that this paper had printed a series of resolutions, passed at a democratic county convention, which were regarded as not truly loyal.

On the same night, Ambrose S. Kimball, editor of the "Essex County Democrat," published once a week, at Haverhill, Mass., was violently taken from his house by an excited crowd, and refusing to give such information as was demanded of him, "he was covered with a coat of tar and feathers, and ridden on a rail through the town." He subsequently was made to take an oath that he would "never again write or publish articles against the North and in favor of secession."

About the same time the printing office of the "Jeffersonian," a weekly paper, published at Westchester, Pa., was destroyed.

On the 16th day of August, the Grand Jury, impanelled for the Circuit Court of the United States for the Southern District of New York, brought into court the following document, asking if certain newspapers could be indicted.

New York, August 16, 1861.

The Grand Inquest of the United States of America for the Southern District of New York, beg leave to present the following facts to the Court, and ask its advice thereon:

There are certain newspapers within this district which are in the frequent practice of encouraging the rebels now in arms against the Federal Government by expressing sympathy and agreement with them, the duty of acceding to their demands, and dissatisfaction with the employment of force to overcome them. These papers are the New York daily and weekly "Journal of Commerce," the daily and weekly "News," the daily and weekly "Day Book," the "Freeman's Journal," all published in the city of New York, and the daily and weekly "Eagle," published in the city of Brooklyn. The first-named of these has just published a list of newspapers in the Free States opposed to what it calls "the present unholy war"—a war in defence of our country and its institutions, and our most sacred rights, and carried on solely for the restoration of the authority of the Government.

The Grand Jury are aware that free governments allow liberty of speech and of the press to their utmost limit, but there is, nevertheless, a limit. If a person in a fortress or an army were to preach to the soldiers submission to the enemy, he would be treated as an offender. Would he be more culpable than the citizen who, in the midst of the most formidable conspiracy and rebellion, tells the conspirators and rebels that they are right, encourages them to persevere in resistance, and condemns the effort of loyal citizens to overcome and punish them as an "unholy war?" If the utterance of such language in the streets or through the press is not a crime, then there is a great defect in our laws, or they were not made for such an emergency.

The conduct of these disloyal presses is, of course, condemned and abhorred by all loyal men; but the Grand Jury will be glad to learn from the Court that it is also subject to indictment and condign punishment.

All which is respectfully presented.

CHARLES GOULD, Foreman.

It is a singular instance of the excitement of the public mind that this document, which simply asks the judge if the press could be indicted, was universally regarded as an indictment.

The clear charge made by Judge Betts to this jury when they were impanelled, placed the question beyond all doubt; and the wording of the document brought in, shows clearly that the jury so understood it. The Judge turned the matter over to the October term, when it was dismissed. The resulting excitement was very great, and on the 22d of August, six days after, Marshal Milward of Philadelphia seized the papers sent from certain New York offices, named in the paper of the Grand Jury, for circulation to their subscribers; on the same day the following order was issued:

Post-Office Department, August 22, 1861.

SIR: The Postmaster-General directs that from and after your receipt of this letter none of the newspapers published in New York city, "which were lately presented by the Grand Jury" as dangerous for their disloyalty, shall be forwarded in the mails. I am respectfully, your obedient servant,

T. P. TROTT, Chief Clerk.

To Postmaster New York City.

Thus the authorities at Washington regarded the action of the Grand Jury as a presentment, and incurred [*sic*] the severe penalties of the post-office laws by excluding the newspapers indicated from the mails.

In consequence of these measures the "Journal of Commerce" changed its editors, and was allowed to circulate through the mails. The publication of the "News" and "Daybook" was stopped, and the "Freeman's Journal" changed its name.

On the 22d of September the Grand Jury of the United States District Court at Trenton, N. Jersey, brought into Court the following presentment:

The Grand Jury came into the United States Court on the 22d, and made a lengthy presentment that complaints have been made before this Grand Inquest concerning certain newspapers published in this State and copies of the following papers, issued during the last few months, have been submitted and carefully examined; namely, the Newark "Evening Journal," the Warren "Journal," the Hunterdon "Democrat," the New Brunswick "Times" and Plainfield "Gazette;" that during the most critical period, while the capital of the nation has been besieged by armed insurgents; while eleven States in actual rebellion, having been striving by invasion and treachery to plunge other States still remaining loyal into open opposition to the National Government, these newspapers have been, up to within a very recent period, persistently denouncing and libelling those to whom this great duty of national defence is necessarily intrusted, in thwarting their efforts for self-preservation, and fomenting rebellion by discouraging and opposing the only means by which it can be put down. While they cherish a due regard for freedom of speech, they feel it their duty to repudiate and denounce the conduct of those journals; that while the press may freely criticize public men and measures in the peaceful contests of party, yet in a war for the life of a nation the press, as well as individuals, should uphold the existing Government, or be treated as its enemies. They consider their duty freely discharged in reference to these newspapers by this presentment, leaving them to the wholesome action of public opinion. They recommend all loyal citizens, all public officers, all municipal corporations, rigorously to withhold all patronage from such newspapers as do not hereafter give their unqualified support to the National Government.

The jurors were then discharged for the term.

Later in the year the "Franklin Gazette," published in Franklin County, New York, was suppressed, and its editor sent to Fort Lafayette, as a State prisoner.

The "Herald," a daily paper, published at Cleveland, Ohio, defended Gen. Fremont from the reports circulating for a time against him, and espoused his cause with earnestness. The packages of this paper were ordered to be taken away from the cars of one of the railroads in the State of Ohio. As they were express packages, the threat was made, that unless they were removed, no express packages should be allowed to go over the road. This threat caused the newspaper packages to be removed. The editor then made a complaint to the president of the road, who had recently been elected Governor of the State of Ohio. The answer was in these words: "That the course of the 'Herald' for the past few weeks has been highly destructive to the best interests of our Government, there can be no question, and so long as its proprietors see proper to continue the same line of policy, I hope the superintendent (who, since my election, has been entrusted with the entire management of the road) will use all legitimate means in his power to suppress its circulation."

29. A RULE OF ACTION FOR THE CENSOR AND THE PRESS

General George B. McClellan and Newsmen, 1861

Not until the last year of the war did government and the Northern press work out a semisatisfactory arrangement for censorship in the field. Attempts in that direction were made, however, as early as mid-1861, after ominous breaches of secrecy by the press and hopelessly confused direction from government. Ineffective though it shortly proved to be, the agreement reached that year between General McClellan and members of the press stands as one of the earliest American efforts to make operative a code of information practices for wartime. Neither side lived up to its bargain, but the principles of voluntary censorship by the press and maximum release of information by government were to have far more success in the world wars of the next century. The House Committee on the Judiciary here states the agreement in a report on telegraphic censorship made to the House of Representatives.

Soon after General McClellan assumed command of the army of the Potomac a series of resolutions were adopted by the rep-

---

From House of Representatives, 37 Cong., 2 Sess., Committee on the Judiciary, Report No. 64 of March 20, 1862, "Telegraph Censorship," pp. 1, 2.

resentatives of the press, and approved by the general, for the purpose of determining a rule for the guidance of the press in the publication of matter which might be connected with the interests of the government. A paper containing said resolutions was produced before the committee by Mr. H. E. Thayer, the present censor, and reads as follows:

At a meeting of the representatives of the newspaper press held at Washington, August 2, 1861, after consultation with Major General McClellan, it was unanimously

Resolved, To accede to the following suggestions from him, and to transmit them to the editors of all newspapers in the loyal States and District of Columbia:

1st. That all such editors be requested to refrain from publishing, either as editorial, or as correspondence of any description, or from any point, any matter that may furnish aid and comfort to the enemy.

2d. That they be also requested and earnestly solicited to signify to their correspondents here and elsewhere their approval of the foregoing suggestion, and to comply with it in spirit and letter.

Also, resolved, That the government be respectfully requested to afford to the representatives of the press facilities for obtaining and immediately transmitting all information suitable for publication, particularly touching engagements with the enemy.

These resolutions were approved by "George B. McClellan, major general; Wm. B. Shaw, New York Herald; W. W. Harding, Philadelphia Inquirer; J. H. Paleston, Philadelphia North American; W. D. Wallach, Washington Evening Star; Adam S. Hill, New York Tribune; George W. Adams, Cincinnati Gazette and Philadelphia Bulletin; C. C. Coffin, Boston Journal; A. R. Spafford, Cincinnati Commercial; D. W. Bartlett, New York Evening Post; L. A. Gobright, reporter for New York associated press; E. C. Stedman, New York World; W. H. Painter, Philadelphia Inquirer."

A majority of the above-named representatives of the press have testified before the committee, and all agree that the resolutions were understood by the government, represented by General McClellan, and by those acting for the press, to constitute a rule of action for the censor and the press. . . .

30. THE PRESIDENT'S DILEMMA: LINCOLN REVOKES AND ORDERS THE SUPPRESSION OF NEWSPAPERS

1863, 1864

Northern newspapers' assault on the North's objectives, on the conduct of the war, and on the integrity of civil and military leaders was widespread, scurrilous, and vehement from the outset. Almost no state was without a potent contingent of "Copperhead" papers, and these were not the weak organs of small and disadvantaged minority groups, as in World War I, but standard newspapers of general and sometimes large circulation. They denounced the war as a failure and the leaders as corrupt and demagogic (Lincoln was the "tyrant" and the "widowmaker"), told the people they were being deceived, and issued stern demands for a suit for peace. Lurid descriptions of sedition and treason were sent to Lincoln, and the pressure on him to suppress the "Copperheads" was unrelenting. His great forbearance was tested time after time. His note to Erastus Corning, a leader of the New York Democrats, put his dilemma poignantly: "Must I shoot a simple-minded soldier boy who deserts, while

I must not touch a hair of a wily agitator who induces him to desert . . . ?"

A. *General A. E. Burnside Orders and President Lincoln Remands the Suppression of the* Chicago Times

1863

Burnside did what he could to warn the *Chicago Times* that its violent "Copperheadism" would not be tolerated forever. Finally, after months of screeds printed in the wake of the Emancipation Proclamation, Burnside issued the order that closed the *Times* for three days and that also curbed the Midwest circulation of the *New York World*. Lincoln reacted at once: His revocation of the order is in the letter to Burnside from Secretary of War E. M. Stanton, and his later reflections are in the letter to I. N. Arnold, below.

General Orders, No. 84. — *Hdqrs. Department of the Ohio, Cincinnati, Ohio,* June 1, 1863.

I. The tendency of the opinions and articles habitually published in the newspaper known as the New York World being to cast reproach upon the Government, and to weaken its efforts to suppress the rebellion, by creating distrust in its war policy, its circulation in time of war is calculated to exert a pernicious and treasonable influence, and is therefore prohibited in this department.

II. Postmasters, news agents, and all others will govern them-

---

Burnside's order is in *War of the Rebellion, Official Records of the Union and Confederate Armies,* Series I, Vol. XXIII, p. 381. Lincoln's order is *ibid.,* Series II, Vol. V, pp. 723–724. Lincoln's later comment is in John G. Nicolay and John Hay (eds.), *Complete Works of Abraham Lincoln* (New York: Francis D. Tandy Company, 1894), X, 108.

selves by this order; as any person detected in forwarding, selling, or in any way circulating the paper referred to will be promptly arrested and held for trial.

III. On account of the repeated expression of disloyal and incendiary sentiments, the publication of the newspaper known as the Chicago Times is hereby suppressed.

IV. Brig Gen. Jacob Ammen, commanding District of Illinois, is charged with the execution of the third paragraph of this order.

By command of Major-General Burnside:

LEWIS RICHMOND,
Assistant Adjutant-General.

War Department, Washington, June 1, 1863.

Maj. Gen. A. E. Burnside,
Commanding Department of the Ohio.

GENERAL. . . . the President has been informed that you have suppressed the publication or circulation of the Chicago Times in your department. He directs me to say that in his judgment it would be better for you to take an early occasion to revoke that order. The irritation produced by such acts is in his opinion likely to do more harm than the publication would do. The Government approves of your motives and desires to give you cordial and efficient support. But while military movements are left to your judgment, upon administrative questions such as the arrest of civilians and the suppression of newspapers not requiring immediate action the President desires to be previously consulted.

EDWIN M. STANTON,
Secretary of War.

Letter to I. N. Arnold

Executive Mansion, May 25, 1864.

My dear Sir: In regard to the order of General Burnside suspending the Chicago "Times," now nearly a year ago, I can only say I was embarrassed with the question between what was due to the military service on the one hand, and the liberty of the press on the other, and I believe it was the despatch of Senator Trumbull and yourself, added to the proceedings of the meeting which it brought me, that turned the scale in favor of my revoking the order.

I am far from certain to-day that the revocation was not right; and I am very sure the small part you took in it is no just ground to disparage your judgment, much less to impugn your motives. I take it that your devotion to the Union and the administration cannot be questioned by any sincere man. Yours truly,

A. LINCOLN

B. President Lincoln Commands the Arrest and Imprisonment of Proprietors of the New York World *and* New York Journal of Commerce

1864

Two of the severely antiadministration newspapers in New York were the *World* and the *Journal of Commerce*. Their political attitudes were not necessarily relevant, however, to their publishing of a bogus presidential proclamation announcing a new draft of 400,000 men, on May 18, 1864. Such an order at this stage of the war would unquestionably have brought serious opposition. Lincoln, after a conference with cabinet officers where he was pressed especially hard by Secretary of State William H. Seward,

---

From *War of the Rebellion, Official Records of the Union and Confederate Armies,* Series III, Vol. IV, pp. 386–395.

ordered the two newspapers closed and their proprietors arrested, and similar treatment was to be accorded the Independent Telegraph System, a firm apparently involved in the transmission of the story. The story unfolds in the orders and replies printed below following the initial query sent to Washington by M. S. Roberts, New York manager of the American Telegraph System which was under federal control. Not shown is the widespread feeling of the time that the victims of a hoax were unjustly suppressed for publishing what appeared to be major news. Howard (Dix's dispatch to Stanton of May 20, below) was indeed the culprit, having distributed the message to the newspapers in the hope of profiting from the stock market reaction to the news.

New York, May 18, 1864.
(*Received* 10 *a. m.*)

Maj. Thomas T. Eckert:

The following is taken from the New York World of this morning. Is it genuine?

M. S. Roberts,
Manager New York Office.

FOUR HUNDRED THOUSAND MORE TROOPS CALLED FOR.

Executive Mansion, May 17, 1864.

Fellow-Citizens of the United States:

In all exigencies it becomes a nation carefully to scrutinize its line of conduct, humbly to approach the Throne of Grace, and meekly to implore forgiveness, wisdom, and guidance.

For reasons known only to Him it has been decreed that this country should be the scene of unparalleled outrage, and this nation the monumental sufferer of the nineteenth century. With a heavy heart, but an undiminished confidence in our cause, I approach the performance of duty, rendered imperative by my sense of weakness before the Almighty, and of justice to the people.

It is not necessary that I should tell you that the first Virginia campaign under Lieutenant-General Grant, in whom I have every confidence, and whose courage and fidelity the people do well to honor, is virtually closed.

He has conducted his great enterprise with discreet ability. He has inflicted great loss upon the enemy. He has crippled their strength and defeated their plans.

In view, however, of the situation in Virginia, the disaster at Red River, the delay at Charleston, and the general state of the country, I, Abraham Lincoln, do hereby recommend that Thursday, the twenty-sixth day of May, in the year of our Lord one thousand eight hundred and sixty-four, be solemnly set apart throughout these United States as a day of fasting, humiliation, and prayer. Deeming, furthermore, that the present condition of public affairs presents an extraordinary occasion, and in view of the pending expiration of the service of 100,000 of our troops, I, Abraham Lincoln, President of the United States, by virtue of the power vested in me by the Constitution and the laws, have thought fit to call forth, and hereby do call forth, the citizens of the United States between the ages of eighteen and forty-five years to the aggregate number of 400,000, in order to suppress the existing rebellious combinations and to cause the due execution of the laws. And furthermore, in case any State or number of States shall fail to furnish by the fifteenth day of June next their assigned quotas, it is hereby ordered that the same be raised by an immediate and peremptory draft. The details for this object will be communicated the State authorities through the War Department. I appeal to all loyal citizens to favor, facilitate, and aid this effort to maintain the honor, the integrity, and the existence of our national Union, and the perpetuity of popular government. In witness whereof I have hereunto set my hand and caused the seal of the United States to be affixed.

Done at the city of Washington this seventeenth day of May, in the year of our Lord one thousand eight hundred and sixty-four, and of the Independence of the United States the eighty-eighth.

ABRAHAM LINCOLN.

By the President:

WILLIAM H. SEWARD,
Secretary of State.

New York, May 18, 1864.
(Received 11.35 *a. m.)*

Hon. W. H. Seward,
Secretary of State:

A proclamation by the President, countersigned by you, and believed to be spurious, has appeared in some of our morning papers calling for 400,000 men, and appointing the 26th instant as a day of fasting, humiliation, and prayer. Please answer immediately for steamer.

JOHN A. DIX,
Major-General.

Department of State,
May 18, 1864.

To the Public:

A paper purporting to be a proclamation of the President, countersigned by the Secretary of State, and bearing date the 17th day of May, is reported to this Department as having appeared in the New York World of this date. The paper is an absolute forgery. No proclamation of that kind or any other has been made or proposed to be made by the President, or issued or proposed to be issued by the State Department or any Department of the Government.

WILLIAM H. SEWARD.

(Sent to New York press and to Charles Francis Adams, London, and William L. Dayton, Paris.)

War Department,
Washington City, May 18, 1864.

Major-General Dix,
New York:

I have just seen a copy of the spurious proclamation referred to in your telegram. It is a base and treasonable forgery.

EDWIN M. STANTON,
Secretary of War.

Executive Mansion,
Washington, May 18, 1864.

Maj. Gen. John A. Dix,
Commanding, New York:

Whereas, there has been wickedly and traitorously printed and published this morning in the New York World and New York Journal of Commerce, newspapers printed and published in the city of New York, a false and spurious proclamation purporting to be signed by the President and to be countersigned by the Secretary of State, which publication is of a treasonable nature, designed to give aid and comfort to the enemies of the United States and to the rebels now at war against the Government, and their aiders and abettors, you are, therefore, hereby commanded forthwith to arrest and imprison in any fort or military prison in your command the editors, proprietors, and publishers of the aforesaid newspapers, and all such persons as, after public notice has been given of the falsehood of said publication, print and publish the same, with intent to give aid and comfort to the enemy, and you will hold the persons so arrested in close custody until they can be brought to trial before a military commission for their offense. You will also take possession, by military force, of the printing establishments of the New York World and Journal of Commerce and hold the same until further orders, and prevent any further publication therefrom.

A. LINCOLN.

War Department,
Washington, D. C., May 18, 1864—2 *p. m.*

Maj. Gen. John A. Dix,
New York:

The President directs that immediately upon receipt of this order you take military possession of the offices of the Independent Telegraph Company at New York (one corner Cedar and Nassau streets, Gold Room, William street, and Brokers' Exchange), and of all the instruments, dispatches, and papers that may be found in the office or upon the person of the manager, superintendent, and operators, and keep possession thereof, and arrest the manager, operators, superintendent, and hold them in close custody until further order, and permit no telegraph to be sent over the line until further orders. Strict diligence, attention, and confidence is desired in the execution of this order, and you are requested to give it your personal attention and employ your best officers.

EDWIN M. STANTON,
Secretary of War.

(Similar orders to General Cadwalader, Philadelphia; Colonel Bomford, Harrisburg, and Captain Foster, Pittsburg.)

New York, May 18, 1864.
(Received 4.35 *p. m.)*

Hon. E. M. Stanton,
Secretary of War:

I am investigating the gross fraud of this morning. The paper purporting to be a proclamation of the President was handed into the offices of the city newspapers at 4 o'clock, written on thin manifold paper of foolscap size, like the dispatches of the Associated Press. In handwriting and every other respect it was admirably calculated to deceive. It was published in the World and Journal of Commerce. None of the responsible editors of either of the papers was present. As soon as the editors of the World discovered the fraud they announced it on their bulletin, and they have offered a reward of $500 for the detection of the author. It was printed by the Herald, but none of the copies were issued, the fraud having been discovered before they left the office. I have sent to all the newspapers for their manuscripts and have received three. They are alike in respect to paper and handwriting. I think the authors will be detected, and I need not add that I shall in that case arrest and imprison them for trifling in so infamous a manner with the authority of the Government and the feelings of the community at this important juncture in our public affairs. Since writing the above the President's order for the arrest of the editors, proprietors, and publishers of the World and Journal of Commerce has come to hand. I shall execute it unless the foregoing information shall be deemed sufficient by the President to suspend it until my investigation is concluded.

JOHN A. DIX,
Major-General.

Major-General Dix, *War Department,* May 18, 1864.
New York:

The President's telegram was an order to you which I think it was your duty to execute immediately upon its receipt. I have no further orders to give you.

EDWIN M. STANTON,
Secretary of War.

New York, May 18, 1864.
Hon. Edwin M. Stanton, *(Received* 5.40 *p. m.)*
Secretary of War:

There will be no delay in the execution of either order. The telegraph offices will be seized immediately, and the newspapers, editors, &c., unless I hear from you before the guards are ready.

JOHN A. DIX,
Major-General.

War Department,
May 18, 1864—6.30 p. m.

Major-General Dix,
New York:

Your telegram of 5.40 is just received. A great national crime has been committed by the publication. The editors, proprietors, and publishers, responsible and irresponsible, are in law guilty of that crime. You were not directed to make any investigation, but to execute the President's order; the investigation was to be made by a military commission. How you can excuse or justify delay in executing the President's order until you make an investigation is not for me to determine.

EDWIN M. STANTON,
Secretary of War.

War Department,
Washington City, May 18, 1864—8.30 p. m.

Major-General Dix,
New York:

The officer in charge of the investigation, respecting the forged proclamation, reports that he is led to believe it originated in this city, and that the New York publishers were not privy to it. If your conclusions are the same you may suspend action against them until developments are made.

EDWIN M. STANTON,
Secretary of War.

New York, May 18, 1864.
(Received 10.40 *p. m.)*

Hon. E. M. Stanton,
Secretary of War:

The investigation was made by me as commanding officer of the department before the President's order was received, as my dispatch showed. There has been none since. I understood the President's orders as commands to be executed, and there has been no unnecessary delay in the execution. The telegraphic offices were seized as soon as my officers could reach them. The World and Journal of Commerce printing offices are in possession of my men. Two of my officers, Major Halpine and Captain Barstow, are engaged in the arrest of the editors, proprietors, and publishers, and a steamer is waiting at Castle Garden to take them to Fort Lafayette. The only delay has been in making proper arrangements to secure, as nearly as possible, simultaneous and effective action.

J. A. Dix,
Major-General.

New York, May 18, 1864.
(Received 10.40 *p. m.)*

Hon. E. M. Stanton,
Secretary of War:

Your dispatch in regard to the probable origin of the forged proclamation is just received. I am satisfied the publishers of the World and Journal of Commerce had no knowledge of it. I shall, therefore, suspend the order as to them, but shall keep possession of their printing offices until you otherwise direct. The manager, superintendent, and operators of the telegraph line will be sent to Fort Lafayette in an hour. They have been in arrest since 5 o'clock.

Jno A. Dix,
Major-General.

Philadelphia, May 18, 1864.
(Received 7.50 *p. m.)*

Hon. E. M. Stanton,
Secretary of War:

The telegram lines indicated in your telegram, and all the instruments, dispatches, and papers have been seized, and the manager, operators, and superintendents arrested and will be held until further orders. A large number of private dispatches are detained. Two other offices than those named by you connected with this line have also been taken possession of. They have through communication everywhere without going through the principal office. It is said that there are also other offices, which I will seize if I can find them. Please inform me if I am not acting correctly.

GEO. CADWALADER,
Major-General, Commanding.

Pittsburg, May 18, 1864.

Hon. E. M. Stanton,
Secretary of War:

Under orders received at 5.30 I have seized papers, instruments, and J. H. Robinson, manager, J. R. Roe, assistant superintendent, George A. Hamilton, operator, W. J. Gill, clerk, Inland Telegraph Line, and all papers. Will send them at 8.35

J. HERON FOSTER,
Capt. and Prov. Mar. Twenty-second District of Pennsylvania.

War Department,
Washington City, May 18, 1864.

Major-General Cadwalader,
Philadelphia:

Accept the thanks of this Department for your prompt action. Secure and forward all the papers, and send the prisoners forward under guard to report to Colonel Wisewell, Military Governor.

EDWIN M. STANTON,
Secretary of War.

(Same to Capt. J. Heron Foster, Pittsburg.)

Harrisburg, May 18, 1864.

Hon. E. M. Stanton:

Have received your important telegram of this date. At 7 p. m. have taken possession of office of Independent Telegraph (self-styled Inland and American Line), also books, papers, instruments, and operators. Am now searching for the president and treasurer. The superintendent, A. J. Baldwin, is in New York City.

J. V. Bomford,
Lieutenant-Colonel Sixteenth Infantry, &c.

Confidential *War Department,*
Washington City, D. C., May 18, 1864.

Maj. Gen. Lew. Wallace,
Baltimore:

A forged treasonable document, purporting to be a proclamation by the President, countersigned by the Secretary of State, appeared in the New York World and Journal of Commerce this morning. Make arrangements and seize all the issues of the papers that may arrive at Baltimore by express or mail and prevent their circulation, and report to this Department.

Edwin M. Stanton,
Secretary of War.

Baltimore, May 18, 1864.
(Received 9 p. m.)

Hon. E. M. Stanton,
Secretary of War:

Your dispatch arrived after the train from New York and the New York World had already been distributed. I have seized all the copies I could find.

Lew Wallace,
Major-General of Volunteers.

Ninth Street Office, Washington, May 18, 1864.
(Received 2.15 p. m.)

Hon. E. M. Stanton,

I have the honor to report that the arrests have been made and offices closed.

THOS. T. ECKERT,
Major and Assistant Superintendent Military Telegraph.

Department of State,
Washington City, May 18, 1864—12.30 p. m.

Charles Francis Adams, Esq.,
U. S. Minister Plenipotentiary, London:

Orders have been given for the arrest and punishment of the fabricators and publishers of the spurious proclamation.

WILLIAM H. SEWARD.

(Same to William L. Dayton, Esq., U. S. Minister Plenipotentiary, Paris.)

New York City, May 19, 1864.
His Excellency A. Lincoln, *(Received 2.30 p. m.)*
President of the United States:

Sir: The undersigned, editors and publishers of a portion of the daily press of the city of New York, respectfully represent that the leading journals of the city sustain very extended telegraphic news arrangements, under an organization established in 1848 and known as the New York Associated Press, which is controlled by its members, acting through an executive committeee, a general agent in this city, and assistant agents immediately responsible to the association at every important news center throughout this country and Europe. Under the above-named organization the rule has always been to transmit by telegraph all intelligence to the office of the general agent in this city, and by him the same is properly prepared for publication, and then written out by manifold process on tissue paper, and a copy of the same is sent simultaneously in sealed envelopes to each of the editors who are entitled to receive the same. From foregoing statement of facts Your Excellency will readily perceive that an ingenious rogue, knowing the manner in which the editors were supplied with much of their telegraphic news, could, by selecting his time and opportunity, easily impose upon editors or compositors the most wicked and fraudulent reports. On Wednesday morning, at about 3 o'clock, a messenger, who well counterfeited the regular messenger of the Associated Press, presented himself at all save one of the editorial rooms of the papers connected with the Associated Press, and delivered to the foreman, in the absence of the night editors, sealed envelopes containing manifold papers similar in all respects to that used by the association, upon which was written a fraudulent proclamation, purporting to be signed by Your Excellency and countersigned by the Honorable Secretary of State. The very late hour at which the fraud was perpetrated left no time for consideration as to the authenticity or genuineness of the document, and the copy in most of the offices was at once cut up into small pieces and given into the hands of the compositors, and in two cases the fraud was not discovered or suspected even till after the whole morning editions of the papers were printed off and distributed. The undersigned beg to state to Your Excellency that the fraud, which succeeded with The World and the Journal of Commerce, was one which, from the circumstances attending it and the practices of the Associated Press, was extremely natural and very liable to have succeeded in any daily newspaper establishment in this city, and inasmuch as, in the judgment of the undersigned, the editors and proprietors of the Journal of Commerce and The World were innocent of any knowledge of wrong in the publication of the fraudulent document, and also in view of the fact that the suspension by Your Excellency's orders of the two papers last evening has had the effect to awaken editors and publishers and news agents, telegraph companies, &c., to the propriety of increased vigilance in their several duties, the undersigned respectfully request that Your

Excellency will be pleased to rescind the order under which The World and the Journal of Commerce were suppressed.

Respectfully, Your Excellency's obedient servants,

SIDNEY HOWARD GAY,
For Tribune.
ERASTUS BROOKS,
New York Express.
FREDERICK HUDSON,
For JAS. G. BENNETT,
New York Herald.
M. S. BEACH,
New York Sun.

New York, May 19, 1864.
(Received 10.40 *a. m.)*

Hon. E. M. Stanton:

Sir: I have the honor to report that the Secretary of State's dispatch to Ministers Adams and Dayton was delivered to the purser of the Scotia, and that he was ordered by Mr. Cunard to telegraph it from Queenstown. Slips were issued by some of the morning papers exposing the forgery, and circulated among the passengers before the vessel sailed.

Very respectfully,

E. S. SANFORD.

War Department,
Washington, D. C., May 19, 1864.

Major-General Wallace,
Baltimore:

The President directs that you take military possession of the telegraph line known as the Independent or Inland Telegraph and its offices and instruments, materials, papers, and dispatches. The principal office is No. 21 South street. The papers and dispatches you will forward to Colonel Wisewell, Military Governor. The agents, superintendents, and operators you will arrest and parole them to appear before you when required. You will place a guard in the offices and prevent any telegraphing.

By order of the President:

EDWIN M. STANTON,
Secretary of War.

New York, May 20, 1864.

Hon. E. M. Stanton:

I have arrested and am sending to Fort Lafayette Joseph Howard, the author of the forged proclamation. He is a newspaper reporter, and is known as " 'Howard,' of the Times." He has been very frank in his confession—says it was a stock-jobbing operation, and that no person connected with the press had any agency in the transaction except another reporter, who took manifolds and distributed the proclamation to the newspapers, and whose arrest I have ordered. He exonerates the Independent Telegraph Line, and says that publication on a steamer day was accidental. His statement in all essential particulars is corroborated by other testimony.

JOHN A. DIX,
Major-General,

War Department,
Washington City, May 20, 1864—9.10 p. m.

Major-General Dix,
New York:

Your telegram respecting the arrest of Howard has been received and submitted to the President. He directs me to say that while, in his opinion, the editors, proprietors, and publishers of The World and Journal of Commerce are responsible for what appears in their papers injurious to the public service, and have no right to shield themselves behind a plea of ignorance or want of criminal intent, yet he is not disposed to visit them with vindictive punishment; and hoping they will exercise more caution and regard for the public welfare in future, he authorizes you to restore to them their respective establishments.

EDWIN M. STANTON,
Secretary of War.

War Department,
Washington City, May 20, 1864—1 p. m.

Major-General Dix,
New York:

You will please proceed immediately to take the examination of the telegraph operators, superintendents, and officers that may have been arrested by you under order of this Department, taking their statements and examination in writing, and, if satisfied that they have had no complicity nor part in the transmission or perpetration of the forgery of the President's proclamation, published in The World and Journal of Commerce, you will discharge them, but holding in arrest any against whom any evidence may appear and reporting the same.

EDWIN M. STANTON,
Secretary of War.

World War I

31. ESPIONAGE ACT OF 1917

When the United States entered World War I, President Woodrow Wilson and his Attorney General found the nation's old

---

From *U.S. Statutes,* XL, 217, 219, 230–231.

conspiracy and treason statutes inadequate to curb antiwar expression. The former law could not reach *individuals* who condemned the war; the latter was of uncertain applicability against words. Partly at their instigation, sedition legislation was incorporated into the Espionage Act of June 15, 1917, within a year to be strengthened by far sterner provisions limiting speech and press in an amendment that came to be called the Sedition Act.

The Espionage Act became a monument to the truism that laws ostensibly barring one kind of criticism of government can be used to bar many kinds. Almost 900 persons were convicted for words spoken or printed. But what the guilty had said was seldom "Don't enlist," or "Resist your superior officers"—the kinds of words that Section 3 seemed aimed at. Often, these persons expressed their opinions about the nation's cause or how the war was managed, and they were punished. Pertinent sections of the Espionage Act, used far more often than the amendment which was not passed until late in the war, appear below.

CHAP. 30.—An Act To punish acts of interference with the foreign relations, the neutrality, and the foreign commerce of the United States, to punish espionage, and better to enforce the criminal laws of the United States, and for other purposes.

Be it enacted by the Senate and House of Representatives of the United States of America in Congress assembled:

TITLE I.

Espionage.

SEC. 3. Whoever, when the United States is at war, shall willfully make or convey false reports or false statements with intent to interfere with the operation or success of the military or naval forces of the United States or to promote the success of its enemies and whoever, when the United States is at war, shall willfully cause or attempt to cause insubordination, disloyalty, mutiny, or refusal of duty, in the military or naval forces of the United States, or shall willfully obstruct the recruiting or enlistment service of the United States, to the injury of the service or of the United States, shall be punished by a fine of not more than $10,000 or imprisonment for not more than twenty years, or both.

SEC. 4. If two or more persons conspire to violate the provisions of sections two or three of this title, and one or more of such persons does any act to effect the object of the conspiracy, each of the parties to such conspiracy shall be punished as in said sections provided in the case of the doing of the act the accomplishment of which is the object of such conspiracy. . . .

TITLE XII.

Use of Mails.

SECTION 1. Every letter, writing, circular, postal card, picture, print, engraving, photograph, newspaper, pamphlet, book, or other publication, matter, or thing, of any kind, in violation of any of the provisions of this Act is hereby declared to be nonmailable matter and shall not be conveyed in the mails or delivered from any post office or by any letter carrier: *Provided,* That nothing in this Act shall be so construed as to authorize any person other than an employe of the Dead Letter Office, duly authorized thereto, or other person upon a search warrant authorized by law, to open any letter not addressed to himself.

SEC. 2. Every letter, writing, circular, postal card, picture, print, engraving, photograph, newspaper, pamphlet, book, or other publication, matter or thing, of any kind, containing any matter advocating or urging treason, insurrection, or forcible resistance to any law of the United States, is hereby declared to be nonmailable.

SEC. 3. Whoever shall use or attempt to use the mails or Postal Service of the United States for the transmission of any matter declared by this title to be nonmailable, shall be fined not more than $5,000 or imprisoned not more than five years, or both. Any person violating any provision of this title may be tried and punished either in the district in which the unlawful matter or publication was mailed, or to which it was carried by mail for delivery according to the direction thereon, or in which it was caused to be delivered by mail to the person to whom it was addressed.

32. TO PROTECT OUR MILITARY FORCES, IT IS REQUESTED THAT SECRECY BE OBSERVED

1917

The voluntary censorship by the press of military information that had been sought with such small success in the Civil War was accomplished to the considerable satisfaction of government and press in World War I. A request by the military departments was issued via the publication put out by the Committee on Public Information and its chairman, George Creel, who was in charge of censorship and propaganda. A short version had been issued in the summer of 1917, and by the end of the year the following detailed statement became the guide for magazines and newspapers.

From "Requests for Censorship by Press of Certain War News," *The Official Bulletin,* Dec. 31, 1917, pp. 10, 16.

THE NEW REQUESTS IN FULL

Following are the new requests in full:

The desires of the Government with respect to the concealment from the enemy of military policies, plans, and movements are set forth in the following specific requests. They go to the press of the United States directly from the Secretary of War and the Secretary of the Navy, and represent the thought and advice of their technical advisers. They do not apply to news dispatches censored by military authority with the Expeditionary Forces or in those cases where the Government itself, in the form of official statements, may find it necessary or expedient to make public information covered by these requests.

For the protection of our military and naval forces and of merchant shipping it is requested that secrecy be observed in all matters of:

1. Advance information of the routes and schedules of troop movements. (See paragraph 5.)

2. Information tending to disclose the number of troops in the Expeditionary Forces abroad.

3. Information calculated to disclose location of the permanent base or bases abroad.

4. Information that would disclose the location of American units or the eventual position of the American forces at the front.

PORTS OF EMBARKATION

5. Information tending to disclose an eventual or actual port of embarkation; or information of the movement of military forces toward seaports or of the assembling of military forces at seaports from which inference might be drawn of any intention to embark them for service abroad; and information of the assembling of transports or convoys; and information of the embarkation itself.

6. Information of the arrival at any European port of American war vessels, transports, or any portion of any expeditionary force, combatant or noncombatant.

7. Information of the time of departure of merchant ships from American or European ports, or information of the ports from which they sailed, or information of their cargoes.

8. Information indicating the port of arrival of incoming ships from European ports or after their arrival indicating, or hinting at, the port at which the ship arrived.

9. Information as to convoys and as to the sighting of friendly or enemy ships, whether naval or merchant.

10. Information of the locality, number, or identity of vessels belonging to our own Navy or to the navies of any country at war with Germany.

11. Information of the coast or anti-aircraft defenses of the United States. Any information of their very existence, as well as the number, nature, or position of their guns, is dangerous.

MINES AND HARBOR DEFENSES

12. Information of the laying of mines or mine fields or of any harbor defenses.

13. Information of the aircraft and appurtenances used at Government aviation schools for experimental tests under military authority, and information of contracts and production of air material, and information tending to disclose the numbers and organization of the air division, excepting when authorized by the Committee on Public Information.

14. Information of all Government devices and experiments in war material, excepting when authorized by the Committee on Public Information.

15. Information of secret notices issued to mariners or other confidential instructions issued by the Navy or the Department of Commerce relating to lights, lightships, buoys, or other guides to navigation.

16. Information as to the number, size, character, or location of ships of the Navy ordered laid down at any port or shipyard, or in actual process of construction; or information that they are launched or in commission.

17. Information of the train or boat schedules of traveling official missions in transit through the United States.

18. Information of the transportation of munitions, or of war material.

PHOTOGRAPHS

Photographs conveying the information specified above should not be published.

These requests go to the press without larger authority than the necessities of the war-making branches. Their enforcement is a matter for the press itself. To the overwhelming proportion of newspapers, who have given unselfish, patriotic adherence to the voluntary agreement, the Government extends its gratitude and high appreciation.

The Com. on Public Information,
By George Creel, *Chairman.*

33. MR. BURLESON, ESPIONAGENT

William Hard, 1919

When World War I arrived, most of the nation's radical elements opposed it as a "capitalists' war"—in fact, only one more device by which to increase the profits of Wall Street and "the Plutocrats" at the expense of labor and the workers' movements. And when these groups now added antiwar talk to several prewar decades of denouncing the capitalist system, they found themselves under increasing attack.

From Hard, William, "Mr. Burleson, Espionagent," *New Republic*, XIX (May 10, 1919), 42–45.

Radical and pacifist newspapers came under the whip of the Espionage Act of 1917 and other statutes, wielded mostly by the Post Office Department. The stunning power of the Postmaster General over the nation's press was never more fully used: the distribution of more than one hundred publications was interfered with. He was empowered by the Espionage Act to bar from the mails that which he thought "seditious." He was largely immune from judicial scrutiny, his acts reviewable only if he was "clearly wrong." And in this period he also asserted and won the crippling power to withdraw the use of the low, second-class mail rates from a newspaper he thought seditious, effectively preventing future mailings on the basis of past actions.

Here an angry William Hard addresses himself to the problem of Postmaster General Burleson.

On May 16th, 1918, a President of the party of Thomas Jefferson signed an act of Congress providing, among other things, that the mails should be closed to any "abusive" writing about the "form of government" of the United States.

Thomas Jefferson said: "If there be any among us who would wish to dissolve this union or to change its form, let them stand undisturbed. Let them stand undisturbed as monuments to the safety with which error of opinion may be tolerated when reason is left free to combat it."

Woodrow Wilson said: "If there is one thing we love more than another in the United States, it is that every man should have the privilege, unmolested and uncriticized, to utter the real convictions of his mind."

Mr. Burleson said: "Newspapers will not be permitted to say that the Government is owned by Wall Street."

Mr. Burleson was right. Mr. Wilson was wrong. He was wrong about the rest of us and wrong about himself. He was all for letting people talk; but he was all for "drawing the line somewhere" as soon as Max Eastman and Floyd Dell began to talk. Mr. Creel drew the line even more rapidly. His Committee on Public Information issued advertisements warning us in effect against criticizing even the physical conduct of the war. "Report the man who spreads pessimistic stories," said the Committee on Public Information. "Report him to the Department of Justice."

We applauded. For one letter coming to Washington resenting suppressions of speech, there were ten urging more suppressions. John Stuart Mill said that no modern democratic elected government was likely ever to attempt any control of opinion "except when in doing so it makes itself the organ of the general intolerance of the public." He described our case.

It had four stages of development and then a fifth stage—in which we now are—a stage of bewilderment. Having dimmed our minds to the intellectual difficulties of the war, we now find them dimmed to the intellectual difficulties of the peace. "The persecutor," said W. H. H. Lecky, "can never be certain that he is not persecuting truth rather than error, but he can always be certain that he is suppressing the *spirit* of truth."

Our first stage was to try to close the mouths of all people hostile to the war. They might think the war unjustifiable. Daniel Webster, in 1847, during the war with Mexico, said: "We are in a most unjustifiable war." In 1847 his spirit was unpopular but tolerated. In 1918 it was non-mailable and criminal. In 1918 we followed the spirit of Judge Aldrich of the District of New Hampshire, who said:

"We must in good faith and with courage accept the reasons which the authorities have deemed sufficient to justify war. We must accept those reasons as altogether sufficient."

The bench approved Mr. Burleson. When Mr. Burleson excluded the Milwaukee Leader from the second-class mails because its "tendency" was "seditious"—that is, against the war—he was sustained by the Supreme Court of the District of Columbia. When he declared the Masses of August of 1917 non-mailable, he was sustained, ultimately, by the New York Circuit Court of Appeals. Ultimately, in all actual decisions of nonmailability, he was always sustained. He was within our spirit and within our law.

We denounced "pacifism" in the same breath with "treason." Boni and Liveright of New York published a book by Andreas Latzko entitled Men in War. It was a descriptive book. It described war's horrors, as seen by an Austrian. Mr. Burleson declared it non-mailable. Censorship is rooted in cowardice, and flowers into cowardice. This book, reporting war, affected reality. Under censorship we came to the idea that we could not face reality without losing our nerve. We came to the idea that if the countrymen of George Washington and of Ulysses S. Grant should read Latzko on war they would quake. Personally we ostracized "pacifists" and mobbed them. Officially we ostracized Latzko and broke his book.

That was the first stage—to try to stop criticisms of the war and also of all war. The second was to try to stop criticisms of certain administrative policies of the government—conscription, for example.

The editor of the Jeffersonian, in the southern district of Georgia, was against conscription. He seemed to think, erroneously, that conscription was unconstitutional. He said: "Does not the President know that the Conscription act, forcing citizens out of the Union to die in France, is every bit as lawless as the action of the Phelps Dodge Copper Company in forcing 1,100 miners out of Arizona?" He made this preposterous comparison, and found himself outside the second-class mails.

Judge Speer decided that he must stay outside. Mr. Burleson had been quite right. The editor of the Jeffersonian could not question the war, and he could not question conscription.

In 1916 conscription existed in England. In 1916 I sent out from England an interview with Mr. W. A. Appleton, a prominent English labor leader, questioning conscription strongly. I did not admire Mr. Appleton's opinion. My own view was that no temporary coercion of men's bodies by act of Parliament could do any lasting political or moral harm, provided only their minds were left free to agitate against that act, if they wanted to agitate against it, and free therefore to secure its repeal if a majority of voters could be persuaded to demand its repeal. Besides, I had a prejudice then, as now, in favor of universal liability to military service as the only possible means of getting an army in the full temperament of the whole nation. Volunteer armies are joined almost exclusively by men who are willing to be strikebreakers and who are willing to be imperialistic adventurers in foreign parts. I thought then, and I think now, that the only democratic revolutionary armies possible are armies drawn from the masses of the people. Therefore I did not admire Mr. Appleton's opinion. But I did admire his interview. It was outright, and able; and it made me work to defend myself against its arguments.

I took it to the authorities in London. They passed it and released it at once. I put it into the mails. And I returned to my country, once England's teacher, and found that no American of Mr. Appleton's opinion had Mr. Appleton's liberty.

We sanctified conscription absolutely and continuously. Many other things we sanctified intermittently. Among them was our revenue system. We suppressed an issue of the Public for saying that Congress ought to raise more money by taxes and less by loans. Once, we almost sanctified Mr. Gompers. He suppressed an issue of the Nation for several days and advertised it to the country as a seditious issue—for doing what? For attacking Mr. Gompers's policy as leader of American labor. By such steps we rose to our third stage. In that third stage we sanctified the policies of our Allies.

Huebsch of New York published a pamphlet by Lajpat Rai of India. It was called An Open Letter to David Lloyd George. It dwelt on evils in India—evils of poverty, evils of inadequate popular education, evils of inadequate popular self-government. It deprecated immediate revolt; but it seemed to advocate ultimate revolt, unless the reasons for revolt should be removed.

Now it is perfectly true that people do exist who, if they are brought into vivid contact with England's crimes, will recoil from a war in which England is an ally. Some few people may even sabotage such a war. They may refuse to help lick the Kaiser till England stops helping to lick him. Among them there may be one who will try to blow up a bridge. The theory of free speech is to increase knowledge, even if a few people have to be jailed for using knowledge badly. The theory of censorship is to de-brain a whole nation in order to prevent a few people from putting us to the trouble of physically stopping them. Lajpat Rai's discussion of Anglo-Indian politics was thrown out of the American mails.

Mr. Burleson, in this stage, protected our minds amply from Indian agitators, and from many other agitators, and from the Pope.

There was a paper in New York called the Freeman's Journal and Catholic Register. There used to be. But it printed too many things noted by Mr. Burleson's assistants and marked with their pencils.

It printed an article earnestly and religiously criticizing the treaty under which the Allies were said to have barred the Pope from having anything to do with "the conclusion of peace"; and it printed a quotation from the Pope, on patriotism, in which the Pope said that "no man can be loyal to his country unless he first be loyal to his conscience and his God." Mr. Burleson's assistants objected to both the article and the quotation. They lifted their pencils and marked the Pope.

The Freeman's Journal and Catholic Register also printed many articles and quotations about Ireland. It printed an opinion by Thomas Jefferson that Ireland should be a republic. Mr. Burleson's assistants marked Thomas Jefferson. It printed George Washington's address against "the insidious wiles of foreign influence." Mr. Burleson's assistants marked George Washington.

Thirteen issues of The Freeman's Journal and Catholic Register were dammed up in the mails. It was a little paper. It ceased. Its editor, Mr. A. Brendan Ford, wrote a farewell editorial in which he showed how he had been "made to realize" that he at least could not speak "regarding self-determination of Ireland" or "in defense of the Vicar of the Prince of Peace." Mr. Ford is an old man, venerable for appearance, venerable for recollection. When he was a boy he worked in the shop of William Lloyd Garrison's Liberator. He has lived to see his own paper destroyed because he could not and would not and did not, on the afternoon of April 6, 1917, suddenly turn his back on Ireland and on the head of his faith.

Mr. Burleson protected us against the Pope and against Mr. Ford on behalf of the British empire and on behalf of a certain anti-Papal policy of the Italian government. It was a logical incident of stage three.

In stage four we went on to deal with our outright military enemies. We were becoming skillful now and ambitious. We were not content, in stage four, with negative protection. We advanced to a protection really positive. We decided that we would make our own pictures of certain of our enemies, through our own bureaus of official enemy portraiture at Washington, and that no other pictures of such enemies would then be either official or patriotic.

Nikolai Lenin, meanwhile, had made a speech in Moscow on The Soviets at Work. It was printed in Izvestia, official organ of the Soviet government. Adventurously it was reprinted, in a pamphlet, by the Rand School in New York. Reading it now, we overhear Lenin speaking to his own people, not to us. We overhear him. We eavesdrop on his incitements of Russia to riot and ruin. What does he say? "Conduct a merciless struggle against chaos." "Raise the productivity of labor." "Establish universal accounting." "Maintain strict discipline at work." "Give no pre-eminence to Red Guard methods." "Pay a high remuneration to specialists." "Pay them 100,000 rubles a year if necessary." "Get rid of grafters." "Execute grafters." "Introduce the Taylor System of Scientific Management." "Make everybody work."

Mr. Burleson declared this pamphlet non-mailable. Then and there he brought censorship to the final flash of the full message of its meaning. Censorship may start as the creature of popular impulse. It ends inevitably as the engine of purely official impulse.

Officially Mr. Lansing and Mr. Creel had contrived a certain explanation of Lenin. Out of the materials at their disposal they had sincerely given us to understand that Lenin was a cheap vulgar crook. The satellite of the Kaiser. Now, with the Kaiser gone, and with Lenin still among us, and with millions of rubles lying at Lenin's disposal in Russian banks for eighteen months, and with Stockholm and foreign exchange and luxury near by, and with Lenin not in Stockholm safe but in Moscow being shot at, we begin to feel that the materials at Mr. Lansing's and Mr. Creel's disposal were quite considerably insufficient. We begin to feel that somehow Lenin has fooled us. But Lenin's own words would have done a great deal to set us right about him, eight months ago.

The Soviets at Work is an unintentional but indubitable self-portrait. It does not flatter. It does not disparage. It reveals a scholastic pedantic man walking the world with a colossal mental stride toward a highly imaginative magnificent mission —or mirage—of perfect technical economic organization, beyond self, beyond personality. It may be the production of an intellectual monster, intellectualizing the world to its ruin. It is not the production of a pickpocket.

But Washington was now master. It helped the Committee on Public Information to circulate the official portrait of Lenin. It would not allow the Rand School to circulate Lenin himself.

We were within striking distance now of the conclusion that no arguments of any sort against any of our public ideas or against any of our public institutions ought ever to be put into circulation in any manner. Judge Wade of the southern district of Iowa struck it first. He made a speech on our schools and said:

"I would not permit an expression which indicated doubt. I would not picture the blessings of other lands except as, by comparison, the blessings of this land might be exalted. I would not discuss the extent of the liberty of any people on earth except as such study would prove that ours is the land of the free. I would have no discussion of the comparative government except in so far as the comparison might be to the absolute advantage of our own form of government."

He used the very words of the Espionage law. His was the mood in which we met the issues of the war, the mood of listening to only our own side; and now we have to meet the issues of the peace in the mental condition consequent. Our general uncertainty, our popular purposelessness, as we look at a conquered world and wonder what to do with it, has many causes, doubtless; but one of them, surely, and a large one, is our ignorance of our opponents, of those who dissent from us, at home and abroad. By weakening our knowledge of their arguments, we have weakened our knowledge of our own purposes. John Stuart Mill said that "He who knows only his own side knows little of that." Once more he described our case.

But it is not our own case only. It is also the case of every other country. England has kept more free speech than America. But in England nevertheless, as everywhere else, the principle of free speech, as a principle, has been deeply undermined, popularly and officially.

Let us not flinch from the fact. We gained no military or intellectual advantage by jailing Bertrand Russell in England or by suppressing Lenin's pamphlet in America. What we accomplished was simply to gratify our growth in the passion of coercion and to exhibit our decline in the sense of liberty.

Free speech seems to be an antique Jeffersonian Victorian liberal sentimental dogma, with few believers left. It thrills our modern scientific radicals as feebly as it thrills our surviving

Tories. Mr. Burleson suppresses a work of Lenin's; and, in the very work suppressed, Lenin says: "We must mercilessly suppress the thoroughly dishonest and insolently slanderous bourgeois press."

Lenin does not believe in natural rights. Mr. Burleson as a Jeffersonian should. Like Lenin he does not. Hardly anybody does any more. But the dogma of free speech rests on the dogma of natural rights and dies without it. Norman Angell can prove that free speech is materially useful to practical progress in society. He proves it in vain. No consideration of ultimate social utility will check a ruler tempted to the immediate demonstrable physical gain of silencing his opponents. All that can check him in any way is an instinct, a fear, a faith which grants to every man a set of rights beyond human recall.

Thomas Jefferson knew what he was about when he grounded his defense of free speech on the absolute assertion that "God created the mind free." If he did not, then Lenin will mould mind as he kneads bread. God has been much invoked, he has even been much kidnapped by the Tories, but some day perhaps we shall see a revival of Thomas Jefferson's God, a God who might be said to differ from the God of the Tories in this: that while he is so known and so explicit that of course we try to live in obedience to his will, he nevertheless remains so altogether unknown and unknowable that he still moves through mysteries to his wonders and we dare not lay the hand of force on his searchings toward his fulfillment in men's minds. The only Easter of free speech in the modern world is in his resurrection.

In the meantime Mr. Burleson has to be exonerated. He did not cause the modern decline in the sense of liberty and he did not conduct his censorship unlawfully or indeed immoderately. The lesson is not in him but in the censorship itself. It shines out from our experiences in information about Russia and in information about many other things, and it tells us emphatically:

Censorship begins by merely controlling the expression of

thought, it finishes by making thought. We start by trying to outwit our opponents. We end by being all of us outwitted by the office-holders.

Even with no belief in free speech as a theory, we may well dislike official mind-moulding as a fact. We have seen that fact in prodigious practice during the war. We have seen it. The question is: Will we remember it when we are urged as we shall be urged to continue a censorship in one form or another, on into peace, over radical book publishers and radical public speakers and radical groups of university professors and radical unions of grade school teachers and other alleged Bolshevists, in the name of alleged Americanism? Will we remember that by our popular intolerance of *certain* people during the war we gave to our office-holders a personal power over *all* people, in cluding ourselves, which we did not really mean to give them, but which is inherent and inevitable in censorship and which is manifestly un-American?

World War II

34. FREEDOM IN WARTIME

American Civil Liberties Union, 1943

In the wake of World War I, suppressions, mob actions, and multiple prosecutions, followed by severe sentences for speaking or printing criticism of America's part in the conflict, there was widespread concern among students of civil liberties that another

---

From American Civil Liberties Union, "Freedom in Wartime," *Annual Report* (New York: 1943), pp. 3–11.

war would spell disaster for freedom of expression. The prospect of ever fiercer wars and attendant greater national need for total commitment by the people seemed to portend the strictest regimentation and control of speech and press.

However, when World War II enveloped America, and a year and then two of fighting passed, those alert to the fate of civil liberties in wartime realized that the apprehensive predictions were not being realized. The American Civil Liberties Union, chronicling each year's state of civil liberties in its annual reports, found a sharp contrast with World War I. In some surprise and with marked gratification, it reported during each war year that freedom of speech and press was in far healthier condition than in the previous conflict. There were dark exceptions—especially in the impounding of Americans of Japanese descent in isolated camps—but in sum, the ACLU found, democracy was maintaining the essentials of liberty even in deep crisis.

Review of the Year

(to June, 1943)

The striking contrast between the state of civil liberty in the first eighteen months of World War II and in World War I offers strong evidence to support the thesis that our democracy can fight even the greatest of all wars and still maintain the essentials of liberty. The country in World War II is almost wholly free of those pressures which in the first World War resulted in mob violence against dissenters, hundreds of prosecutions for utterances; in the creation of a universal volunteer vigilante system, officially recognized, to report dissent to the F.B.I.; in hysterical hatred of everything German; in savage sentences for private expressions of criticism; and in suppression of public debate of the issues of the war and the peace.

No such atmosphere marks the present war. We experience no hysteria, no war-inspired mob violence, no pressure for suppressing dissent, no activity of a secret political police, no organization of virtuous patriots seeking out seditious opinion, and no hostility to persons of German or Italian origin. Hostility to persons of Japanese ancestry, while painfully in evidence, is largely confined to the Pacific Coast and smaller communities in the west.

The government has not resorted to prosecution or censorship on any appreciable scale. War-time prosecutions brought by the Department of Justice for utterances, and publications barred by the Post Office Department as obstructive, have so far numbered about forty-five, involving less than two hundred persons, compared with over a thousand persons involved in almost as many cases in World War I. Even though some of the proceedings were hardly justified by any reasonable interpretation of the "clear and present danger" test laid down by the Supreme Court, the Department of Justice has on the whole shown commendable restraint.

A striking test of our progress in war-time tolerance is the much more favorable attitude to Jehovah's Witnesses, whose anti-war propaganda and public activities are calculated to provoke patriotic opposition. Yet in contrast with World War I, when their leaders were jailed and their propaganda curbed, and with outbursts against them in 1940, they have been accorded by the courts and by public opinion even greater liberties than in time of peace.

Conclusions as to our comparative freedom are supported not only by observation of the larger national aspects, but by local observers all over the country. A check-up early in 1943 with 112 correspondents of the Union in 41 states showed remarkable unanimity on the almost complete absence of repressive tendencies, and a surprising freedom of debate and criticism of war measures. Many of them reported the general climate of freedom in their localities as much better than even a year ago.

The record of violations of civil liberties shows the extraordinary fact that more issues and cases have arisen from the normal conflicts in our democracy than from the pressures of war, though some have been accentuated by war-time strains. In that continuing field, the record, particularly in May and June with the agitation over the miners' strikes and the outbreaks of racial mob violence, has been far from encouraging.

The causes of the heartening contrast with World War I in war-inspired issues are to be found in the comparatively slight opposition to the war,—concealed and unorganized,—against a vigorous radical and pacifist opposition then; in the widespread opposition to the Administration from powerful sources acting in the conventional democratic pattern, which tends to keep open the channels of debate and criticism; in the concentration of public attention not on attitudes to the war but on the debate as to what kind of a post-war world we are in process of creating; in the liberal policies of the Administration; and in the much firmer foundations put under the Bill of Rights in the last decade by numerous Supreme Court decisions.

The measures taken by the government to intern dangerous enemy aliens, to denaturalize the disloyal who acquired citizenship by fraud, to control espionage and sabotage—virtually nonexistent,—the centralization of controls in Washington, have all tended to allay fear and to create the conviction that any movements obstructive of the war are well in hand.

But this encouraging war record is not without its inevitable exceptions. From the viewpoint of both the numbers affected and the seriousness of the rights violated, undoubtedly the worst single invasion of citizens' liberties under war pressures was the wholesale evacuation from the Pacific Coast of over 70,000 Americans of Japanese ancestry and their subsequent confinement in what are virtually concentration camps. The evils and injustices of that desperate move, dictated by race prejudice and military precaution, have been somewhat relieved by permitting those found to be loyal to leave the centers and resettle outside the military zones; by recently accepting into the army volunteers of Japanese ancestry after excluding them from Selective Service, and even by permitting soldiers in uniform to return to the evacuated area. But none of the measures are as yet nearly adequate to restore the rights of American citizens nor to offer a long-range solution. . . .

In the larger arena of communication an exception to the excellent record of war-time control of press and radio under voluntary codes must be recorded in the censorship of non-military news cabled to allied nations. Undue caution as to what news and opinion might feed the Axis propaganda machine has led to unreasonable restraints, particularly on news of race conflicts, and to frequent complaints by foreign correspondents.

The treatment of conscientious objectors, so much better in principle than in World War I, has nevertheless resulted in imprisoning more than three times as many, in large part because of a narrow interpretation of "religious training and belief" and reluctance to parole men to useful occupations. The administration of the Selective Service law has resulted in jailing hundreds of Jehovah's Witnesses, who demand a status as ministers although they are not employed full-time in that occupation and who, when that status is denied, prefer jail to any form of compulsory war service. The Supreme Court has, however, agreed to review one case in which draft boards denied the ministerial status. More Jehovah's Witnesses are in prison today for their particular brand of conscience than any other minority in the country.

Although the government has generously freed all Italian enemy aliens of war-time restrictions, it has not yet moved to free a class with an even greater claim on our democracy—the anti-Nazi German refugees who are still under the same restrictions as apply to all enemy aliens.

In addition to these exceptions to the generally favorable administration of war-time controls, apprehension is expressed in many quarters over the effects on our liberties of the vastly expanded war-time powers of government. Many, indeed, profess to see in measures already taken the outlines of a totalitarian state. But these measures largely concern economic controls which do not directly affect freedom of opinion and debate, nor the right of opposition or of criticism. Apprehension is also expressed over the prospects of the passage of a civilian compulsory war-service act, and its presumed effects in regimenting the entire population. But fear for the future of our democracy does not negate the plain facts of a record so far generally encouraging. . . .

This survey of the record justifies, we believe, our opening assertion that "our democracy can fight even the greatest of all wars and still maintain the essentials of liberty." Indeed, this is not the whole of the story, for we witness in this war not only the substantial maintenance of our rights but vigorous campaigns to strengthen and extend them. Thus, even with a conservative Congress, the movement for abolition of the poll tax makes headway; the attacks on the various censorships yield results; campaigns waged by Negroes, by labor, and by other minority groups register advances; court decisions have considerably enlarged constitutional guarantees; and the executive departments of the government have on the whole shown a growing response to the protection of minority rights.

But in the midst of so vast a conflict, with uncertain shifts in national and international policy in the war and post-war periods, it would be folly to let any encouragement lead to complacency. Dangers remain great. Undue prolongation of the war, reaction from war weariness or the growth of reaction in other fields, a sudden change in the public temper, might easily reverse the record of these months.

Today, as always, only "eternal vigilance" and activity protects our liberties. Sensitive and alert awareness by all liberal forces, instant and determined resistance to every encroachment, and the foresight to anticipate and effectively to meet whatever new forces of repression and reaction may appear—these will alone preserve the democratic process of change.

Part Six

SEX AND OBSCENITY

35. DEATH TRAPS BY MAIL

Anthony Comstock, 1884

The attack on the obscene—and on countless allegedly obscene works of high literary and artistic worth, of social and scientific importance—started in earnest in America with the career of the famous Anthony Comstock. From 1873 until his death in 1915, he was the unquestioned leader of the zealots in the assault upon Eros. He began his work in 1868 and soon became the agent of the New York Society for the Suppression of Vice; tested his powers early as the chief lobbyist in the passage of the federal "Comstock Act" of 1873; developed his techniques of seizure and arrest as a special, unpaid agent of the Post Office; and battled the "liberals" (as he called the colleagues and followers of Robert G. Ingersoll) throughout his life. His name gave the language "Comstockery"—a synonym for a bundle of attitudes that include prudery, fear of sex, shame, and the inclination to suppress.

From Anthony Comstock, *Traps for the Young* (3rd edition; New York: Funk & Wagnalls, 1884), pp. 131–142.

Just what spurred the widespread public approval of his work is hard to determine, but that legislators felt it and that courts read it in the temper of the times seems difficult to dispute. And what drove Comstock himself is hard to know, but that his writings reveal a mind obsessed with images and practices that he considered "impure" or "lustful" is patent. He declared that an agony of soul, mind, and body was the fate of young people caught in the "death trap" of sex, and he described their torment in the vivid detail known to the experienced.

In the selection below, two themes that recur in his writing are striking: that exposure to a pornographic work means moral and physical ruin for countless young people, and that he and his supporters could suppress the offending materials of sex faster than printing presses could produce them.

As has been seen, Satan is permitted to place his traps where they will do him most good and the children most harm. The sickening details of crimes, infidel scoffings, cheap works of fiction, newspaper advertisements, "blood-and-thunder" story papers—all are freely admitted around the hearthstones and under the roof-trees of the land.

We now come to a class that is thrust upon the youth in secret. The favorite method is under the sanctity of the seal in the United States mail. By means of it the most infamous scoundrel may send the vilest matter to the purest boy or girl. And *this is being done systematically*. If the facts of the business of obscene publications and indecent articles could be published here, a shock would be given to the sensitive and decent in the community that would make their blood run cold, while a wave of indignation would roll over the country that would sweep away any person found engaging in the business. The evils we have been considering travel openly, and are seen on all sides. But here comes a more subtle and insidious snare. To one acquainted with the history, the variety, and extent of this evil, it does not seem possible that man could sink so low as to edit such foulness, while it appears impossible for the human mind to invent the variety of indecencies which formerly existed before the effectual efforts of the New York Society for the Suppression of Vice had suppressed them.

Secrecy marks these operations. In the darkness of attic-room, of basement or cellar, is the favorite salesroom. The message of these evil things is death—socially, morally, physically, and spiritually.

This moral vulture steals upon our youth in the home, school, and college, silently striking its terrible talons into their vitals, and forcibly bearing them away on hideous wings to shame and death. Like a cancer, it fastens itself upon the imagination, and sends down into the future life thousands of roots, poisoning the nature, enervating the system, destroying self-respect, fettering the will-power, defiling the mind, corrupting the thoughts, leading to secret practices of most foul and revolting character, until the victim tires of life, and existence is scarcely endurable. It sears the conscience, hardens the heart, and damns the soul. It leads to lust and lust breeds unhallowed living, and sinks man, made in the image of God, below the level of the beasts. There is no force at work in the community more insidious, more constant in its demands, or more powerful and far-reaching than lust. *It is the constant companion of all other crimes.* It is honeycombing society. Like a frightful monster, it stands peering over the sleeping child, to catch its first thoughts on awakening. This is especially true where the eye of youth has been defiled with the scenes of lasciviousness in the weekly criminal papers, or by their offsprings, obscene books and pictures. The peace of the family is wrecked, homes desolated, and society degraded, while it curses more and more each generation born into the world.

Think of the homes that are wrecked by unbridled passion, of the curse that falls upon any community when there is spread before the eyes of all classes by the newspaper gossip, the inner secrets of those whited sepulchres, those moral monsters, who, stripped of all sense of shame, parade their foul living in the courts.

From the first impure thought till the close of the loathsome life of the victim of lust, there is a succession of sickening, offensive, and disgusting scenes before the mind, until life, to such a one, must be made up of disease, wounds, and putrefying sores. Suicide dances before his vision in his moments of despondency as the only means by which to hide his shame, and the sole cure for his wretched condition. The turgid waters speak louder with the death stillness which they promise than does hope, with its beckonings to a better life. Turn as he will, the chains of habit permit him to go but a short distance before they clank their hold upon him. The brightest sun over his head seems scarcely able to penetrate the gloom of despair that youthful indiscretions have often woven into his life. His one cry is, "Who shall deliver me from the body of this death?"

As the jackal follows in the wake of its equally ferocious yet stronger foe, so murder haunts the pathway of lust. There are in a neighboring city, at this writing, three youths on trial for murder. It is charged that after a most monstrous conspiracy, a young and beautiful maiden was ruined and then murdered to hide their shame. Lust has but to whistle, and red-handed murder quickly responds, obedient to his master.

I repeat, *lust is the boon companion of all other crimes.* There is no evil so extensive, none doing more to destroy the institutions of free America. It sets aside the laws of God and morality; marriage bonds are broken, most sacred ties severed, State laws ignored, and dens of infamy plant themselves in almost every community, and then reaching out like immense cuttlefish, draw in, from all sides, our youth to destruction.

Obscene literature may be said to be the favorite agency of the evil one to recruit these dens. City houses of ill-fame, in many instances, are filled with the daughters of country homes. Often children are scarcely able to walk before a curse and blight has been attempted by some foul-minded nurse upon these buds of humanity. Scarcely have they become able to observe what is passing about them before the seeds of impurity meet their eyes in the licentious papers that line their pathway. Then when the critical period approaches when they emerge from youth to manhood or womanhood, when those mysterious changes in nature take place, and they become aware of new emotions within, then the wily one stands ready to capture and pervert them to his own hellish purposes.

Consider some of his devices in this respect. Many a parent, before sending the child away from home to school, canvasses the country over for a proper and desirable institution where the child shall have all the comforts and advantages of home and culture. All the details are inquired into with greatest care. At last the child reaches the school, and his or her name appears upon the roll and is printed in the catalogue. These catalogues are sought for by those who send circulars through the mails advertising obscene and unlawful wares.

The obscenity dealer, the quacks, the lottery managers, and the frauds all adopt the same method of advertising, to wit, either as above, or by buying old letters from other dealers for the sake of the names, or by sending circulars to postal clerks and others through the country, offering prizes for a list of the names of youth of both sexes under twenty-one years of age, or by purchasing addressed envelopes of those who make a business of collecting names, and then addressing envelopes to supply parties doing business through the mails. These are some of the devices in vogue to secure names.

In one instance a professor of a female seminary of great prominence informed me that some party had obtained surreptitiously of one of his assistants some fifteen or more catalogues of other female seminaries and colleges. After a long search I discovered the party, and when I called for the catalogues he brought out a pile of about one hundred different ones, and we selected the ones he had borrowed. I wrote immediately to each of the heads of these institutions, and before the close of that year I received complaints from more than one half of the number written to, who had detected noxious matter sent to the students. From two of these came almost direct replies, containing circulars of death-dealing articles of a most infamous character sent to young ladies. These are unfit for description. One lady teacher wrote, "Not only must this scoundrel have the catalogue of the present, but of the last term as well, as he has sent to the graduates of last term, besides sending to those of the present."

These catalogues then are directories for the venders of obscene matter, etc., which furnish them the names of our boys and girls. *Children have thrust upon them, unsolicited, these death-traps.* Their curiosity is piqued, and unconscious of danger, they often send for the matter advertised, simply to gratify inquisitiveness.

Let us suppose that a boy who has been brought up in a Christian home is thus placed at school, and has one of these vile circulars sent him by mail. He has never heard of this matter before. His curiosity "to just see what it is," is the first allurement of the devil. This is made to seem laudable to the child's simple mind. He promises himself that he will not show it to any one, he will just see what it is, and then destroy it. He thus silences conscience. He sends the money as requested or directed on the circular. In a few days the cursed thing comes by mail. The recipient hies away to his room in secret, to open it, to see what it is. Conscience tells him he is doing wrong. A sense of guilt and shame, a feeling that he is doing a mean thing, come over him before the seal is broken. He knows his teacher would disapprove, and that it would break his mother's heart if she knew of it. As he thinks of her his first impulse is to throw the package unopened in the fire. Blessed is the boy who acts thus wisely, for he shall escape a lasting curse.

But the tempter is watching intently. This momentary delay worries him. It will not do to loose his victim, when thus almost in his trap, and all that is necessary is just a nibble at his bait for a sure capture. He whispers, "Just look at it a moment so as to see what it is, and then you can destroy it." So urged, the boy breaks the seal and lets the monster loose. The hideous appearance at first shocks the pure mind, and the poor victim would fain put it out of existence. But the tempter says, "It can't hurt you; you are strong. Look it over and see what it is. Don't be afraid." Thus beguiled, a second look, and then a mighty force from within is let loose. Passions that had slumbered or lain dormant are awakened, and the boy is forced over a precipice, and death and destruction are sure, except the grace of God saves him. An indelible stain has been placed upon the boy's imagination, and this vision shall be kept like a panorama, moving to and fro before his mind until it has blotted out moral purity, and the lamentable condition before described is experienced.

Intemperance marks its victim by the bleared eye, bloated face, red nose, tainted breath, reeling form, and tottering step. The effects of this evil are not so easily discerned. *Its most deadly effects are felt by the victims in the habit of secret vices, before their course is marked by external appearances.*

Many a parent sends away the child pure, fresh, and vigorous. He comes back, after a few years' absence, with pale cheeks, lustreless and sunken eyes, enervated body, moody, nervous, and irritable—a moral wreck—and the parents mourn "that the child has studied too hard." If they could get at the real trouble, it would be found that the child had fallen into one of these lust-traps, or death traps by mail. Habits thus formed many a youth promises himself he will check at a certain date; that when he is a man, or twenty-one years of age, he will stop his vicious practices. Ah! silly boy, the shackles of habit you will never be able to throw off by your own unaided strength. The longer indulgence continues, the weaker you become to will and do against the force within. The standard of self-respect is being constantly lowered, and the will weakened. *The time to stop is before you begin.*

Where does this evil exist? Where are these traps set? I

reply, everywhere. Children of all grades in society, institutions of learning in all sections of the land, and the most select homes, are invaded by the evil of licentious literature. The danger is not so great as it was ten years ago, as there is not so much of this grossest business done as in former years, as the tabular statement from the last annual report of the New York Society for the Suppression of Vice shows, to wit:

TABULAR STATEMENT, SHOWING A PART OF THE WORK OF THE NEW YORK SOCIETY FOR THE SUPPRESSION OF VICE, FROM ITS ORGANIZATION.

DESCRIPTION.	Prior to January, 1882.	1882.	Total.
Persons arrested in U. S. Courts	248	10	258
Persons arrested in State Courts	334	108	442
Discharged by committing magistrates	27	8	35
Discharged by juries	9	8	17
Convicted or plead guilty	281	30	311
Sentenced	251	22	273
Prisoners absconded	19	1	20
Prisoners rearrested	25	3	28
Disagreement by juries	12	. . . .	12
Convicted on second trial	5	. . . .	5
Bail bonds forfeited	$50,900	$2,500	$53,400
	yrs. mos. days.	years. days.	years. days.
Years of imprisonment imposed	151 11 23	3 20	155 13
Amount of fines imposed	$63,931	$1,325.97	$65,256.97
Convicts pardoned	17		17
STOCK CONFISCATED			
Books and sheet stock seized and destroyed	27,584 lbs.	2 lbs.	27,586 lbs.

DESCRIPTION.	Prior to January, 1882.	1882.	Total.
Obscene pictures and photos ..	203,238	1,301	204,539
Microscopic pictures for charms, knives, etc.	7,400	....	7,400
Negative plates for making obscene photographs	1,700	....	1,700
Engraved steel and copper plates	352	....	352
Woodcuts and electro-plates ..	536	3	539
Stereotype plates for printing books, etc.	14,495 lbs.	....	14,495 lbs.
Number of different books	165	....	165
Lithographic stones destroyed .	50	....	50
Articles for immoral use, of rubber, etc.	64,836	....	64,836
Lead moulds for making obscene matter	700 lbs.	....	700 lbs.
Establishments for making same closed	5	....	5
Indecent playing cards destroyed	6,122	....	6,122
Boxes of pills, powders, etc., used by abortionists	4,185	....	4,185
Circulars, catalogues, songs, poems, etc.	1,376,939	50	1,376,989
Newspapers containing unlawful advertisements or obscene matter	22,354	....	22,354
Open letters seized in possession of persons arrested	105,280	181	105,461
Names of dealers as revealed by account-books of publishers .	6,000	....	6,000
Obscene pictures, framed on walls of saloons	27	....	27
Figures and images seized and destroyed	569	93	662

DESCRIPTION.	Prior to January, 1882.	1882.	Total.
Letters, packages, etc., seized in hands of dealers ready for mailing at the time of arrest	3,421	....	3,421
Names and P. O. addresses to whom circulars, etc., may be sent, that are sold as matters of merchandise, seized in hands of persons arrested ...	976,125	2,885	979,010
Obscene plays stopped, or places of amusement closed	4	....	4
Miles travelled by agent outside N. Y. City	173,992 mi.	16,106	190,098 mi.

. . . To say that twenty-five tons of weight of contraband matter has been seized by the Society for the Suppression of Vice, while it sums up the facts, does not present to the ordinary mind the fearful magnitude of this evil.

In 1872, when the work of extermination against this evil commenced, there were 165 different books published in New York and Brooklyn. Numerous establishments were in full blast, turning out obscene pictures and articles for indecent purposes, and of the vilest character. In all the so-called sporting papers, in many otherwise respectable weekly journals, in the daily, and sometimes covertly in the religious papers, these foul articles and things were advertised. According to the account-books of the publishers and manufacturers seized by the above society, there were about 4000 dealers scattered throughout the country. These supplied themselves from the headquarters for the production of these nefarious goods in New York and Brooklyn. All the known manufactories and publishing houses of these obscene articles have been closed. The plates for printing and illustrating 163 of the 165 books have been seized and destroyed, and there is the best of evidence that the owner suppressed the other two from fear. A vigilant watch is kept to discover any new enterprises. There are traces of the old stock, and this is supplemented by leaflets, poems, songs, doggerel, and other cheap forms of nastiness, at the present time. Here and there some amateur printer or clerk in a printing establishment issues a small lot of vileness, but the immense stock-in-trade formerly carried by dealers no longer exists. Many now have taken to writing out copies of this old matter. I arrested a young man away up in Maine, who, living on a farm, advertised in some of the papers, and then for $1 would copy and send by mail a four-page notesheet of this filth.

Of twenty varieties recently seized, all but one or two were copies in writing from old printed matter.

Night and day this evil has been pursued by the agents of the society referred to in this chapter. Eternal vigilance is the price of moral purity. Let the efforts of this society be relaxed, or allow it to be known that its efforts will cease, and there are hundreds of villains ready to embark in this soul-destroying business. . . .

36. LIBERTY OF CONSCIENCE, SPEECH, AND PRESS

Theodore Schroeder, 1906

Theodore Schroeder was probably the most prolific champion of free speech and press in American history. From the 1890's almost until the mid-twentieth century, his articles and books

From Theodore Schroeder, "Liberty of Conscience, Speech and Press" (1906), pp. 3–15. Pamphlet. Republished for the author from *The Liberal Review*, August and September 1906.

ranged into philosophical, psychological, sociological, anthropological, cultural, and legal aspects of control of expression. Natural rights and moral and social progress underlay his insistence on unrestricted and unpunished speech and press except when it could be determined that words had "inseparably accompanied" some attempted or achieved violence to person or property. It was anathema to Schroeder for authorities to have power to decide whether words were criminal, on the basis of an "*ex post facto* guess" about the words' "psychologic tendency" to do damage.

While Schroeder wrote untiringly against punishing radical attacks on government and "blasphemous" attacks on religion, his first concern was with the law of obscenity and the attitudes, activities, suppressions, and long-term effects of the nation's Comstocks. Until 1906, his output was small; that year marked the start of his major commitment to writing about free speech and press.

The desire to persecute, even for mere opinion's sake, seems to be an eternal inheritance of humans. We naturally and as a matter of course encourage others in doing and believing whatever for any reason, or without reason, we deem proper. Even though we have a mind fairly well disciplined in the duty of toleration, we quite naturally discourage others and feel a sense of outraged propriety, whenever they believe and act radically different from ourselves. Our resentment becomes vehement just in proportion as our reason is impotent and our nerves diseasedly sensitive. That is why it is said that "man is naturally, instinctively intolerant and a persecutor."

From this necessity of our undisciplined nature comes the stealthy but inevitable recurrence of legalized bigotry, and its rehabilitation of successive inquisitions. From the days of pagan antiquity to the present hour, there has never been a time or country wherein mankind could claim immunity from all persecution for intellectual differences. This cruel intolerance has always appealed to a "sacred and patriotic duty," and masked behind an ignorantly made and unwarranted pretense of "morality."

"Persecution has not been the outgrowth of any one age, nationality or creed; it has been the ill-favored progeny of all." Thus, under the disguise of new names and new pretensions, again and again we punish unpopular, though wholly self-regarding, non-moral conduct, imprison men for expressing honest intellectual differences, deny the duty of toleration, destroy a proper liberty of thought and conduct, and always under the same old false pretenses of "morality," "law and order."

Whenever our natural tendency toward intolerance is reinforced by abnormally intense feelings, such as diseased nerves produce, persecution follows quite unavoidably, because the intensity of associated emotions is transformed into a conviction of inerrancy. Such a victim of diseased emotions, even more than others, "knows because he feels, and is firmly convinced because strongly agitated." Unable to answer logically the contention of his neighbor, he ends by desiring to punish him as his enemy. Because of the close interdependence of the emotional and the generative mechanism, it is probable that superstitious opinions about the relation of men and women will be the last superstition to disappear.

The concurrence of many in like emotions, associated with and centered upon the same focus of irritation, makes the effective majority of the state view the toleration of their opponents as a crime, and their heresy, whether political, religious, ethical or sexual, is denounced a danger to civil order, and the heretic must be judicially silenced. Thus all bigots have reasoned in all past ages. Thus do those afflicted with our present sex superstition again defend their moral censorship of literature and art.

These are the processes by which we always become incapable of deriving profit from the lessons of history. That all the greatest minds of every age believed in something now known to be false, and in the utility of what is now deemed injurious or immoral, never suggests to petty intellects that the future generations will also pity us for having entertained our most cherished opinions.

The presence of these designated natural defects, which so very few have outgrown, makes it quite probable that the battle for intellectual freedom will never reach an end. The few, trained in the duty of toleration, owe it to humanity to re-state, with great frequency, the arguments for mental hospitality. Only by this process can we contribute directly toward the mental discipline of the relatively unevolved masses, and prepare the way for those new and therefore unpopular truths by which the race will progress. The absolute liberty of thought, with opportunity, unlimited as between adults for its oral or printed expression is a condition precedent to the highest development of our progressive morality.

Men of strong passions and weak intellects seldom see the expediency of encouraging others to disagree. Thence came all of those terrible persecutions for heresy, witchcraft, sedition, etc., which have prolonged the midnight of superstition into "dark ages." The passionate zeal of a masterful few has always made them assume that they only could be trusted to have a personal judgment upon moral questions, while all others must be coerced, unquestioningly to accept them upon authority.

Such egomania always resulted in the persecution of those who furnished the common people with the materials upon which they might base a different opinion, or outgrow their slave-virtues.

One of Queen Mary's first acts was an inhibition against reading or teaching the Bible in churches and against printing books. In 1530, the king, pursuant to a memorial of the House of Commons, issued a proclamation requiring every person "which hath a New Testament or the Old, translated into English or any other boke of Holy Scripture, so translated, beinge in printe," to surrender them within fifteen days, "as he will avoyde the Kynge's high indignation and displeasure," which meant death.

Another and similar proclamation was issued, covering the New Testament and writings of many theologians. The act passed in the 3rd and 4th Edward VI, repeated this folly. So thousands of Bibles were burned under the personal supervision and benediction of priests and bishops, because of the immoral tendency of reading the "Divine Record" by which ordinary persons might acquire a private judgment as to its meaning.[1]

Poor William Tyndale, who took the infinite trouble of translating the scriptures into English, found that, "his New Testament was forthwith burnt in London;" and he himself, after some years, was strangled and burnt at Antwerp. (1536.[2])

So now we have many who likewise esteem it to be of immoral tendency for others than themselves to secure such information as may lead to a personal and different opinion about the physiology, psychology, hygiene, or ethics of sex, and by law, we make it a crime to distribute any specific and detailed information upon the subject, especially if it be unprudish in the manner of its presentation or is accompanied with unorthodox opinions about marriage or sexual ethics. This is repeating the old folly that the adult masses cannot be trusted to form an opinion of their own. The "free" people of the United States cannot be allowed to have the information which might lead to a change of their own statute laws upon sex.

There will always be those thoughtless enough to believe that truth may be properly suppressed for considerations of expediency. I prefer to believe with Professor Max Muller, that "The truth is always safe, and nothing else is safe;" and with Drummond that "He that will not reason, is a bigot; he that

---

[1] Vickers' "Martyrdom of Literature," pp. 190, 225 to 227.

[2] Books Condemned to be Burnt, page 9.

cannot reason is a fool, and he that dares not reason is a slave;" and with Thomas Jefferson when in his inaugural address he wrote "Error of opinion may be tolerated, when reason is left free to combat it;" and I believe these are still truisms even though the subject is sex.

We have only to go back a few centuries to find an influential clique of pious men trying to maintain a monopoly of "truth." Those who disputed their affirmations whether about geology or theology, were promptly beheaded or burnt. The clerical monopolists denied common people the right not only of having an independent judgment as to the significance, or value, or truth of "holy writ," but even denied them the right to read the book itself, because it would tempt them to independent judgment, which might be erroneous, and thus make them "immoral."

The contents and the interpretation of the Bible, together with the political tyranny founded on these, must, "with humble prostration of intellect," be unquestioningly accepted. Those who disputed the self-constituted mouthpieces of God were promptly killed. And now, those who dispute, without "humble prostration of intellect," any of the ready-made ignorance on the physiology, hygiene and psychology or ethics of sex, are promptly sent to jail. Yet we call this a "free" country, and our age a "civilized" one.

By the same appeal to a misguided expediency, we find that only a few years ago it was a crime to teach a Negro slave how to read or write. Education would make him doubt his slave-virtues, and with a consciousness of the injustice being inflicted upon him, he might disturb the public order to secure redress. So, imparting education became immoral, and was made a crime.

An effort was made to make it a crime to send anti-slavery literature through the mails because of its immoral tendency, and southern postmasters often destroyed it without warrant of law, before delivery to those to whom it was addressed.

Within the past century, married women had no rights

which their husbands need respect, and education to women was made impossible, though the imparting of it was not penalized. Now they may acquire an education about everything, except what ought to be the most important to them, if married, namely: a scientific knowledge of the ethics, physiology, hygiene, and psychology of sex. To furnish them with literature of the highest scientific order, even though true and distributed from good motives, or in print to assert their "natural right and necessity for sexual self-government," is now a crime, and we call it "obscenity" and "indecency."

Formerly, when bigots were rampant and openly dominant, the old superstition punished the psychological crime of "immoral thinking," because it was irreligious, and it was called "sedition," "blasphemy," etc. Under the present verbal disguise, the same old superstition punishes the psychological crime of immoral thinking, because it may discredit the ethical claims of religious asceticism, and now we call it "obscenity" and "indecency." What is the difference between the old and the new superstition and persecution?

Strange to say, there are hundreds of thousands of the unchurched, who, for want of clear mental vision or adequate moral courage, are fostering the suppression of unconventional thinking, and justify it, upon considerations of expediency.

The argument against the expediency of truth is ever the last refuge of retreating error, the weakest subterfuge to conceal a dawning consciousness of ignorance. In all history, one cannot find a single instance in which an enlargement of opportunity for the propagation of unpopular allegations of truth has not resulted in increased good.

"If I were asked, 'What opinion, from the commencement of history to the present hour, had been productive of the most injury to mankind?' I should answer, without hesitation: 'The inexpediency of publishing sentiments of supposed bad tendency.' " It is this infamous opinion which has made the world a vale of tears, and drenched it with the blood of martyrs.

I am fully mindful of the fact that an unrestricted press

means that some abuse of the freedom of the press will result. However, I also remember that no man can tell *a priori* what opinion is of immoral tendency. I am furthermore mindful that we cannot argue against the use of a thing, from the possibility of its abuse, since this objection can be urged against every good thing, and I am not willing to destroy all that makes life pleasant. Lord Littleton aptly said: "To argue against any breach of liberty from the ill use that may be made of it is to argue against liberty itself, since all is capable of being abused."

Everyone who believes in the relative and progressive morality of scientific ethics, must logically believe in the immorality of a code which preaches absolutism in morals upon the authority of inspired texts, instead of deriving moral precepts from natural, physical law. But that is no warrant for the scientific moralist suppressing the teaching of religious morality, as inexpedient, even if he believed it to be so and had the power. Neither can the religious moralist justify himself in the suppression of the opinions of his scientific opponents. It is alone by comparison and contrast, that each perfects his own system, and in the end all are better off for having permitted the disputation.

No argument for the suppression of "obscene" literature has ever been offered which will not justify by unavoidable implication, and which has not already justified, every other limitation that has ever been put upon mental freedom. No argument was ever made to justify intolerance, whether political, theological, or scientific, which has not been restated in support of our present sex superstitions and made to do duty toward the suppressing of information as to the physiology, psychology, or ethics of sex. All this class of arguments that have been made have always started with the false assumption that such qualities as morality or immorality could belong to opinions, or to a static fact.

Because violence is deemed necessary to prevent a change, or the acquisition of an opinion concerning the hygiene, physiology or ethics of sex, we must infer that those who defend the press censorship are unconsciously claiming omniscient infallibility for the present sexual intelligence. If their sex opinions were a product of mere fallible reason, they would not feel the need or duty to suppress rational criticism. By denying others the right of publishing either confirmation or criticism, they admit that their present opinions are a matter of superstition and indefensible as a matter of reason. To support a sex superstition by law is just as reprehensible as, in the past, it was to support the, now partially exploded, governmental, scientific and theological superstitions, by the same process. This be it remembered, was always done in the name of "morality," "law and order," etc.

There may still be those, who, like Dr. Johnson, argue that the persecutors of Christians were right, because the persecution of an advocate is a necessary ordeal through which his truth always passes successfully; legal penalties, in the end, being powerless against the truth, though sometimes beneficially effective against mischievous error.

It may be a historical fact that all known truths, for a time, have been crushed by the bigot's heel, but this should not make us applaud his iniquity. It is an aphorism of unbalanced optimists, that truth crushed to earth will always rise. Even if this were true, it must always remain an unprovable proposition, because it postulates that at every particular moment we are ignorant of all those suppressed truths, not then resurrected, and since we do not know them, we cannot prove that they ever will be resurrected. It would be interesting to know how one could prove that an unknown truth of past suppression is going to be rediscovered, or that the conditions which alone once made it a cognizable fact will ever again come into being. And yet a knowledge of it might have a very important bearing on some present controversy of moment.

Surely, many dogmas have been wholly suppressed which were once just as earnestly believed to be as infallibly true as some that are now accepted as inspired writ. Just a little more strenuosity in persecution would have wiped out Christianity. How can we prove that all the suppressed, and now unknown, dogmas were false? If mere survival after persecution is deemed evidence of the inerrancy of an opinion, then which of the many conflicting opinions, each a survivor of persecution, are unquestionably true, and how is the choice to be made from the mass? Is it not clear that neither a rediscovery, nor a survival after persecution, can have any special relation to truth as such? If it is, then let us unite to denounce as an unprovable hallucination the statement that truth crushed to earth will rise again.

The abettors of persecution are more damaged than those whom they deter from expressing and defending unpopular opinions, since as between these, only the former are depriving themselves of the chief means of correcting their own errors. But the great mass of people belong neither to the intellectual innovators, nor to their persecutors. The great multitude might be quite willing to listen to or read unconventional thoughts if ever permitted, amid opportunity, to exercise an uncoerced choice.

Much of the justification for intolerance derives its authority from false analogies, wrongfully carried over from physical relations into the realm of the psychic.

Thus some argue that because we, by laws, protect the incompetent against being (unconsciously) infected with contagious disease, therefore the state should also protect them (even though mature and able to protect themselves by mere inattention) against the literature of infectious moral poison. Here a figure of speech is mistaken for an analogy. "Moral poison" exists only figuratively and not literally in any such sense as strychnine is a poison.

Ethics is not one of the exact sciences. Probably it never will be. Until we are at least approximately as certain of the existence and tests of "moral poison," as we are of the physical characteristics and consequences of carbolic acid, it is folly to talk of "moral poison" except as a matter of poetic license.

In the realm of morals no age has ever shown an agreement, even among its wisest and best men, either as to what is morally poisonous, or by what test it is to be judged as morally deadly. Moral concepts are a matter of geography and evolution. The morality of one country or age is viewed as the moral poison of another country or age. The defended morality of one social or business circle is deemed the immorality of another. The ideals which attach to one man's God, are those of another man's devil. Furthermore, our best scientific thinkers concur in the belief that all morality is relative and progressive, whereas numerous other men deem a part or all of our conduct to be *per se* moral or immoral. Some deem the source of authority in matters of morals to be God, as his will is manifested through the revelations or prophets of his particular church, or that interpretation of them, which some particular branch of some particular church promulgates. Others find morality only in the most health-giving adjustment to natural law, and still others find their authority in unrestrained conscience. Only the generous exercise of the most free discussion can help us out of this chaos.

Philosophers tell us that life is "the continuous adjustment of internal relations to external relations." The use of conscious effort toward the achievement of the fullest life through our most harmonious conformity to natural laws, is the essential distinction between the human and other animals.

Observance of natural law is the unavoidable condition of all life, and a knowledge of those laws is a condition precedent to all effort for securing well-being, through conscious adjustment to them. It follows that an opportunity for an acquaintance with nature's processes, unlimited by human coercion, is the equal and inalienable right of every human being, because an essential to his life, liberty, and the pursuit of happiness. No exception can be made for the law of our sex nature.

It also follows that in formulating our conception of what is the law of nature, and in its adjustment or application by us to our infinitely varied personal constitutions each sane adult human is the sovereign of his own destiny and never properly within the control of any other person, until some one, not an undeceived voluntary participant is directly affected thereby to his injury.

The laws for the suppression of "obscene" literature as administered, deny to adults the access to part of the alleged facts and arguments concerning our sex nature, and therefore are a violation of the above rules of right and conduct.

We all believe in intellectual and moral progress. Therefore, whatever may be the character or subject of a man's opinions, others have the right to express their judgments upon them; to censure them, if deemed censurable; or turn them to ridicule, if deemed ridiculous. If such right is not protected by law, we should have no security against the exposition or perpetuity of error, and therefore we should hamper progress.

It follows that the believer in a personal God or in the Trinity, the Mormon with his "Adam God," the Agnostic with his "Unknowable," the Christian-scientist with his impersonal "All mind and all love" God, the Unitarian with his "Purposeful Divine Imminence," the Theosophist with his godless "Nirvana," and the Atheist, all have an equal right to vie with each other for public favor; and, incidentally, to censure or ridicule any crudities which they may believe they see in any or all rival conceptions.

It is only by recognition and exercise of such a liberty that humanity has evolved from the primal sex-worship through the innumerable phases of nature worship to our present relatively exalted religious opinion. Even though we reject all, or all but one, of the numerous modern anthropomorphic and deistic conceptions of God, we must still admit that each of these is based upon a more enlightened and enlarged conception of the Universe and man's relation to it than can possibly be implied in the worship of the phallus. Thus liberty of thought and of its expression has been and will continue to be the one indispensable condition to the improvement of religions.

If we are not thus far agreed as to the equal moral rights of each, then which one has less right than the rest? It is beyond question that the solitary man has an unlimited right of expressing his opinion, since there is no one to deny him the right. With the advent of the second man surely he still has the same right with the consent of that second man. How many more persons must join the community before they acquire the moral warrant for denying the second man the right and the opportunity to listen to or to read anything the other may speak or write, even though the subject be theology or sex-morality? By what impersonal standard (not one based merely upon individual preferences) shall we adjudge the forfeiture of such individual rights, if forfeiture is to be enforced by a limitation?

If such impersonal standard cannot be furnished then the argument must proceed as follows:

If all disputants have the equal right to question and deride the conceptions of all the rest as to the existence, nature or knowableness of their respective God, then they have an equal right to question the divine origin or interpretation of that which others believe to be divine revelation.

If men have a right to cast doubt upon the source and fact of divine revelation, then, of course, they must have an equal right to discredit that which others believe to have been taught by such divine revelation, even though the subject be the relation of the sexes.

More specifically, that means this: The Catholic priest may advocate, as others deny, the superior morality of his celibacy; the Bible Communists of Oneida may advocate, as others deny, the superior morality of "free love;" the Episcopalians and Felix Adler may advocate, as others deny, the superior morality of indissoluble monogamy; the Agnostic or liberal religionist may advocate, as many deny, the superior morality of easy divorce; the Utilitarian may advocate, as others deny, the superior morality of stirpiculture with or without monogamic marriage; the Mormon may advocate, as others deny, the superior morality of polygamy, etc., etc.

I assume for the present that they do not advocate the violation of existing marriage laws, but limit their demand and argument to a repeal or amendment of those laws, so as to make them comformable to their respective ideals.

Those who hold to any one of these ideals necessarily believe all others to be of immoral tendency; and it seems to me that ridicule, fact and argument, unrestricted as to adults, are the only means by which the race can secure that progressive clarification of moral vision which is essential to higher moral development.

The vaunted morality of one age is the despised superstition and barbarism of succeeding ages. Thus we have proceeded, as far as our sexual morality is concerned, through irresponsible, indiscriminate promiscuity, group marriage, female slavery, the sacred debauchery of sex-worship, polyandry, polygamy, the abhorrent ideas of asceticism and sex-perverts, to our present standards, and the course of moral evolution is not yet ended.

Since, then, the very superiority of our present morality is due to the liberty of thinking and of exchanging thoughts, how absurd and infamous it is now to impair or destroy the very basis upon which it rests, and upon which must depend the further development of our progressive morality.

Since advancement in the refining of our ethical conceptions is conditioned upon experimentation and the dissemination of its observed results, it follows that the most immoral of present tendencies is that which arrests moral progress by limiting the freedom of speech and press. When viewed in long perspective it also follows that we must conclude that the most immoral persons of our time are those who are now successfully stifling discussion and restricting the spread of sexual intelligence, because they are most responsible for impeding moral progress, as to the relations of men and women.

Those who in these particulars deny a freedom of speech and press and the correlative right to hear, unlimited as to all sane adults, by their very act of denial, exercise a right which they would suppress in others. The true believer in equality of liberty allows others the right to speak against free speech, though he may not be so hospitable as to its actual suppression. No man is truly liberal who is unwilling to defend the right of others to disagree with him, even about free-love, polygamy or stirpiculture.

If our conceptions of sexual morality have a rational foundation, then they are capable of adequate rational defense, and there is no need for legislative suppression of discussion. If our sex ethics will not bear critical scrutiny and discussion then to suppress such discussion is infamous, because it is a legalized support of error. In either case the freest possible discussion is a condition of the progressive elimination of error. . . .

37. U.S. v. ONE BOOK CALLED "ULYSSES"

Judge John Woolsey, 1933

The suppression of literature that treated the serious social and psychological problems connected with sex or that examined its liberating and creative forces marched ahead with the curbing

---

From *U.S.* v. *One Book Called "Ulysses,"* 5 Federal Supplement 182.

of hard-core pornography for sixty years and more after passage of the Comstock Act in 1873. The "Hicklin test" of obscenity, laid down in 1868 in the English case of *Regina* v. *Hicklin,* was approved by American state and federal courts. Its focus on protecting the most susceptible minds and its finding of guilt in isolated passages rather than requiring the assessment of a "whole work" made convictions easy. Meanwhile, Customs and Post Office employed informal procedures, largely immune from court review or censure, for confiscating books that their officials thought obscene. The roster of works banned from entry into the country or from the mails grew by the score.

Congress and the courts were not wholly insensitive to the suppression. Senator Bronson Cutting of New Mexico in 1929 delivered a basic attack on the customs barriers, and the law was modified to provide for closer scrutiny by the courts of administrators' seizures. Then in 1933, the principles of *Regina* v. *Hicklin* were ignored as a rule for defining "obscenity" in a decision by Federal Judge John Woolsey, who ruled that James Joyce's *Ulysses* might legally be admitted to the United States. Not the most susceptible mind, but the normal person, was to be the standard; not the isolated passage, but the entire book, was to be taken into account.

Following a first section on procedural matters, Judge Woolsey wrote:

II. I have read "Ulysses" once in its entirety and I have read those passages of which the government particularly complains several times. In fact, for many weeks, my spare time has been devoted to the consideration of the decision which my duty would require me to make in this matter.

"Ulysses" is not an easy book to read or to understand. But there has been much written about it, and in order properly to approach the consideration of it it is advisable to read a number of other books which have now become its satellites. The study of "Ulysses" is, therefore, a heavy task.

[1] III. The reputation of "Ulysses" in the literary world, however, warranted my taking such time as was necessary to enable me to satisfy myself as to the intent with which the book was written, for, of course, in any case where a book is claimed to be obscene it must first be determined, whether the intent with which it was written was what is called, according to the usual phrase, pornographic, that is, written for the purpose of exploiting obscenity.

If the conclusion is that the book is pornographic, that is the end of the inquiry and forfeiture must follow.

But in "Ulysses," in spite of its unusual frankness, I do not detect anywhere the leer of the sensualist. I hold, therefore, that it is not pornographic.

IV. In writing "Ulysses," Joyce sought to make a serious experiment in a new, if not wholly novel, literary genre. He takes persons of the lower middle class living in Dublin in 1904 and seeks, not only to describe what they did on a certain day early in June of that year as they went about the city bent on their usual occupations, but also to tell what many of them thought about the while.

Joyce has attempted—it seems to me, with astonishing success—to show how the screen of consciousness with its ever-shifting kaleidoscopic impressions carries, as it were on a plastic palimpsest, not only what is in the focus of each man's observation of the actual things about him, but also in a penumbral zone residua of past impressions, some recent and some drawn up by association from the domain of the subconscious. He shows how each of these impressions affects the life and behavior of the character which he is describing.

What he seeks to get is not unlike the result of a double or, if that is possible, a multiple exposure on a cinema film, which would give a clear foreground with a background visible but somewhat blurred and out of focus in varying degrees.

To convey by words an effect which obviously lends itself more appropriately to a graphic technique, accounts, it seems to me, for much of the obscurity which meets a reader of "Ulysses." And it also explains another aspect of the book, which I have further to consider, namely, Joyce's sincerity and his honest effort to show exactly how the minds of his characters operate.

If Joyce did not attempt to be honest in developing the technique which he has adopted in "Ulysses," the result would be psychologically misleading and thus unfaithful to his chosen technique. Such an attitude would be artistically inexcusable.

It is because Joyce has been loyal to his technique and has not funked its necessary implications, but has honestly attempted to tell fully what his characters think about, that he has been the subject of so many attacks and that his purpose has been so often misunderstood and misrepresented. For his attempt sincerely and honestly to realize his objective has required him incidentally to use certain words which are generally considered dirty words and has led at times to what many think is a too poignant preoccupation with sex in the thoughts of his characters.

The words which are criticized as dirty are old Saxon words known to almost all men and, I venture, to many women, and are such words as would be naturally and habitually used, I believe, by the types of folk whose life, physical and mental, Joyce is seeking to describe. In respect of the recurrent emergence of the theme of sex in the minds of his characters, it must always be remembered that his locale was Celtic and his season spring.

Whether or not one enjoys such a technique as Joyce uses is a matter of taste on which disagreement or argument is futile, but to subject that technique to the standards of some other technique seems to me to be little short of absurd.

Accordingly, I hold that "Ulysses" is a sincere and honest book, and I think that the criticisms of it are entirely disposed of by its rationale.

V. Furthermore, "Ulysses" is an amazing tour de force when

one considers the success which has been in the main achieved with such a difficult objective as Joyce set for himself. As I have stated, "Ulysses" is not an easy book to read. It is brilliant and dull, intelligible and obscure, by turns. In many places it seems to me to be disgusting, but although it contains, as I have mentioned above, many words usually considered dirty, I have not found anything that I consider to be dirt for dirt's sake. Each word of the book contributes like a bit of mosaic to the detail of the picture which Joyce is seeking to construct for his readers.

If one does not wish to associate with such folk as Joyce describes, that is one's own choice. In order to avoid indirect contact with them one may not wish to read "Ulysses"; that is quite understandable. But when such a great artist in words, as Joyce undoubtedly is, seeks to draw a true picture of the lower middle class in a European city, ought it to be impossible for the American public legally to see that picture?

To answer this question it is not sufficient merely to find, as I have found above, that Joyce did not write "Ulysses" with what is commonly called pornographic intent, I must endeavor to apply a more objective standard to his book in order to determine its effect in the result, irrespective of the intent with which it was written.

VI. The statute under which the libel is filed only denounces, in so far as we are here concerned, the importation into the United States from any foreign country of "any obscene book." Section 305 of the Tariff Act of 1930, title 19 United States Code, § 1305 (19 USCA § 1305). It does not marshal against books the spectrum of condemnatory adjectives found, commonly, in laws dealing with matters of this kind. I am, therefore, only required to determine whether "Ulysses" is obscene within the legal definition of that word.

[2] The meaning of the word "obscene" as legally defined by the courts is: Tending to stir the sex impulses or to lead to sexually impure and lustful thoughts. . . .

[3] Whether a particular book would tend to excite such impulses and thoughts must be tested by the court's opinion as to its effect on a person with average sex instincts—what the French would call *l'homme moyen sensuel*—who plays, in this branch of legal inquiry, the same role of hypothetical reagent as does the "reasonable man" in the law of torts and "the man learned in the art" on questions of invention in patent law.

The risk involved in the use of such a reagent arises from the inherent tendency of the trier of facts, however fair he may intend to be, to make his reagent too much subservient to his own idiosyncrasies. Here, I have attempted to avoid this, if possible, and to make my reagent herein more objective than he might otherwise be, by adopting the following course:

After I had made my decision in regard to the aspect of "Ulysses," now under consideration, I checked my impressions with two friends of mine who in my opinion answered to the above-stated requirement for my reagent.

These literary assessors—as I might properly describe them—were called on separately, and neither knew that I was consulting the other. They are men whose opinion on literature and on life I value most highly. They had both read "Ulysses," and, of course, were wholly unconnected with this cause.

Without letting either of my assessors know what my decision was, I gave to each of them the legal definition of obscene and asked each whether in his opinion "Ulysses" was obscene within that definition.

I was interested to find that they both agreed with my opinion: That reading "Ulysses" in its entirety, as a book must be read on such a test as this, did not tend to excite sexual impulses or lustful thoughts, but that its net effect on them was only that of a somewhat tragic and very powerful commentary on the inner lives of men and women.

[4] It is only with the normal person that the law is concerned. Such a test as I have described, therefore, is the only proper test of obscenity in the case of a book like "Ulysses" which is

a sincere and serious attempt to devise a new literary method for the observation and description of mankind.

I am quite aware that owing to some of its scenes "Ulysses" is a rather strong draught to ask some sensitive, though normal, persons to take. But my considered opinion, after long reflection, is that, whilst in many places the effect of "Ulysses" on the reader undoubtedly is somewhat emetic, nowhere does it tend to be an aphrodisiac.

"Ulysses" may, therefore, be admitted into the United States.

38. ROTH v. UNITED STATES

1957

The *Ulysses* decision was to have its long-term effect outside the Customs realm, although at the time there was hardly a ripple in the defining of obscenity under state statutes or by postal administrators. A notable addition to the definition of the word came in 1940 in the case of *Parmelee* v. *United States.* There the Federal Court of Appeals adopted the "community standard" test—suggested a quarter century earlier by Federal Judge Learned Hand in *U.S.* v. *Kennerley*—as a limiting factor in calling a work "obscene." And in 1957 the Supreme Court stated flatly in *Butler* v. *Michigan* that a state statute incorporating the Hicklin test violated the First Amendment by reducing "the adult population of Michigan to reading what was fit for children."

The tests in *Ulysses* and *Parmelee* were brought together in a major Supreme Court decision that also appeared in 1957. *Roth* v. *United States* (in which *Alberts* v. *California* was also settled) is

---

From *Roth* v. *United States,* 354 U.S. Reports 476.

notable as much for the combining formula as for its ruling that the Comstock Act—revised, refined, and amended, but the lineal descendant of the measure of 1873—was indeed constitutional. While much remained to be settled in the realm of obscenity, in *Roth* v. *United States*, the Supreme Court had ruled that the First Amendment did not protect obscenity and had launched what promised to be a long search in tangled thickets for a stable definition of the term.

Mr. Justice Brennan delivered the opinion of the Court:

The constitutionality of a criminal obscenity statute is the question in each of these cases. In *Roth*, the primary constitutional question is whether the federal obscenity statute violates the provision of the First Amendment that "Congress shall make no law . . . abridging the freedom of speech, or of the press . . . ." In *Alberts*, the primary constitutional question is whether the obscenity provisions of the California Penal Code invade the freedoms of speech and press as they may be incorporated in the liberty protected from state action by the Due Process Clause of the Fourteenth Amendment. . . .

Roth conducted a business in New York in the publication and sale of books, photographs and magazines. He used circulars and advertising matter to solicit sales. He was convicted by a jury in the District Court for the Southern District of New York upon 4 counts of a 26-count indictment charging him with mailing obscene circulars and advertising, and an obscene book, in violation of the federal obscenity statute. His conviction was affirmed by the Court of Appeals for the Second Circuit. We granted certiorari.

Alberts conducted a mail-order business from Los Angeles. He was convicted by the Judge of the Municipal Court of the Beverly Hills Judicial District (having waived a jury trial) under a misdemeanor complaint which charged him with lewdly keeping for sale obscene and indecent books, and with writing, composing and publishing an obscene advertisement of them in violation of the California Penal Code. The conviction was affirmed by the Appellate Department of the Superior Court of the State of California in and for the County of Los Angeles. We noted probable jurisdiction.

The dispositive question is whether obscenity is utterance within the area of protected speech and press. Although this is the first time the question has been squarely presented to this Court, either under the First Amendment or under the Fourteenth Amendment, expressions found in numerous opinions indicate that this Court has always assumed that obscenity is not protected by the freedoms of speech and press. . . .

The guaranties of freedom of expression in effect in 10 of the 14 States which by 1792 had ratified the Constitution, gave no absolute protection for every utterance. Thirteen of the 14 States provided for the prosecution of libel, and all of those States made either blasphemy or profanity, or both, statutory crimes. As early as 1712, Massachusetts made it criminal to publish "any filthy, obscene, or profane song, pamphlet, libel or mock sermon" in imitation or mimicking of religious services. Acts and Laws of the Province of Mass. Bay, c. CV, § 8 (1712), Mass. Bay Colony Charters & Laws 399 (1814). Thus, profanity and obscenity were related offenses.

In light of this history, it is apparent that the unconditional phrasing of the First Amendment was not intended to protect every utterance. This phrasing did not prevent this Court from concluding that libelous utterances are not within the area of constitutionally protected speech. *Beauharnais* v. *Illinois,* 343 U. S. 250, 266. At the time of the adoption of the First Amendment, obscenity law was not as fully developed as libel law, but there is sufficiently contemporaneous evidence to show that obscenity, too, was outside the protection intended for speech and press.

The protection given speech and press was fashioned to assure unfettered interchange of ideas for the bringing about of political and social changes desired by the people. This objective was made explicit as early as 1774 in a letter of the Continental Congress to the inhabitants of Quebec:

"The last right we shall mention, regards the freedom of the press. The importance of this consists, besides the advancement of truth, science, morality, and arts in general, in its diffusion of liberal sentiments on the administration of Government, its ready communication of thoughts between subjects, and its consequential promotion of union among them, whereby oppressive officers are shamed or intimidated, into more honourable and just modes of conducting affairs." 1 Journals of the Continental Congress 108 (1774).

All ideas having even the slightest redeeming social importance—unorthodox ideas, controversial ideas, even ideas hateful to the prevailing climate of opinion—have the full protection of the guaranties, unless excludable because they encroach upon the limited area of more important interests. But implicit in the history of the First Amendment is the rejection of obscenity as utterly without redeeming social importance. This rejection for that reason is mirrored in the universal judgment that obscenity should be restrained, reflected in the international agreement of over 50 nations, in the obscenity laws of all of the 48 States, and in the 20 obscenity laws enacted by the Congress from 1842 to 1956. This is the same judgment expressed by this Court in *Chaplinsky* v. *New Hampshire,* 315 U. S. 568, 571–572:

". . . There are certain well-defined and narrowly limited classes of speech, the prevention and punishment of which have never been thought to raise any Constitutional problem. *These include the lewd and obscene. . . . It has been well observed that such utterances are no essential part of any exposition of ideas, and are of such slight social value as a step to truth that any benefit that may be derived from them is clearly outweighed by the social interest in order and morality. . . .*" (Emphasis added.)

We hold that obscenity is not within the area of constitutionally protected speech or press.

It is strenuously urged that these obscenity statutes offend the constitutional guaranties because they punish incitation to impure sexual *thoughts,* not shown to be related to any overt antisocial conduct which is or may be incited in the persons stimulated to such *thoughts.* In *Roth,* the trial judge instructed the jury: "The words 'obscene, lewd and lascivious' as used in the law, signify that form of immorality which has relation to sexual impurity and has a tendency to excite lustful *thoughts.*" (Emphasis added.) In *Alberts,* the trial judge applied the test laid down in *People* v. *Wepplo,* 78 Cal. App. 2d Supp. 959, . . . namely, whether the material has "a substantial tendency to deprave or corrupt its readers by inciting lascivious *thoughts* or arousing lustful desires." (Emphasis added.) It is insisted that the constitutional guaranties are violated because convictions may be had without proof either that obscene material will perceptibly create a clear and present danger of antisocial conduct, or will probably induce its recipients to such conduct. But, in light of our holding that obscenity is not protected speech, the complete answer to this argument is in the holding of this Court in *Beauharnais* v. *Illinois, supra,* at 266:

> "Libelous utterances not being within the area of constitutionally protected speech, it is unnecessary, either for us or for the State courts, to consider the issues behind the phrase 'clear and present danger.' Certainly no one would contend that obscene speech, for example, may be punished only upon a showing of such circumstances. Libel, as we have seen, is in the same class."

However, sex and obscenity are not synonymous. Obscene material is material which deals with sex in a manner appealing to prurient interest. The portrayal of sex, *e. g.,* in art, literature and scientific works, is not itself sufficient reason to deny material the constitutional protection of freedom of speech and press. Sex, a great and mysterious motive force in human life, has indisputably been a subject of absorbing interest to mankind through the ages; it is one of the vital problems of human interest and public concern. As to all such problems, this Court said in *Thornhill* v. *Alabama,* 310 U. S. 88, 101–102:

"The freedom of speech and of the press guaranteed by the Constitution embraces at the least the liberty to discuss publicly and truthfully *all matters of public concern* without previous restraint or fear of subsequent punishment. The exigencies of the colonial period and the efforts to secure freedom from oppressive administration developed a broadened conception of these liberties as adequate to supply the public need for *information and education with respect to the significant issues of the times.* . . . Freedom of discussion, if it would fulfill its historic function in this nation, must embrace *all issues about which information is needed or appropriate to enable the members of society to cope with the exigencies of their period.*" (Emphasis added.)

The fundamental freedoms of speech and press have contributed greatly to the development and well-being of our free society and are indispensable to its continued growth. Ceaseless vigilance is the watchword to prevent their erosion by Congress or by the States. The door barring federal and state intrusion into this area cannot be left ajar; it must be kept tightly closed and opened only the slightest crack necessary to prevent encroachment upon more important interests. It is therefore vital that the standards for judging obscenity safeguard the protection of freedom of speech and press for material which does not treat sex in a manner appealing to prurient interest.

The early leading standard of obscenity allowed material to be judged merely by the effect of an isolated excerpt upon particularly susceptible persons. *Regina* v. *Hicklin,* [1868] L. R. 3 Q. B. 360. Some American courts adopted this standard but later decisions have rejected it and substituted this test: whether to the average person, applying contemporary community standards, the dominant theme of the material taken as a whole appeals to prurient interest. The *Hicklin* test, judging obscenity by the effect of isolated passages upon the most susceptible persons, might well encompass material legitimately treating with sex, and so it must be rejected as unconstitutionally restrictive of the freedoms of speech and press. On the other hand, the substituted standard provides safeguards adequate to withstand the charge of constitutional infirmity.

Both trial courts below sufficiently followed the proper standard. Both courts used the proper definition of obscenity. . . .

It is argued that the statutes do not provide reasonably ascertainable standards of guilt and therefore violate the constitutional requirements of due process. . . . The federal obscenity statute makes punishable the mailing of material that is "obscene, lewd, lascivious, or filthy . . . or other publication of an indecent character." The California statute makes punishable, *inter alia,* the keeping for sale or advertising material that is "obscene or indecent." The thrust of the argument is that these words are not sufficiently precise because they do not mean the same thing to all people, all the time, everywhere.

Many decisions have recognized that these terms of obscenity statutes are not precise. This Court, however, has consistently held that lack of precision is not itself offensive to the requirements of due process. ". . . [T]he Constitution does not require impossible standards"; all that is required is that the language "conveys sufficiently definite warning as to the proscribed conduct when measured by common understanding and practices. . . ." *United States* v. *Petrillo,* 332 U. S. 1, 7–8. These words, applied according to the proper standard for judging obscenity, already discussed, give adequate warning of the conduct proscribed. . . .

In summary, then, we hold that these statutes, applied according to the proper standard for judging obscenity, do not offend constitutional safeguards against convictions based upon protected material, or fail to give men in acting adequate notice of what is prohibited. . . .

Part Seven

RADICALS, LABOR, AND SEDITION

---

39. MOB VIOLENCE IN WORLD WAR I

National Civil Liberties Bureau, 1919

Threat and violence have almost always arisen to frighten or still American newspapers that have violated consensus in times of severe social and political stress: the American Revolution, the War of 1812, abolition, the Civil War, World War I, and the mid-twentieth-century Negro protest, all called forth the club or the axe, the whip or the tar brush, the rail or the rope and gun, to punish unorthodoxy.

In World War I, apart from persons of German descent considered loyal to the Kaiser, those who took the brunt of illegal

---

From National Civil Liberties Bureau, "War-Time Prosecutions and Mob Violence" (New York City: NCLB, March 1919), pp. 1–13. Pamphlet.

physical outrage were the radical International Workers of the World, the Socialists, and the farmers' Nonpartisan League. Generally the targets were not printers of newspapers but the spokesmen for groups that considered themselves denied a reasonable life by America and so were skeptical about supporting its war. Their attempts to modify or change drastically the private enterprise system had made them suspect to much of middle-class America before the war, and now their opposition to the war fed the widespread impression that they were un-American and should be silenced.

In 1919, the National Civil Liberties Bureau, forerunner of the American Civil Liberties Union, compiled a list of incidents of violence for a two-year period beginning April 1, 1917. It was "by no means a complete record," the NCLB said.

The cases are set forth under the following classifications:

I. Mob Violence 164
  1. For alleged personal disloyalty 123
    a. General Cases 101
    b. Forced by mobs to kiss the flag (a special group of cases so classified because of their number) 22
  2. Industrial causes: involving primarily the I. W. W. 18
  3. Political causes: involving primarily the Non-Partisan League .... 23. . . .

1. FOR ALLEGED PERSONAL DISLOYALTY

a. General Cases

4/8/17. **Baltimore, Md.**—Peace meeting addressed by **David Starr Jordan** attacked by mob.

——— **New York City.**—During the summer of 1917 many meeting[s] of the Socialist Party and the Friends of Irish Freedom were broken up by soldier mobs.

7/2/17. **Boston, Mass.—Peace parade** of Socialist Party

broken up and headquarters wrecked by mob of soldiers and sailors.

8/23/17. **York, S. C.—Rev. W. T. Sims,** negro preacher, lynched for alleged opposition to the draft.

9/9/17. **Milwaukee, Wis.—Several Italians** shot in street riot after a loyalty meeting.

10/2/17. **Pasadena, Cal.**—Conference of **Christian Pacifists** broken up by mob of Home Guards.

10/18/17. **New York, N. Y.**—Two meeting[s] of Columbia students to protest against the expulsion of **Professors Cattell** and **Dana** broken up by mob of Naval Reserves.

10/30/17. **Newport, Ky.—Rev. Herbert S. Bigelow,** a pro-war radical, kidnapped and horsewhipped by mob "in the name of the women and children of Belgium."

11/15/17. **Newport, Ark.—Rev. J. H. Ellis,** negro preacher, held for 96 days on flimsy charge of "treason." When released from jail beaten by mob of white citizens and officials.

11/18/17. **New York, N. Y.**—Dry goods store on upper east side wrecked by mob of Italians because proprietor was alleged not to have paid proper respect to the Italian flag.

11/22/17. **Osakis, Minn.—E. H. Stratemeyer** tarred and feathered for alleged disloyalty.

12/4/17. **Hugo, Colo.—Henry Dutsch,** tarred and feathered by Vigilantes for alleged seditious utterances.

12/10/17. **St. Louis, Mo.—Emmett Oburn** beaten for neglect to stand up while Star Spangled Banner was being played at a meeting.

12/17/17. **Clayton, N. J.—Albert M. Canter,** school teacher, driven from town by mob of citizens for alleged disloyal remarks.

12/25/17. **Brenham, Tex.—Six German farmers** whipped to make them subscribe to the Red Cross.

12/28/17. **Audobon, Ia.—Rev. W. A. Starck** and **Fred Tennegkeit** beaten and nearly hanged for alleged seditious utterances. Saved from mob by dupty [*sic*] sheriffs.

1/5/18. **Hartford, Conn.—Maximilian Von Hoegen** beaten, nose broken, forced to kiss flag.

1/13/18. **Philadelphia, Pa.—Paul Beilfuss,** rescued by police from mob which threatened to lynch him for disloyal remarks.

1/22/18. **Mitchell, S. D.—Wm. C. Rempfer,** deported after Socialist State Convention broken up by police.

1/28/18. **Elkins, W. Va.—L. H. Keenan,** Socialist lawyer, tarred and feathered for alleged disloyalty.

2/12/18. **Staunton, Ill.—Severino Oberden,** a labor organizer, and **J. L. Metzen,** his attorney, beaten by mob in police station at Staunton, Ill. Later tarred. Many other cases of violence in this mining region for alleged disloyalty, notably Marysville, Hillsboro, Worden, Mt. Olive, Gillespie and Williamson.

3/13/18. **Ottumwa, Ia.—Leon Battig,** a teacher, painted yellow by a mob on suspicion of disloyalty.

3/16/18. **Scotland, S. D.—Wm. Rempfer,** Socialist State Secretary, and **August Friederich** driven out of town by threat of tar and feathers.

3/21/18. **Altus, Okla.—O. F. Westbrook and Henry Hoffman** beaten, tarred and feathered for alleged disloyalty.

3/20/18. **Yerington, Nev.—Elmer White** beaten with iron cat-o'-nine tails for disloyal remarks.

3/23/18. **Christopher, Ill.—Rev. John Kovalsky** and two others tarred and feathered for alleged disloyalty.

3/25/18. **Benton, Ill.—Mrs. Frances Bergen,** a Bohemian, ridden on a rail by mob of Loyalty Leaguers for alleged pro-Germanism.

3/25/18. **Duluth, Minn.—Gust Lundin,** Socialist, tarred and feathered by Knights of Liberty.

3/28/18. **Clarksville, Ark.—Frank Oberlee,** tarred, feathered and driven out of town.

3/28/18. **Hartford, Ark.—Six alleged pro-Germans** who

were later declared loyal by agents of Dept. of Justice, beaten, forced tȯ kiss the flag and thrown into jail.

3/31/18. **Ashland, Wis.—Prof. E. A. Schimmel**, tarred and feathered by mob.

4/2/18. **Lasalle, Ill.—Dr. J. C. Bienneman** ducked in canal and ordered out of town after being forced to kiss the flag. The stores of **Henry Mueller** and **Regas Bros.** were painted yellow.

4/2/18. **Emerson, Neb.—Rudolph Schwopke** tarred and feathered for alleged refusal to contribute to Red Cross.

4/3/18. **Sioux Falls, S. D.**—Windows of the **Deutscher Herold**, edited by **Conrad Kornmann**, painted yellow by mob.

4/4/18. **Sulphur, Okla.—H. C. Capers**, 72 years old, head shaved by crowd of men awaiting draft call, for alleged pro-Germanism.

4/5/18. **Sioux Falls, S. D.**—Offices of ex-U. S. Senator **R. F. Pettigrew** painted yellow by mob.

4/5/18. **Collinsville, Ill.—Robert P. Prager**, lynched by mob because of alleged pro-German utterances. Mob leaders tried and acquitted.

4/6/18. **Jefferson City, Mo.—Fritz Monal** whipped and forced to kiss the flag.

4/7/18. **Seward, Neb.—William Grats** tarred and feathered for alleged pro-Germanism.

4/8/18. **Mounds, Ill.—Norman M. Harris**, editor, beaten by a mob for alleged disloyal utterances.

4/8/18. **Hartford, Conn.**—Home Guards broke up Socialist rally.

4/8/18. **West Salisbury, Pa.—Charles Klinge** beaten, made to walk along the street with a dog chain around his neck, forced to kiss the flag and ducked for alleged disloyal remarks.

4/9/18. **Monroe, N. Y.—A. C. Richter**, beaten until unconscious for remarks opposing the draft.

4/10/18. **Elk City, Okla.—Rev. Wm. M. Hicks**, tarred and feathered for promoting World Peace League.

4/11/18. **Ashland, Wis.—Adolph Anton**, tarred and feathered for alleged pro-Germanism.

4/11/18. **Salt Lake City, Utah.—Wm. Prisse**, thrown into a dough bin and nearly smothered for alleged pro-German remarks.

4/12/18. **Omaha, Neb.—Mrs. Margaret Selby**, beaten by Lithuanian women for alleged insult to the flag.

4/12/18. **Muskogee, Okla.—James Holt** tarred and feathered for refusal to buy liberty bonds.

4/13/18. **Santa Fe, N. M.—John M. Birkner**, tarred and feathered by convicts in prison while held on charge of disloyalty.

4/13/18. **Medford, Ore.—George Maynard**, member International Bible Students' Assn., iron cross painted on body, driven from town. **Rev. E. P. Taliaferro** driven out.

4/13/18. **Montrose, Mich.—Mrs. Harley Stafford**, tarred and feathered for "disloyal remarks."

4/14/18. **Lincoln, Neb.**—House of **Rev. George Allenbach** painted yellow for his refusal to participate in a liberty loan rally.

4/14/18. **Holland, O.—Three men** tarred and feathered and made to kiss the flag.

4/15/18. **Kansas City, Mo.—Three men** painted yellow by fellow workmen for alleged remark, "To hell with the Liberty Loan."

4/15/18. **Clovis, N. M.—T. Smith**, a Socialist, tarred and feathered for refusal to buy Liberty Bonds.

4/16/18. **Woodlawn, Pa.—Three Austrian workmen** tarred for alleged disloyalty.

4/16/18. **Tulsa, Okla.—John Kubecka**, beaten, tarred and feathered by the "Knights of Liberty" for alleged disloyal remarks.

4/17/18. **Pittsburg[h], Pa.—Leo J. Eschman**, mobbed by 300 munition workers, led by girls.

4/17/18. **Newellton, La.—Wm. A. Hunter,** 68 years old, tarred and feathered for not buying Liberty Bonds, though he had bought $5,000 worth.

4/19/18. **Collinsville, Okla.—Henry Rheimer,** hanged by mob till almost dead because suspected of disloyalty.

4/19/18. **Arlington, S. D.**—Buildings, trees and fence posts on the farm of **August Lieske** painted yellow for refusal to buy bonds.

4/20/18. **Berkeley, Cal.**—Tent tabernacle of the Church of the Living God burnt down by mob of men and boys because of alleged pacifist beliefs of the sect. **Rev. Josiah Sykes** and two elders ducked in the baptismal tank.

4/20/18. **El Centro, Cal.—J. E. Morgan,** announced to speak at a Mooney meeting, kidnaped and run out of town in an automobile by a so-called citizens' committee.

4/21/18. **Firewater, Ore.—Unknown person,** rescued from mob which threatened to lynch him for distributing circular attacking suppression of "The Finished Mystery."

4/22/18. **McPherson, Kan.—Walter Cooperider,** tarred and feathered for alleged seditious remarks. His father, a bed-ridden man of 90 years, forced to kiss the flag.

4/22/18. **Las Vegas, N. M.—Louis A. Lee** painted yellow by fellow employes for refusal to buy Liberty Bonds.

4/22/18. **Canonsburg, Pa.—Stephen Melanos,** a Greek, thrown into a creek for refusing to buy a Liberty Bond.

4/22/18. **Pendleton, Ore.—Clifford T. Metz,** attacked by mob for distributing circulars attacking the suppression of "The Finished Mystery."

4/23/18. **Wynnewood, Okla.—Claud Watson,** a farmer, tarred and feathered by 50 drafted men waiting to entrain. Negro was hired to lash his back.

4/25/18. **Bessemer, Ala.—J. Will McNabb,** handcuffed to a post for three hours for alleged disloyalty.

4/26/18. **New Bru[n]swick, N. J.—S. H. Chovenson,** Rutgers student, secretary Socialist local, covered with molasses and feathers by a mob of business men for refusal to buy a bond and to aid the Red Cross.

4/27/18. **Pittsburg [h], Pa.—Unknown foreigner,** tarred and feathered for making remarks against the Liberty Loan.

4/27/18. **San Francisco, Cal.—Carl Schultz,** intimidated by "Knights of Liberty" who placed rope around his neck and caused him to leave town.

4/27/18. **Excelsior Spring, Mo.—Otto Scharf and Rudolph Gustoff,** painted yellow and forced to kiss the flag by mob.

4/30/18. **Walnut Ridge, Ark.—Charles Franke, E. J. French, W. B. Duncan and C. B. Griffen,** taken from jail and tarred and feathered for selling "The Kingdom News," a periodical of the International Bible Students' Assn.

4/30/18. **Robinson, Pa.—Albert Phillips,** tarred and feathered by Austrians for refusal to buy bonds and support Y. M. C. A. and Red Cross.

5/2/18. **San Jose, Cal.—George Koetzer,** tarred, feathered and tied to a cannon in a public park by "Knights of Liberty" for alleged disloyal remarks.

5/2/18. **Richmond, Cal.—Guido Poenisch,** tarred and feathered by masked "Knights of Liberty" for alleged disloyalty.

5/2/18. **San Jose, Cal.—H. Steinmolz** hanged until unconscious, tied to a tree and later taken away in an auto by "Knights of Liberty" for alleged disloyalty.

5/6/18. **Birmingham, Alabama.**—The home of **M. V. Hale** dynamited for refusal to cease activities as A. F. of L. organizer.

5/7/18. **Avoca, Pennsylvania—Barney Walukus** strung up thirty feet from the ground and a fire hose played on him by fellow employes for refusing to buy a bond.

5/7/18. **San Rafael, Cal.—Henry Zang,** an alleged pro-German, kidnapped, his hair was clipped in the shape of a cross and he was tied to a tree in front of the courthouse.

5/8/18. **Klamath Falls, Mont.—J. W. Tyrrel** driven out of town for alleged disloyalty.

5/10/18. **Henrietta, Oklahoma.—Cris Wagoner** taken from jail, painted a bright red and given 20 lashes for alleged disloyalty.

5/21/18. **Spencer, S. D.—Hart Duxbury** tarred and feathered for refusal to buy Liberty Bonds or contribute to the Red Cross.

5/23/18. **Seattle, Wash.—Joe Polaris** tarred and feathered and placed on interurban trolley clad only in a gunnysack for alleged seditious remarks.

5/23/18. **St. Paul, Minn.—Gus Tummerscheit** bound, dragged several hundred feet and tied to a telegraph pole by fellow workmen for alleged disloyal utterances.

5/25/18. **El Paso, Texas—Lubi Lara** and **Jose Villareal** tarred and feathered by fellow employes for refusal to buy Liberty Bonds.

5/27/18. **New York, N. Y.—Carl Peterson** badly beaten by mob for alleged remark that he hoped Germany would win the war.

6/10/18. **Buffalo, N. Y.—Jacob W. Oswald** painted yellow by mob of fellow workmen for alleged seditious remarks.

6/22/18. **San Francisco, Cal.—George Mattel** tarred and feathered by fellow employes for alleged refusal to buy war saving stamps.

7/6/18. **Muskogee, Okla.—James Holt**, ex-U. S. deputy marshal tarred and feathered for alleged seditious statements, refusal to buy bonds or contribute to war activities.

7/23/18. **Vicksburg, Miss.—Dave Cook** tarred and feathered for alleged disloyalty.

7/23/18. **Vicksburg, Miss.—Dr. J. C. Miller** tarred and feathered for alleged disloyalty.

7/24/18. **Vicksburg, Miss.—**Two negro women tarred and feathered because they were said to have refused to work.

7/27/18. **New York, N. Y.—Carl Netreba** beaten by mob who accused him of tearing down an American flag.

10/1/18. **Fort Wayne, Ind.**—Mob of 600 forced **Max Vonderau to raise flag in front of his house.**

10/17/18. **Appleton, Wis.—Dan Schultze, Wm. Bates, Charles Drenks, August Julius, H. A. Holzman, Louis Becker** and **Frank Julius** coerced into buying their "quota" of Liberty Bonds by a committee of the Council of Defense.

11/—/18. **Brawley, Cal.—James Ross** dragged behind an automobile, beaten, tarred and feathered supposedly for refusal to buy Liberty Bonds but probably because of his opposition to the vice interests of the town.

b. Mob Violence—Forced by Mobs to Kiss the Flag.

12/20/17. **Pine Bluff, Ark.—George Carlisle.**

2/2/18. **Canton, O.—Harry Rogalski.**

2/28/18. **Connellsville, Pa.—Tony Senkis,** also painted green by the mob.

2/28/18. **Trenton, N. J.—Eliz. and Margaret Paine.**

3/3/18. **Boston, Mass.—Unknown** young man.

3/28/18. **Lewistown, Mont.—Edward Foster.**

3/28/18. **Brooklyn, N. Y.—Harry Meyer.**

4/2/18. **Canton, O.—Wm. Zerbe.**

4/2/18. **Fremont, O.—Fred K. Bollman, Fred Kolbe.**

4/4/18. **Athens, Ill.—John W. Rynders.**

4/8/18. **Reno, Nev.—W. Merriman.**

4/9/18. **Lincoln, Neb.—C. H. Peter.**

4/17/18. **Portchester, N. Y.—Louis Dudas.**

4/18/18. **Van Houten, N. M.—Constantinus Koch.**

4/27/18. **Anaconda, Mont.—H. C. Lind.**

4/29/18. **Cleveland, O.—German musician,** name unknown.

5/1/18. **Camden, N. J.—Harry A. Fay.**

5/15/18. **Fremont, Neb.—Frank Somejkal.**

5/28/18. **Paterson, N. J.—George R. Rem.**
6/3/18. **Williamsport, Pa.—Peter Smabel.**
7/18/18. **Cincinnati, O.—Unknown man.**
7/20/18. **Indianapolis, Ind.—Charles C. Hickman.**

2. INDUSTRIAL CAUSES

Involving primarily the I. W. W.

7/10/17. **Jerome, Ariz.—Seventy miners** loaded into cattle cars and sent into California by gunmen of the United Verde Copper Co.

7/12/17. **Bisbee, Ariz.—Over 1,000 miners** forcibly deported from their homes to the desert by loyalty league organized by employers. Many deported were I. W. W. members. Officials of the Phelps-Dodge Corporation and other prominent citizens of Bisbee were subsequently indicted but the indictments were later dismissed without trial.

7/23/17. **Aberdeen, S. D.—G. J. Bourg,** I. W. W. organizer, seized and taken to jail, later put into an auto with Chief of Police and two others, taken outside of town where mob of business men beat him with clubs while he was held face to the ground.

8/1/17. **Butte, Mont.—Frank Little,** member executive board I. W. W. hanged by masked mob until dead.

8/11/17. **Oakland, Cal.—I. W. W. headquarters** wrecked by mob of soldiers.

8/22/17. **Duluth, Minn.—I. W. W. hall** wrecked by mob of soldiers.

8/29/17. **Franklin, N. J.—John Avilla,** I. W. W. organizer, taken in an auto to the woods and hung to a tree by Chief of Police and mob of business men. Cut down when unconscious.

10/4/17. **Stuttgart, Ark.—Luck Laur,** whipped, tarred and feathered and driven out of town for being an I. W. W.

11/9/17. **Tulsa, Okla.—17 I. W. W. prisoners** taken forcibly from the police, beaten, tarred and feathered "in the name of the women and children of Belgium," by mob of citizens and officials calling themselves "The Knights of Liberty."

11/17/17. **Red Lodge, Mont.—Sec'y Finnish I. W. W.**, and several other labor leaders beaten and tortured by mining company representatives, after mock hearing in the court house.

11/28/17. **Red Lodge, Mont.—Emil Koski**, I. W. W. member, beaten by Liberty Committee.

1/5/18. **Seattle, Wash.—Piggott Printing Co.** (printer of Industrial Worker and Seattle Call), plant wrecked by mob of sailors.

2/20/18. **Butte, Mont.—Mell Hathaway**, I. W. W. member, horse-whipped and driven out of town.

3/17/18. **Yerington, Nev.—I. W. W. organizer**, tarred and feathered for "incendiary remarks."

3/9/18. **Yakima, Wash.—H. B. Myers**, Sec'y I. W. W., tarred and feathered.

4/10/18. **Aberdeen, Wash.—Six I. W. W.** leaders tarred, feathered and ordered out of town.

4/13/18. **Muskogee, Okla.—J. A. Lewis**, I. W. W. organizer, taken from jail and deported.

4/15/18. **Jerome, Ariz.—Wm. Waldrop**, I. W. W. organizer, tarred and feathered.

3. POLITICAL CAUSES

Involving primarily the Non-Partisan League.

10/4/17. **Lake City, Minn.**—Meeting of Non-Partisan League broken up by business men who closed the hall and threatened to play a fire hose on the crowd.

10/19/17. **Rock Creek, Minn.—N. S. Randall** and **Perry Aronson**, Non-Partisan League organizers, kidnapped by mob that threatened to lynch them but released them after deporting them.

1/19/18. **Norwood, Minn.—T. Tharaldson**, Non-Partisan League organizer deported by "loyalty league" mob.

1/19/18. **Jasper, Minn.—Non-Partisan League representa-**

tive kidnapped and deported by mob while arranging for a meeting.

1/23/18. **Lakefield, Minn.—Non-Partisan League** meeting broken up by mob composed of county attorney and other officials.

1/25/18. **Akely, Minn.—C. W. Barnes** and **R. R. Hamilton** deported by mob.

2/12/18. **Lakefield, Minn.—James Manahan,** Non-Partisan League attorney, driven out of town.

3/8/18. **Kenyon, Minn.—George Breidel,** N.-P. League organizer, dragged from a moving picture show and put on an outgoing train.

3/23/18. **Rock Creek, Minn.**—Office of **Madelia News,** a League newspaper, painted yellow by a mob.

4/—/18. **New Prague, Minn.—Wm. Wright** painted yellow by mob for League activity.

4/4/18. **Mineola, Texas.**—Several organizers of Non-Partisan League badly beaten and driven out of town.

4/26/18. **Winlock, Wash.—Alfred Knutson** and **W. R. Edwards,** organizers for the Non-Partisan League, tarred and driven out of town.

4/28/18. **Dodge Center, Minn.**—Organizers of the League and farmers who were members driven out of town by a mob.

4/29/18. **Winlock, Wash.—W. R. Edwards,** tarred and driven out of Toledo, near Winlock, second time.

4/29/18. **Sultan, Wash.—Joseph O. Golden,** Non-Partisan League organizer, seized and taken in an auto by young thugs, tarred, feathered and beaten with a revolver.

4/30/18. **Red Wing, Minn.**—Chief witness in the trial of a League organizer driven out of town at point of guns by a mob.

6/—/18. **Madison Lake, Minn.**—Fire hose played by a mob on League parade.

6/—/18. **Rock County, Minn.**—Two farmers that would not renounce League membership driven out of the county.

Office of a paper friendly to the League boarded up and editor driven out of the county. One of the deported farmers, John Meents, tarred and feathered upon his return.

6/—/18. **Rock County, Minn.**—Houses and stores of League supporters painted yellow by mob.

6/—/18. **Pipestone, Minn.**—Farmers' co-operative store painted yellow by mob for displaying League candidates' pictures in the window.

6/11/18. **Anoka, Minn.**—A parade of 1,500 League sympathizers broken up by a mob. Many women and children, as well as men beaten.

6/22/18. **Belle Fourche, S. D.—W. W. Callen,** Non-Partisan League organizer, kidnapped by home guards and taken to another town.

40. THE ALIEN REGISTRATION ACT OF 1940

In 1939 and 1940 a flood of bills for the control of aliens and sedition was introduced in Congress, the product of the fears of approaching war and threatening totalitarianisms. One came to fruition, the Alien Registration Act of 1940 (the "Smith Act," named for Rep. H. W. Smith of Virginia). Little of it dealt with registration; it was primarily a sedition act, and the first federal peacetime sedition law since the Alien and Sedition Acts of 1798–1800. Its provisions making advocacy of violent overthrow of government a crime resembled an act sought unsuccessfully by Attorney General A. Mitchell Palmer in his zealous deporta-

---

From Alien Registration Act of 1940, 54 *U.S. Statutes* 670.

tion activity of 1919–1920; but Smith Act supporters met almost none of the vigorous public protest that had helped defeat the Palmer bill. Large majorities approved it in Congress. Sections 2 and 3 of Title I were to become the basis for the prosecution of Communists in the 1940's and 1950's, the most noteworthy being that under which Eugene Dennis and ten other Communist Party leaders were sentenced to prison in 1951.

An Act

To prohibit certain subversive activities; to amend certain provisions of law with respect to the admission and deportation of aliens; to require the fingerprinting and registration of aliens; and for other purposes.

Be it enacted by the Senate and House of Representatives of the United States of America in Congress assembled,

TITLE I

SECTION 1. (a) It shall be unlawful for any person, with intent to interfere with, impair, or influence the loyalty, morale, or discipline of the military or naval forces of the United States—

(1) to advise, counsel, urge, or in any manner cause insubordination, disloyalty, mutiny, or refusal of duty by any member of the military or naval forces of the United States; or

(2) to distribute any written or printed matter which advises, counsels, or urges insubordination, disloyalty, mutiny, or refusal of duty by any member of the military or naval forces of the United States. . . .

SEC. 2. (a) It shall be unlawful for any person—

(1) to knowingly or willfully advocate, abet, advise, or teach the duty, necessity, desirability, or propriety of overthrowing or destroying any government in the United States by force or violence, or by the assassination of any officer of any such government;

(2) with the intent to cause the overthrow or destruction of any government in the United States, to print, publish, edit, issue, circulate, sell, distribute, or publicly display any written or printed matter advocating, advising, or teaching the duty, necessity, desirability, or propriety of overthrowing or destroying any government in the United States by force or violence;

(3) to organize or help to organize any society, group, or assembly of persons who teach, advocate, or encourage the overthrow or destruction of any government in the United States by force or violence; or to be or become a member of, or affiliate with, any such society, group, or assembly of persons, knowing the purposes thereof. . . .

SEC. 3. It shall be unlawful for any person to attempt to commit, or to conspire to commit, any of the acts prohibited by the provisions of this title. . . .

SEC. 5. (a) Any person who violates any of the provisions of this title shall, upon conviction thereof, be fined not more than $10,000 or imprisoned for not more than ten years, or both.

(b) No person convicted of violating any of the provisions of this title shall, during the five years next following his conviction, be eligible for employment by the United States, or by any department or agency thereof (including any corporation the stock of which is wholly owned by the United States).

41. THIRTY-FIVE YEARS WITH FREEDOM OF SPEECH

Zechariah Chafee, Jr., 1952

When Zechariah Chafee, Jr., gave the talk printed in large part below, he had been deeply committed to the study of free speech and press since World War I. He spoke at a time when much of the United States was undergoing paroxysms of apprehension over domestic communism, when "loyalty committees" were at high tide, and when administrative agencies of government were purging their ranks of men concerning whom only a hint of suspicion might be raised.

What struck Chafee about the period after 1945 was the diminishing of judicial safeguards for speech and press; the growth in punishments inflicted by agencies and instruments of less visible, less palpable nature than courts; the vagueness of new intellectual and verbal offenses; and the irregularity of procedure that often accompanied punishment for words. In this analysis the close relation between free speech and press and other fundamental liberties of Americans is striking. His emphasis on the recent period and on the "new suppression" is given here, and his short beginning section on the circumstances which brought him to his long study of free speech and press.

It is one hundred and sixty years since the United States Constitution was first amended, to declare "Congress shall make

---

From Zechariah Chafee, Jr., "Thirty-Five Years with Freedom of Speech" (New York: Roger N. Baldwin Civil Liberties Foundation, 1952), pp. 1–3, 18–34. Pamphlet.

no law . . . abridging the freedom of speech, or of the press. . . ." For a century and a quarter, however, the meaning of those words remained conjectural. There was hot discussion at long intervals—over the Sedition Act of 1798 and the exclusion of Abolitionist pamphlets from the mails and the treatment of Copperheads, and legal treatises did some speculating, but nobody knew what the First Amendment did or did not protect. Such knowledge could come only from court decisions, and there was little occasion for these until the day when the United States declared war against Germany for the first time. The thirty-five years since April 6, 1917, have given us all the authoritative judicial interpretation of freedom of speech and press we have, and they have also brought forth a host of restrictions on open discussion, which whether constitutional or not were never dreamed of in the United States before we went to war to save freedom.

It happens that my career as a law teacher is spanned by the same thirty-five years. I have chanced to be an observer of the whole constitutional development of freedom of speech. Consequently, it may be interesting to describe these events and trends as seen through one man's eyes. Though this intrudes myself, I am claiming no credit for anything. I feel about the suppression I shall describe like William James giving his impression of the San Francisco earthquake. I did not start it, and I did very little to stop it, but at any rate I was there.

My connection with freedom of speech is due to two accidents. Before beginning to teach law in the autumn of 1916, I was like most Americans, who, as the polls indicate, have no enthusiasm or even interest in the importance of free speech. It is, I suspect, an acquired taste like olives. The only previous contacts with the subject that I can recall were signing a petition to have my Law School eating club in 1912 stop subscribing to a Boston newspaper which was full of boring admiration of Theodore Roosevelt, and worrying about a play called "The Easiest Way." This depicted a young woman escaping from the rigors and low wages of a department store into an expansive life of sin. I talked in favor of closing down the performances in Providence for fear they might persuade real salesgirls to follow the heroine's example.

Such was my general outlook when unexpectedly invited to desert my law-partners and teach a course on injunctions against those various types of wrongs which we lawyers call Torts. This course had for years dealt with such humdrum matters as smoking factories and people piling rocks on somebody else's land. Then my predecessor in it, Dean Pound, brightened it up by including the problem of enjoining libels. So I set to work to master this novel topic. One of the cases in Pound's book was about Dr. Brandreth, a New York vendor of patent medicines, whose pills were a household word in 1839 like Bayer's Aspirin today. This prosperous medicine merchant had a salesman named Lance, whom he discharged for misconduct. Lance vowed revenge. He advertised a purported autobiography of Brandreth, including his "Comical Adventures and Amorous Intrigues . . . , interspersed with racy descriptions of scenes of life in London and New York." Brandreth sought to enjoin this book. The judge said he could wait till after publication and then try to get damages, but he could not strangle the book at birth by an injunction, that would infringe upon "the liberty of the press."

Being thus accidentally called on to discuss the case with my students, I felt obligated to find out what this "liberty of the press" really was. I read all the cases through 1916—there were only a few—and I remained almost as unenlightened as when I started. Everybody seemed to be for free speech, just as everybody was then for "freedom of the seas," but there was the same semantic vagueness.

Then the halcyon days of uninterrupted teaching were driven

away by war, never to return. Soon my task of reading current court decisions turned up many cases of prosecutions under the Espionage Act for speeches and articles. I woke up to the fact that constitutional freedom of speech was getting interpreted by judges at a great pace. It was certainly in my line of duty to learn what the courts were doing and pass on the information to my class, which I proceeded to do with youthful diligence.

The whole matter might have stayed inside the walls of Harvard Law School except for a second accident. Harold Laski was then tutoring in Harvard College and writing on the staff of the *New Republic*. When he learned of my researches into the war cases, he asked me to put the results into a *New Republic* article. Doctor Johnson says that "Nobody but a fool ever wrote except for money," and the prospect of $75 was a sharp spur to an assistant professor. It was the first cash I earned by writing. This article ripened into a longer technical paper in the *Harvard Law Review*, and that led to other articles and discussion at the many forums of those days. Walter Lippmann, who was then advising the new publishing firm of Harcourt Brace & Co., suggested the expansion of these articles into a book. So I started something I could not ever stop.

As I look back, the development of free speech in the United States since 1917 falls roughly into four periods. The dividing lines are blurred, but it is convenient to place them in 1920, 1930, and 1945. First came the Period of Struggle and Criminal Prosecutions, running from the outbreak of the First World War until 1920. Second was the Period of Growth, ending in 1930. The third period of a decade and a half until about V-J Day was the Period of Achievement. Now we are in the midst of a Period of Renewed Struggle and Subtle Suppressions. After passing each of the first three periods in review, I shall concentrate on the last. This most deserves our attention because it is the only one we can do something about. . . .

4. The Period of Renewed Struggle and Subtle Suppressions, Since 1945

The closing years of the Period of Achievement gave several indications of a bad time ahead for freedom of discussion. It was not clear that the inspiring opinions of the Supreme Court under Hughes were having much effect on the man in the street. Perhaps Americans had not become more tolerant than in 1920, but were merely more indifferent and less frightened. When fear returned, suppression might return with it. As in the opening years of the Period of Growth, the forces of suppression and the forces of freedom were both increasing, but this time the forces of suppression were increasing faster and eventually they got ahead.

The year 1938, which produced the Bill of Rights Committee of the American Bar Association, also gave the country a very different committee in the House of Representatives. Today this House Committee on Un-American Activities is flourishing like the green bay tree, while the Bill of Rights Committee has done little except render a legal opinion in favor of the McCarran Act. In 1940, Congress passed the first peace-time federal sedition law since the detested Act of 1798. The Smith Act contained practically everything which A. Mitchell Palmer wanted at the height of the Red Menace. Soon afterwards came Pearl Harbor. As in the First World War, we were faced with two staggering sets of problems. Again we had to defend ourselves against German military might, with the Japanese added; and again we were perplexed by the revolutionary rulers of Russia. For four years it was essential to cement the coalition with the Soviet Union against Hitler which is now commonly forgotten when any American is denounced for the merest gesture of friendship in 1942 or 1943, but when the fighting was over, apprehensions about Russia flared, as in 1919, into panic and suppression.

All the water that ran under the bridge for a quarter of a century after 1917 is now coming back under the bridge in waves of intolerance.

So we are in a Period of Struggle once more. The old arguments for restrictions are repeated. Jefferson's First Inaugural again needs quoting in reply. Yet the present situation differs from conditions in 1919–20. . . .

The most striking difference from the earlier Period of Struggle lies in the subtlety of the suppressions now employed. During and after the First World War, the chief method for controlling the speech and publications of American citizens was criminal trials. These trials often ran wild, as everybody now agrees, but at least they had several safeguards against abuses. Determination of guilt in a criminal prosecution is made by a jury, and reviewed by judges; and the test of guilt is defined in a statute with considerable clearness. All these safeguards are conspicuously lacking in the novel methods of suppression which have recently sprung up. We do still have criminal trials, with an even wider scope than in 1920 because of the Smith Act and the new McCarran Act crime of facilitating a totalitarian dictatorship; but there is ever so much more suppression today through proceedings which have no juries, no substantial supervision by judges, and vague definitions of wrongdoing.

Ever since the Zenger case in colonial New York, Americans have insisted it is essential to freedom of speech that only a jury should be able to punish a man for expressing questionable views. Even if the jury acquits in disregard of the letter of the law, this is accepted as right, because a man ought not to suffer for saying what a cross-section of the community believes the community has a right to hear. And if the jury goes too far the other way and convicts the man improperly, its action is subjected to substantial supervision by judges, up to the Supreme Court of the United States.

Any proceeding was abhorrent to our ancestors which allowed active members of the government in power to determine the wrongfulness of speech and printing so as to impose various types of penalties. For this reason our ancestors detested censorship by officials and taxes on knowledge imposed by legislatures.

Run rapidly over some of the current methods of suppression and see what persons do the deciding and penalizing instead of jurymen. In legislative investigations, the denouncing and ousting from jobs is done by legislators with an eye on reelection and party axes to grind. Loyalty programs in federal and state governments are run by administrative officials, who can drive men out of their chosen careers and often make it hard for them to get any private work. If loyalty programs are extended to industry, the decision is made by businessmen who are often afraid of losing government contracts. In public schools and universities, the loss of a career is inflicted by educational officials, who are sometimes threatened by the statute with being severely punished themselves if they decide the teacher innocent and are afterwards ruled to have been mistaken. Many efforts are made to extend the same system to private schools and colleges. Books are weeded out from schools and colleges by officials. The extensive outlawing of organizations contemplated by the McCarran Act will be done by a board of five men specially selected as watch-dogs of sedition. Administrators can also stifle organizations by choking off the financial contributions which are essential to their existence; they can deprive potential givers of exemptions from income taxes and sometimes threaten them with prosecution if they give money to a red-listed group. The denial of passports is chiefly left to the uncontrolled discretion of one official whose name is unknown to the public. If a war or declared emergency exists, administrators will decide who shall be sent to concentration camps under the McCarran Act. And over and above all these penalties imposed on American citizens by officials is the constant smearing of them by single speakers on the floor of the legislature and single columnists, who now exercise the power to take away any man's good name and blackmail his customers and sponsors with threats of boycotts and very likely ruin his chances of supporting himself, his wife and his children.

Not only do jurymen have almost nothing to do with the suppressions just listed, but judges too are pretty much out of the picture. The importance of active judicial supervision over governmental restrictions on speech and press is obvious when we remember what the Supreme Court did under Hughes. Nevertheless, the McCarran Act gives judges little more than perfunctory tasks, and there is as yet no evidence that a majority of the Supreme Court Justices will give any protection to freedom of thought and expression from legislative investigations, loyalty programs, purges of teachers, and test oaths. In criminal prosecutions, too, the Court has nearly abdicated the control over sedition laws which it exercised under Hughes. This is to me the most disquieting feature of the Dennis case. It cut down the First Amendment to mean about this: "Congress shall make no law abridging the freedom of speech and of the press unless Congress does make a law abridging the freedom of speech and of the press."

Anybody who has studied the enactment of the Smith Act and subsequent sedition statutes can see that the indispensable balance of the values of free speech against the danger of violent acts, etc., does not take place in a legislature today. Instead, free speech gets little attention and the dangers are everything. The legislative judgment is not reached "after due deliberation." So the indispensable balancing will have to be done by the courts or not at all. If judges cannot or will not review suppressions, then legislators and officials are left free to penalize speech and even thoughts as much as they may desire, and they desire a great deal.

The definition of wrongful speech and assembly in the new kinds of suppression is not confined, as in the older criminal statutes, to advocacy of force and violence. The new legislation is indeed put through by arguments that it is badly needed to get rid of Communists. Yet its enforcement rarely stops with Communists or other violent revolutionists.

Look at the authoritative definition of "subversive activity" by a House Committee as the basis for throwing federal officials out of their jobs: "Subversive activity . . . derives from conduct intentionally destructive of or inimical to the Government . . . which seeks to undermine its institutions, or to distort its functions, or to impede its projects, or to lessen its efforts . . . the ultimate end being to overthrow it all." This goes far beyond support of violent revolution. The same is true of the vague characterization of "communist-front organizations" in the McCarran Act. This Act also allows citizens to be sent to concentration camps without having committed any crime at all. Citizens can be put behind barbed wire for years merely because some official has "reasonable ground to believe" that they will commit or conspire with others to commit espionage or sabotage. Such an official belief can of course be based on all sorts of heterodox opinions, etc., which would never support a conviction in a criminal trial. The tests of wrongdoing which will throw federal officials out of their jobs are "disloyalty" or "a poor security risk." The American Bar Association has called for disbarment proceedings against any lawyer who, without having the remotest connection with the Communist Party, is suspected of embracing "Marxism-Leninism," a doctrine which may mean to his accusers something quite different from what it means to economists. An American citizen can be denied a passport for no other reason than that his "travel abroad at this time would be contrary to the best interests of the United States." Perhaps the most extreme departure from the old criminal-law tests of guilt appears in the recommendations of a California investigating committee for barring text-books from public schools. A book is condemned, apart from anything the author writes, because its bibliography happens to list a book by Charles A. Beard or myself, or because the book refers casually to Senator Frank P. Graham. Then I am condemned because I joined Beard and Graham in exercising my constitutional right of petition, and because I was on the mailing-list of organizations whose communications promptly went into the waste-basket, while Beard and Graham are condemned for associating with me. *In short, anything which is found to be "subversive" can be penalized in some way or other, and "subversive" is rapidly coming to mean anything which the powers that be don't like.*

. . . It is important during this crisis to have three general guides for our thinking.

In the first place, there is a strong need for everybody to keep firmly in mind both sides of the balance, which I described early in this address as essential to the proper solution of all free speech problems. On one side are the great values of open discussion, and we ought to start with them. If we begin with the vivid dangers, it is easy to stop there. However, people who are devoted to the First Amendment should avoid the opposite error of ignoring the genuine dangers which confront the nation today. The ruling groups in the Soviet Union and its satellites seem determined not to maintain any normal human relations with other countries. During my experiences in the United Nations, it was impossible to get anywhere with them. The chief impression I carried away was of men who had masks instead of faces. And they have despicable clever allies in our midst, as several spy cases prove.

Supporters of freedom of speech who adequately understand such dangers will be better able to correct exaggerated versions of them by which the advocates of suppression are scaring the American people into throwing overboard our most cherished liberties. They will be better able to show how those dangers can be combatted effectively by other weapons than sedition laws. This existence of good alternatives is constantly getting overlooked. For example, Chief Justice Vinson gave as a main reason for sustaining the constitutionality of the Smith Act: "We reject any principle of governmental helplessness in the face of preparation for revolution. . . ." Yet there was no helplessness if the Smith Act had been set aside. The government could crush any real preparation for revolution by using the Conspiracy Act of 1861, which punishes severely any two or more persons who conspire "to overthrow, put down, or to destroy by force the Government of the United States, or to levy war against them, or to oppose by force the authority thereof, or by force to prevent, hinder, or delay the execution of any law of the United States." This old statute carried us safely through the terrible dangers of the Civil War, the unrest of the Red Menace, the suffering and resentment of the Great Depression. . . .

The second important principle is more complex. Just because you think a certain kind of person or speech or organizational activity is very objectionable, it does not necessarily follow that force and suppression are the right ways to deal with the situation. For example, people ask, "Do you want an extreme Marxist to teach your children?" And when you answer "No," they regard this as a conclusive reason why you should acquiesce in a test oath or inquisition for all school teachers in order to get rid of a few Marxists, if they should thus be turned up. The trouble is that only part of the situation has been stated. I don't want my children to be run over by automobiles, and I could keep them completely safe by never letting them go out of doors. Yet the losses would obviously far outweigh the gain. I am also anxious to have my children grow into active, courageous, and useful citizens. So I must take chances of automobile accidents, and minimize those chances in some better way. . . . Moreover, suppression will often do more harm than good. Thus after zealous patriots had thrown the University of California into months of turmoil in order to get rid of a score of professors who were not Communists at all, a dean remarked: "No conceivable damage to the university at the hands of the hypothetical Communists among us could have equaled the damage resulting from the unrest, ill will, and suspicion engendered by this series of events." Aside from the fact that students don't absorb all they hear anyway, there were plenty of orthodox professors available to offset the teaching of occasional heretics, to say nothing of parents, newspaper editors, and numberless other influences off the campus. . . .

Third, what is constitutional may still be very unwise. Most people have fallen into almost exactly the opposite attitude. Every time the Supreme Court refuses to upset one more kind of suppression, this decision is regarded as a green light to dash ahead. Yet nobody acts on the idea that everything constitutional is good when he is discussing income-tax rates or the size of old-age benefits or the regulation of collective bargaining. There constitutionality is sure, but we talk much about wisdom. We insist one plan will work well and another plan will work badly. We are all aware of many sorts of conflicting interests that require careful consideration.

So it ought to be when we are dealing with free speech problems. The reluctance of the Supreme Court to block loyalty programs, investigating committees, etc., simply puts constitutional objections out of the way. Other very serious objections to what is actually done under the law may still remain and call urgently for careful consideration.

Take legislative investigating committees. So far as the Constitution goes, "No holds are barred." Because their proceedings are not criminal trials, they are not bound by several of the procedural safeguards of prosecutions in the Sixth Amendment. Nevertheless, the First and Sixth Amendments set forth principles of wisdom which are highly relevant to legislative investigations. Therefore it is very regrettable that almost nothing has been done by Congress or the American bar to work out rules of decent procedure for investigating committees.

Because of my principle about the need for scrutinizing the

wisdom and practical consequences of suppressive measures regardless of their constitutionality, I am going to ignore constitutional law for the rest of this talk. There is no time to review in detail the operation of the various novel types of suppression. I shall attempt to state some aspects of what is going on now which disturb a man who loves the kind of country in which he grew up and fears that that kind of country will soon disappear unless present trends are checked.

I am disturbed by the gradual erosion of many fundamental human rights which were cherished by the Americans of 1791. It is not just a question of inroads on freedom of speech and press, freedom of assembly, and freedom of petition (through the deterring effect of red-listing). Equally disquieting is what those inroads are doing to our traditions of a fair trial. A person who is subpoenaed into a legislative investigation, where his reputation and perhaps his livelihood are at stake, is denied much of the protection long enjoyed by those who risk imprisonment or a fine. He is not told what he is charged with before he prepares his defense and starts answering questions; the investigators have a roving commission to find out anything whatever that will damage him. He cannot demand to be confronted with the witnesses against him, for they may be spies whose identity the secret police do not want disclosed. So he may not know who his accusers are, and in any event he cannot cross-examine them. The normal right to counsel is denied. Sometimes he cannot even bring a lawyer into the room with him. When a lawyer is graciously admitted, he must usually be just a bystander with no chance to conduct the defense. Investigating committees even propose the disbarment of lawyers who defend persons suspected of subversive activities.

One frequent line of questioning by investigating bodies is to me abominable. After the investigated person has been asked whether he ever belonged to some "subversive" organization—remember that the range goes far beyond the Communist Party—the next question may be, "Name your associates" or

"Were X and Y also in this organization?" The law, of course, gives no privilege against betraying one's friends, and yet no decent American would request such a betrayal, so long as no heinous crime is involved. It is ingrained in school-boys not to "peach" on a comrade, and any school-teacher who asked them to do so is not fit for his job. . . .

It is this "mean and unworthy thing" which investigators are now trying to force citizens to do, in the name of Americanism. The only sure way to evade this dirty question is to remain silent throughout the whole hearing, through claiming a privilege against self-incrimination regardless of the very damaging effect of such a claim on a person's career. I am told that often the reason for setting up this privilege at the outset of a hearing is not because the questioned man is unwilling to tell anything he has done himself, but in order to prevent his being forced to inculpate old friends.

Congressional committees who fling around frequent threats of committing such reluctant witnesses for "contempt of Congress" would do well to remember the old story of a Justice of the Peace. He met a man against whom he had lately decided a case. The defeated litigant started to upbraid the J.P., who said he would sentence him for contempt. "You're not in your court. What I say on the street isn't contempt. You can't punish me." "Yes, I can. A Justice of the Peace is always an object of contempt." . . .

I am disturbed by the common assumption that deprivation of a job connected with the government is not a substantial loss of freedom. The theory is that governmental activity is a special sort of thing and not a general privilege; hence the ousted individual is simply thrust out of a small corner of life, with plenty of other places left open to him. Thus, in sustaining the New York Feinberg Law, the Supreme Court reasoned that a school teacher is not deprived of freedom of speech and assembly when he is thrown out of the public schools. In short, when a teacher can think and talk as much as he likes by merely giving up a government job, this is freedom.

Such a theory seems to me to assume what is not so. The man was trained to be a public school teacher and to spend his life in that profession. Since thinking and talking are his business, restrictions on them as a condition of holding his job are peculiarly repugnant, while it is like cutting off his hand for him to go elsewhere. And where else? Private schools are fully staffed and unlikely to take a man who has quit in a controversy. A school teacher is not prepared for a trade and he is too old to make a fresh start. The Court's reasoning would logically make out that disbarment of a lawyer with heterodox opinions is no infringement of freedom of speech and thought.

And there is a still larger fallacy in this attitude. It was all very well for Justice Holmes to say that no man has "a constitutional right to be a policeman," because policemen are a small fraction of the population. But as soon as you begin to apply loyalty tests to anybody connected with the government, you embrace an enormous range of activities. The number of federal, state, and municipal employees is a substantial part of the working population. Add workmen in factories with government contracts and professors teaching in universities with an ROTC or a government grant for scientific research or an unassigned unit from the army or the navy, and hardly anybody is left out. . . .

I am disturbed by the growing inclination to turn spies into heroes. One of the earliest lessons learned by children, is as I have already said, that tale-bearing on one's comrades is a dirty business. No doubt, there are several long-recognized crimes very harmful to the community, like counterfeiting, where convictions would often be hard to obtain without stool-pigeons and spies. Here the need for the betrayer's evidence is so great as to outweigh the evils of spies. But when one is considering a novel crime, it is a question whether the game is worth the candle. The use by employers of spies in labor unions shows what can happen. And when it comes to political crimes, historians of the Popish Plot and sedition laws in England during the French Revolution have demonstrated that spies were a black blot on such affairs. Spies sometimes become *agents provocateurs,* who incite the very crimes they are hired to report. Hence it is very disquieting to read the evidence against the eleven Communists in New York two years ago by at least three spies working under the direction of the FBI, who joined the Communist Party and served on its recruiting committees. Thus these government employees were actively inducing American citizens to become members of a conspiracy against the United States. . . .

I am disturbed by the strong tendency to establish an American party-line. Loyalty and integrity are more and more getting tested by mental qualifications going far beyond the old-fashioned determination to support and defend the Constitution of the United States. One prominent lawyer asserts that the Constitution "contemplates a free enterprise system" and hence everything inconsistent with that system deserves condemnation. The trouble is that the competition of small farmers and shopkeepers which the Founding Fathers knew was not quite the same as a nation of giant corporations. There is no definition of "free enterprise" suitable for application in any sort of legal proceeding. Yet this lawyer's proposal has been put into operation by the school authorities of Englewood, New Jersey, where every teacher or school-head who proposed to use a text-book must certify in writing that the book does not "advocate . . . a doctrine inimical to the principles of government established by the Constitution . . . and further that it does not advocate a principle or doctrine inimical to the American system of free enterprise." To some administrative officials this might well include a book which pointed out the advantages of new federal hospitals for everybody or free college education or the abolition of holding-companies in public utilities. Such a vague phrase can mean what anybody wants it to mean. It is a deviation from the American party-line to want democracy. "Ours is a republic. Under a democratic government the major party can put the minority into slavery," said the chairman of the California investigating committee to Florence Eldridge, the actress, before he red-listed her as "typical of the individuals within the various Stalinist orbits." It is becoming a tenet of the American party-line that there was only one right policy in the frightful tangle of Chinese affairs. If I were a cartoonist, I would picture a new recruit in the State Department holding up his right hand and swearing to defend the Constitution of the United States and Chiang Kai-Shek. Belief in natural law is becoming essential to the American party-line. This is a highly controversial philosophical doctrine, as to which devoted and law-abiding citizens hold contrary views. Yet because Justice Holmes did not believe in natural law, he is now denounced as a totalitarian.

In short, honest differences of opinion are treated like moral differences. The common framework of discussion is getting torn to pieces. Instead of an orderly and enlightened search for facts and sound judgment, public opinion is getting framed by coercion and intrigue and insinuations. Government by representation is giving way to government by misrepresentation.

What can we in this hall do to help turn this nation back toward the freedoms which Englishmen and Americans attained through centuries of struggle and privations and hard thinking? For years to come, I fear, there is a very small chance of our being able to affect decisions in specific cases or the enactment of sedition laws or the behavior of subversive control boards and legislative investigating committees. Little can we do there, but much can we do to aid in the formation of a sounder public opinion, which will revert to the courage of Thomas Jefferson.

Free speech problems are arising constantly in private lives. They are not limited to courtrooms and Congressional offices. Shall I let my child read this book? Shall I sit silent while the school committee dismisses an unpopular teacher? Shall this meeting take place in a local hall or a vacant lot? Shall I vote against a man because some Senator calls him subversive? Am I reading both sides of a controversy? These are questions presented to common or garden people all the time, and the way they are answered can give us more freedom or less.

And it is very fruitful to keep discussing, in season and out of season, the great advantages of open discussion. Of all the arguments against restrictions on speech, the strongest of all (I have come to think) is that it gives us a better country to live in, with fewer suspicions, animosities, informers, heresy trials, and more scope for initiative and originality.

Although freedom cannot be maintained by expositions alone, in the end they furnish the main strength of liberty. A people gets sooner or later as much freedom as it wants. This want is partly created by prophets on or off the bench, but partly by constant discussion from plain citizens like us. The best safeguard against inroads on freedom of speech lies in the ferment in the thoughts of the young and of those who will not let themselves grow old.

Part Eight

THE ECONOMIC FACTOR

Government

42. CHANNELS FOR GRAFT

1877–1878

Reconstruction in South Carolina brought a story of gross fraud and corruption in the Republican-controlled government, involving public lands, bonds, and mining rights, and railroads, banks, and important segments of the press. Of all areas of fraud investigated after the Democrats returned to power in 1876, the "printing frauds" were declared by investigators to be the worst. State officers and legislators found willing editors and established newspapers as channels for carrying huge sums of public monies to themselves and "friends." Other newspapers were in effect bribed to assure a friendly press. The amount of money "appro-

---

From *South Carolina Reports and Resolutions, 1877–1878*, "Report of the Joint Investigating Committee on Public Frauds," (Columbia, S. C.: Public Printing, 1878).

priated and paid" for public printing from 1868 to 1876, when the debacle came to an end, totaled $1,326,589—a total greater than the State had paid in all the years between its establishment and 1868.

After having reported on other matters referred to them, your Committee have now to consider the matter of public printing. Before entering into the details of the system of fraud by which, under this guise, the State Treasury was depleted more effectually than by any other scheme, (unless it be through the issuing of legislative pay certificates,) the Committee desire to engage in advance the public indulgence. Whilst fraud, bribery and corruption were rife in every department of the State government, nothing has equaled the magnitude and infamy attending the management of public printing. So much of comment is necessary, even though each statement we shall make is verified by reliable testimony.

The corruption was everywhere prevalent, and the division of the spoils extended from the highest officials to the humblest members of the General Assembly. Indeed, it embraced a majority of the State officials and two-thirds of the members of the General Assembly. In addition to the amounts expended for the benefit of those persons, the fund obtained was devoted to the establishment and support of various Republican journals, daily and weekly, but principally to aid the Charleston Daily Republican, the Columbia Daily Union and the Columbia Union-Herald. A large amount of money was expended annually for the support of these and kindred papers without any legal authority; and bills purporting to be presented under or by virtue of law, illegally and fraudulently increased in amount to many thousands of dollars, were paid year after year from the State Treasury. At first, as will appear from the testimony, under Mr. Denny's contract the division of the spoils was confined to a few of the leading members of the General Assembly, but a majority did not like Denny's close manner of conducting business. Hence the Carolina Printing Company was formed, composed of certain State officials and the editors of the Columbia Union and Charleston Republican. After this, the system of issuing pay certificates for public printing for division became almost universal, resulting in many thousands of dollars worth of printing pay certificates being issued annually without any consideration, to be paid out of any money not otherwise appropriated, unless the taking of it by the officials and members can be construed as an appropriation, which it literally was. Not content with this, claims when paid by the Treasurer for permanent and current printing were in several instances raised to three times the original amounts, and thus paid and divided. These payments thus raised were added to the printing accounts in order that this ring should not lose thereby. The checks and evidence show that Woodruff, the Clerk of the Senate, was to take care of the "circle of friends" in the Senate, and Clerk Jones of "the friends" in the House, and they were jointly to take care of State officials.

Your Committee experienced great difficulty in arriving at the amounts actually paid for public printing, as the sum was largely in excess of that charged on the books of the State Treasurer. We ascertained that large payments had been made ostensibly for printing which were charged to other convenient accounts, and hence we were obliged to examine and go through all the vouchers from 1868 to 1876, at the expense of much time and labor. The amount appropriated and paid during this time, including the publication of the general laws and claims for printing, was $1,326,589, a sum largely in excess of the cost of public printing from the establishment of the State government up to 1868, including all payments made during the war in Confederate currency. In this connection we respectfully invite attention to paper annexed to the evidence with this report marked "Exhibit E, F, G," in further illustration of the extravagant and enormous cost of public printing during these flush times of the so-called Printing Ring; also, to the appropriations made at the sessions of 1872–73, when appropriations for public printing and amounts paid newspapers for printing Acts reached $450,000, or $171,759 more than the printing cost the State for twenty-five years, commencing at 1840–41 and ending 1865–66, including $42,141.63 paid during the war in 1864 in Confederate currency for one year's printing. This statement includes payments made throughout the war when the true value of labor and materials ascended in ratio with the depreciation of Confederate currency, and included also the amounts paid for printing at the session of 1865–6, when, owing to the destruction of our railroads, the freights upon printing material alone cost more than the material and freights combined in 1872–3. The public printing in this State cost $450,000 in one year, exceeding the cost of like work in Massachusetts, Pennsylvania, Ohio, Maryland and New York by $122,932.13, embracing as they do five of the largest and most populous of the Northern, Eastern, Western and Southern States. . . .

Your Committee herewith submit a portion of Mr. Woodruff's testimony bearing upon this subject, so that some idea may be had of the system and results of this stupendous plundering of the Treasury of the State. Mr. Woodruff swears that he was elected Clerk of the Senate in 1868. J. W. Denny was then State Printer. "Senators composing the circle of friends" became dissatisfied with Mr. Denny's close manner of conducting business and his failure to meet their expectations in the division of the profits arising from the public printing. In the Fall or Winter of 1870 the Carolina Printing Company was organized by Messrs. J. W. Denny, R. K. Scott, N. G. Parker, D. H. Chamberlain, J. W. Morris and L. Cass Carpenter. This company owned the Daily Union of Columbia and the Charleston Republican. Senator Leslie told Woodruff that "the friends" in the Senate thought that as this was a matter of Senate patronage they should have a percentage of the profits from the printing. In order to carry out the wishes of "the friends," Mr.

Leslie proposed that pay certificates for various amounts, ranging from three to five thousand dollars, for current printing be drawn, and one-third or one-fourth of the amount realized be given to the Chairman of the Committee on Printing for division among "the friends," including some fifteen or sixteen Senators. This system was carried out as long as moneys could be paid out of any sums in the Treasury *not otherwise appropriated,* and was only checked and stopped when the law for specific appropriations and payments was enacted. Besides this, Woodruff testifies that a vast deal of unofficial and dead-head work was done by the company for State officials, friends and members of the General Assembly. . . .

Your Committee find that huge frauds were committed under the head of newspaper advertising, and that the people were loaded with an oppressive tax to subsidize a venal press. These frauds were equal in proportion to those of the Carolina or Republican Printing Company. Not satisfied with the large sums paid them as leading Senators and Representatives, many of the same parties filched considerable sums from the Treasury for printing laws in country newspapers established for that purpose. Several instances are on record where a Senator received five thousand dollars for publishing the Acts, whilst a paper not owned or controlled by a Senator would have received for the same work about five hundred dollars. It is a matter of proof that daily newspapers were established in Charleston and Columbia and run in the personal interest of the members of the Ring, and frauds were perpetrated in the making up and collecting of such accounts scarcely equalled by any other. With a view of satisfying the General Assembly of the truth of this statement, we will briefly recite some instances: James H. Diseker, Edwin Forde and Edwin A. Nelson, all experienced and practical printers, have carefully and minutely measured all the official advertisements of every description contained in the files of the Charleston Republican (large amounts of which were made out and collected in the name of the Carolina Printing Company.) They find, and so state, that, according to the contract made with the two Clerks for publishing the laws and the rates charged by such paper for advertising, the sum due the paper would be $24,538.20. On examination of the vouchers paid and in the State Treasurer's office, it is shown that there was paid said paper the extraordinary sum of $60,982.14 during its existence and at times there was paid the monstrous sum of *twenty-five cents a line* each for both Daily and Weekly Republican for publishing the Acts. This contract is attached to the evidence marked "Exhibit E, D," as a remarkable curiosity in business matters.

Thus it is seen that the State paid $36,443.94 over and above the legitimate sum due, in order that "the organ" of the party in power might subsist. In deed and in truth, the Charleston Republican was a *lively bonanza,* that never failed to prove a grand source of revenue to some of the *modern statesmen.* This is established by the large amounts paid as claims to the "friends" of the Republican, passed from time to time, reaching several thousand dollars, when at the time of the passage of the claim the company had drawn largely in excess of any amount properly due it. We refer to paper marked "Exhibit A" as a specimen claim of this character, being only one of many in the Treasurer's office. We also refer to the evidence of the printers above named, who say they have examined the files of the Columbia Daily Union, and find there was due L. Cass Carpenter, editor and proprietor, the sum of $17,174.05, from November, 1870, to May, 1873, under contract to publish the laws at 20 cents per line and the advertised rates for other official advertisements. Nevertheless, the vouchers in the Treasurer's office show that Mr. Carpenter was paid $59,987.64 for advertising in his paper, including $9,286 claimed to have been due for publications made in the weekly issue, thus defrauding the State out of $33,527.59 in less than three years. In addition to this, Mr. Carpenter was paid a claim of $2,500 for publishing Acts in 1874. He was also paid more than $5,000 for furnishing papers to State officials, members of the Assembly and other lesser lights of *the party*. The vouchers show that he received over $10,000 for publishing two Acts known as "Insurance Laws." The evidence of Dr. Neagle, then Comptroller General, and his letter to Mr. Carpenter, herewith submitted as "Exhibit I, L," show that the amounts thus collected were without any authority of law. . . .

43. GROSJEAN v. AMERICAN PRESS COMPANY

1936

Huey P. Long found unacceptable the tendencies toward independence of large Louisiana newspapers in the early and mid-1930's. At his instance the Louisiana legislature passed a law in 1934 placing a two per cent tax on gross advertising receipts of every newspaper that had a circulation of more than 20,000 a week. Of the state's 163 newspapers, this affected thirteen, of which twelve had opposed Senator Long's reign. In a note over the name of Senator Long, legislators were informed that the tax on newspapers "will help their lying some."

The publishers of the thirteen newspapers brought suit to enjoin the supervisor of public accounts of Louisiana from enforcing the tax. The United States District Court granted the injunction, Supervisor Grosjean appealed, and the Supreme Court decided the case squarely on free press grounds. Justice Sutherland's de-

---

From *Grosjean* v. *American Press Company*, 297 U.S. Reports 233.

cision said that in operating to curtail advertising revenue and circulation, the measure amounted to a tax on knowledge of a kind odious to England and America for more than two centuries. It was beyond belief, he said, that such taxes were thought by the authors of the Bill of Rights to be acceptable within the meaning of a free press. The narrow view of the English common law that freedom of the press consisted only in immunity from prepublication censorship, Sutherland declared, could not have been all that the framers of the First Amendment intended the term to mean. A state government may tax newspapers with any of the ordinary forms of taxation for the support of government, but not with a tax devised to limit the circulation of information to which the public is entitled.

Mr. Justice Sutherland delivered the opinion of the Court:

. . . The validity of the act is assailed as violating the Federal Constitution in two particulars—(1) that it abridges the freedom of the press in contravention of the due process clause contained in § 1 of the Fourteenth Amendment; (2) that it denies appellees the equal protection of the laws in contravention of the same Amendment.

1. The first point presents a question of the utmost gravity and importance; for, if well made, it goes to the heart of the natural right of the members of an organized society, united for their common good, to impart and acquire information about their common interests. The First Amendment to the Federal Constitution provides that "Congress shall make no law . . . abridging the freedom of speech, or of the press . . ." While this provision is not a restraint upon the powers of the states, the states are precluded from abridging the freedom of speech or of the press by force of the due process clause of the Fourteenth Amendment. . . .

That freedom of speech and of the press are rights of . . . fundamental character, safeguarded by the due process of law clause of the Fourteenth Amendment against abridgement by state legislation, has . . . been settled by a series of decisions of this Court beginning with *Gitlow* v. *New York*, 268 U. S. 652, 666, and ending with *Near* v. *Minnesota*, 283 U. S. 697, 707. The word "liberty" contained in that amendment embraces not only the right of a person to be free from physical restraint, but the right to be free in the enjoyment of all his faculties as well. *Allgeyer* v. *Louisiana*, 165 U. S. 578, 589. . . .

The tax imposed is designated a "license tax for the privilege of engaging in such business"—that is to say, the business of selling, or making any charge for, advertising. As applied to appellees, it is a tax of two per cent. on the gross receipts derived from advertisements carried in their newspapers when, and only when, the newspapers of each enjoy a circulation of more than 20,000 copies per week. It thus operates as a restraint in a double sense. First, its effect is to curtail the amount of revenue realized from advertising, and, second, its direct tendency is to restrict circulation. This is plain enough when we consider that, if it were increased to a high degree, as it could be if valid . . . , it well might result in destroying both advertising and circulation.

A determination of the question whether the tax is valid in respect of the point now under review, requires an examination of the history and circumstances which antedated and attended the adoption of the abridgement clause of the First Amendment, since that clause expresses one of those "fundamental principles of liberty and justice which lie at the base of all our civil and political institutions" (*Hebert* v. *Louisiana*, 272 U. S. 312, 316), and, as such, is embodied in the concept "due process of law" . . . , and, therefore, protected against hostile state invasion by the due process clause of the Fourteenth Amendment. . . .

For more than a century prior to the adoption of the amendment—and, indeed, for many years thereafter—history discloses a persistent effort on the part of the British government to prevent or abridge the free expression of any opinion which seemed to criticize or exhibit in an unfavorable light, however truly, the agencies and operations of the government. The struggle between the proponents of measures to that end and those who asserted the right of free expression was continuous and unceasing. As early as 1644, John Milton, in an "Appeal for the Liberty of Unlicensed Printing," assailed an act of Parliament which had just been passed providing for censorship of the press previous to publication. He vigorously defended the right of every man to make public his honest views "without previous censure"; and declared the impossibility of finding any man base enough to accept the office of censor and at the same time good enough to be allowed to perform its duties. Collett, History of the Taxes on Knowledge, vol. I, pp. 4–6. The act expired by its own terms in 1695. It was never renewed; and the liberty of the press thus became, as pointed out by Wickwar (The Struggle for the Freedom of the Press, p. 15), merely "a right or liberty to publish *without* a license what formerly could be published only *with* one." But mere exemption from previous censorship was soon recognized as too narrow a view of the liberty of the press.

In 1712, in response to a message from Queen Anne (Hansard's Parliamentary History of England, vol. 6, p. 1063), Parliament imposed a tax upon all newspapers and upon advertisements. Collett, vol. I, pp. 8–10. That the main purpose of these taxes was to suppress the publication of comments and criticisms objectionable to the Crown does not admit of doubt. Stewart, Lennox and the Taxes on Knowledge, 15 Scottish Historical Review, 322–327. There followed more than a century of resistance to, and evasion of, the taxes, and of agitation for their repeal. In the article last referred to (p. 326), which was written in 1918, it was pointed out that these taxes constituted one of the factors that aroused the American colonists to protest against taxation for the purposes of the home government; and that the revolution really began when, in 1765, that government sent stamps for newspaper duties to the American colonies.

These duties were quite commonly characterized as "taxes on knowledge," a phrase used for the purpose of describing the effect of the exactions and at the same time condemning them. That the taxes had, and were intended to have, the effect of curtailing the circulation of newspapers, and particularly the cheaper ones whose readers were generally found among the masses of the people, went almost without question, even on the part of those who defended the act. May (Constitutional History of England, 7th ed., vol. 2, p. 245), after discussing the control by "previous censure," says: ". . . a new restraint was devised in the form of a stamp duty on newspapers and advertisements,—avowedly for the purpose of repressing libels. This policy, being found effectual in limiting the circulation of cheap papers, was improved upon in the two following reigns, and continued in high esteem until our own time." Collett (vol. I, p. 14), says, "Any man who carried on printing or publishing for a livelihood was actually at the mercy of the Commissioners of Stamps, when they chose to exert their powers."

Citations of similar import might be multiplied many times; but the foregoing is enough to demonstrate beyond peradventure that in the adoption of the English newspaper stamp tax and the tax on advertisements, revenue was of subordinate concern; and that the dominant and controlling aim was to prevent, or curtail the opportunity for, the acquisition of knowledge by the people in respect of their governmental affairs. It is idle to suppose that so many of the best men of England would for a century of time have waged, as they did, stubborn and often precarious warfare against these taxes if a mere matter of taxation had been involved. The aim of the struggle was not to relieve taxpayers from a burden, but to establish and preserve the right of the English people to full information in respect of the doings or misdoings of their government. Upon the correctness of this conclusion the very characterization of the exactions as "taxes on knowledge" sheds a flood of corroborative light. In the ultimate, an informed and enlightened public opinion was the thing at stake; for, as Erskine, in his great speech in defense of Paine, has said, "The liberty of opinion keeps governments themselves in due subjection to their duties." Erskine's Speeches, High's ed., vol. I, p. 525. See May's Constitutional History of England, 7th ed., vol. 2, pp. 238–245.

In 1785, only four years before Congress had proposed the First Amendment, the Massachusetts legislature, following the English example, imposed a stamp tax on all newspapers and magazines. The following year an advertisement tax was imposed. Both taxes met with such violent opposition that the former was repealed in 1786, and the latter in 1788. Duniway, Freedom of the Press in Massachusetts, pp. 136–137.

The framers of the First Amendment were familiar with the English struggle, which then had continued for nearly eighty years and was destined to go on for another sixty-five years, at the end of which time it culminated in a lasting abandonment of the obnoxious taxes. The framers were likewise familiar with the then recent Massachusetts episode; and while that occurrence did much to bring about the adoption of the amendment (see Pennsylvania and the Federal Constitution, 1888, p. 181), the predominant influence must have come from the English experience. It is impossible to concede that by the words "freedom of the press" the framers of the amendment intended to adopt merely the narrow view then reflected by the law of England that such freedom consisted only in immunity from previous censorship; for this abuse had then permanently disappeared from English practice. It is equally impossible to believe that it was not intended to bring within the reach of these words such modes of restraint as were embodied in the two forms of taxation already described. Such belief must be rejected in the face of the then well known purpose of the exactions and the general adverse sentiment of the colonies in respect of them. . . .

In the light of all that has now been said, it is evident that the restricted rules of the English law in respect of the freedom of the press in force when the Constitution was adopted were never accepted by the American colonists, and that by the First Amendment it was meant to preclude the national government, and by the Fourteenth Amendment to preclude the states, from adopting any form of previous restraint upon printed publications, or their circulation, including that which had theretofore been effected by these two well-known and odious methods.

This court had occasion in *Near* v. *Minnesota, supra,* at pp. 713 *et seq.*, to discuss at some length the subject in its general aspect. The conclusion there stated is that the object of the constitutional provisions was to prevent previous restraints on publication; and the court was careful not to limit the protection of the right to any particular way of abridging it. Liberty of the press within the meaning of the constitutional provision, it was broadly said (p. 716), meant "principally although not exclusively, immunity from previous restraints or [from] censorship."

Judge Cooley has laid down the test to be applied—"The evils to be prevented were not the censorship of the press merely, but any action of the government by means of which it might prevent such free and general discussion of public matters as seems absolutely essential to prepare the people for an intelligent exercise of their rights as citizens." 2 Cooley's Constitutional Limitations, 8th ed., p. 886.

It is not intended by anything we have said to suggest that the owners of newspapers are immune from any of the ordinary forms of taxation for support of the government. But this is not an ordinary form of tax, but one single in kind, with a long history of hostile misuse against the freedom of the press.

The predominant purpose of the grant of immunity here invoked was to preserve an untrammeled press as a vital source of public information. The newspapers, magazines and other journals of the country, it is safe to say, have shed and continue to shed, more light on the public and business affairs of the nation than any other instrumentality of publicity; and since informed public opinion is the most potent of all restraints upon misgovernment, the suppression or abridgement of the publicity afforded by a free press cannot be regarded otherwise than with grave concern. The tax here involved is bad not because it takes money from the pockets of the appellees. If that were all, a wholly different question would be presented. It is bad because, in the light of its history and of its present setting, it is seen to be a deliberate and calculated device in the guise of a tax to limit the circulation of information to which the public is entitled in virtue of the constitutional guaranties. A free press stands as one of the great interpreters between the government and the people. To allow it to be fettered is to fetter ourselves.

In view of the persistent search for new subjects of taxation, it is not without significance that, with the single exception of the Louisiana statute, so far as we can discover, no state during the one hundred fifty years of our national existence has undertaken to impose a tax like that now in question.

The form in which the tax is imposed is in itself suspicious. It is not measured or limited by the volume of advertisements. It is measured alone by the extent of the circulation of the publication in which the advertisements are carried, with the plain purpose of penalizing the publishers and curtailing the circulation of a selected group of newspapers.

2. Having reached the conclusion that the act imposing the tax in question is unconstitutional under the due process of law clause because it abridges the freedom of the press, we deem it unnecessary to consider the further ground assigned that it also constitutes a denial of the equal protection of the laws.

Decree affirmed.

The Public

44. EVERYTHING MORTGAGED UP TO THE NECK

George B. Leonard, 1930

The retreat of the *Minnesota Daily Star* in the early 1920's from its position as an informed and militant reporter and oracle for labor and farmers, to policies of heavily popularized content and a barely identifiable editorial position, tells part of the story of freedom's reliance on economics. Financed and repeatedly rescued though it was by a great force of loyalty in the form of organized farmers and labor unions, that was not enough to offset bad business management and weak circulation and advertising support. It trimmed its sails to attract more readers and advertising but could not stave off disaster.

The Star's story was duplicated by almost a dozen other "labor dailies" of the first quarter of the twentieth century. But as its splendid early editor, Herbert E. Gaston, said, it is not only radical publications whose first duty is to live. Mass media of communications established as business propositions in a business society must find accommodation with audience and advertisers. Much of the financial struggle of the Northwest Publishing Company, which published the *Star,* is told below by the attorney for its receiver, six years after its death.

"To Stockholders of The Northwest Publishing Company," *Seaman Paper Company of Minnesota* v. *The Northwest Publishing Company,* Hennepin County, Minn., District Court File #222466.

To Stockholders of The Northwest Publishing Company

There are some stockholders who are not familiar with the events leading up to the appointment of the Receiver or what has been accomplished by the Receiver since his appointment. I was not attorney for the Northwest Publishing Company before its failure. Mr. Dollenmayer, who was appointed Receiver by the Court, was not in any way connected with the Company. He is in the advertising business. He has also a wide knowledge of the newspaper business.

An examination of the records of the Company discloses substantially this history: The Company was organized in 1919 under the laws of the State of Minnesota. Its chief object was the publication of a daily paper, presumably to represent the progressive farmer and labor point of view. Its capital stock was a million dollars. The promoters, chiefly Mr. Arthur Townley and Mr. Thomas Van Lear, evidently realized that the starting of a paper of this kind in the face of opposition of big advertisers would involve losses of several hundred thousand dollars before the paper could be made financially self-supporting. They went out to raise a million dollars therefore. By August, 1920, they had raised only about $700,000, and after paying the solicitors' commissions, they were left with about $600,000, in cash, notes, and Liberty bonds. The Non-Partisan League was in need of headquarters, and of help in the publication of its weekly NON-PARTISAN LEADER. These leaders and their associates decided to erect a building to serve all the three purposes,—as headquarters of the Non-Partisan League, a place to publish the NON-PARTISAN LEADER, and a place to publish the Daily. The Daily was started in the Summer of 1920. It is very apparent that there were at least three fundamental errors committed; provided of course that the establishment of a Daily at such sacrifice was at all advisable.

First: The paper was started before the whole million dollars was raised.

Second: Almost half of the moneys thus raised was sunk in a lot and building, thereby freezing up half of the Company's capital. Adequate quarters for the publication of the paper could have been rented for a few hundred dollars a month; and

Third: The first issue of the paper came out in August, 1920, when paper was at its highest, commanding 16 cents a pound, as against an average of a normal price of 4 cents or so per pound.

After using up more than $250,000 in the lot and building, most of the balance was used in the purchase of machinery and equipment, leaving the Company with a comparatively small working capital of about $100,000. For the first 110 days, the Company lost at an average rate of $1,000 a day, so that its working capital was exhausted in less than four months. Thereupon the building was mortgaged for $150,000, and the bond issue disposed of mostly to International Unions, some of which are still holding these bonds. While the monthly losses were less as time went on, the money raised on the bond issue melted away in less than eight months. Thereupon, the machinery and equipment were mortgaged and when the money raised on that was gone, in the latter part of 1922, appeals went out to the public to buy development notes. Intimations were given out by the management that the Company had reduced its losses to a minimum, and was about to turn a new page, and get on the profit side of the ledger, when, as a matter of fact, the paper was then losing at the rate of between $13,000 to $15,000 a month, or approximately $500 a day. Besides these losses, it was also burdened with the publication of the NON-PARTISAN LEADER, which was not self-sustaining. About $200,000 was raised from the sale of these development notes from more than 900 farmers, labor organizations, union men and other progressives. At the rate of these losses, it took the year 1923 to melt this fund away. In the meantime, the debt of the Non-Partisan League and the Non-Partisan Leader to the Company was mounting. With everything mortgaged up to the neck, and with no further moneys in sight with which to continue the publication of the paper, the appointment of a receiver was inevitable. One of the chief assets of the Company was an indebtedness of the Non-Partisan Leader and of the National Non-Partisan League in the amount of $52,373.64 and accumulated interest, not a cent of which could be collected. The Receiver was appointed on February 25, 1924.

It was then that I stepped in and helped to finance and unscramble a most difficult situation. There were about 63,000 names on the subscription list. It cost a lot of money to build it up. To stop the publication of the paper would have meant a great disaster to the progressive cause. It would have meant the loss of the subscription list. It would have meant an immediate assessment of the stockholders. It would have meant the complete collapse of the biggest undertaking of the progressives of this State. To save the stockholders from an immediate assessment as well as the loss to the bondholders and noteholders, I obtained an order of the Court to authorize the Receiver to borrow money from the stockholders at the rate of $10 per share, hoping to raise $60,000 with which to continue the publication of the paper, even at a loss, until it could be sold as a going-concern. In the meantime I borrowed $10,000 and advanced it to the Receiver, with which to pay half of the wages of the employees for the first four weeks, after obtaining the consent of the employees to stand by the paper and trust the other half of the wages to the Receiver until the paper could be sold. The stockholders did not respond to the appeal generously and less than a thousand of them bought Receiver's certificates. These Receiver's Certificates have practically all been paid by the Receiver since the sale. I kept advancing the Receiver more money as it was needed, until the plant and business were finally sold on May 26, 1924.

The property of the Company was appraised in the Receivership proceedings as follows:

Building and Real Estate, appraised at.	$200,000.00
Machinery and Equipment, appraised at.	120,883.92
Supplies, appraised at.	3,077.06
Subscription list, and good-will, appraised at.	190,000.00
Treasury bonds, held by creditors as collateral to loans, par value.	33,600.00
Total	$547,560.98

Between the time of the appraisal and the time of the sale, the following reductions were made:

On supplies.	$ 900.70
On buildings, etc., depreciation.	2,911.08
On good-will.	12,107.60

It left the property appraised at $531,641.59. The Receiver and I insisted that whoever purchased it should pay a hundred cents on the dollar, including the good-will, that is the circulation list, which was appraised at a little better than $3 a subscriber. The purchaser agreed to pay the full price, but was given 4½ years within which to pay it up.

At the time of the appointment of the Receiver, the liability of the Company on unexpired subscriptions, amounted to $80,625.00. At the time of the sale it was reduced to $57,674.26. It would have been impossible to realize on the circulation list without filling all the subscriptions, and it may be noted that during the Receivership, the balance of prepaid subscriptions was reduced by some $23,000. The Receiver was in no position to stop sending out some 36,000 papers every day to country subscribers, who had paid in advance. It paid to run the paper in order to preserve the names and the going value of the business. The sale of the circulation list justified those expectations.

We urged that if the new company could make the paper go, it could afford to pay this price. The plant and business were sold on May 26, 1924, to a new corporation organized under the laws of Delaware, for $531,641.59.

The purchase price was paid in the following manner: By the Company assuming

First mortgage gold bonds	$150,000.00	
Second mortgage on building	21,152.48	
Accrued interest on secured indebtedness	12,786.26	
Taxes	7,667.66	
Chattel mortgage on machinery and equipment	67,427.19	
City Carriers' bonds, moneys deposited in trust to secure faithful performance	4,091.19	
Balance on contracts for machinery, equipment and loans secured by Treasury bonds	60,842.55	
Unexpired subscriptions	57,674.26	
And agreeing to pay the Receiver an additional	150,000.00	
		$531,641.59

At that time there was outstanding and owing to unsecured creditors as follows:

Commissions to solicitors	$ 4,981.93
Accounts payable	34,199.74
To noteholders	182,988.66
	$222,170.33

These unsecured debts were not assumed by the new Company. There are 909 noteholders. A good many of them loaned the Company $500 and as high as $2,000 each. 310 of them are also stockholders who lost their money with the other stockholders during the first two years of the paper's publication. A partial list of persons who loaned $500 or more to the Company and who are creditors in such amounts is appended. They are all people of very modest means. The Minneapolis Daily Star

Company, organized by a new group of people with fresh money, has finally been able to put the paper on a paying basis largely by cutting the country subscriptions in two but doubling its city circulation. Department stores and other large advertisers are guided more by the size of the city circulation than country in choosing their advertising medium. Likewise the rates are accordingly made by the papers. How important that is to a newspaper is evident from the well known fact that less than one-third of the gross income of a daily paper is derived from subscriptions, the other two-thirds or more is derived from advertising.

From the above, it is readily seen that an exceptionally good sale was made. Not only were the tangible assets disposed of at the highest possible price, but a handsome sum was realized on the good-will, which would have been of no value had the paper ceased to be published. In order to accomplish that, we had to take long chances in financing the Receivership. I had faith that we could realize on the good-will if we ran the paper uninterruptedly, and was therefore ready to help finance the Receivership to the extent of many thousands of dollars, until a profitable sale could be made, which was done. By doing so, we were able to relieve the stockholders of an immediate full assessment. Only fifty of the hundred-fifty thousand dollars which was to be paid to the Receiver, was paid in cash or short time notes. The balance of one hundred thousand dollars was made payable over a period of 42 months, commencing with April 15, 1925. The Receiver took a blanket mortgage on all of the property, including the good-will. Out of the money received, first had to be deducted the losses sustained in the operation of the paper during the Receivership. In addition, back payrolls are preferred claims, and had to be taken care of in full. It would leave, however, a shortage of more than $125,000, besides the expenses of the Receivership, which could only be made up from an assessment of stockholders. In view of the large number of stockholders and the small amounts held by each, the expense of collection would necessarily be large, and therefore a full 100% assessment was inevitable.

With the sanction of the court, a plan was devised by the Receiver and the undersigned to enable the stockholders to settle their stockholders' liability for 25% of the par value of the stock held by them. It was submitted to the stockholders. At first about 850 offered to settle. As letter after letter went out, more offers came in. But many held aloof. Finally an application was made to the Court for a full assessment. It was granted. The Court filed its order on November 20, 1929, assessing all stockholders a hundred per cent on the par value of stock held. Those who settled were released by the Court. Eliminating dead and gone, more than 80% have now settled. The other 20% have to be sued. The Receiver has no choice. Out of the moneys paid in by stockholders in settlement of their liability, the Receiver has already paid to those noteholders and other creditors the sum of more than $65,000 in a 30% dividend distributed to them on December 20th last. From what may be further realized from the collection or settlement of the assessment against the balance of the stockholders, he hopes to pay another dividend to these noteholders and others.

George B. Leonard,
Attorney for A. Dollenmayer, Receiver,
Northwest Publishing Company,
1036 Andrus Building,
Minneapolis, Minn.

Dated: January 15, 1930

The Press

45. THE OBVIOUS ANXIETY OF RICH PUBLISHERS ABOUT FREEDOM OF THE PRESS

William Allen White, 1939

William Allen White, one of America's foremost journalists, despite the fact that his Emporia, Kansas, *Gazette* was printed in a small Midwestern town, was concerned to interpret to publishers and editors how their pocketbooks affected their journalistic performance. In the selection here, he states for the public as well as for publishers his fears about the newspaper institution's internal threat to freedom of the press.

The most serious danger that menaces the freedom of the American press is the obvious anxiety of rich publishers about the freedom of the press. They make so much noise about the threat to the freedom of the press that they have persuaded many people, particularly unthinking people, that the freedom of the press is merely a private snap for editors who wish to exploit the public by selling poisoned news. It is not a universal rule, but the rule is fairly workable that a newspaper which is eternally agonizing about the freedom of the press is a newspaper which is endangering the freedom of the press by abusing that freedom.

William Allen White, "Canons of Journalism—IX," *Chicago Times*, July 2, 1939, p. 13.

In the last 50 years the cost of printing machinery—by that I mean presses, linotypes, stereotypes and photoengraving machinery—has risen so that a publisher has to be a capitalist with real standing at the town or city bank. For instance, the machinery to publish a paper in a village of 1,000 would cost, if bought new, $3,000 to $4,000. The machinery necessary to print a decent little daily newspaper in a town of 10,000 would cost from $25,000 to $40,000. The machinery to publish a daily newspaper in a town of 50,000 would cost nearly $100,000 and as towns grow into cities these figures advance until the publisher of a daily newspaper in a town of half a million needs an investment in machinery and working capital of two or three million dollars if he expects to compete with an established daily. So the publisher becomes a capitalist.

If he is a smart go-getting-up-and-acoming publisher in a town of 100,000 to 1,000,000 people, the publisher associates on terms of equality with the bankers, the merchant princes, the manufacturers, and the investing brokers. His friends unconsciously color his opinion. If he lives with them on any kind of social terms in the City club or the Country club or the Yacht club or the Racquet club, he must more or less merge his views into the common views of the other capitalists. The publisher is not bought like a chattel. Indeed he often is able to buy those who are suspected of buying him. But he takes the color of his social environment.

He is pretty generally against organized labor. He is too often found opposing the government control of public utilities. He instinctively fears any regulation of the stock exchange. The right to strike seems to the rich publisher and his Chamber of Commerce friends to be sheer anarchy. It is inevitable that the managing editor and the editorial writers, who want to hold their jobs, take their professional views and get their professional slant from their boss, the man who signs the payroll check.

So it often happens, alas too often, that a newspaper publisher, reflecting this unconscious class arrogance of the consciously rich, thinks he is printing the news when he is doctoring it innocently enough. He thinks he is purveying the truth when much that he offers seems poison to hundreds of thousands of his readers who don't move in his social and economic stratosphere. So when this rich publisher sees any kind of a threat to the freedom of the press and when he protests in big black type at what he sees or at what he thinks he sees in the menace to his freedom, the net of it is that thousands of his readers get a notion that the freedom of the press is merely a political gadget to allow rich publishers to make money by coloring the news against the poor folk! This is unfair to the rich publisher.

That it is unfair is not the worst of it. The worst of it is that, bad as he is, the crookedest, rich, property-minded publisher is vastly better than he would be if he was operating under a government controlled press. For on seven sides out of ten, the most prejudiced, unscrupulous publisher is fair and his columns in those areas are reasonably dependable.

In a government controlled press, nothing is fair, nothing is left to the routine professional judgment of the editor. A crooked, kept press, privately owned and operated, dominated by an arrogant, class conscious individual or group of individuals, at its worst blinds only one eye of the public. But a government censored press blinds both eyes. And sometimes one objectionable newspaper in a community is mean only on one side and another mean newspaper is good on its rival's bad side. So by shopping around, the public gets the truth in a free press.

Take the worst of the newspapers. I mean the newspapers which color every political item, for instance affecting the New Deal or President Roosevelt, newspapers which are known to be sympathetic to all the inequities and iniquities of business in their home towns, newspapers which are rabid in their anti-labor attitudes, newspapers which refer to men on the left with whom they disagree as Reds, newspapers which imply that every man is a Communist who wants to see a just and equitable order established under the evolutionary democratic process—still, even those publishers' papers are better than a censored press.

At least the readers of a biased press have got the editor's number. They have taken his measure. They know how to get the truth out of his paper by discounting at a certain per cent and allowing certain dependable margins for lying. Then this biased, class-conscious editor is most enterprising in realms that do not affect his social bias and economic position. After all, bad as the biased editor is, his faults are not fatal. For there are chinks in his armor of untruth through which the facts leak out. That is not true in the press of Russia or Italy or Japan or Germany. Moreover, if the press is free—free even to be biased, mean and truculent—then the more arrogant the editor is, the wider field he leaves for another paper to come in and take his subscribers.

But the sad thing is that the biased editor—whether he is a plutocrat or a proletarian—by his continual blatting about the freedom of the press deafens people to the truth that the freedom of the press is not primarily for the newspapers, that it is not primarily to give purse-proud publishers a chance to make money by lying to the poor. If the unthinking minorities grow into majorities who are persuaded by the property-minded editors or radicals clamoring for a free press that the free press is only a license for class conscious lying on one side or the other, then these unthinking minorities may not protest when real freedom of the press is menaced.

So whenever I read a rabid editorial by a reactionary newspaper whooping it up for the freedom of the press I am scared stiff. For every boost that kind of a paper makes for freedom is a knock against it. That kind of press in czarist Russia, in prewar Germany and Italy of the Kingdom must have made the public sentiment that stood by and let the freedom of the press on continental Europe go to pot. A kept government press is a kept press whether it is kept by the dictatorship of the proletariat or by the dictatorship of the military plutocracy of Germany or by the dictatorship of state capitalism in Italy. A kept press is the first sign that human liberty is being crushed.

46. THE SELF-INTERESTS OF THE NEWSPAPER INDUSTRY ARE NOT CONCLUSIVE

Judge Learned Hand, 1943

The bylaws of the Associated Press, the largest American newsgathering service, provided in part that newspaper applicants for membership could be admitted to a "field" (morning, evening, or Sunday) in which a member already published, by majority vote of all AP members. The applicant further was required to pay ten percent of all assessments that had been paid to AP by members in the "field" since 1900. The money would go to those in the "field" at the time of an applicant's admission, but they might waive the payment if they wished.

Marshall Field wanted an AP membership for his *Chicago Sun,* established as a business and ideological competitor to Robert R. McCormick's *Chicago Tribune.* He protested the severe membership barriers; the government brought an action against the AP under the antitrust laws; and the courts required the AP

From *U.S.* v. *Associated Press,* 52 Federal Supplement 362.

to open its membership to newspapers regardless of competitive factors.

Judge Learned Hand wrote the lower court's decision. He found that the bylaws of the great news agency were designed to prevent competition in restricting applicants' access to the news report. Society's vital stake in "the dissemination of news from as many different sources, and with as many different facets and colors as is possible," he held, was too little regarded by the bylaws. As for freedom of the press, he said, the effect of the judgment would be "not to restrict AP members as to what they shall print, but only to compel them to make their dispatches accessible to others."

The by-laws of AP are in effect agreements between the members: that one which restricts AP to the transmission of news to members, and that which restricts any member to transmitting "spontaneous" news to the association, are both contracts in restraint of commerce. They restrict commerce because they limit the members' freedom to relay any news to others, either the news they learn themselves, or that which they learn collectively through AP as their agent. The commerce which they restrict is interstate commerce. . . . However, as everyone now agrees . . . restriction alone is not enough to stamp a combination as illegal; it must be "unreasonable" in the sense that the common law understood that word; and that never has been, and indeed in the nature of things never can be, defined in general terms. Courts must proceed step by step, applying retroactively the standard proper for each situation as it comes up. . . .

There are some situations in which the liabilities have now become settled. No combination fixing prices is valid; it is no excuse that some such arrangement may be necessary to prevent destructive price wars or the like. . . . Again, if a combination effectively excludes, or tries to exclude, outsiders from the business altogether, it is a monopoly, or an incipient monopoly, and it is unconditionally unlawful. . . . Finally, a combination may be illegal because of the means used to effect purposes lawful in themselves; and the means may be unlawful although it would not be, if used by a single person. It is arguable that a boycott, for instance, is always such a means: i.e., any use by a combination of its economic power to force a third person not to deal with another whom the combination wishes to coerce. . . .

But these settled instances are not exhaustive; they are only illustrations of a general doctrine, whose scope they do not measure. When a situation does not fall within one of them, a court is forced to weigh the advantages gained by the combination against the injury done to the public, and apparently in this connection the public is the "purchasers or consumers" whom the combination will deprive "of the advantages which they derive from free competition." Apex Hosiery Co. v. Leader, 310 U.S. 469, 501. . . .

As we have said, the crucial by-laws of the AP are those which deal with the admission of members, for the fate of the others which the plaintiff challenges depends upon them. They give power to the directors to admit an applicant without condition of any sort and without the consent of any of the members, whenever he is publishing a paper in a "field" in a city in which there are no existing members: that is, in cases where the applicant is not competing with members directly, and does not propose to do so. So far the plaintiff does not object, for while it is true that such an applicant may still remotely compete, that competition may be disregarded, as the defendants themselves disregard it. When however the applicant is competing in the same "field" in a city with existing members, the directors have no power to admit him except upon the consent ("waiver") of his competitors; and while these have no longer their former absolute veto, they retain what we may fairly call a conditional veto. They may require the applicant to get the vote of a majority of all regular members and to fulfill the entrance conditions which we have described. To put the power into the hands of the majority, of whom only a very few can be competitors of the applicant, certainly gives the appearance of liberalizing admission: and unquestionably it has somewhat done so. Indeed, there have at times been sharp election contests, whose conduct was incidentally not always edifying. But, although the change was some abatement of the competitors' earlier control, it by no means opened membership to all those who would be entitled to it, if the public has an interest in its being free from exclusion for competitive reasons, and if that interest is paramount. Although, as we have said, only a few members will have any direct personal interest in keeping out an applicant, the rest will not feel free to judge him regardless of the effect of his admission on his competitors. Each will know that the time may come when he will himself be faced with the application of a competitor; and that will be true even as to those in whose "field" no applicant has as yet appeared. Unless he supports those who now object to the admission of their competitor, he will not in the future be likely to get their support against his own. A by-law which leaves it open to members to vote solely as their self-interest may dictate, disregards whatever public interest may exist. . . .

So much for the power of competing members to insist upon a vote of the majority. The conditions which they may exact when an applicant secures such a vote are plainly designed in the interest of preventing competition. The first is the payment of ten per cent of all the assessments paid by members in the same "field" for a period of over forty years: the payment to be distributed among those who have paid the assessments. This upon its face appears an exaction designed to compensate the applicant's competitors for the loss of their differential advantage, and incidentally to act as a deterrent. The defendants seek to justify it, however, upon the theory that it merely reimburses the competitors for that share in the capital assets which they must yield to him out of their collective interest.

There are two answers to this. First, no such payment is required of an applicant who does not compete with any member, though he becomes equally a co-owner of the capital assets, and entitled to his share on any distribution. Second, the percentage was not in fact computed upon the value of the share in the capital assets to which an applicant becomes entitled on admission, even though we include in capital such questionable items as the employees' benefit fund (which, it would seem, could hardly be regarded as beneficial to members) or the value of the good-will (which, in part at any rate, must be dependent upon the power to exclude competitors). The evidence proves beyond doubt that, although the putative value of the assets, tangible and intangible, was a factor, the payments as a whole were also designed to compensate competitors for the loss in value of their membership, arising out of the applicant's improved position as a competitor. This was consistent enough with AP's position that membership is a purely personal privilege; but if that position be ill taken, the condition makes necessary the appraisal of the public interest. The other condition is that an applicant shall relinquish any exclusive right of his own to any news, and news picture, service; and shall "require" such service to be given on the same terms as he enjoys it, to any one of his competitors who demands it. To require him to relinquish his own exclusive rights may perhaps be "reasonable," but certainly it is not so to require him to secure similar rights to others. That may prove a complete bar to the admission of any applicant who is already a member of a news service not automatically open to all comers.

Is it permissible to treat membership in AP as a purely proprietary privilege? It is not a monopoly in the sense that membership is necessary to build up, or support, even a great newspaper. Such papers have been founded and have thriven without it; they have abandoned it, after they have used it. Indeed, there appear to be some who think that UP is a better service, at least in some departments, perhaps in all. But monopoly is a relative word. If one means by it the possession of something absolutely necessary to the conduct of an activity, there are few except the exclusive possession of some natural resource without which the activity is impossible. Most monopolies, like most parents, give control over only some means of production for which there is a substitute; the possessor enjoys an advantage over his competitors, but he can seldom shut them out altogether; his monopoly is measured by the handicap he can impose. . . . And yet that advantage alone may make a monopoly unlawful. It would be possible, for instance, to conduct some kind of a newspaper without any news service whatever; but nobody will maintain that, if AP were the only news service in existence, the members could keep it wholly to themselves and reduce all other papers to such news as they could gather by their own efforts. The very virtues of the founders which had achieved their unique position, would force upon them hospitality to applicants. Nor need AP be even the best of all existing services; it might be enough that it was the largest and most popular, and that there was a substantial body of opinion in the calling which believed it to be the best. Its popularity is proved by the enormous preponderance of its members, both in number and in circulation; as well as by the fact that, out of nearly a thousand members of UP almost a third are also AP members. No decision of ours as to the relative merits of the two would convince those who may chance to prefer it; the grievance of being unable to choose his own tools is not assuaged, when a court finds that the user does not understand his interest. And so, even if this were a case of the ordinary kind: the production of fungible goods, like steel, machinery, clothes or the like, it would be a nice question whether the handicap upon those excluded from the combination, should prevail over the claim of the members to enjoy the fruits of their foresight, industry and sagacity. But in that event the only interest we should have to weigh against that of the members would be the interest of the excluded newspapers. However, neither exclusively, nor even primarily, are the interests of the newspaper industry conclusive; for that industry serves one of the most vital of all general interests: the dissemination of news from as many different sources, and with as many different facets and colors as is possible. That interest is closely akin to, if indeed it is not the same as, the interest protected by the First Amendment; it presupposes that right conclusions are more likely to be gathered out of a multitude of tongues, than through any kind of authoritative selection. To many this is, and always will be, folly; but we have staked upon it our all.

News is history; recent history, it is true, but veritable history, nevertheless; and history is not total recall, but a deliberate pruning of, and culling from, the flux of events. Were it possible by some magic telepathy to reproduce an occasion in all its particularity, all reproductions would be interchangeable; the public could have no choice, provided that the process should be mechanically perfect. But there is no such magic; and if there were, its result would be immeasurably wearisome, and utterly fatuous. In the production of news every step involves the conscious intervention of some news gatherer, and two accounts of the same event will never be the same. Those who make up the first record—the reporters on the spot—are themselves seldom first hand witnesses; they must take the stories of others as their raw material, checking their veracity, eliminating their irrelevancies, finally producing an ordered version which will evoke and retain the reader's attention and convince him of its truth. And the report so prepared, when sent to his superiors, they in turn "edit," before they send it out to the members; a process similar to the first. A personal impress is inevitable at every stage; it gives its value to the dispatch, which without it would be unreadable. So much for those items which actually appear in all the larger news services, and which include all events of major interest. But these are not all: the same personal choice which must figure in preparing a dispatch, operates in deciding what events are important enough to appear at all; and about that men will differ widely; as we often find, when one service "carries" what others have thought too trivial; or may indeed have missed altogether.

For these reasons it is impossible to treat two news services as interchangeable, and to deprive a paper of the benefit of any service of the first rating is to deprive the reading public of means of information which it should have; it is only by cross-lights from varying directions that full illumination can be secured. Nor is it an answer that the by-law challenged only applies to a "field," in which by hypothesis there is already an AP newspaper in which AP dispatches will appear. That is true, but the final product to the reader is not the AP dispatch simpliciter; but how and where it appears in the paper as it comes before him. That paper may print it verbatim, or a summary of it, or a part of it. The last two are certainly as authentically new and original as the dispatch itself; they bear somewhat the same relation to it that it does to the first report, or that the first report does to the event or occasion. And, even though the whole dispatch be printed verbatim, its effect is not the same in every paper; it may be on the front page, or it may be in an obscure corner; depending upon the importance attached to it. The headlines may plangently call it to readers' attention, or they may be formal and unarresting. There is no part of a newspaper which is not the handiwork of those who make it up; and their influence is often most effective when most concealed.

But what, it is asked, are the limits of such a doctrine? Does it apply to the engagement of a single reporter by a single editor? Suppose the only source of information about momentous events in some remote region is a single exceptionally gifted correspondent: must any paper which engages him agree to admit all others on equal terms? Consistently, must we not recognize the overriding public interest in his reports, particularly since in such a case his employer will otherwise have a monopoly? The answer to such questions need not embarrass us: their true pertinency presupposes that whatever is true in small matters, must be true in large; and the greater part of the law is founded upon a denial of exactly that; for in law differences in quantity again and again become decisive differences in quality. We need not therefore say how important the control of news in any supposititious case must be in order to demand relief; it is enough that in the case at bar AP is a vast, intricately reticulated, organization, the largest of its kind gathering news from all over the world, the chief single source of news for the American press, universally agreed to be of prime consequence. Wherever may be the vanishing point of public concern with any particular source of information, that point is far beyond this service. . . .

We conclude therefore that the present by-laws of AP unlawfully restrict the admission of members; and that further enforcement of them should be enjoined. We shall not attempt to say what conditions may be imposed; we hold no more than that members in the same "field" as the applicant shall not have power to impose, or dispense with, any conditions upon his admission, and that the by-laws shall affirmatively declare that the effect of admission upon the ability of an applicant to compete with members in the same "field" shall not be taken into consideration in passing upon his application. It is of course true that the members may disregard the last provisions in practice; but that is not to be assumed. At any rate, we think that the plaintiff is entitled to that much positive assurance in the organic law; and it is as far as we can go. . . .

In conclusion it is perhaps proper that we should say a word about the freedom of the press, since that question has been mentioned in the briefs. The effect of our judgment will be, not to restrict AP members as to what they shall print, but only to compel them to make their dispatches accessible to others. We do not understand on what theory that compulsion can be thought relevant to this issue; the mere fact that a person is engaged in publishing, does not exempt him from ordinary municipal law, so long as he remains unfettered in his own selection of what to publish. All that we do is to prevent him from keeping that advantage for himself. The argument appears to be that if all be allowed to join AP, it may become the only news service, and get a monopoly by driving out all others. That is perhaps a possibility, though it seems to us an exceedingly remote one; but even if it became an actuality, no public injury could result. For, if AP were open to all who wished the service, could pay for it, and were fit to use it, it would be no longer a monopoly: a monopoly of all those interested in an activity is no monopoly at all, for no one is excluded and the essence of monopoly is exclusion. AP would then be only a collective effort of the calling as a whole. If other services were incidentally driven out, that would not be an actionable wrong.

A judgment may therefore be entered enjoining the defendants from continuing to enforce the by-laws regulating the admission of members in their present form, but leaving it open to them to adopt substitutes which will restrict admission, provided that members in the same "field" as the applicant shall not have power to impose, or dispense with, any conditions upon his admission, and that the by-laws shall affirmatively declare that the effect of admission upon the ability of an applicant to compete with members in the same "field" shall not be taken into consideration in passing upon his application. . . .

Part Nine

THE PROBLEM OF SECRECY IN GOVERNMENT

---

47. THE JOURNALS ARE TO THE MODERN FREEMAN WHAT THE AGORA WAS TO THE ATHENIAN

Francis Lieber, 1853

Many American newsmen found the greatest threat to freedom of the press during the period following World War II in secrecy in government. Arguing from the standpoint of society's right to know, they asserted that a war-born tendency to secrecy burgeoned in the fears of the cold war with communism, and at every level of government blocked access to information that a self-governing society must have. They spun and re-spun the

---

From Francis Lieber, *On Civil Liberty and Self-Government* (Philadelphia: Lippincott, Grambo and Co., 1853), I, 149–157.

theory of an informed electorate as the only safe basis for the democratic process.

Among those who had stated it for an earlier America was the political theorist Francis Lieber, a leader in higher education through the middle decades of the nineteenth century and the author of a half-dozen major works on government, law, and politics. The selection below identifies the principle of publicity primarily with the legislative and judicial branches of government; Lieber's twentieth-century counterparts, citizens of an age when executive and administrative branches of government had grown to proportions undreamed of by most nineteenth-century Americans, found the central threat to "the right to know" in the branches that Lieber stressed least.

We now approach those guarantees of liberty which relate more especially to the government of a free country, and the character of its polity. The first of all we have to mention under this head is publicity of public business. This implies the publicity of legislatures and judicial courts, as well as of all minor transactions that can in their nature be transacted publicly, and also the publication of all important documents and reports, treaties, and whatever else can interest the people at large. It farther implies the perfect freedom with which reporters may publish the transactions of public bodies. Without the latter, the admission of the public would hardly amount in our days to any publicity at all. We do not assemble in the markets as the people of antiquity did. The millions depending upon public information, in our national states, could not meet in the market, as was possible in the ancient city-states, even if we had not a representative government. The journals are to modern freemen what the agora was to the Athenian, the forum to the Roman.

Important as the printing of transactions, reports, and documents is, it is nevertheless true that oral discussions are a most important feature of Anglican publicity of legislative, judicial, and of many of the common administrative transactions. Modern centralized absolutism has developed a system of writing and secrecy, and consequent pedantry, abhorrent to free citizens who exist and feed upon the living word of liberty.[1] Bureaucracy is founded upon writing, liberty on the breathing word. I do not hesitate to point out orality, especially in the

[1] The following passage is given here for a twofold purpose. Everything in it applies to the government of the pen on the continent of Europe, and it shows how similar causes have produced similar results in India and under Englishmen, who at home are so adverse to government-writing and to bureaucracy. In the Notes on the North-western Provinces of India, by Charles Raikes, Magistrate and Collector of Mynpoorie, London, 1853, we find the following passage:

"Action, however, and energy, are what we now lay most stress upon, because in days of peace and outward tranquillity these qualities are not always valued at their true price, and their absence is not so palpably mischievous as in more stirring times. There is more danger now of men becoming plodding, methodical, mere office functionaries, than of their stepping with too hasty a zeal beyond the limits of the law. There is truth, too, in Jacquemont's sneer—India *is* governed by stationery, to a more than sufficient extent; and one of the commonest errors of our magistrates, which they imbibe from constant and early Indian associations, is to mistake *writing* for *action,* to fancy that *dictation* will supply the place of *exertion.* In no other country are so many written orders issued with so much confidence, received with such respect, and broken with such complacency. In fact, as for writing, we believe the infection of the 'cacoethes scribendi' must first have grown up in the East. It pervades everything, but is more rampant and more out of place in a police office than anywhere else. It was not the magistrates who originated this passion for scribbling; but they have never succeeded in repressing it, nor, whilst the law requires that every discontented old woman's story shall be taken down in writing, is it to be expected they ever will. The Khayeths worship their pen and ink on certain festivals, and there is a sort of 'religio' attaching to written forms and statements, which is not confined to official life, but pervades the whole social polity of the writing tribes. An Indian scribe, whose domestic expenditure may average sixpence a day, will keep an account-book with as many columns, headings, and totals, as would serve for the budget of a chancellor of the exchequer. To Tudor Mul and such worthies we owe, no doubt, a great deal for the method and order which they infused into public records; but we have also to thank these knights of the pen for the plaguiest long-figured statements, and the greatest number of such statements, which the world ever saw." Well may the continental European, reading this, exclaim: C'est tout comme chez nous!

administration of justice, in legislation and local self government, as an important element of our civil liberty. I do not believe that a high degree of liberty can be imagined without widely pervading orality; but oral transaction alone is no indication of liberty. The patriarchal and tribal governments of Asia, the chieftain government of our Indians, indeed all primitive governments are carried on by oral transaction without any civil liberty.

Publicus, originally Populicus, meant that which relates to the Populus, to the state, and it is significant that the term gradually acquired the meaning of public, as we take it—as significant, as it is that a great French philosopher, honored throughout our whole country, lately wrote to a friend: "Political matters here are no longer public matters."[2]

In free countries political matters relate to the people, and therefore ought to be public. Publicity informs of public matters; it teaches, and educates, and it binds together. There is no patriotism without publicity, and though publicity cannot always prevent mischief, it is at all events an alarm bell, which calls the public attention to the spot of danger. In former times secrecy was considered indispensable in public matters; it is still so where cabinet policy is pursued, or monarchical absolutism sways; but even these governments have been obliged somewhat to yield to a better spirit, and even Russia publishes occasionally government reports.

That there are certain transactions which the public service requires to be withdrawn for a time from publicity, is evident. We need point only to diplomatic transactions when not yet brought to a close. But even with reference to these, it will be observed that a great change has been wrought in modern times, and comparatively a great degree of publicity now

---

[2] This observation followed a request to write henceforth with caution, because, said he, choses politiques ne sont plus ici choses publiques.

prevails even in the foreign intercourse of nations—a change of which the United States have set the example. A state secret was formerly a potent word, while one of our first statesmen wrote to the author, many years ago: I would not give a dime for all the secrets that people may imagine to be locked up in the United States archives.

It is a remarkable fact that no law insures the publicity of the courts of justice, either in England or the United States. Our constitution insures neither the publicity of courts nor that of congress, and in England the admission of the public to the commons or the lords is merely by sufferance. The public may at any time be excluded merely by a member observing to the presiding officer that strangers are present, while we all know that the candid publication of the debates was not permitted in the times of Dr. Johnson. Yet so thoroughly is publicity now ingrained in the American and Englishman that a suppression of this precious principle cannot even be conceived of. If any serious attempt could be made to carry out the existing law in England, and the public were really excluded from the house of commons, a revolution would be unquestionably the consequence, and publicity would be added to the declaration of rights. We can no more imagine England or the United States without the reporting newspapers, than nature without the principle of vegetation.

The principle of publicity so pervaded all the American politics, that the framers of our constitution probably never thought of it, or if they did, they did not think it worth while to provide for it in the constitution, since no one had doubted it. It is part and parcel of our common law of political existence. They did not trouble themselves with unnecessaries, or things which would have had a value only as possibly completing a certain symmetry of theory.

It is, however, interesting to note that the first distinctly authorized publicity of a legislative body in modern times, was that of the Massachusetts house of representatives, which adopted it in 1766.[3]

Publicity of speaking has its dangers, and occasionally exposes to grave inconveniences, as all guarantees do, and necessarily in a greater degree as they are of a more elementary character. It is the price at which we enjoy all excellence in this world. The science of politics and political ethics must point out the dangers as well as the formal and moral checks which may avert or mitigate the evils arising from publicity in general, and public oral transaction of business in particular. It is not our business here. We treat of it in this place as a guarantee of liberty, and have to show its indispensableness. Those who know liberty as a practical and traditional reality and as a true business of life, as we do, know that the question is not whether it be better to have publicity or not, but, being obliged to have it, how we can best manage to avoid its dangers while we enjoy its fullest benefit and blessing. It is the same as with the air we breathe. The question is not whether we ought to dispense with a free respiration of all-surrounding air, but how, with free inhalation, we may best guard ourselves against colds and other distempers caused by the elementary requisite of physical life, that we must live in the atmosphere.[4]

---

[3] I follow the opinion of Mr. Robert C. Winthrop, late speaker of the American house of representatives, and believe him to be correct, when, in an able Address before the Maine Historical Society (Boston, 1849), he says: "The earliest instance of authorized publicity being given to the deliberations of a legislative body in modern days, was in this same house of representatives of Massachusetts, on the 3d day of June, 1766, when, upon motion of James Otis, and during the debates which arose on the question of the repeal of the stamp act, and of compensation to the sufferers by the riots in Boston, to which that act had given occasion, a resolution was carried 'for opening a gallery for such as wished to hear the debates.' The influence of this measure in preparing the public mind for the great revolutionary events which were soon to follow, can hardly be exaggerated."

[4] . . . Having mentioned the inconvenience of prolix speaking, it may not be improper to add another passage of the address of Mr. Winthrop. . . .

Liberty, I said, is coupled with the public word, and however frequently the public word may be abused, it is nevertheless true that out of it arises oratory—the æsthetics of liberty. What would Greece and Rome be to us without their Demosthenes and Cicero? And what would their other writers have been, had not their languages been coined out by the orator? What would England be without her host of manly and masterly speakers? Who of us could wish for a moment to see the treasures of our own civilization robbed of the words contributed by our speakers, from Patrick Henry to Webster? The speeches of great orators are a fund of wealth for a free people, from which the school-boy begins to draw when he declaims from his Reader, and which enriches, elevates, and nourishes the souls of the old.

Publicity is indispensable to eloquence. Who can speak in secret before a few? Orators are in this respect like poets—their kin, of whom Goethe, "one of the craft," says that they cannot sing unless they are heard.

All governments hostile to liberty are hostile to publicity, and parliamentary eloquence is odious to them, because it is a great power which the executive can neither create nor control. Mr. de Morny, brother of Napoleon the Third, issued a circular to the prefects, when minister of the interior, in

---

It will be recollected that this gentleman has been speaker. He knows, therefore, the inconvenience in its whole magnitude. "Doubtless," he says, "when debates were conducted with closed doors there were no speeches for Buncombe, no claptrap for the galleries, no flourishes for the ladies, and it required no hour rule perhaps to keep men within some bounds of relevancy. But one of the great sources of instruction and information, in regard both to the general measures of government and to the particular conduct of their own representatives, was then shut out from the people, and words which might have roused them to the vindication of justice or to the overthrow of tyranny were lost in the utterance. The perfect publicity of legislative proceedings is hardly second to the freedom of the press, in its influence upon the progress and perpetuity of human liberty, though, like the freedom of the press, it may be attended with inconveniences and abuses."

1852, in which the publicity of parliamentary government is called theatricals. It is remarkable that this declaration should have come from a government which, above all others, seems, in a great measure, to rely on military and other shows.

48. THE EXECUTIVE POWER TO WITHHOLD INFORMATION

Dwight D. Eisenhower, 1954

The frustration of the news fraternity after 1950 over blocked access to government information arose partly in trying to learn where the "power to withhold" lay. It was like wrestling with eels; statutes and administrative rules upon which withholding of information rested were many, and often specific to single agencies. After 1954, however, the least "public" branch of government—the executive—relied more and more on one document. It was a directive from President Dwight D. Eisenhower to the Secretary of Defense. Its immediate purpose was to inform Secretary of the Army Robert Stevens that his subordinates were not to give certain information in testimony before a subcommittee of the Senate that was investigating a controversy between the Army and Senator Joseph McCarthy. It stands today as a major document in the executive power to withhold information, both from other branches of government and from the press.

House Report, No. 2947, 84 Cong., 2 Sess., July 27, 1956. "Availability of Information from Federal Departments and Agencies." Dwight D Eisenhower to Secretary of Defense, May 17, 1954, pp. 64–65.

The White House,
May 17, 1954

The honorable the Secretary of Defense,
Washington, D. C.

Dear Mr. Secretary: It has long been recognized that to assist the Congress in achieving its legislative purposes every executive department or agency must, upon the request of a congressional committee, expeditiously furnish information relating to any matter within the jurisdiction of the committee, with certain historical exceptions—some of which are pointed out in the attached memorandum from the Attorney General. This administration has been and will continue to be diligent in following this principle. However, it is essential to the successful working of our system that the persons entrusted with power in any one of the three great branches of Government shall not encroach upon the authority confided to the others. The ultimate responsibility for the conduct of the executive branch rests with the President.

Within this constitutional framework each branch should cooperate fully with each other for the common good. However, throughout our history the President had withheld information whenever he found that what was sought was confidential or its disclosure would be incompatible with the public interest or jeopardize the safety of the Nation.

Because it is essential to efficient and effective administration that employees of the executive branch be in a position to be completely candid in advising with each other on official matters, and *because it is not in the public interest that any of their conversations or communications, or any documents or reproductions, concerning such advice be disclosed, you will instruct employees of your Department that in all of their appearances before the subcommittee of the Senate Committee on Government Operations* regarding the inquiry now before it they are not to testify to any such conversations or communications or to produce any such documents or reproductions. This principle must be maintained regardless of who would be benefited by such disclosures. [Italic added.]

I direct this action so as to maintain the proper separation of powers between the executive and legislative branches of the Government in accordance with my responsibilities and duties under the Constitution. This separation is vital to preclude the exercise of arbitrary power by any branch of the Government.

By this action I am not in any way restricting the testimony of such witnesses as to what occurred regarding any matters where the communication was directly between any of the principals in the controversy within the executive branch on the one hand and a member of the subcommittee or its staff on the other.

Sincerely,

DWIGHT D. EISENHOWER.

Part Ten

FREEDOM AND RESPONSIBILITY

49. THE PROBLEM AND THE PRINCIPLES OF FREEDOM AND RESPONSIBILITY

Commission on Freedom of the Press, 1947

The Commission on Freedom of the Press was a group of thirteen men, all but two of them scholars and teachers, who during the middle 1940's, inquired into, pondered, and discussed the problems of freedom and responsibility in the American mass media of communications. The chairman was Robert M. Hutchins, then

---

From Commission on Freedom of the Press, *A Free and Responsible Press* (Chicago: The University of Chicago Press, 1947), pp. 1–19. Reprinted from *A Free and Responsible Press* by permission of The University of Chicago Press.

chancellor of the University of Chicago. Out of their effort came a group of books, one of them the product of all thirteen members: *A Free and Responsible Press*, published in 1947 as their general report.

Probably no part of the report had not been said before in some form, much of it by personnel of the mass media. But nowhere had there appeared a single statement at once so complete, so basic, and so ordered. The heart of the conclusions was that unless the mass media improved their performance, society ultimately would undertake to regulate and control them.

Major representatives of the mass media from around the nation assailed the report as unfair, ill-informed, and hostile to freedom of speech and press. But as the years passed, first a few and then more owners, editors, and reporters concluded that much of what the Commission had said needed saying, or even agreed with substantial parts of its conclusions.

Chapter 1 of the report states relationships between freedom and responsibility, and is printed below.

The Problem and the Principles

THE PROBLEM

The Commission set out to answer the question: Is the freedom of the press in danger? Its answer to that question is: Yes. It concludes that the freedom of the press is in danger for three reasons:

First, the importance of the press to the people has greatly increased with the development of the press as an instrument of mass communication. At the same time the development of the press as an instrument of mass communication has greatly decreased the proportion of the people who can express their opinions and ideas through the press.

Second, the few who are able to use the machinery of the press as an instrument of mass communication have not provided a service adequate to the needs of the society.

Third, those who direct the machinery of the press have engaged from time to time in practices which the society condemns and which, if continued, it will inevitably undertake to regulate or control.

When an instrument of prime importance to all the people is available to a small minority of the people only, and when it is employed by that small minority in such a way as not to supply the people with the service they require, the freedom of the minority in the employment of that instrument is in danger.

This danger, in the case of the freedom of the press, is in part the consequence of the economic structure of the press, in part the consequence of the industrial organization of modern society, and in part the result of the failure of the directors of the press to recognize the press needs of a modern nation and to estimate and accept the responsibilities which those needs impose upon them.

We do not believe that the danger to the freedom of the press is so great that that freedom will be swept away overnight. In our view the present crisis is simply a stage in the long struggle for free expression. Freedom of expression, of which freedom of the press is a part, has always been in danger. Indeed, the Commission can conceive no state of society in which it will not be in danger. The desire to suppress opinion different from one's own is inveterate and probably ineradicable.

Neither do we believe that the problem is one to which a simple solution can be found. Government ownership, government control, or government action to break up the greater agencies of mass communication might cure the ills of freedom of the press, but only at the risk of killing the freedom in the process. Although, as we shall see later, government has an important part to play in communications, we look principally to the press and the people to remedy the ills which have chiefly concerned us.

But though the crisis is not unprecedented and though the cures may not be dramatic, the problem is nevertheless a problem of peculiar importance to this generation. And not in the United States alone but in England and Japan and Australia and Austria and France and Germany as well; and in Russia and in the Russian pale. The reasons are obvious. The relation of the modern press to modern society is a new and unfamiliar relation.

The modern press itself is a new phenomenon. Its typical unit is the great agency of mass communication. These agencies can facilitate thought and discussion. They can stifle it. They can advance the progress of civilization or they can thwart it. They can debase and vulgarize mankind. They can endanger the peace of the world; they can do so accidentally, in a fit of absence of mind. They can play up or down the news and its significance, foster and feed emotions, create complacent fiction and blind spots, misuse the great words, and uphold empty slogans. Their scope and power are increasing every day as new instruments become available to them. These instruments can spread lies faster and farther than our forefathers dreamed when they enshrined the freedom of the press in the First Amendment to our Constitution.

With the means of self-destruction that are now at their disposal, men must live, if they are to live at all, by self-restraint, moderation, and mutual understanding. They get their picture of one another through the press. The press can be inflammatory, sensational, and irresponsible. If it is, it and its freedom will go down in the universal catastrophe. On the other hand, the press can do its duty by the new world that is struggling to be born. It can help create a world community by giving men everywhere knowledge of the world and of one another, by promoting comprehension and appreciation of the goals of a free society that shall embrace all men.

We have seen in our time a revival of the doctrine that the

state is all and that the person is merely an instrument of its purpose. We cannot suppose that the military defeat of totalitarianism in its German and Italian manifestations has put an end to the influence and attractiveness of the doctrine. The necessity of finding some way through the complexities of modern life and of controlling the concentrations of power associated with modern industry will always make it look as though turning over all problems to the government would easily solve them.

This notion is a great potential danger to the freedom of the press. That freedom is the first which totalitarianism strikes down. But steps toward totalitarianism may be taken, perhaps unconsciously, because of conditions within the press itself. A technical society requires concentration of economic power. Since such concentration is a threat to democracy, democracy replies by breaking up some centers of power that are too large and too strong and by controlling, or even owning, others. Modern society requires great agencies of mass communication. They, too, are concentrations of power. But breaking up a vast network of communication is a different thing from breaking up an oil monopoly or a tobacco monopoly. If the people set out to break up a unit of communication on the theory that it is too large and strong, they may destroy a service which they require. Moreover, since action to break up an agency of communication must be taken at the instance of a department of the government, the risk is considerable that the freedom of the press will be imperiled through the application of political pressure by that department.

If modern society requires great agencies of mass communication, if these concentrations become so powerful that they are a threat to democracy, if democracy cannot solve the problem simply by breaking them up—then those agencies must control themselves or be controlled by government.

If they are controlled by government, we lose our chief safeguard against totalitarianism—and at the same time take a long step toward it.[1]

THE PRINCIPLES

Freedom of the press is essential to political liberty. Where men cannot freely convey their thoughts to one another, no freedom is secure. Where freedom of expression exists, the beginnings of a free society and a means for every extension of liberty are already present. Free expression is therefore unique among liberties: it promotes and protects all the rest. It is appropriate that freedom of speech and freedom of the press are contained in the first of those constitutional enactments which are the American Bill of Rights.

Civilized society is a working system of ideas. It lives and changes by the consumption of ideas. Therefore it must make sure that as many as possible of the ideas which its members have are available for its examination. It must guarantee freedom of expression, to the end that all adventitious hindrances to the flow of ideas shall be removed. Moreover, a significant innovation in the realm of ideas is likely to arouse resistance. Valuable ideas may be put forth first in forms that are crude, indefensible, or even dangerous. They need the chance to develop through free criticism as well as the chance to survive on the basis of their ultimate worth. Hence the man who publishes ideas requires special protection.

The reason for the hostility which the critic or innovator may expect is not merely that it is easier and more natural to suppress or discourage him than to meet his arguments. Ir-

---

[1] A third possibility is that government itself may come into the field with an alternative system of communications. The Commission has given little consideration to this possibility, except in international communications. Yet the example of Station WNYC, controlled by New York City, suggests what government may do in domestic communications if it regards private service as inadequate.

rational elements are always present in the critic, the innovator, and their audience. The utterance of critical or new ideas is seldom an appeal to pure reason, devoid of emotion, and the response is not necessarily a debate; it is always a function of the intelligence, the prejudice, the emotional biases of the audience. Freedom of the press to appeal to reason may always be construed as freedom of the press to appeal to public passion and ignorance, vulgarity and cynicism. As freedom of the press is always in danger, so is it always dangerous. The freedom of the press illustrates the commonplace that if we are to live progressively we must live dangerously.

Across the path of the flow of ideas lie the existing centers of social power. The primary protector of freedom of expression against their obstructive influence is government. Government acts by maintaining order and by exercising on behalf of free speech and a free press the elementary sanctions against the expressions of private interests or resentment: sabotage, blackmail, and corruption.

But any power capable of protecting freedom is also capable of endangering it. Every modern government, liberal or otherwise, has a specific position in the field of ideas; its stability is vulnerable to critics in proportion to their ability and persuasiveness. A government resting on popular suffrage is no exception to this rule. It also may be tempted—just because public opinion is a factor in official livelihood—to manage the ideas and images entering public debate.

If the freedom of the press is to achieve reality, government must set limits on its capacity to interfere with, regulate, or suppress the voices of the press or to manipulate the data on which public judgment is formed.

Government must set these limits on itself, not merely because freedom of expression is a reflection of important interests of the community, but also because it is a moral right. It is a moral right because it has an aspect of duty about it.

It is true that the motives for expression are not all dutiful. They are and should be as multiform as human emotion itself, grave and gay, casual and purposeful, artful and idle. But there is a vein of expression which has the added impulsion of duty, and that is the expression of thought. If a man is burdened with an idea, he not only desires to express it; he ought to express it. He owes it to his conscience and the common good. The indispensable function of expressing ideas is one of obligation—to the community and also to something beyond the community—let us say to truth. It is the duty of the scientist to his result and of Socrates to his oracle; it is the duty of every man to his own belief. Because of this duty to what is beyond the state, freedom of speech and freedom of the press are moral rights which the state must not infringe.

The moral right of free expression achieves a legal status because the conscience of the citizen is the source of the continued vitality of the state. Wholly apart from the traditional ground for a free press—that it promotes the "victory of truth over falsehood" in the public arena—we see that public discussion is a necessary condition of a free society and that freedom of expression is a necessary condition of adequate public discussion. Public discussion elicits mental power and breadth; it is essential to the building of a mentally robust public; and, without something of the kind, a self-governing society could not operate. The original source of supply for this process is the duty of the individual thinker to his thought; here is the primary ground of his right.

This does not mean that every citizen has a moral or legal right to own a press or be an editor or have access, as of right, to the audience of any given medium of communication. But it does belong to the intention of the freedom of the press that an idea shall have its chance even if it is not shared by those who own or manage the press. The press is not free if those who operate it behave as though their position conferred on them the privilege of being deaf to ideas which the processes of free speech have brought to public attention.

But the moral right of free public expression is not unconditional. Since the claim of the right is based on the duty of a man to the common good and to his thought, the ground of the claim disappears when this duty is ignored or rejected. In the absence of accepted moral duties there are no moral rights. Hence, when the man who claims the moral right of free expression is a liar, a prostitute whose political judgments can be bought, a dishonest inflamer of hatred and suspicion, his claim is unwarranted and groundless. From the moral point of view, at least, freedom of expression does not include the right to lie as a deliberate instrument of policy.

The right of free public expression does include the right to be in error. Liberty is experimental. Debate itself could not exist unless wrong opinions could be rightfully offered by those who suppose them to be right. But the assumption that the man in error is actually trying for truth is of the essence of his claim for freedom. What the moral right does not cover is the right to be deliberately or irresponsibly in error.

But a moral right can be forfeited and a legal right retained. Legal protection cannot vary with the fluctuations of inner moral direction in individual wills; it does not cease whenever a person has abandoned the moral ground of his right. It is not even desirable that the whole area of the responsible use of freedom should be made legally compulsory, even if it were possible, for in that case free self-control, a necessary ingredient of any free state, would be superseded by mechanism.

Many a lying, venal, and scoundrelly public expression must continue to find shelter under a "freedom of the press" built for widely different purposes, for to impair the legal right even when the moral right is gone may easily be a cure worse than the disease. Each definition of an abuse invites abuse of the definition. If the courts had to determine the inner corruptions of personal intention, honest and necessary criticisms would proceed under an added peril.

Though the presumption is against resort to legal action to curb abuses of the press, there are limits to legal toleration. The already recognized areas of legal correction of misused liberty of expression, libel, misbranding, obscenity, incitement to riot, sedition, in case of clear and present danger—have a common principle; namely, that an utterance or publication invades in a serious, overt, and demonstrable manner personal rights or vital social interests. As new categories of abuse come within this definition, the extension of legal sanctions is justified. The burden of proof will rest on those who would extend these categories, but the presumption is not intended to render society supine before possible new developments of misuse of the immense powers of the contemporary press.

THE PRINCIPLES IN THE PRESENT SITUATION

The principles we have attempted to state are those general truths which are valid as goals for all civilized societies. It must be observed that freedom of the press is not a fixed and isolated value, the same in every society and in all times. It is a function within a society and must vary with the social context. It will be different in times of general security and in times of crisis; it will be different under varying states of public emotion and belief.

The freedom we have been examining has assumed a type of public mentality which may seem to us standard and universal but which is in many respects a product of our special history—a mentality accustomed to the noise and confusion of clashing opinions and reasonably stable in temper in view of the varying fortunes of ideas. But what a mind does with a fact or an opinion is widely different when it is serene and when it is anxious; when it has confidence in its environment and when it is infected with suspicion or resentment; when it is gullible and when it is well furnished with the means of criticism; when it has hope and when it is in despair.

Further, the citizen is a different man when he has to judge his press alone, and when his judgment is steadied by other social agencies. Free and diverse utterance may result in bewilderment unless he has access—through home, church, school, custom—to interpreting patterns of thought and feeling. There is no such thing as the "objectivity" of the press unless the mind of the reader can identify the objects dealt with.

Whether at any time and place the psychological conditions exist under which a free press has social significance is always a question of fact, not of theory. These mental conditions may be lost. They may also be created. The press itself is always one of the chief agents in destroying or in building the bases of its own significance.

If we now fix our problem in space and time and look at the press in the United States today, we see that the conditions of our society and of the press in our society require new applications of the principles we have stated.

The aim of those who sponsored the First Amendment was to prevent the government from interfering with expression. The authors of our political system saw that the free society they were seeking to establish could not exist without free communication. As Jefferson put it: "The basis of our governments being the opinion of the people, the very first object should be to keep that right; and were it left to me to decide whether we should have a government without newspapers or newspapers without a government, I should not hesitate a moment to prefer the latter. But I should mean that every man should receive those papers and be capable of reading them."

Our ancestors were justified in thinking that if they could prevent the government from interfering with the freedom of the press, that freedom would be effectively exercised. In their day anybody with anything to say had comparatively little difficulty in getting it published. The only serious obstacle to free expression was government censorship. If that could be stopped, the right of every man to do his duty by his thought was secure. The press of those days consisted of hand-printed sheets issuing from little printing shops, regularly as newspapers, or irregularly as broadsides, pamphlets, or books. Presses were cheap, the journeyman printer could become a publisher and editor by borrowing the few dollars he needed to set up his shop and by hiring an assistant or two. With a limited number of people who could read, and with property qualifications for the suffrage—less than 6 per cent of the adult population voted for the conventions held to ratify the Constitution—there was no great discrepancy between the number of those who could read and were active citizens and those who could command the financial resources to engage in publication.

It was not supposed that any one newspaper would represent all, or nearly all, of the conflicting viewpoints regarding public issues. Together they could be expected to do so, and, if they did not, the man whose opinions were not represented could start a publication of his own.

Nor was it supposed that many citizens would subscribe to all the local journals. It was more likely that each would take the one which would reinforce his prejudices. But in each village and town, with its relatively simple social structure and its wealth of neighborly contacts, various opinions might encounter each other in face-to-face meetings; the truth, it was hoped, would be sorted out by competition in the local market place.

Those circumstances which provide variety and interchange of opinion and easy individual access to the market place of ideas have changed so radically as to justify us in saying that this country has gone through a communications revolution.

Literacy, the electorate, and the population have increased to such a point that the political community to be served by the press includes all but a tiny fraction of the millions of the American people. The press has been transformed into an enormous and complicated piece of machinery. As a necessary accompaniment, it has become big business. There is a marked reduction in the number of units of the press relative to the total population. Although in small communities we can still see a newspaper plant and product that resemble their Colonial prototypes, these are no longer the most characteristic or the most influential agencies of communication.

The right of free public expression has therefore lost its earlier reality. Protection against government is now not enough to guarantee that a man who has something to say shall have a chance to say it. The owners and managers of the press determine which persons, which facts, which versions of the facts, and which ideas shall reach the public.

This is one side of the shield—the effect of the communications revolution on the right of the citizen to publish his beliefs. The other side is the effect of the communications revolution on the press as the agency through which the members of a free society receive, as well as exchange, the judgments, opinions, ideas and information which they need in order to participate in the management of that society. The press has become a vital necessity in the transaction of the public business of a continental area.

In local affairs there is still a chance for face-to-face observation to get in its work. Many private groups, formal and informal, throw an extensive web of alternative communication over the country or over parts of it. But there is obviously less opportunity for direct observation and news by word of mouth in a metropolitan region, in a great nation, or in a world society than there is in a village, a small state, or a single country. For the most part the understanding of the leaders and people of China, Russia, England, and Argentina possessed by the citizens of New Hampshire, Kansas, Oregon, and Alabama will be gained from the agencies of mass communication. Hardly less is the dependence on these agencies of midwest farmers for their understanding of a strike in Detroit or a change in the discount rate of the Federal Reserve Board in Washington.

The complexity of modern industrial society, the critical world situation, and the new menaces to freedom which these imply mean that the time has come for the press to assume a new public responsibility.

Through concentration of ownership the variety of sources of news and opinions is limited. At the same time the insistence of the citizen's need has increased. He is dependent on the quality, proportion, and extent of his news supply, not only for his personal access to the world of event, thought, and feeling but also for the materials of his duties as a citizen and judge of public affairs. The soundness of his judgment affects the working of the state and even the peace of the world, involving the survival of the state as a free community. Under these circumstances it becomes an imperative question whether the performance of the press can any longer be left to the unregulated initiative of the few who manage it.

The moral and legal right of those who manage it to utter their opinions must remain intact; this right stands for the valid kernel of individualism at the heart of all social life. But the element of duty involved in the right requires a new scrutiny; and the service of news, as distinct from the utterance of opinion, acquires a new importance. The need of the citizen for adequate and uncontaminated mental food is such that he is under a duty to get it. Thus his interest also acquires the stature of a right.

To protect the press is no longer automatically to protect the citizen or the community. The freedom of the press can remain a right of those who publish only if it incorporates into itself the right of the citizen and the public interest.

Freedom of the press means freedom from and freedom for.

The press must be free from the menace of external compulsions from whatever source. To demand that it be free from pressures which might warp its utterance would be to demand that society should be empty of contending forces and beliefs. But persisting and distorting pressures—financial, popular, clerical, institutional—must be known and counterbalanced. The press must, if it is to be wholly free, know and overcome any biases incident to its own economic position, its concentration, and its pyramidal organization.

The press must be free for the development of its own conception of service and achievement. It must be free for making its contribution to the maintenance and development of a free society.

This implies that the press must also be accountable. It must be accountable to society for meeting the public need and for maintaining the rights of citizens and the almost forgotten rights of speakers who have no press. It must know that its faults and errors have ceased to be private vagaries and have become public dangers. The voice of the press, so far as by a drift toward monopoly it tends to become exclusive in its wisdom and observation, deprives other voices of a hearing and the public of their contribution. Freedom of the press for the coming period can only continue as an accountable freedom. Its moral right will be conditioned on its acceptance of this accountability. Its legal right will stand unaltered as its moral duty is performed.

50. A NEED FOR SELF-RESTRAINT

Warren Commission, 1964

The assassination of President John F. Kennedy on November 22, 1963, and the subsequent killing of the suspected assassin, Lee Harvey Oswald, brought to national attention one of the most intractable problems in the realm of freedom and responsibility of the press. The statements of police and prosecutors that Oswald was indeed the assassin were carried by television, radio, and newspaper to almost every adult in the nation. "Trial by publicity" had occurred in its most spectacular form: Oswald had been "tried" in the court of public opinion and millions were convinced of his guilt. Had he lived, it would have been a real question whether an unprejudiced jury could have been found for a court trial.

The problem was old; courts and journalists had wrestled with it for decades. Increasingly in its decisions since the 1940's, the Supreme Court had delivered stern criticisms of the mass media. The conviction of an accused murderer in *Irvin* v. *Dowd* had been reversed in 1962 solely on the ground that pretrial publicity had made fair trial by an impartial jury impossible.

The Commission to investigate the circumstances of the incredible events of November 22–24, 1963, under Chief Justice of the United States Earl Warren, placed on the police first responsibility for trial by publicity. But the mass media shared in the fault, the Commission said. A code of professional conduct "would be welcome evidence" that the Dallas tragedy had provided a lesson.

Report of the President's Commission on the Assassination of President John F. Kennedy (Washington, D.C.: Government Printing Office, 1964), pp. 240–242.

While appreciating the heavy and unique pressures with which the Dallas Police Department was confronted by reason of the assassination of President Kennedy, primary responsibility for having failed to control the press and to check the flow of undigested evidence to the public must be borne by the police department. It was the only agency that could have established orderly and sound operating procedures to control the multitude of newsmen gathered in the police building after the assassination.

The Commission believes, however, that a part of the responsibility for the unfortunate circumstances following the President's death must be borne by the news media. The crowd of newsmen generally failed to respond properly to the demands of the police. Frequently without permission, news representatives used police offices on the third floor, tying up facilities and interfering with normal police operations. Police efforts to preserve order and to clear passageways in the corridor were usually unsuccessful. On Friday night the reporters completely ignored [Police Chief] Curry's injunction against asking Oswald questions in the assembly room and crowding in on him. On Sunday morning, the newsmen were instructed to direct no questions at Oswald; nevertheless, several reporters shouted questions at him when he appeared in the basement.

Moreover, by constantly pursuing public officials, the news representatives placed an insistent pressure upon them to disclose information. And this pressure was not without effect, since the police attitude toward the press was affected by the desire to maintain satisfactory relations with the news representatives and to create a favorable image of themselves. Chief Curry frankly told the Commission that

> I didn't order them out of the building, which if I had it to do over I would. In the past like I say, we had always maintained very good relations with our press, and they had always respected us.

Curry refused Fritz' request to put Oswald behind the screen in the assembly room at the Friday night press conference because this might have hindered the taking of pictures. Curry's subordinates had the impression that an unannounced transfer of Oswald to the county jail was unacceptable because Curry did not want to disappoint the newsmen; he had promised that they could witness the transfer. It seemed clear enough that any attempt to exclude the press from the building or to place limits on the information disclosed to them would have been resented and disputed by the newsmen, who were constantly and aggressively demanding all possible information about anything related to the assassination.

Although the Commission has found no corroboration in the video and audio tapes, police officials recall that one or two representatives of the press reinforced their demands to see Oswald by suggesting that the police had been guilty of brutalizing him. They intimated that unless they were given the opportunity to see him, these suggestions would be passed to the public. Captain King testified that he had been told that

> A short time after Oswald's arrest one newsman held up a photograph and said, "This is what the man charged with the assassination of the President looks like. Or at least this is what he did look like. We don't know what he looks like after an hour in the custody of the Dallas Police Department."

City Manager Elgin Crull stated that when he visited Chief Curry in his office on the morning of November 23, Curry told him that he "felt it was necessary to cooperate with the news media representatives, in order to avoid being accused of using Gestapo tactics in connection with the handling of Oswald." Crull agreed with Curry. The Commission deems any such veiled threats to be absolutely without justification.

The general disorder in the Police and Courts Building during November 22–24 reveals a regrettable lack of self-discipline by the newsmen. The Commission believes that the news media, as well as the police authorities, who failed to impose conditions more in keeping with the orderly process of justice, must share responsibility for the failure of law enforcement which occurred in connection with the death of Oswald. On previous occasions, public bodies have voiced the need for the exercise of self-restraint by the news media in periods when the demand for information must be tempered by other fundamental requirements of our society.

At its annual meeting in Washington in April 1964, the American Society of Newspaper Editors discussed the role of the press in Dallas immediately after President Kennedy's assassination. The discussion revealed the strong misgivings among the editors themselves about the role that the press had played and their desire that the press display more self-discipline and adhere to higher standards of conduct in the future. To prevent a recurrence of the unfortunate events which followed the assassination, however, more than general concern will be needed. The promulgation of a code of professional conduct governing representatives of all news media would be welcome evidence that the press had profited by the lesson of Dallas.

The burden of insuring that appropriate action is taken to establish ethical standards of conduct for the news media must also be borne, however, by State and local governments, by the bar, and ultimately by the public. The experience in Dallas during November 22–24 is a dramatic affirmation of the need for steps to bring about a proper balance between the right of the public to be kept informed and the right of the individual to a fair and impartial trial.

51. OWNERS DEFINE RESPONSIBILITIES

The Commission on Freedom of the Press stated philosophical relationships between freedom and responsibility in detail. When newsmen and owners spoke of responsibilities they were not likely to elaborate differences between moral and legal rights or to discuss the duty of the thinker to his thought and to his conscience; they spoke in rather specific terms of what they conceived to be right and wrong for their communities in newspaper and magazine practice, and of their duty to the public.

They had been at this for a long time—about as long as American critics had lamented the "abuses" of the press. Abuses were there always, but performance and thoughts ran also to the public weal and were not—as some have always had it—exclusively characterized by an extravagant rugged individualism, a public-be-damned cast, and an obsession with "my freedom of the press" untempered by recognition of the reader's stake.

A. Canons for the Management of the Press

Editors of the Richmond Compiler, 1817

The American Society of Newspaper Editors in 1923 produced what became the best-known American code for newspaper conduct—the "Canons of Journalism." Its initiators had had forebears of similar stripe. The editors of the Richmond, Virginia, *Compiler* had proposed the idea and a similar title to the editor of the great "depot of facts," Hezekiah Niles, whose weekly *Niles' Register* was a journalistic leader of the early nineteenth

From *Niles' Register,* XIII (Nov. 29, 1817), 210–211.

century. Niles refused, but the proposal remains today as a clue to some early thinking about self-regulation of the press.

Sir—We present you the respects of a weak brother—for weak is our wing, and humble our pretentions. We thank you for the work you have given to the American public—*We* regard it as the most valuable *depot of facts* which issues from the press. . . .

One of the most useful things you are wont to do, is to sketch a *list* of passing transactions, which are capable of being reduced to numbers, and from time to time sum up the whole, and present them in one collective point of view. Such was the list of prize-vessels you collected during the late war. Such is the list of emigrations you have lately furnished.

We beg leave to turn your attention to another quarter—one in which both of us are deeply interested. We mean our *public journals, their condition, multiplication, declension* and *fall.*

In the first place, we *want,* what we may call, *canons for the management of the press,* a sort of "*codification,*" as Jeremy Bentham calls it, of those *rules,* which ought to guide the conductor of the press—to regulate its *liberty,* and restrain its *licentiousness.* Not rules enacted by the laws of the land; but *rules,* drawn from the sound principles of discussion, and forming a sort of *moral legislation* for the press; rules, which every editor ought to observe, and which none should violate without an offence to decency and good taste. These rules will prescribe the rights and duties which one editor owes to another, or which editors and correspondents own [sic] to each other. They would teach us the species of *manner* which editors ought to use towards each other; the *species of matter,* which they ought to publish, and those which they ought not; in other words, what is fit for the public eye, and what is not; the species of *evidence* they ought to require and furnish for their statements; with other cases, which are apt to occur in the editorial line.

We hold, that the number of well regulated papers is a species of *test* of the state of the public mind; their multiplication, is an indirect proof of the growth of a liberalizing spirit among the people; their declension, of a depreciation of that spirit. Hence we should like to see a Register of the numbers of newspapers; which should notice every newspaper that is set up, or the discontinuance of every old one—with the change of editors, &c. &c. Thus you would take notice of every typographical star that rose above or set below the horizon. . . .

B. Joseph Pulitzer's Credo

1907

Joseph Pulitzer had been in bad health and almost blind for a dozen years when in 1907 he concluded—mistakenly, as it was to prove—that he could no longer be an active force in the direction of his newspapers. He cabled this famous "credo" to his two newspapers, the *New York World* and the *St. Louis Post-Dispatch.* While less than a decade earlier, Pulitzer had been engaged with William Randolph Hearst in the nation's most celebrated spree of "yellow journalism," he was now in the middle years of making his papers among the finest in the nation. The credo spoke an understanding of public responsibility that was to guide the *World* until its sale in 1931, and the *Post-Dispatch* on its long, persistent, and still vigorous course of journalistic excellence.

From Program, Birthday Anniversary Dinner, Given by Joseph Pulitzer, April 10, 1907 (St. Louis: Woodward S. Tiernan Printing Co.), pp. 11–13.

Cap Martin, France, April 10

White, Post-Dispatch, St. Louis:

In retiring from the presidency in favor of my son, Ralph, I want to express to you and the editors, managers and entire staff my sincere appreciation for the integrity and ability with which the Post-Dispatch has been so successfully conducted. My grateful thanks are also due to the people of St. Louis for their generous approval of the principles and character of the paper. I know that my retirement will make no difference in its cardinal principles, that it will always fight for progress and reform, never tolerate injustice or corruption, always fight demagogues of all parties, never belong to any party, always oppose privileged classes and public plunderers, never lack sympathy with the poor, always remain devoted to the public welfare, never be satisfied with merely printing news, always be drastically independent, never be afraid to attack wrong, whether by predatory plutocracy or predatory poverty.

JOSEPH PULITZER

C. Responsibility and Freedom

Arthur Hays Sulzberger, 1947

Perhaps shortly after World War I, the American newspaper world came to recognize that, if a single newspaper could be called the craft's leader, it was the *New York Times.* No other paper could match its breadth and depth of news coverage, and its integrity and devotion to public interest proved unsurpassed as the decades under Adolph S. Ochs progressed. His successor, Arthur Hays Sulzberger, had been president and publisher for twelve years when he agreed to the "complimentary but definitely embarrassing" request of the American Society of Newspaper

---

From "Sulzberger Discusses Ethics of Journalism," *Editor & Publisher,* LXXX, No. 18 (April 26, 1947), 86, 88.

Editors to talk to them about ethics in journalism. His statements on the relation between a newspaper's freedom and its responsibility to the public follow.

As I see it we, as a newspaper, have one paramount responsibility and that is to the public. I, in turn, as the publisher, have a second great responsibility and that is to the staff.

As a newspaper we live under certain guarantees of freedom, and it is important to point out that there is no quid pro quo written into the constitution. Freedom is granted—responsibility is not required. Despite that, more and more of us have come to recognize that responsibility is the Ruth to freedom's Naomi.

I would define a responsible press as one which admits that the manner in which it covers and presents the news is a matter of legitimate public concern.

It seems to me that the public has a right to demand this. It has a right to protection from unscrupulous advertising; it has the right to demand as accurate, full and impartial a news service as the public itself is prepared to support. It has this right because freedom of the press is one of its own fundamental freedoms which, in effect, it vests with a relatively small number of its citizenry. And the press suffers, and freedom everywhere suffers, where a community fails to demand and receive its rights in this respect.

Now I know full well that freedom of the press implies the right to be biased. A sectarian periodical, naturally, is biased in favor of the particular faith which it is produced to serve, and it should be protected in its right to be so prejudiced. I speak rather of newspapers of general circulation which seek to serve all elements of our democratic communities.

I hold that it is the duty of every newspaper of general circulation to inform its readers on *all* sides of *every* important issue, and that it fails in its responsibilities when it does not do so.

One of the most serious threats to the nation's freedom may lie in this failure. There is no point in reviewing here the four fundamental freedoms our citizens cherish. We are *concerned* with all; we are *responsible* in larger measure for one, and that one happens to be the most sensitive. If freedom of the press were to fall, then all freedoms would die. . . .

Now, fundamental to the picture is the fact that in our country, and in many other lands, the press is privately owned, and sincerely good democrats can well ask how any industry vested with so much public interest can proceed with fairness to the community without some form of governmental control. Of course, the answer is that government control would destroy freedom, and the question these good people ask is actually an impossible one—you cannot have outside control of a free press and have it free. *Control must come from within.*

That seems to me to be the nub of the issue—call it newspaper ethics or responsibility. It is a code of some kind and here, ladies and gentlemen, are some of the points in that code that guide us:

We recognize that the freedom we enjoy imposes responsibility on us.

We interpret responsibility in part as meaning that when a member of the community complains about our handling of the news we do not consider him as butting in where he has no business. It is his business and we wish more people knew it.

We believe it to be our duty to give all available sides to a story, and to present the news without any criterion except objective news judgment.

We try to keep our standards of news as broad as possible, and in so doing know that we are serving our readers.

We admit that there is news in crime and violence, but we do not believe that either crime or violence is normal, and we proceed on the theory that our readers desire information rather than entertainment.

We recognize the difficulties in obtaining strictly factual information although we constantly try to achieve it. We recognize as well the need for interpretive writing in these days of complex issues. Always, however, we make the distinction between interpretation and opinion, and we earnestly seek to exclude the latter from our news columns.

We hold the date line sacred and any copyreader who updates without checking with the source, or who combines under one date line stories which came from different places violates a cardinal principle of ours. The reader is entitled to know precisely where and when a dispatch originated.

We endeavor to be helpful in community problems, and to raise the level of underprivileged groups by *fair* treatment. We bend over backwards to use the word 'Negro' when it is associated with worthy acts, and to eliminate it from our reports of discreditable deeds unless, as in the case of a race riot, or in describing a missing criminal, it is an important part of the news story.

I have heard it said that when *you* adhere strongly to an opinion which differs from *mine* it is an evidence of prejudice, but that when *I* adhere firmly to an opinion that differs from *yours* that is a principle. Maybe so. At any rate, we believe we are actuated by principle when we consistently refuse to grant a closed shop to the newspaper guild. I believe we are the only newspaper with a contract which contains an affirmative statement for the open shop with that union. Clause one provides that "membership in the guild shall not be a prerequisite to employment in the Times." We do not fight unionism and, in the past, have not objected to the closed shop in any place except the editorial departments. We are steadfast, however, in our unwillingness to turn over the writing and editing of the news to any single group which has any smaller common denominator than its Americanism.

We try to report the news of communism as fairly as the news of any other movement or party; but I would not knowingly employ a communist or any other type of totalitarian in our news or editorial departments or any place of influence.

We have long recognized a responsibility to our readers in keeping our advertising columns clean and truthful. At the same time, we admit the right of advertisers to express views with which we are not in sympathy, provided they do not overstep certain bounds. This applies particularly to editorial advertising. . . .

I have a profound and deep faith in democracy, and that unless the spirit of man is free I find no point in existence. Man finds his noblest expression in his desire for knowledge, and in supplying that knowledge ours is a sacred and special mission. The manner in which we perform our duties may well determine the destiny of the world. We can give strength to liberty or selfishly destroy it and ourselves. Let us fight for a free press. Let us make it a responsible one.

Index

THE AMERICAN HERITAGE SERIES

THE COLONIAL PERIOD

Adams, John *The Political Writings of John Adams: Representative Selections* AHS 8 George A. Peek, Jr.
The English Libertarian Heritage: From the Writings of John Trenchard and Thomas Gordon in The Independent Whig *and* Cato's Letters AHS 32 David L. Jacobson
The Great Awakening AHS 34 Alan Heimert, Perry Miller
Puritan Political Thought AHS 33 Edmund S. Morgan

THE REVOLUTIONARY ERA

The American Revolution as a Democratic Movement AHS 36 Alfred Young
The Antifederalists AHS 38 Cecelia Kenyon
Early American Libertarian Thought: Freedom of the Press from Zenger to Jefferson AHS 41 Leonard W. Levy
Franklin, Benjamin *The Political Thought of Benjamin Franklin* AHS 64 Ralph Ketcham
Paine, Thomas *Common Sense and Other Political Writings* AHS 5 Nelson F. Adkins

THE YOUNG NATION

Calhoun, John C. *Disquisition on Government and Selections from the* Discourse AHS 10 C. Gordon Post
Channing, William Ellery *Unitarian Christianity and Other Essays* AHS 21 Irving H. Bartlett
Democracy, Liberty, and Property: The State Constitutional Conventions of the 1820's AHS 43 Merrill D. Peterson

The Federal Convention and the Formation of the Union of American States AHS 19 Winton U. Solberg

From the Declaration of Independence to the Constitution: The Roots of American Constitutionalism AHS 6 Carl J. Friedrich, Robert G. McCloskey

Gallatin, Albert *Selected Writings* AHS 40 E. James Ferguson

Hamilton, Alexander *Papers on Public Credit, Commerce, and Finance* AHS 18 Samuel McKee, Jr., J. Harvie Williams

Hamilton, Madison, and Jay on the Constitution: Selections from the Federalist Papers AHS 7 Ralph H. Gabriel

Jefferson, Thomas *The Political Writings of Thomas Jefferson: Representative Selections* AHS 9 Edward Dumbauld

Social Theories of Jacksonian Democracy: Representative Writings of the Period 1825–1850 AHS 1 Joseph L. Blau

The Writings of Justice Joseph Story AHS 45 Henry Steele Commager

THE MIDDLE PERIOD

The Antislavery Argument AHS 44 Jane and William Pease

Lincoln, Abraham *The Political Thought of Abraham Lincoln* AHS 46 Richard Current

The Radical Republicans and Reconstruction AHS 47 Harold Hyman

THE LATE NINETEENTH CENTURY

Bryan, William Jennings *The Mind and Thought of William Jennings Bryan* AHS 52 Ray Ginger

The Forging of American Socialism: Origins of the Modern Movement AHS 24 Howard H. Quint

Late Nineteenth-Century American Liberalism AHS 26 Louis Filler

The Populist Mind AHS 50 Norman Pollack

THE TWENTIETH CENTURY

Addams, Jane *The Social Thought of Jane Addams* AHS 69 Christopher Lasch

The American Writer and the Great Depression AHS 63 Harvey Swados

Negro Protest Thought in the Twentieth Century AHS 56 Francis Broderick, August Meier
New Deal Thought AHS 70 Howard Zinn
The Progressives AHS 54 Carl Resek
Roosevelt, Theodore *The Writings of Theodore Roosevelt* AHS 53 William H. Harbaugh
The Supreme Court: Law Versus Discretion AHS 72 Wallace Mendelson
Wilson, Woodrow, *The Political Thought of Woodrow Wilson* AHS 68 E. David Cronon

TOPICAL VOLUMES

The American Economic System: Representative Selections AHS 27 Massimo Salvadori
American Military Thought AHS 75 Walter Millis
The Church and the City AHS 61 Robert Cross
Freedom of the Press: 1800–1965 AHS 74 Harold L. Nelson
Nonviolence in America: A Documentary History AHS 60 Staughton Lynd